The Sakya School of Tibetan Buddhism

Dhongthog Rinpoche

The Sakya School of Tibetan Buddhism

A History

Dhongthog Rinpoche

Translated by Sam van Schaik

Wisdom

Wisdom Publications
199 Elm Street
Somerville, MA 02144 USA
wisdompubs.org

Library of Congress Cataloging-in-Publication Data
Names: Dhongthog, T. G., 1933–2015, author. | Van Schaik, Sam, translator.
Title: The Sakya school of Tibetan Buddhism : a history / Dhongthog Rinpoche ; Translated by Sam van Schaik.
Other titles: Byang phyogs Thub pa'i rgyal tshab Dpal ldan Sa-skya-pa'i bstan pa rin po che ji ltar byung ba'i lo rgyus rab 'byams zhing du snyan pa'i sgra dbyangs zhes bya ba bzhugs so. English
Description: Somerville, MA : Wisdom Publications, 2016. | Includes bibliographical references and index.
Identifiers: LCCN 2015037521| ISBN 1614292523 (hardcover : alk. paper) | ISBN 1614292671 (ebook)
Subjects: LCSH: Sa-skya-pa (Sect—History.
Classification: LCC BQ7672.2 .D4813 2016 | DDC 294.3/92309—dc23
LC record available at http://lccn.loc.gov/2015037521

ISBN 978-1-61429-252-4 ebook ISBN 978-1-61429-267-8
20 19 18 17 16 5 4 3 2 1

Cover and interior design by Gopa & Ted2. Set in Diacritical Garamond Pro 11/14.1.
Frontispiece photo by Kurt Smith. Author photo of Dhongthog Rinpoche by Kurt Smith.
Author photo of Sam van Schaik by Imre Galambos.

Wisdom Publications' books are printed on acid-free paper and meet the guidelines for permanence and durability of the Production Guidelines for Book Longevity of the Council on Library Resources.

This book was produced with environmental mindfulness.
For more information, please visit wisdompubs.org/wisdom-environment.

Printed in the
United States of America.

MIX
Paper from responsible sources
FSC® C044104
FSC www.fsc.org

Please visit fscus.org.

Contents

Foreword to the Translation *by Lama Jampa Thaye* vii
Translator's Introduction 1

Sweet Harmonies for Infinite Realms:
The History of the Precious Teachings of the Glorious Sakyapas,
the Regents of the Sage in the North

Foreword *by His Holiness Sakya Trizin* 7
Author's Preface 9
1. The Dharma in India and Tibet 13
2. The Sakya Family Lineage 53
3. The Lamdre 77
4. The Thirteen Golden Dharmas and the Protectors 107
5. The Ngor Tradition 125
6. Biographies of Great Scholars 135
7. The Tsar Tradition 159
8. The Essential Sakya Teachings 171
9. Masters of the Nineteenth and Twentieth Centuries 183
10. Conclusion 219

Notes 235
Bibliography 259
Index 273
About the Author 313

Publisher's Acknowledgment

THE PUBLISHER gratefully acknowledges the generous contribution of the Hershey Family Foundation toward the publication of this book.

Foreword to the Translation by Lama Jampa Thaye

It is with great pleasure that I introduce this fine English translation of the *History of the Sakya Tradition* composed in 1976 by the eminent Tibetan scholar Dhongthog Rinpoche. Until now only brief accounts of this tradition, such as that authored by the late Chogye Trichen, have appeared in English. Now Dhongthog Rinpoche has presented Sakya history in its full richness and glory.

The present work commences with an examination of the development of Buddhism in India and Tibet, setting the scene for the establishment in the eleventh century of the Sakya school by the precious Khon family. Subsequently, Dhongthog Rinpoche provides magisterial accounts of the transmission of the Lamdre, the very heart of Sakya contemplative practice, and other major streams of esoteric instruction such as the Thirteen Golden Dharmas and the ritual cycles of the "greater" and "lesser" Dharma protectors.

As well as supplying accounts of the Ngor and Tsar branches of the Sakya tradition, Dhongthog Rinpoche's history contains important material on the great Sakya masters such as Rongtongpa and Gorampa, who made an invaluable contribution to religious and intellectual life in Tibet and whose work is just beginning to be appreciated in the West. Fittingly the history concludes with a survey of the great Sakya and nonsectarian masters Jamyang Khyentse Wangpo and Khyentse Chokyi Lodro, whose labors did so much to ensure the continuing vitality of the Sakya tradition.

With this work Dhongthog Rinpoche has performed a great service to all who cherish the Sakya tradition in particular and Buddhism in general. It will be hard to surpass his achievement. I would also like to congratulate Dr. van Schaik for his splendid translation and pray that it may contribute to the flourishing of our tradition in these modern times.

Translator's Introduction

When Dhongthog Rinpoche completed his history of the Sakya school in 1976, he was living in New Delhi, India. He was born in 1933 in the eastern region of Tibet known as Kham, in the Trehor region, which is in the present-day Garze (Kardze) Tibetan Autonomous Prefecture in China. He was identified as the fifth in the tulku lineage of Dhongthog Monastery and given the religious name Tenpai Gyaltsen, "Victory Banner of the Teachings." Outside of Tibet he has often used a Westernized form of his name: T. G. Dhongthog. He studied under many teachers but counted two—Ngawang Lodro Zhenpen Nyingpo (Khenchen Dampa) and Dzongsar Khyentse Jamyang Chokyi Lodro—as his main teachers, studying for three years at Dzongsar Monastery under the latter. However, due the deterioration of the situation in eastern Tibet under the rule of the Chinese Communist Party, he chose to leave for India in 1957.

While living in New Delhi, Dhongthog Rinpoche played several different roles in the Tibetan exile community, often involved with the preservation of Tibetan culture. For example, he worked closely with Lokesh Chandra, copying by hand texts that had been brought out of Tibet for new editions published in India. He also worked as the librarian of Tibet House in New Delhi, during which time he wrote several works, including the present history. Then in 1979 he accepted an invitation from Dagchen Rinpoche, the head of the Puntsog Palace of the Sakya family lineage, who was resident in Seattle with his family.

In Seattle Dhongthog Rinpoche established the Sapan Center, named after the great scholar Sakya Paṇḍita, as a base for his activities. He continued to write and worked closely with Dezhung Rinpoche before the latter's death in 1987. The works written during Dhongthog Rinpoche's time in Seattle attest to his wide learning in many areas of Tibetan culture, including history, biography, grammar, and astrology, as well as Buddhist teachings transmitted in the Sakya lineage. His publications in English include *The New Light English-Tibetan Dictionary* (1988) and *The Earth-Shaking Thunder of the True Word* (2000). The latter, a translation of his Tibetan text of 1996, is one of several polemical works he had written in the debate surrounding the deity Dorje Shugden, supporting the position of the Fourteenth Dalai Lama that practices focusing on this deity are illegitimate and harmful to Buddhism. Other recent works included a Tibetan translation of the English biography of Dezhung Rinpoche written by David Jackson and published by Wisdom. Dhongthog Rinpoche passed away in January 2015 at his home in Seattle.

Dhongthog Rinpoche's history of the Sakya school—the full title of which is *Sweet Harmonies for Infinite Realms: The History of the Precious Teachings of the Glorious Sakyapas, the Regents of the Sage in the North* (*Byang phyogs thub pa'i rgyal tshab dpal ldan sa skya pa'i bstan pa rin po che ji ltar byung ba'i lo rgyus rab 'byams zhing du snyan pa'i sgra dbyangs*)—is the only work of its kind, giving an overview of the whole history of the Sakya school and the wealth of ritual and meditative traditions of Vajrayāna Buddhism that have been passed down through generations of scholars and practitioners. The Sakya school has a strong tradition of keeping historical accounts of its own lineages, and Dhongthog Rinpoche drew upon a variety of these when composing this work.

In the traditional manner of Tibetan authorial practice, much of this work is a compilation of previous sources, selectively edited and abridged. For example, the section on the Lamdre is largely an abridged version of Ame Zhab's (1597–1659) history of the Lamdre, while the section on Śākya Chogden is an abridged version of the extensive biography by Jonang Kunga Drolchog (1507–66). The biographies of more recent masters such as Gaton Ngawang Legpa are based on Dhongthog Rinpoche's own work and, as he states in his closing remarks, from conversations with other learned lamas who were educated in Tibet such as Chogye Trichen Rinpoche (1920–2007).

I began this translation of Dhongthog Rinpoche's history of the Sakya school in 2005 at the request of my teacher Lama Jampa Thaye. When I wrote to Dhongthog Rinpoche expressing my wish to translate his work, he gave his full support to the project and was both helpful and encouraging. Along the way I received a great deal of generous assistance from Ronald Davidson, David Jackson, and Cyrus Stearns, for which I am immensely grateful. Volker Caumanns, Tsering Gonkatsang, and Burkhard Quessel gave valuable advice on specific aspects of the translation. Lama Jampa Thaye kindly offered corrections and clarifications across the whole text, greatly improving the accuracy of the translation. I would finally like to thank David Kittelstrom at Wisdom Publications for his enthusiasm for, and editing of, this translation. The responsibility for any errors and infelicities is of course mine.

Notes on the Translation

The present translation generally follows the usual conventions of modern English translations of Buddhist texts. Names of Tibetan people and places have been rendered phonetically in the translation, and the Wylie transliteration can be found in the index. In general, the names of Indian texts appear in the original Sanskrit, while Tibetan titles are translated, with the original title appearing in the bibliography. Official titles are usually translated, except where these refer to specific positions that often take the place of personal names, such as Tartse Khenchen.

Dhongthog Rinpoche's original Tibetan text was, in the usual style of a Tibetan treatise, laid out in a nested heirarchical structure of headings and subheadings. These have been retained but somewhat simplified into a structure of ten chapters with subheadings. In the notes to the translation I have attempted where possible to clarify references in the text to aspects of Sakya Buddhism that may not be known to the general reader and to point the reader to other relevant publications. Where the historical sources conflict, I have sometimes pointed out alternative accounts to those given in this history. The Tibetan text also contains some interlinear notes by Dhongthog Rinpoche himself, and these are translated and included in the notes here, marked as "DR's note."

One of the most important aspects of Sakya teaching and practice is the Lamdre (*lam 'bras*), a contraction of *lam 'bras bu dang bcas pa*, "the path that includes the result." Since the Tibetan term has become familiar in itself, I have not translated it. I have on the other hand translated the names of the two versions of Lamdre transmission as "the explication for the assembly" (*tshogs bshad*) and "the explication for disciples" (*slob bshad*). In the Sakya tradition the Lamdre is sometimes even more fully referred to as "the precious oral instructions of the path that includes the result" (*gsung ngag rin po che lam 'bras bu dang bcas pa*). In the present work the Lamdre is often referred to as "the precious oral instructions" or simply "the oral instructions." The phrase "oral precepts" (*gdams ngag*) is also sometimes used, though this phrase also often refers to other tantric traditions. At points where it is not clear in the context, I have added ". . . of the Lamdre" to "oral instructions" and "oral precepts."

For most of the dates in the original text, the Tibetan system of sixty-year cycles has been used, with the modern Western dates added in parentheses. Of the many systems for naming the lunar months in Tibet, at least three appear in the text. The first is seasonal, with each of the four seasons divided into early, middle, and late. The first day of the year, early spring, is February/March. The second system, derived from the *Kālacakra Tantra*, has twelve months with the following names: Chu (*mchu*, Skt. *māgha*), Wo (*dbo*, Skt. *phālguna*), Nagpa (*nag pa*, Skt. *caitra*), Saga (*sa ga*, Skt. *vaiśākha*), Non (*snron*, Skt. *jyeṣṭha*), Chuto (*chu stod*, Skt. *āṣāḍha*), Drozhin (*gro bzhin*, Skt. *śrāvaṇa*), Trum (*khrums*, Skt. *bhādrapada*), Takar (*tha skar*, Skt. *āśvina*), Mindrug (*smin drug*, Skt. *kārttika*), Go (*mgo*, Skt. *mārgaśīrṣa*), and Gyal (*rgyal*, Skt. *pauṣa*). The third system is the Mongolian method of naming the same twelve months. The seasonal names, which generally appear in the earlier part of the history, have been retained, but the others have been converted to give the number of the month, with the first month being equivalent to February/March. An exception is made in the discussion of the dates of the historical Buddha, because these are so closely linked to the *Kālacakra Tantra* itself.

Sweet Harmonies for Infinite Realms:
The History of the Precious Teachings of the Glorious
Sakyapas, the Regents of the Sage in the North

༄། །བྱང་ཕྱོགས་ཐུབ་པའི་རྒྱལ་ཚབ་དཔལ་ལྡན་ས་སྐྱ་པའི་བསྟན་པ་རིན་པོ་ཆེ་
ཇི་ལྟར་བྱུང་བའི་ལོ་རྒྱུས་རབ་འབྱམས་ཞིང་དུ་སྙན་པའི་སྒྲ་དབྱངས། །

གདོང་ཐོག་བསྟན་པའི་རྒྱལ་མཚན།

Sakya Paṇḍita Kunga Gyaltsen on the left and his nephew Chogyal Pagpa on the right surrounded by the lineage teachers of the Guhyasamāja tantra and the deities Akṣobhyavajra, Mañjuvajra, and Avalokita.

CENTRAL TIBET, SIXTEENTH CENTURY, 28.5 X 24 INCHES, COLLECTION OF SHELLEY & DONALD RUBIN

Foreword by His Holiness Sakya Trizin

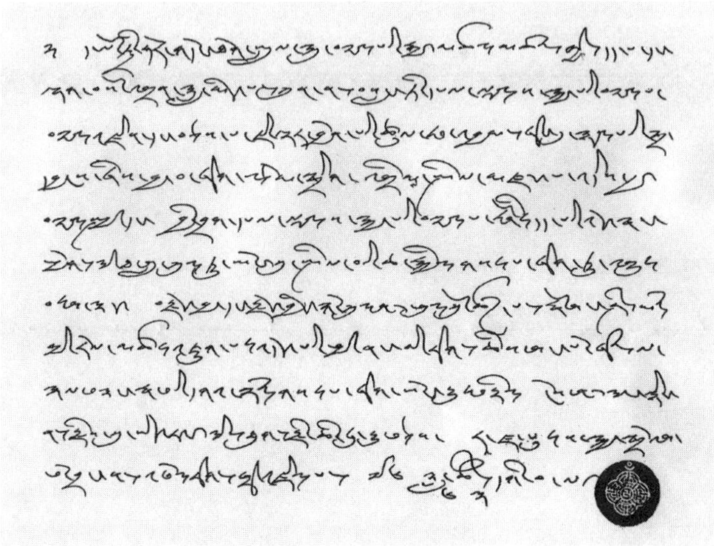

RECENTLY, Trehor Dhongthog Tulku Tenpai Gyaltsen, motivated by supreme faith and unrivaled sincere aspirations, has composed and published *Sweet Harmonies for Infinite Realms*, an account of how the teachings and teachers of the glorious Sakya came to be. Thanks to this, the light of faith in the precious Sakya teachings—the general and special teachings of the Conqueror—can now spread to every corner of the world. Since what is written here and the person who has written it are so thoroughly excellent, this is a new feast of auspiciousness for all people, both Buddhists and non-Buddhists, who wish to enter the ocean of all there is to learn. Knowing this and rejoicing from the heart, this foreword was written in gratitude by the throne holder of the Khon family line in the Sakya Podrang in Rajpur on June 3, 1976.

Author's Preface

BECAUSE A HEAP of faults like me lacks any of the qualities of an author of treatises, I am not worthy of the respect due to a writer. Many marvelous Dharma histories have already been written by previous Sakya scholars, and the difficulty involved in a new composition is quite unnecessary. Therefore at no stage have I felt any pride in writing this new Dharma history.

Nowadays when trivialities are elevated to the level of the Dharma, an ordinary person like myself who has been helplessly caught in the trap of bustle and distraction may have a little desire for hearing and contemplating but doesn't have the time to examine the vast ocean of scriptures, and has little diligence anyway. At a place and time like this, it is difficult even to gather the books one needs, so it is merely wishful thinking to hope that this afflicted body might be the basis for a perception of reality. Those of lesser intellect like myself need to begin by awakening faith and pure vision based on a concise history of the Dharma. Then they need to gradually exert themselves in listening and contemplating, and having trained their intelligence, practice according to the way of this stainless tradition, ultimately achieving the great result. I have been motivated by the idea that this book may be a beneficial contributing factor, either directly or indirectly, to such people.

What appears below has been gathered from the authoritative texts. Apart from a few necessary supplements, and some new sentences added to fill in the gaps, I have left everything as it is, as the blessed words of our sacred forefathers. I have asked advice from the lord of the teachings, the glorious Sakya Trizin Vajradhara, from the holder of the treasury of the spoken transmission, Chetsun Chogye Trichen Rinpoche, and from Khenpo Deno Changwa Yonten Zangpo of the glorious Sakya College. Having had the confirmation of their gracious words and having obtained permission from them, I have had no doubts about compiling this history with the appropriate expansions and summaries.

This book has been well produced, and the publication process—writing, correcting, printing, and so on—has been scrupulously checked from beginning to end. Therefore I hope that those who approach it with the attitude of placing confidence in the Dharma rather than the person will find it to be a reliable source.

This preface was written by the author on the first day of the tenth month of the fire-dragon year (December 20, 1976). May there be virtue.

I prostrate with my three gates at the feet of my glorious root lama in whom all of the body, speech, mind, qualities, and activities of the buddhas of the three times are gathered, Choje Palden Sakya Paṇḍita Kunga Gyaltsen Palzangpo. I pray that he will stay close to me throughout all future time.[1]

Due to his compassion he displayed the body of a spiritual guide without moving from the unelaborated mind that is the dharmakāya,
and then he showed the methods for liberation appropriate to the different levels of intellect among trainees:
I place the top of my head at the feet of my lama, who is supremely kind and learned.

The illusory wisdom emanations that miraculously unify emptiness and compassion,
the lords of all that is animate and inanimate in the variety of peaceful, lustful, and wrathful forms,
those who bestow the two kinds of accomplishment, ordinary and supreme, such as the glorious Hevajra:
with faith I rely on the principal deities of the maṇḍalas of the four classes of tantra.

The perfect Buddhas, the Teacher who taught the path of liberation to limitless beings,

the Dharma of scripture and realization, the final pacification that completely pacifies the three kinds of suffering and their causes,
the Saṅgha of noble ones, the students who study well the three superior disciplines:
I faithfully rely on the Three Supreme Jewels, supreme undeceiving refuges for all beings including the gods.

Though renunciation and realization are the same for all buddhas,
because he made five hundred prayers of aspiration for the great undertaking,
he is praised as a white lotus amid a thousand guides:
I pay homage to the king of the Śākyas.

As a symbol of his conquest of unawareness and his teaching of thusness,
he is supported by an *utpala* flower, and a book adorns his hand.
His youthful body has the radiance of the rising sun:
heroic Mañjuśrī, be my protector throughout all my lifetimes.

The two supreme ones and the six ornaments of Jambudvīpa,
among them the chariots of view and activity, Nāgārjuna and Asaṅga,
and those supreme ones who maintained the teachings by performing austerities,
such as Virūpa: to them I bow down.

Illuminating the sūtra and mantra teachings of the perfect Conqueror,
they traveled the globe to lead others to the mind of enlightenment,
thus causing the realm of Tibet to be pervaded by the light of the Dharma:
I remember with devotion the benevolence of the Dharma kings, lotsāwas, and paṇḍitas.

The jeweled *adarśa* (mirrors) that taught the great secret,
whose miraculous forms were purified and cleansed by learning and accomplishment,
the eight chariots of the practice lineage in the snowy lands of the far east:

I have heartfelt faith in those sages who established the tradition.

The hundred thousand rivers of the personally transmitted tradition of
sūtra, mantra, and instruction,
brought through the canals of hearing, thinking, and meditating,
are kept by the lords of the teachings in the lakes of their intellects:
the five Sakya forefathers are the conquerors at the crown of my head.

The exalted ones who understood and disseminated the long tradition
of Ānanda,
the all-knowing second Buddha, Ewampa,
the great Tsar father and sons who were masters of the spoken
transmission:
such are the supreme sages who have come to us one after another.[2]

Once the benevolent father and sons established the textual tradition in
their hearts,
they vanquished the enemies of the teaching and bound them by oath
to be protectors;
Pañjaranātha, the four-faced guardian and sisters, Begtse, and the rest—
stay always near and dispel inner, outer, and intermediate obstacles.

When we begin by spreading these clouds of verse in praise of the sacred objects of refuge, the doors to good fortune are flung open. This unconfused history of the stainless tradition of the Sakyapas, who like second Teachers full of enlightened activities brought the precious teachings of the Conqueror to the land of snows, is gathered from the words of our forefathers. I set it down here with unwavering faith.

· 1 ·

The Dharma in India and Tibet

FOUR SCHOOLS of the Hīnayāna and Mahāyāna appeared in India, the land of the noble ones, and the Old and New mantra systems of the four main schools, along with their subdivisions, appeared in Tibet. We should have confidence that these are all part of the Conqueror's inconceivable and unobjectified activity, derived from his compassion and appropriate to the various abilities of students. Holding the Three Jewels as our refuge, we should accomplish the unique teaching of the Buddha by means of the cause that resembles its effect, practicing the four mudrās that authenticate the view.

With this in mind I will establish the context by teaching how our guide, the precious teacher, the sage who possessed the ten powers, appeared in our worldly realm. Then I will write a preliminary historical account of the gradual propagation of the teachings in the noble land of Tibet. In order that this may be a cause for intelligent readers to develop conviction, and be relevant and coherent, it will be taught in three parts: the origin of the precious teachings of the Buddha in the world in general, the propagation of the teachings in Tibet in particular, and the duration of the teachings.

The first of these is in four parts: the life of the Teacher, the way he expounded the Dharma, the way the teachings were compiled, and the lives of the saints who upheld the teachings.

The Life of the Teacher

According to the definitive meaning, the Conqueror should not be a subject of calculation, reduced to no more than an enumeration that constructs and measures a series of lifetimes as periods of time in a particular world. As was said by the saint Jamgon Sakya Paṇḍita:

> To say that he lived only at this particular point
> entails that he was limited to that particular point,
> which runs contrary to the scriptures of the Leader of Beings;
> therefore we should analyze his limitless intention.

On the other hand, according to the indirect meaning, in this fortunate eon a thousand nirmāṇakāyas have appeared in succession at the self-arisen vajra seat in Magadha, which is in the middle of the land beautified by the tree of Jambu, located in this enduring world system. They have shown the way to buddhahood and then turned the wheel of the Dharma. Then came our teacher, the Lord of Sages, the Fourth Guide.

The divisions of this enduring world system in which the Conqueror appeared are usually made according to the *Abhidharmakośa*:

> The four continents, the sun and moon,
> Mount Meru, the gods' desire realm,
> and the thousand worlds of Brahmā—
> a thousand of these worlds form the upper part.
> A thousand sets of these form the second thousand,
> which is the middle world system.
> And a thousand sets of those form the third thousand;
> these worlds all come into being together.

These billion world systems, each of which contains four continents, are encircled by a single iron ring. Our system of a thousand worlds to the power of three is called the *enduring world system*. The creation, abiding, and destruction of these worlds occur simultaneously.

So the conditions for the appearance of a nirmāṇakāya are known as "this enduring world system" and "this golden age." *Enduring* means "to withstand," for it withstands the three poisonous defilements and cannot be stolen away by them. It is enduring due to the mental fortitude of the Sage. As is said in the *Karuṇāpuṇḍarīka Sūtra*:

> Why is this world system called *enduring*? These sentient beings endure attachment, they endure aversion, and they endure ignorance. They endure the chains of affliction. That is why this world system is known as *enduring*. In this world system there

> arises what we call the *great golden age*. Why is it called the great golden age? Because in this great golden age, among sentient beings performing acts of attachment, aversion, and ignorance, a thousand perfect buddhas, blessed ones endowed with great compassion, will appear.

There are also omens of the coming of the thousand buddhas. Before they came to this very world and this corrupt age, a thousand golden lotuses appeared in the middle of a lake. The gods of the pure abodes examined them and knew them to be an omen of the coming of a thousand buddhas. "Amazing!" they said. "This is the golden age." And that is why, according to the *Karuṇāpuṇḍarīka Sūtra*, this became known as the golden age.

So how did our teacher, the Lord of Sages, come into this world? According to Nāgārjuna's *Aṣṭamahāsthānacaityastotra*:

> First he roused the supreme awakening mind
> and gathered the accumulations over three incalculable eons.
> Subsequently he conquered the four Māras.
> Homage to the lionlike Conqueror.

There are many ways of teaching the way in which he roused his mind. According to the Mahāyāna, it was when he was born as a chariot puller in the hell realms. When he tried to protect his weaker companions, he was stabbed again and again by the guards of hell. At this point he developed the awakening mind. He spoke of this in the *Sūtra on Repaying Kindness* and the *Bhadrakalpika Sūtra*:

> In a previous life, I had been born into the lower realms,
> yet because I made an offering
> to the Tathāgata Śākyamuni,[3]
> this was the first time I roused the supreme awakening mind.

Subsequently he gathered the accumulations; the Mahāyāna account of this is given in the *Sūtrālaṃkāra*:

> This bhūmi is stated to be the first.
> On it for an incalculable eon . . .

And:

> By perfecting his practice for three incalculable eons,
> he completed the path of meditation.

One incalculable eon is reckoned to be sixty calculable eons. For three of these periods, he gathered the accumulations of merit and wisdom and actualized the tenth bhūmi. For the first incalculable eon, he attained the first bhūmi through devoted conduct.[4] In the second eon he reached the seventh bhūmi, and in the third he attained the tenth bhūmi.

The way he attained final liberation, as understood in the Lesser Vehicle, is set out in the *Abhidharmakośa*:

> The Teacher and the solitary ones achieve enlightenment
> purely on the basis of the final contemplation;
> prior to that they are merely in accord with liberation.

And:

> He became a buddha after three incalculable eons.

While on the path of accumulation, he gathered the virtues conducive to liberation. Then in his final life as Prince Siddhārtha, in the body of an ordinary person, he conquered Māra at Bodhgaya as twilight fell. In the middle period, relying on the four absorptions as his main practice, he advanced to the path of application. From dusk until dawn he perfected the six perfections, completing them at the moment of sunrise. Then he reached full enlightenment and became glorified by the marks and signs of a fully ripened rūpakāya. Having understood all, he resolved to come to the aid of those who could be taught, bringing everyone throughout space to nirvāṇa.

According to the ordinary Mahāyāna, three incalculable eons after he developed the awakening mind, he was born on the tenth bhūmi as the sacred child of the god Śvetaketu, just a single birth away from enlightenment. After this existence as a bodhisattva of the tenth bhūmi, he was born as Prince Siddhārtha and achieved buddhahood in this realm of ours.

In the tradition of the extraordinary Mahāyāna, each of the thousand buddhas of the golden age achieve buddhahood in the richly adorned realm of Akaniṣṭha, and only then do they display the activities of a buddha in Jambudvīpa. As it says in the *Ghanavyūha Sūtra*:

> All buddhas reside in Akaniṣṭha;
> they do not achieve buddhahood in the realm of desire,
> nor do they carry out the activities of a buddha.

And in *Laṅkāvatāra Sūtra*:

> Transcending even the pure heavens,
> the perfect buddha achieved buddhahood
> in Ghanavyūha Akaniṣṭha,
> and a nirmāṇakāya became a buddha here.

Other examples can be seen in sūtras like *Pitāputrasamāgama Sūtra*. This sūtra tells how the tathāgata Indraketu attained buddhahood three incalculable great eons in the past. He too displayed like a magical illusion the activities of developing the awakening mind, training in the path, and awakening. According to these sūtras, all buddhas achieve buddhahood while based in Akaniṣṭha. In buddhahood the saṃbhogakāya possessing the five certainties and the dharmakāya possessing the two purities are inseparable. Without moving from that state, like the appearance of the moon in ten million jugs of water, they display the activities of transferring from the Tuṣita heaven and so on in a billion Jambudvīpas.

In the sūtras, the main activities of these emanated compassionate teachers are summarized in twelve sections. These stages are given in Maitreya's *Uttaratantraśāstra*:

> He knew the world through his great compassion;
> having seen all worlds,
> without moving from the dharmakāya,
> through its manifold nature of emanation,
> he was born into the highest birth:
> transferring from his abode in Tuṣita,
> he entered the womb and was born.
> He became skilled in the arts,
> sported with princesses,

renounced all and practiced asceticism.
Coming to the seat of enlightenment,
he vanquished Māra's hosts and became fully enlightened.
Then he turned the wheel of the Dharma and went to nirvāṇa.
And so in impure lands,
he teaches for as long as saṃsāra remains.

Let us tell the story according to these stages. The first stage is the encouragement of the buddhas of the ten directions. Our teacher was once born into an exalted family of brahmans. After he died, he was reborn in Tuṣita as the sacred child of the god Śvetaketu, a bodhisattva who was one life away from enlightenment. While he was residing as a Dharma teacher of the Mahāyāna, sitting on a lion throne in a high mansion, he was encouraged by the buddhas of the ten directions. Their words of encouragement spontaneously came forth as a melodious song: "The time has come to train the beings of Jambudvīpa. Do you realize that you possess oceans of merit due to the power of your previous aspirations and the blessings of the conquerors of the ten directions? Your limitless intelligence produces light rays of wisdom! You have a multitude of unequaled powers and vast magical skills! Consider the prophecy that was made by Dīpaṃkara!" When the bodhisattva thought about these words and considered their meaning, he realized that the time had come.

The second stage is the transference from Tuṣita. As we have seen, the bodhisattva was residing on the Dharma throne. He taught his devoted entourage of divine beings the 108 doorways to the Dharma, such as "the doorway to the Dharma is single-mindedness." Then he introduced the awakening mind, patience, and the pure vision of Dharma. Then the bodhisattva took his own crown and placed it on the head of Maitreya, empowering him as his regent.

The bodhisattva had five visions: that he would live one hundred years, that he would be born in the continent of Jambudvīpa, in the country of India, and into the royal caste, and that an exceptional woman was to bear him. Then with a voice like a lion, he said to his entourage: "The time has come for me to go to train the beings of Jambudvīpa." Thus he made them aware of his intentions.

Then he assumed the form of a sacred elephant and was visited by countless gods from the mountain realms of the Four Great Kings, the heaven of the Thirty-Three, the heaven Free from Strife, the heaven of Controlling Others' Emanations, Brahmā's heaven, and Akaniṣṭha. They came bearing a multitude of different kinds of offerings.

The third stage is the entry into his mother's womb. He saw that Jambudvīpa was superior to the other three continents. He also saw that when sentient beings live a long time, it is rare for them to become disenchanted, and when they live for less than a hundred years their impurities increase so quickly that they have no opportunities. Thus he considered a hundred years an appropriate span of time for training. He saw that in Magadha the royal caste was highly esteemed. So on the fifteenth day of the last month of spring, the *vaiśākha* month of the fire-hare year, he entered the left side of Queen Mahāmāya, the wife of King Śuddhodana of Kapila, when she was observing the fast of repentance. Due to the bodhisattva's previously acquired merit, he perceived the queen's womb as a palace of sandalwood, richly arrayed with many different luxurious offerings. While the bodhisattva resided in her womb, his mother's realization came to equal his own.

The fourth stage is his birth. During the ten months spent in his mother's womb, he ripened 3.6 billion gods and men in the three vehicles. When the thirty-two omens of birth arose simultaneously, his mother was observing the fast of repentance (*poṣadha*) in the majestic heights of the forests of Lumbini. On the full-moon day of the eleventh lunar mansion in the earth-dragon year, known as *the treasury*, his mother grasped a pāla tree, and without any harm coming to her, the bodhisattva was born from her left side, unstained by the uterus, and fully clothed. The gods and nāgas offered him ablutions of nectar, while Brahmā gave him garments of Benares cotton. Then he took seven steps in each of the four directions, at every seventh step proclaiming himself the greatest in the world. There was the sound of cymbals, and everywhere was filled with light. In Magadha, the bodhi tree began to grow. All of the realms were filled with a billion billion omens of virtue, such as the spontaneous surfacing of five thousand treasures. Therefore he was given the name Sarvārthasiddha, "he who accomplishes all aims." Even the gods worshiped him and honored him with the name Devātideva, "god among gods." The learned astrologers predicted that if the prince stayed inside the palace, he would become a universal sovereign, but if he renounced it he would become a buddha. He was cared for by eighty-four nursemaids.

The fifth stage is his training in the arts. When he had grown into boyhood, he learned the alphabet from the writing instructor Viśvāmitra. In a similar way he learned astrology, archery, and swimming. With his knowledge, prowess, beauty, and learning, he overpowered every arrogant person he met. When he rested under the Jambu tree, the shade did not leave his body.

The sixth stage is his sporting with the princesses. The bodhisattva understood that all of the objects of desire are like optical illusions. However, in order to guide sentient beings and show how to abandon that which is improper, he decided to train in the same way as previous conquerors. He chose the daughter of Śākya Daṇḍapāṇi to be his wife. Then he took part in contests of writing, counting, archery, strength, and magical feats and destroyed the arrogance of all challengers. Thereafter he lived surrounded by an entourage of sixty thousand princesses, including Yaśodharā-Gopā, and Mṛgajā, achieving the benefit of beings through pleasure and play.

The seventh stage is his leaving the palace and practicing asceticism. When the bodhisattva was twenty-nine and living in the palace, the blessings of the tathāgatas of the ten directions brought forth a song to tell him that the time had come to renounce it all. This produced in him the wish to leave home. When he was on his way to the pleasure grove of Udyāna, he saw a man exhausted and tormented by old age at the eastern gate of the city of Kapila. At the southern gate he saw a man oppressed by illness. At the western gate he saw the body of a man who had died being lifted onto a bier and taken away to the charnel ground. At the northern gate he saw a calm renunciate wearing saffron-colored religious robes. These sights made him understand the shortcomings of saṃsāra and the noble qualities of renunciation. He returned to the palace and began to get ready to leave home.

The king, having heard of this, had powerful warriors guard the four gates of the city and commanded the attendant princesses to delay the bodhisattva by behaving in seductive ways. But the bodhisattva's mind was firm and could not be swayed. Seeing this, the king gave his permission. The bodhisattva ascended to the top of the royal residence and accepted the fabled steed that was offered to him by Chandaka. The guardians of the four directions bowed at his feet, and Brahmā and the other gods came from the sky to worship him in the same way. Then he set off toward the holy stūpa at Vaiśālī, twelve *yojana* to the east.[5]

There the bodhisattva gave his clothes, ornaments, and horse back to

Chandaka. He accepted a set of saffron-colored robes from a god who had taken the form of a hunter and cut off his own hair. These were taken to the god realms by Indra, where a stūpa was erected.

In Vaiśālī and Rājagṛha he studied with Arāḍakālāma and Udraka, eventually equaling the attainments of his teachers in the absorptions on nothingness and the pinnacle of worldly existence. Yet he came to realize that this would not free him from saṃsāra. On the banks of the river Nairañjanā, with five disciples, he practiced asceticism for six years, resting in the all-pervading absorption. After this time he wished to free himself from the limits of asceticism itself, so he ate some coarse bread to fortify his body. The five disciples lost faith in him and left for Vārāṇasī.

The eighth stage is his coming to the seat of enlightenment.[6] On his way to the vajra throne, the bodhisattva was offered the refined cream of a thousand cows by a farmer's daughter, which was the ultimate auspicious sign, and he became surrounded by light to a distance of six feet. Then he accepted the gift of some grass from a mower called Svastika. Then he laid the grass at the foot of the bodhi tree, circumambulated the tree, and sat down. Then he made the following oath:

> I will remain here for long as it takes to attain enlightenment;
> even if my body withers away,
> even if my skin, bones, and flesh decay,
> I will not move my body from this seat.

And he remained there unmoving until he attained enlightenment.

The ninth stage is his conquest of Māra's hosts. The bodhisattva summoned Māra's maṇḍala by projecting light from between his eyebrows. Māra the evil one arrived to mock the bodhisattva, surrounded by millions of soldiers from his mountain realm. They took on horrifying forms and with fearful illusions attempted to overwhelm the bodhisattva. The beautiful daughters of Māra attempted to beguile him with their deceitful ways. But through his blessings the weapons turned into flowers, and the daughters of Māra became old and decrepit. With his loving kindness, the bodhisattva overcame them all. Then Sthāvarā the earth goddess came and gave witness to the bodhisattva's accomplishment and completion of the two accumulations over many eons.

The tenth stage is his attainment of full enlightenment. It was the night of the fifteenth day of the water-tiger year, known as the *virtuous*. During the first part of the night, the bodhisattva produced the four kinds of absorption,[7] and during the middle period, the three kinds of knowledge.[8] Then in the later part of the night, in the time it takes to beat a royal drum, he attained the inexhaustible wisdom, complete buddhahood. He grew to the height of seven palm trees and announced: "My path has come to an end."

The gods laid flowers that piled up to his knees, worshiped, and exalted him. All the world became filled with light, and the earth shook six times. The gods of the ten directions sang his praises.

The eleventh stage is his turning the wheel of the Dharma. Seven weeks after the attainment of buddhahood, the merchants Trapuṣa and Bhallika gave him honey. The four great kings offered him vessels made from precious stones, but he rejected them and took the honey in an ordinary vessel. Then he spoke auspicious words to them, explaining that this nectar is not experienced by mere philosophers, and announced that despite the merit of turning the wheel of the Dharma, he would not do it:

> I have found a Dharma that is like nectar,
> profound, peaceful, free from elaboration, luminous, and
> uncompounded;
> even if I taught it, nobody would understand it.
> So I will stay here in the forest, without speaking.

Having thus taught a little on his state of being, he remained there for seven weeks without expounding the Dharma. Then Brahmā and six million others brought a thousand-spoked golden wheel, while the lord of the gods, Indra, came with an entourage of ten million to offer a right-turning conch shell. They asked the Buddha to turn in this world the wheel of the Dharma, this miraculous nectar that he had discovered. The Buddha accepted their gifts immediately.

The Buddha spoke the words, "I agree to turn the wheel of the Dharma!" He was heard as far away as the heaven of Akaniṣṭha, and every god came bearing offerings to present to the Buddha. Remembering his previous aspirations, he saw that his five worthy disciples were in Vārāṇasī, and so he traveled there. When he arrived at the deer park called Ṛṣipatana, the five disciples were there. They had agreed not to bow to the Tathāgata, but that agreement was destroyed by the sight of his brilliance.

Then a thousand jeweled thrones appeared all around the Buddha. He circumambulated those of the three previous buddhas and sat down on the fourth. The throne on which he sat radiated light, and the others disappeared. Then to his five excellent disciples and eighty thousand gods, he turned the Dharma wheel with four truths that expound the middle way that is free from the two extremes. He taught these three times and then turned the wheel of the twelve aspects of dependent origination. After this the whole of his audience saw the truth, and the five disciples each attained the level of an arhat.

Then on Gṛdhrakūṭa Mountain, for those of an appropriate mindset, he turned the Dharma wheel teaching non-identity. Then in an indeterminate location he turned the final Dharma wheel that fully disclosed his intention. At the same time as these marvelous wheels were being turned, the Buddha taught in solitary places, turning limitless Dharma wheels concerning the general Mahāyāna and the special secret mantra in four classes. In between teachings he displayed an inconceivable number of miraculous activities, such as reuniting a father and son, displaying magical emanations, taming a wild elephant, and pacifying the avaricious Nanda, the aggressive Aṅgulimālā, and the ignorant Jaṭilakāśyapa.

The twelfth stage is his passing into nirvāṇa. To encourage those who believe in permanence to turn to the Dharma, and to make people understand the rarity of a buddha, the Buddha traveled to the land of Kuśinagara, the land of the Mallas, where he set up a throne between two śāla trees and concentrated his mind upon nirvāṇa. He performed his final activities of personally training the king of the gandharvas, Sunanda, and his disciple Subhadra.

Then the Buddha removed the garment covering the upper part of his body and said: "O monks, it is rare to see a tathāgata, so look upon the body of the Tathāgata! O monks, after this I shall speak no more. O monks, everything that is compounded is subject to destruction. These are the final words of the Tathāgata." Then, at the very beginning of the earth-bird year, known as the *all-embracing*, his bodily form passed away.

Then Ānanda crossed the river Vasumatī, where a stūpa was erected, girded round with the crowns of the Mallas, and the body was placed before it. When the body was cleansed it was transformed into a heap of relics. The Mallas of Kuśinagara and others each took one eighth of the relics away to their own kingdoms, building stūpas for them, instituting worship at the stūpas, and declaring the Buddha's passing a holy day. A portion of the relics that had been given to Rāvaṇa was stolen by the nāgas and worshiped by them. Thus the Tathāgata, the greatest of beings, the source of all refuge, remained for eighty years in Jambudvīpa. From the *Vibhāṣākośa*:

> The Sage, supreme being,
> lived for one year each
> at the place where he turned the wheel of the Dharma,
> at Vaiśālī, Makkolam, and in the god realms,
> Śiśumāra Hill, Kauśāmbī,
> Āṭavī, Caityagiri,
> Veṇapura, Sāketu,
> and in the city of Kapilavastu.
> He passed twenty-three years in Śrāvastī,
> four years in Bhaiṣajyavana,
> two years in the Jvālinī Cave,
> and five years in Rājagṛha.
> He had spent six years practicing austerity
> and twenty-nine years in the palace.
> So it was that the Conqueror,
> the supreme and holy sage,
> passed into nirvāṇa at the age of eighty.[9]

The way he expounded the Dharma

Initially the Bhagavan turned the wheel of the four truths in Vārāṇasī in order to guide his five disciples, who were of the śrāvaka lineage. He said: "Monks, there is the burden, and there is the one who carries the burden," teaching thus the existent nature of the apprehender and the apprehended. If he had taught unreality from the beginning, the disciples would have been terrified. So as to avoid this problem, he taught an indirect meaning that requires interpretation. By doing so, he averted any clinging to nonexistence. However, clinging to existence came to prevail, so in places like Gṛdhrakūṭa Mountain, he turned the intermediate Dharma wheel of non-identity for those trainees who had entered the Mahāyāna. In the Prajñāpāramitā sūtras he taught that all phenomena, from form to omniscience, are in their very essence without any inherent nature. By doing so, he averted any clinging to existence. However, clinging to the nonexistence of phenomena came to prevail, so in places like Śrāvastī he turned the Dharma wheel of final disclosure for those trainees who had entered into both the Hīnayāna and Mahāyāna.

In the second and third Dharma wheels, distinctions can be made between indirect and definitive meanings, and between hidden and clear intentions. The Buddha first taught that the imputed nature does not exist, the dependent nature exists conventionally, and the absolute nature exists ultimately. He then clarified the great path of the Madhyamaka in order to avert clinging to the extremes of existence and nonexistence.

The first of the three wheels is contained in the scriptural collections (*piṭaka*) of the Hīnayāna, and the second and third are in the scriptural collections of the Mahāyāna. The first wheel presents the view of the śrāvakas, the intermediate wheel presents the view of the Mādhyamikas, and the final wheel presents the view of the Cittamātrins. Therefore the intermediate wheel is the definitive meaning, and the other two are the indirect meaning. The correct understanding of this is taught in the *Sandhivyākaraṇa Tantra*:

> Without conceptualization or delusion,
> the unique vajra words that please the mind
> come forth in a multitude of specific forms
> in dependence on the dispositions of trainees.

And from the *Avataṃsaka Sūtra*:

> A single sermon contains the voices of an ocean of different
> aspects.
> Therefore, in the pure melodious speech of all the conquerors,
> there are as many melodies as there are dispositions among all
> beings.

Thus in a single sermon delivered without conceptualization by the Bhagavan, he taught every aspect of the Dharma, both sequentially and simultaneously.

How was the Dharma wheel of the extraordinary Vajrayāna turned? Were the tantras of secret mantra expounded by our Teacher or not? They were expounded by his emanations in three ways. First, the tantras that were heard in an ordinary place and by an ordinary audience, such as the five disciples, were expounded through the display of the Buddha's speech. The exposition of the *Kālacakra Tantra* was heard in an extraordinary place, the stūpa of Dhānyakaṭaka, and by an extraordinary audience, the Dharma king Sucandra. It was expounded through the display of the Buddha's body.

The second way involves tantras like *Tattvasaṃgraha* and *Cakrasaṃvara*. It says at the beginning of the *Tattvasaṃgraha* that as soon as it was completed it descended into the realms of men. This means that the Teacher came to Jambudvīpa to teach it. This is explained by the master Bhavyakīrti in his commentary on the *Cakrasaṃvara Tantra*:[10]

> This enumeration of Dharma is a beginningless continuum, in which the Bhagavan Śākyamuni has abided from the dawn of time. When teachings like the Prajñāpāramitā decline at the end of the eon in which everything is burned up by the power of time's passing, the Bhagavan Śākyamuni will expound them again. But the glorious *Cakrasaṃvara* is not like this. The tantra was received by heroes and heroines in a buddha realm beyond verbalization, and because it remains there it can never decline. This is how it was taught. On the other hand, most tantras, such as the *Guhyasamāja*, were expounded here by emanations of the Buddha himself.

Thus the third way is exposition by an emanation of the Buddha himself. The Bhagavan Śākyamuni displayed the bodily form of Guhyasamāja and taught the *Guhyasamāja Tantra*. He displayed the bodily form of Yamāri and taught the *Yamāri Tantras*. As it says in the *Guhyasamāja*:

> Then Vajrapāṇi, lord of all tathāgatas, spoke to all of the tatāgatas and all of the bodhisattvas: "This is how the *Guhyasamāja* was expounded. When the Bhagavan was residing in the city of Śrāvastī, there was a country called Oḍḍiyāna three hundred leagues to the west. There lived a king called Indrabhūti. One morning the king saw a multitude of monk-like forms flying through the sky. Not knowing what they were, he consulted his ministers. The ministers did not know either, so they asked the people. One person said: 'Three hundred *yojana* to the east

of here, in the city of Śrāvastī, there resides a son of King Śuddhodana who has attained buddhahood. Those monks are his followers.' The king was overjoyed, and bowed down in that direction while holding a flower in his hand.

"Traveling to Śrāvastī, the king saw the Teacher with his followers and became full of devotion. 'O Bhagavan, omniscient and compassionate one, illusion-like honored one, please come to my kingdom at midday tomorrow,' the king requested. So at midday on the following day, the Bhagavan and his followers arrived in Oḍḍiyāna. The king and his entourage worshiped the Buddha and made a formal request: 'We are tormented by the objects of desire. May we have a method for liberation that does not require us to abandon them?' At that moment the Buddha, in order to help ordinary beings who are full of desire, entered the *bhaga* of the vajra queen and gave empowerment to Indrabhūti in the middle of a circle of his queens. At the moment of empowerment Indrabhūti was liberated, the Vajrayāna was expounded, and the king's entourage was liberated as well. So it is spoken."

As for the *Hevajra Tantra*, it was expounded first by the Saṃbhogakāya, in the middle by the supreme emanation, Hevajra, and finally by Śākyamuni himself in Jambudvīpa. As it says in the *Commentary to the Vajramālā*:

> Subsequently, in order to subdue the four Māras, the glorious *Hevajra Tantra* was taught here in Jambudvīpa. This teaching included the extensive tantra, the concise tantra, and the explanatory tantra.

And the master Kāmadhenu has said:[11]

> In his eighty years in Jambudvīpa, the Bhagavan did not expound the precious tantras one after another. There was a unique exposition that happened all at once in a single moment. Therefore that time, and no other, is the uniquely special one.

According to these authors, the Buddha taught a limitless array of secret tantras in a variety of ordinary experiential domains such as Akaniṣṭha, on top of mountains, and in Oḍḍiyāna, the land of ḍākinīs, to various marvelous audiences all at the same time. On the other hand, the *Mañjuśrīnāmasaṃgīti* teaches that the secret mantra is expounded by the buddhas of the three times:

> This was expounded by the buddhas of the past,
> it will be expounded again by the buddhas of the future,
> and it is the source of the perfect Buddha of the present.
> Again and again, it will be expounded.

According to the *Guhyasamāja*, the tantra had previously been expounded by the bhagavan, the tathāgata, the arhat, the perfect Buddha Dīpaṃkara, and then in the intermediate period by the great sage Kāśyapa Buddha. One may object: "How can this be? The Bhagavan taught the essential points of the great secret, but because sentient beings were lacking good fortune at the time of Dīpaṃkara and Kāśyapa, they did not expound the secret mantra when they taught." The teaching that all of the buddhas of the three times expounded the secret mantra is intended for superior trainees. The teaching that they did not expound it is intended for ordinary trainees. This was explained by that protector of beings, Chogyal Pagpa.

The way the teachings were compiled

With regard to the ordinary vehicles, it is generally agreed that three councils were convened. The first council is summarized in the *Vinayakṣudrāgama*:

> During the summer that followed the Teacher's nirvāṇa,
> in a secret cave in Rājagṛha,
> Ajātaśatru provided sustenance
> for a council of five hundred arhats,
> and the Tripiṭaka was compiled.[12]

As it says, shortly before the compassionate Teacher had passed into nirvāṇa, his two supreme disciples (Śāriputra and Maudgalyāyana) and their entourages had passed into nirvāṇa. The gods chastised the monks, saying: "The words of the Teacher are now just smoke from a dead fire. Since the best of the monks have passed away, there is nobody to proclaim the Sūtras, the Vinaya, or the Abhidharma." In response to this, Elder Mahākāśyapa convened a meeting of the saṅgha in the Nyagrodha cave at Rājagṛha during the summer monsoon retreat in the year following the Buddha's nirvāṇa, under the patronage of King Ajātaśatru.

When Gavāṃpati heard that the Teacher had passed away, he passed into nirvāṇa. This meant that the arhats were one short of the five hundred needed to convene a council of the saṅgha. Mahākāśyapa made the remaining monks agree not to pass away into nirvāṇa, and he saw that Ānanda could be cultivated through censure. He chastised Ānanda thus:

> You are guilty of eight faults: (1) asking [for women to be admitted to the saṅgha], (2) not asking [the Buddha to prolong his life], (3) commenting inappropriately [on the Buddha's teachings], (4) [treading on the Budddha's] robe, (5) [offering the Buddha muddy] water, (6) [not querying when] the precepts can be relaxed, and (7, 8) displaying [to women the secret parts of the Buddha and the Buddha's golden body].[13]

Having accused Ānanda of these eight faults, he sent him away. Due to this, and encouraged by Vṛjiputra, Ānanda freed himself from mental contamination by actualizing the instructions of the Teacher and attained the state of an arhat. He returned to the gathering of the saṅgha, where Mahākāśyapa appointed him to gather the sūtras. Ānanda sat upon the lion throne, on which the five hundred arhats had placed their garments, and recited the entire collection of sūtras as they had been spoken by the Buddha. Everyone was overjoyed that every single word had been preserved.

Then in order to collect the Vinaya, Upāli ascended the lion throne and recited where the Bhagavan had first established the discipline, for whose sake, for what reason, and in what way. Then the saṅgha established the scriptures, including the two Prātimokṣa sūtras and the four collections of Āgamas.[14] Then Mahākāśyapa ascended to the lion throne. He recited the essential recollections[15] and all of the other parts of the scriptual collection known as the *mātṛkā* or Abhidharma.

At that time the gods proclaimed aphorisms like: "How wonderful! Noble Kāśyapa and the other arhats have gathered together the three scriptural collections of the Sugata. Now the numbers of the gods will increase, and the numbers of the demigods will decline." This is the account of how the first council was convened by the five hundred arhats. Afterward Mahākāśyapa entrusted the teachings to Ānanda, who entrusted them to Śāṇavāsa, who entrusted them to Upagupta, who entrusted them to Dhītika, who entrusted them to Ārya Kṛṣṇa, who entrusted them to Sudarśana.[16] These are spoken of in the Vinaya as the "seven holders of the teaching." Thus the teaching of the Buddha spread through the central and outlying regions of Jambudvīpa.

The second council was 110 years after the passing of the Teacher, during the time that Dhītika was the upholder of the teachings and the monks of Vaiśālī were engaging in ten basic improper activities. These were: exclamations of "alas!" rejoicing, cultivating the earth, drinking beer, eating salt, eating on the road, eating with two fingers, mixing foods, using new mats, and begging for gold.[17] These activities deviated from the sūtras, contradicted the Vinaya, and took the monks far from the Teacher's teaching. Therefore a council of seven hundred arhats was convened by the arhat Yaśas under the patronage of King Aśoka. The ten basic improper activities were rejected, the breaches of the monks were purified, and the correct teaching was established.

Starting from the time of King Vīrasena, the grandson of the Dharma King Aśoka and son of Vigatāśoka, and continuing over the reigns of four kings, the monks Mahādeva, Bhadra, Elder Nāga, and Sthiramati, all of whom had come under the influence of Māra, appeared in succession. They proclaimed five basic points:

> Arhats may answer others, remain unknowing,
> harbor doubts, enquire discursively,
> and they may support themselves;
> this is the Teacher's teaching.[18]

Through teaching this false Dharma they caused disharmony, and a number of different versions of the sūtras came to coexist, which brought about divisions into different sects. According to the explanations of Vinītadeva and Lodri Khenpo, there were four main schools:[19] (1) the Sarvāstivāda, (2) the Mahāsaṃgika, (3) the Saṃmitīya, and (4) the Sthavira. Some of these underwent further divisions, making a total of eighteen sects.

There were four divisions of the Sarvāstivāda: the (1) Kaśyapīya, (2) Mahīśāsaka, (3) Dharmaguptaka, and (4) Mūlasarvāstivāda. They became separate because some people held conflicting views, not because they followed a different teacher. There were six divisions of the Mahāsaṅgika: the (1) Pūrvaśaila, (2) Aparaśaila, (3) Haimavata, (4) Vibhajyavāda, (5) Prajñaptivāda, and (6) Lokottaravāda. Then there were the five divisions of the Saṃmitīya: (1) Tāmraśatiya, (2), Avantaka, (3) Kaurukullaka, (4) Bahuśrutīya, and (5) Vatsīputrīya. Then there are the three divisions of the Sthavira: (1) Jetavanīya, (2) Abhayagirivāsa, and (3) Mahāvihāravāsa.

The third council was convened to clear up disagreements regarding the transmission of the Buddha's word between the eighteen sects. It was sponsored by King Kaniṣka and held in Kuvana Monastery in the country of Gandhāra.[20] It was attended by five hundred arhats including Pūrṇika, five hundred bodhisattvas including Vasumitra, and five hundred ordinary paṇḍitas. They established that all of the eighteen sects held the pure teachings, based on the following passage drawn from the *Savapnanirdeśa Sūtra*:

> The perfect buddha Kāśyapa said to King Kṛkī, "Your majesty, the dream in which you saw eighteen men pulling on a sheet of cloth means that the teaching of Śākyamuni will become divided into eighteen sects. But the cloth itself, which is liberation, will remain undamaged."[21]

At this point the scriptural collection of the Vinaya was written down for the first time, the parts of the scriptural collection of the Sūtras and the Abhidharma that had not previously been recorded were written down, and those parts that had already been recorded were revised and corrected. This is how the third council is explained by the scholars of Magadha. The Kashmiris say that the site of the compilation of the word of the Buddha was in the Karṇikāvana monastery in Kashmir.

The Mahāyāna tradition

At Vimalasvabhāva in southern Rājagṛha, 900 million bodhisattvas assembled, and the Abdhidharma, Vinaya, and Sūtras were compiled by Mañjuśrī, Maitreya, and Vajrapāṇi respectively. It is said in Bhāvaviveka's *Tarkajvālā* that the original compilers who gathered the whole of the Mahāyāna scriptures were Samantabhadra, Mañjuśrī, the Lord of Secrets (Vajrapāṇi), Maitreya, and other bodhisattvas.

In the ultimate truth, the Buddha's word in the form of sūtra and mantra was given as an empowerment to Vajrapāṇi, the owner of the secrets of all the tathāgatas. The compiler was the Lord of Secrets alone. This can be seen in the *Vajrapāṇyabhiṣeka Tantra*.

In the Vajrayāna too, the one who requested the teachings was also the compiler. The main *Hevajra Tantra* and its explanatory tantras as well as the *Kālacakra Tantra* agree on this. Furthermore, it is taught that the Buddha's word was initially compiled by Vajrapāṇi and then later compiled by others. According to sources such as the commentary to the *Ḍākārṇavamahāyoginī Tantra*, certain tantras were received from the Bhagavan by an assembly including Vajravārāhī.[22] The way this was done was that the Bhagavan answered the questions put to him, and these answers were then compiled into the essential vajra topics. The way the teachings were compiled is explained in the commentary to the *Sitātapatrādhāraṇī*:[23]

> The teachings were requested by an assemblage of bodhisattvas in Changlochen and compiled by Vajrapāṇi.

It is also explained in the *Guhyasiddhi*:

> He assumed the form of one whose vajra mind has the nature of illusion-like wisdom, ornamented with the thirty-two signs of a saint. Then saying "Thus have I heard . . ." and so on, he taught the ultimate truth of suchness to the buddhas and bodhisattvas.

In a similar way, when the Bhagavan ripened King Indrabhūti of Oḍḍiyāna and his entourage in the maṇḍala of emanation, Vajrapāṇi compiled all of the tantras and gave them to the king. They all achieved accomplishments and became what is known as "inherently established heroes and yoginīs." Then the realm of Oḍḍiyāna became deserted. In time there appeared a great lake, under which lived nāgas. The Lord of Secrets ripened them with an emanated maṇḍala and entrusted them with a multitude of books containing the tantras. Gradually the nāgas began to take on human form and to build many cities on the shores of the lake, in which they lived. Because they practiced the Vajrayāna, accomplishments appeared in most of them. Thereafter Oḍḍiyāna came to be known as "the land of ḍākinīs" and was a unique treasury of secrets, and it is said that every one of its kings followed the Dharma.

Following this the Dharma gradually spread through the noble land of India. The king of the southern regions, Visukalpa, had a prophetic dream in which he visited Oḍḍiyāna, the residence of the ḍākinīs. The nāga yoginīs bestowed on him the *Guhyasamāja* and *Tattvasaṃgraha* tantras as well as instructions and permissions. As a result of this, the secret mantra spread throughout the southern regions. Similarly Kukkuripa introduced the *Mahāmāya Tantra*, Master Lalitavajra introduced the *Vajrabhairava Tantra*, and so on. The tantras of Hevajra in particular are said in one history to have been introduced by Virūpa, while another states that they were introduced by Ḍombī Heruka; however, there is no contradiction between these two accounts. In the same way as this, other adepts introduced a vast multitude of secret tantras from Oḍḍiyāna.

The Lives of the Saints Who Upheld the Teachings

In addition to the seven successors to whom the teachings were entrusted mentioned earlier, the commentary to the *Laṅkāvatāra Sūtra* has: Dhṛṭaka, Bidhaka, Buddhanandi, Buddhamitra, Bhikṣu Pārśva, Sunaśata, Aśvaghoṣa, Amṛta, Nāgārjuna, Āryadeva, Rāhula, Saṅghanandi, Ghalaśa, Kumārata, Shāyanta, Vasubandhu, Manota, and Haklenayaśas.[24] Each one of these entrusted the teaching to his successor, and it is said that these arhats along with the sixteen noble elders, each with his own entourage of numerous arhats, did not pass into nirvāṇa and still continue to teach and protect the teachings.

Those who are chiefly responsible for propagating the teaching of the Teacher across an ever-greater area of Jambudvīpa are known as the six ornaments and the two supreme ones.

Nāgārjuna

The noble Nāgārjuna was prophesied in scriptures such as the *Laṅkāvatāra Sūtra* and *Mañjuśrīmūla Tantra*. Four hundred years after the Buddha's passing, he was born into a brahman family. He was taken as a disciple by the great adept Saraha. He learned and put into practice the great *Guhyasamāja* and every other tantra. He traveled to the land of the nāgas and brought about the benefit of vast numbers of beings. There he discovered the *Prajñāpāramitā in a Hundred Thousand Verses*.

Nāgārjuna composed several treatises on worldly matters such as the *Jantupoṣaṇabindu* and several treatises on science such as the *Yogaśataka*. He composed the six logical treatises on the Madhyamaka, eighteen hymns, and two compendiums (the *Sūtrasamuccaya* and the *Tantrasamuccaya*). He composed sūtra literature such as the *Suhṛllekha*, and on the mantra side, the *Pañcakrama* and an inconceivable number of sādhanas of Guhyasamāja. He is said to have lived in the land of men for six hundred years.

Āryadeva

Āryadeva was born miraculously on the island of Siṃhala. As a disciple of the master Nāgārjuna he learned by heart all of the topics of the outer and inner sciences and the meaning of every sūtra and tantra. He defeated with logic those who spread falsehoods, such as Aśvaghoṣa, converting them into his own disciples. He composed the *Madhyamakacatuḥśataka*, the *Jñānasārasamuccaya*, and many distinguished treatises on the tantric side of the teachings.

Nāgabodhi

The master Nāgabodhi was born into a family of herdsmen. He was ordained by Ārya Nāgārjuna and obtained from him the initiation and instructions for the maṇḍala of Guhyasamāja. It is said that he attained the accomplishment of long life and even now resides in Śrīparvata. He composed many distinguished treatises on mantra, such as the *Guhyasamāja-maṇḍalopāyikā-viṃśatividhi*.

Aśvaghoṣa

The master Aśvaghoṣa, also known as Vīra, was a follower of Āryadeva who attained learning and accomplishments. He composed the hundred stories of the Buddha's previous lives (the *Jātakamālā*) and many commentaries on the difficult points of sūtra and mantra, such as the commentary on the fourteen root downfalls, the *Vajrayāna-mūlāpatti-saṃgraha*.

Candrakīrti

The master Candrakīrti was born in the south, in Samantara. Learning the instructions on sūtra and tantra from Nāgārjuna and Āryadeva, he attained accomplishments. With his miraculous powers, such as being able to extract milk from a painted cow, he overturned peoples' clinging to the reality of external objects. He composed many commentaries elucidating the sūtras and tantras, including the *Madhyamakāvatāra* root text and commentary, and the *Pradīpodyotana*, his great commentary on the *Guhyasamāja*.

Śāntideva

Prince Śāntideva was born the son of a king of the southern realms called Mañjuśrīvarman.[25] He gave up the kingdom and received instructions and initiations in the forests of Bengal from a master who had attained the absorption of Mañjuvajra. He attained accomplishments and defeated those who preached erroneous views, such as the non-Buddhist scholar Śaṃkara, leading them to the correct teachings. He was ordained in Nālandā, where he dedicated himself to accomplishment while acting as a layabout.[26] His activities are known as the seven miraculous stories:

> He abandoned his kingdom and attained accomplishment,
> becoming king over the realms of the two branches of science;
> he was ordained and saw the truth, and came to possess magical powers.
> I bow down to the one endowed with these seven miracles.

This master elucidated the teachings by composing the *Bodhicaryāvatāra* and the two compendiums (the *Sūtrasamuccaya* and the *Śikṣāsamuccaya*).

Asaṅga

The great master Ārya Asaṅga, who had been prophesied in the *Mañjuśrīmūla Tantra*, was born into a royal family exactly nine hundred years after the passing of the Buddha. On Mount Kukkuṭapāda he meditated upon the exalted Maitreya, eventually seeing his actual face and attaining the absorption in the stream of truth (*srotānugata-samādhi*). Asaṅga took hold of Maitreya's robes and was taken to Tuṣita, where he remained for twenty-five human years. He studied the five Dharmas of Maitreya and many sūtras, of which the most important were the Prajñāpāramitā sūtras. Thereafter he returned to the human realm. He lived for a hundred and fifty years and clarified the teachings of the Mahāyāna with his numerous treatises including the five works on the bhūmis.[27] Nāgārjuna and Asaṅga are widely renowned as the two chariots of profundity and vastness, and were both founders of traditions.

Vasubandhu

The master Vasubandhu was the brother of Asaṅga. He was born into a brahman family. At Saṅghabhadra in Kashmir he became learned, studying works such as the *Vibhāṣākośa* and the seven works of the Abhidharma.[28] Later he studied the Dharma with his elder brother, learning by heart the ninety-nine divisions of the scriptural system of the *Śatasāhasrikā*.[29] It is said that after the Teacher's nirvāṇa, there was nobody who was more learned than Vasubandhu. All of the monks of the Hīnayāna and Mahāyāna respected him, and he became known as a second Buddha.

Vasubandhu composed fifty treatises, including the root text and commentary of the *Abhidharmakośa* and the eight dissertations[30] that expounded his own system. He carried out a vast number of activities for the benefit of the teachings, setting up 654 Dharma establishments and gathering a following of 60,000 Mahāyāna monks.

Dignāga

Vasubandhu's student Dignāga, the inventor of the system of logic, defeated non-Buddhists who spread falsehoods, such as Kṛṣṇamunirāja. He composed works explaining his system of logic, such as the *Pramāṇasamuccaya*. Dignāga was able to ask Mañjuśrī himself questions about the Dharma. Over the course of his life he composed a hundred treatises and taught a wide variety of sūtras, propagating and spreading all of the teachings, even the Abhidharma. He repaired many Dharma establishments that had become derelict and assembled a group of students too numerous to count.

Dharmakīrti

Glorious Dharmakīrti became learned in logic by studying with Īśvarasena, a student of Dignāga. From the glorious Heruka he received the accomplishment of victory in debate. He clarified the system of logic by writing seven treatises, including the *Pramāṇavārttika*.[31] He became the king of all debaters and defeated numerous non-Buddhists, after which he clarified the teachings for them. He learned the Abhidharma directly from a student of Vasubandhu, and he received the blessing of a firm intellect from Lady Tārā, thus becoming a scholar without rival. He also wrote commentaries on the Abhidharma and on the *Pramāṇasamuccaya*.

Other teachers

Vimuktisena, a self-taught scholar of the Prajñāpāramitā, composed works such as the *Pañcaviṃśatisāhasrikāloka*, and the so-called *Great Commentary on the Pañcaviṃśatisāhasrikā by Venerable Vimuktisena.*[32] His student Haribhadra wrote the great commentary on the *Aṣṭasāhasrikā* and a clarification of the meaning of the *Abhisamayālaṃkāra*, among other works.[33] The self-taught scholar of Vinaya, the brahman master Venerable Guṇaprabha, clarified the teachings of the Vinaya with works such as his root text, the *Vinaya Sūtra*. Śākyprabha composed the *Triśatakārikā*, among other works.

Nāgārjuna, Asaṅga, and Dignāga authored original works, while Āryadeva, Vasubandhu, and Dharmakīrti authored commentaries. Together they are known as the six ornaments of Jambudvīpa. In addition Nāgārjuna and Asaṅga are known as the two chariots, and when certain later figures are included, the masters Guṇaprabha and Śākyprabha are added to the six ornaments. Prince Śāntideva, who was endowed with the seven miraculous stories, and Candragomin, who was learned in all the branches of science and attained accomplishments, are praised together as the two wondrous masters. In addition there is Saraha and the other eighty-four adepts. Those known as scholars at the six gates are: Śāntipa, guardian of the eastern gate of Vikramaśīla; Prajñākara, guardian of the southern gate; Vāgīśvarakīrti, guardian of the western gate; Nārotapa, guardian of the northern gate; and the brahman Ratnavajra and Jñānaśrīmitra, the two central pillars.[34] And there is also Atiśa Dipaṃkāra Śrījñāna.

I have not got as far as writing about those great sages who attained learning and accomplishments, such as the senior and junior Kālacakrapādas.[35] I have not been able to write more than a little about these biographies of teachers who in their immeasurable worthiness held, protected, and spread the precious teachings of sūtra and mantra, established others in the state of ripening and liberation, and performed inconceivable numbers of other miracles. Their full biographies should be studied in the elegant writings of previous scholars.

The propagation of the teachings in Tibet in particular

This is in three parts: the earlier propagation of the teachings, the later propagation of the teachings, and an account of the schools of those who upheld the teachings.

The earlier propagation of the teachings

According to the prophecy in the *Mañjuśrīmūla Tantra*:

> When the lake in the land of snows has dried,
> a forest of sal trees will appear.

So at first there was a lake, which gradually dried up, after which a forest spread throughout the land. A monkey who was an emanation of Avalokiteśvara and a rock ogress who was an emanation of Lady Tārā copulated, and the children they produced gradually became human beings. This account of the first human beings of Tibet is given in the Dharma cycles of the Great Compassionate One such as the *Kachem Kakholma* and the *Maṇi Kabum*.

According to the commentary on the *Devātiśayastotra* by Prajñāvarman, over two thousand years before the Buddha came to India, at the very beginning of the age of the present degenerate eon, the five Pāṇḍavas were at war with their enemies, the twelve armies of the Kauravas. A king called Rūpati and a thousand of his troops disguised as women fled into the Himālaya and spread from there.

At first this land was ruled by nonhuman beings. Gradually they took on human form, and the land came to be ruled by twelve minor kingdoms and forty principalities. Then came Nyatri Tsenpo, the first human king and the ruler of all Tibet. Some say that he was the fifth descendent of Prasenajit, the king of Kosala. Others say that he was the fifth descendent of the weakest son of Bimbisāra. Others say that he was the son of Udayana, the king of Vatsa. However, according to the transmission of the *Mañjuśrīmūla Tantra*, he came from the Śākya Licchavi clan.

In any case, a wonderful superhuman being appeared on Mount Lhari Rolpa in the land of snows. When he reached Tsentang Gozhi, the Bonpos called him a god because he arrived on a sky cord and a sky ladder. When they asked who he was, he replied, "I am the Tsenpo." When they asked him where he had come from, he pointed to the sky. "He should be our ruler," they said and placed him on a wooden throne (*tri*) that was carried on the necks (*nya*) of four men. Therefore he became known as Nyatri Tsenpo, the first ruler of Tibet.

In the succession there were seven heavenly kings called Tri including Nyatri Tsenpo, two higher kings called Teng, six middle kings called Lek, eight earthly kings called De, and five lower kings called Tsen. Throughout these five dynasties the continuity of the kingdom was sustained by means of traditional narratives and Bon.

In the *Vimaladevīvyākaraṇa* it says:

> Two thousand five hundred years after my parinirvāṇa, the true Dharma will be propagated in the land of the red-faced men.[36]

In accordance with this prophecy, when the twenty-eighth king, Lha Totori Nyentsen, who was an emanation of the bodhisattva Samantabhadra, was living in the palace of Yumbu Lagang, a casket fell onto the roof of the palace. When it was opened it was found to contain the *Pangkong Sūtra of a Hundred Homages*, a mould for the Cintāmaṇi form of Avalokiteśvara, the *Karaṇḍavyūha Sūtra*, the six-syllable mantra, and a golden stūpa. Although the king did not know what they were, he understood that they were auspicious and gave them the name Fearsome Secret. Due to the blessing of worshiping and venerating them, the king, a man of sixty-one years, became a healthy youth of sixteen again. He lived on for sixty more years and so reached the age of one hundred and twenty. The king obtained a prophecy that the kingdom would go from strength to strength, and after five reigns the meaning of the Fearsome Secret would be understood.

According to Nelpa Paṇḍita, the Bonpos say that the casket fell from the sky because they revere the sky, but in actual fact those two texts were brought by the paṇḍita Losemtso and the Khotanese lotsāwa Tese. When they arrived they found that the king could neither read the writing nor understand the meaning, so paṇḍita and lotsāwa went back again.[37] This is corroborated by the *Testimony of Ba*'s account of Ba Selnang's visit to Nepal. When he met the abbot Śāntarakṣita, the abbot said to him: "While the Buddha Kāśyapa was teaching, the Tsenpo of Tibet, you, and I were the three sons of a woman who kept poultry, and we made a vow to disseminate the teachings in Tibet. I have been sitting and waiting here for nine reigns for the Tsenpo to be born and for you to come of age."[38] Some scholars believe this version to be correct. However, the Fifth Dalai Lama says:

> Nelpa Paṇḍita's belief that it is absurd for a casket to fall from the sky is proof of his stupidity. In the auspicious circumstances in which the teachings were first discovered, the magical activities and compassion of noble individuals is beyond ordinary thought.[39]

Thus scholars hold different positions on this matter. I think that it is possible that ordinary and extraordinary trainees perceive events differently.[40]

According to the prophecy in the *Mañjuśrīmūla Tantra*:

> In the place surrounded by snowy mountains
> called the Land of Gods,
> a king called God Among Men will be born
> into the Licchavi race.

Totori was followed by three successors, and then by Namri Songtsen, the fourth. After the latter's death, the Dharma king Songtsen Gampo, an emanation of Avalokiteśvara, inherited the kingdom at the age of thirteen. When he was fifteen he invited an emanated monk called Akaramati to bring a spontaneously manifested image of Avalokiteśvara. He also invited Nepalese and Chinese princesses, emanations of Tārā and Bhṛkuṭī. They both came with a wish-fulfilling image of the Teacher.

The king also sent his minister Tumi Sambhoṭa to gather the necessary elements for writing Tibetan from writing experts in the noble land of India and to create an alphabet.[41] Thereafter translations were made of the *Karaṇḍavyūha Sūtra*, the *Pangkong Sūtra of a Hundred Homages*, the *Ratnamegha Sūtra*, and the twenty-one sūtras and tantras of Avalokiteśvara.

Then Songtsen Gampo established two temples to hold the two images of Śākyamuni, called Trulnang and Ramoche. He used these along with his own palace as models for the border-taming and further-taming temples and their contents. He assured the happiness of all of his Tibetan subjects with a system of law based on the ten virtuous teachings of the gods and the sixteen pure teachings of men.

The king invited masters from India, including Kusara, the brahman Śaṃkara, and the Nepalese master Śīlamañju, and masters from China such as Heshang Mahāyāna. They translated portions of the three scriptural collections and the tantras, thus introducing the teachings into Tibet. Though nobody actually taught or studied, the king himself secretly bestowed the precepts of the peaceful and wrathful forms of the Great Compassionate One to a lucky few. There were about a hundred long-haired yogins based at Nyangdren Pabongkha and elsewhere who passed down the transmission of the mahāyoga of the Great Compassionate One.

After Songtsen Gampo came Gungri Guntsen, Mangsong Mangtsen, Dusong Mangpoje, and "the bearded ancestor" Tride Tsugtsen. Then in the fifth generation came the emanation of Mañjuśrī called Trisong Detsen. His ancestor Songtsen Gampo had made the following prophecy: "Five generations from now, in the lifetime of a descendant called King De, the true Dharma will appear." In accordance with this, Trisong Detsen inherited the kingdom at the age of thirteen. At the age of twenty he developed the aspiration to spread the true Dharma, and he invited the bodhisattva Śāntarakṣita and the great master Padmasambhava into order to build the immutable and spontaneously arisen great temple of Samye.

Several intelligent young Tibetans trained as lotsāwas, and many great paṇḍitas were invited from the holy land of India, including the masters Jinamitra, Buddhagupta, Vimalamitra, and Śāntigarbha. Twelve Sarvāstivādin monks were also invited. To begin with, seven men, including Ba Rinchen Sungwa, were ordained in order to test whether the Tibetan people were suitable for ordination. These were the first ordained Tibetans. Following them 108 lotsāwas, including Kawa Paltseg, and then a 1008 lotsāwas, including Chogro Lui Gyaltsen, were ordained and trained their minds.

The Buddha's word, in the form of sūtra and mantra, and the major commentaries and treatises elucidating his intentions were translated into Tibetan by paṇḍitas like the abbot Śāntarakṣita and the master Padmasambhava, along with lotsāwas like Bairotsana and the trio of Ka, Chog, and Zhang.[42] Bairotsana, Namkhai Nyingpo, and others were sent to India, where they studied and attained accomplishments in doctrines like the Great Perfection, which they then disseminated in Tibet.

Furthermore, after the great master Padmasambhava arrived in Tibet, he sent forth magical emanations to visit each of the central and border areas of Tibet in succession, where he bound with oaths all of the powerful non-human beings of Tibet, including the twelve earth goddesses, the thirteen hunter gods, and the twenty-one laymen. He also blessed the mountains, rocks, caves, and lakes of Tibet as places for meditation, and he ripened and liberated the king and many of his fortunate subjects with initiations and instructions. In short, he carried out an inconceivable number of enlightened activities.

In the latter part of this Dharma king's life, he invited the master Kamalaśīla, who refuted the philosophy and false views of the Chinese Heshang and placed the people of Tibet in the correct philosophy and view. Through works like these the Buddha's teaching was made to shine like the sun. Thus it is said that during the life of Trisong Detsen, the true Dharma was propagated and spread throughout Tibet. Due to the great kindness of the abbot, the master, and the Dharma king, their fame reached the ears of every person in the snowy land of Tibet.

Three princes were born to the Dharma king Trisong Detsen. The eldest was Mune Tsepo, the middle one was Murug Tsepo, and the youngest was Mutig Tsepo, also known as Senaleg Jingyon. They continued and extended the propagation of the Dharma. During the reign of Mune in particular, the four great cycles of worship were instituted, and the gap between poverty and wealth among the Tibetan people was equalized three times.

Mutig built the Dorje Ying temple at Karchung. Five sons were born to him, the most important of whom was Tri Ralpachen, an emanation of noble Vajrapāṇi also known as Tritsug Detsen. The king is famed for appointing seven householders to look after each monk in his kingdom and for building a thousand temples. He worshiped and honored the two orders of clergy, the followers of sūtra and mantra, by laying at their feet the ends of the silken ribbons tying up his hair. Such were his limitless activities in honor of the high and precious victory banner of the teachings.

In the lower valley of the Kyichu River, Ralpachen built the Onchangdo Peme Trashi Gepel temple. He invited many paṇḍitas from India, including Surendrabodhi, Śīlendrabodhi, and Dānaśīla. Together with the Tibetan abbots Ratnarakṣita, Dharmatāśīla, and others, they revised most of the scriptures that had been translated in earlier times, using new terminology.

When Langdarma, another son of Senaleg, ascended to the throne, he developed an antipathy toward the Buddha's teachings due to his ambitiousness. He dissolved all of the monasteries; those who did not want to give up all the elements of monkhood, he sent out as hunters. All those who were not considered useful were killed, and after a while even the name of the true Dharma, the teaching that tames, was no longer heard in U and Tsang.

Some time later a monk called Lhalung Palgyi Dorje, who was meditating in the Yerpa caves, could no longer bear the destruction of the teachings. Going undercover, he assassinated the king and fled to Kham, taking with him the *Abhidharmasamuccaya*, the Vinaya treatise called *Prabhāvati*, and the *Karmaśataka*.

Langdarma's younger queen gave birth to a son named Namde Osung. The elder queen took a beggar's child and claimed it as her own; hence the child was given the name Tride Yumten ("on the mother's word"). As the two could not come to an agreement over the kingdom of Ngari, a major civil war erupted. Thereafter Tibet as a whole was no longer ruled by the descendents of the first king Nyatri Tsenpo. Popular uprisings soon spread from Kham across the whole of the country.

The son of Namde Osung was Ngadag Palkhortsen. His sons were Tri Trashi Tsegpapal and Trikyi Nyimagon. The first of these two ruled a kingdom and had three sons, Palde, Ode, and Kyide, who became known as the three De of eastern Tibet. Trikyi Nyimagon traveled to Ngari and established his territory there. The eldest of his three sons, Palde Rigpagon, established Mangyul; the middle son, Trashigon, established Puhrang; and the youngest son, De Tsugon, established Zhangzhung. Thus they came to be known as the three Gon of western Tibet.

De Tsugon had two sons, Khore and Tronge. The eldest became famous under his ordination name, Yeshe O. In this period the early propagation of the Dharma had come to an end, and the tradition of inviting paṇḍitas had disappeared some time ago. In Yeshe O's time a learned Nepalese lotsāwa called Padmaruci invited two paṇḍitas called Sūkṣmadīrgha and Smṛtijñānakīrti. By the time they arrived the lotsāwa had died, and the two paṇḍitas, who initially did not understand the Tibetan language, wandered around for a long time. Smṛti worked for a while as a shepherd in Tanag before eventually arriving in Kham and settling in the Tārā temple at Denyul Langtang, where he performed great deeds of instruction and learning, such as teaching Vasubandhu's *Abhidharmakośa* and composing the treatise known as *Vacanamukhāyudhopama*.

The later propagation of the teachings

This is in two parts: how the flame of the teachings was kept in eastern Tibet, and how the teachings spread from western Tibet.

How the flame of the teachings was kept in eastern Tibet

When Langdarma snuffed out the teachings, three men called Mar Śākyamuni, Yo Gejung, and Tsang Rabsal put a load of Vinaya books onto a mule and fled to Kham. When they were living and meditating at the Crystal Retreat in Dantig, a man called Muzug saw their fire and came to ask faithfully for ordination.[43] He was ordained by Mar, acting as the abbot, and Yo, acting as the preceptor, and given the name Gewa Rabsal. Later, because of his good heart, he came to be known as Lachen ("the great lama") Gongpa Rabsal.

A year later Gewa Rabsal asked for the full ordination, but this required five monks. Therefore he zealously searched for and found the residence of Lhalung Palgyi Dorje, who said, "Since I killed the evil king I can't come to complete the group, but I will find others and send them to you." He delegated the Chinese monks Kewang and Gyipen, and Gewa Rabsal was fully ordained by this group of five. Thereafter Gewa Rabsal studied the Vinaya for fifteen years with the abbot and the master.

Five years after Gewa Rabsal's full ordination, ten men from central Tibet, including one called Lume, arrived in Kham. They obtained the complete ordination by receiving the three aspects of ordination one by one in a single sitting. Because he did it all at once in this way, and because he had not completed the required ten years studying all aspects of the teachings, Lachen became known as one who performs the activities of a bodhisattva. Mar, Yo, and Tsang were also extraordinary people, and this was a time of great need, when the teachings were in decline. So it is said, and some lamas have concluded that there was no fault in the way Gewa Rabsal bestowed the ordinations. According to some other people, however, the practice of the Vinaya became faulty through this improper practice.

In any case, when the ten men of central Tibet arrived in Yar, many monastic settlements spread, and this became known as the lineage of the Vinaya from eastern Tibet. Much later Lochen Dharmaśrī encouraged the exposition and practice of this lineage of the vows, the very same one that is to be found in the monastic university Orgyen Mindroling and its subsidiaries, where the traditions of the early propagation of the Dharma are upheld.

This teaching lineage passed from Jinamitra and Dānaśīla to Chogro Lui Gyaltsen, then to Mar, Yo, and Tsang, then to Lachen, then to Drum Yeshe Gyaltsen, then to Lume Tsultrim Wangchug, and then to Zu Dorje Gyaltsen. After that it merged with the transmission of the Vinaya from western Tibet.[44]

How the Teachings Spread from Western Tibet

Lha Lama Yeshe O invited the paṇḍita Dharmapāla from Eastern India, who encouraged the exposition and practice of the Vinaya. Dharmapāla had three students each called Pāla, one of whom, Prajñāpāla, was the teacher of the king of Zhangzhung, Gyalwai Sherab. From the latter's students, such as the lotsāwa Paljor, the lineage known as *the western Vinaya* was gradually propagated throughout Tibet. The teaching lineage passed from Jinamitra and Dānaśīla to Śākyasena, then to Dharmapāla, then to Lub Lotsāwa and Kyog Duldzin, then from those two to Zu Dorje Gyaltsen. From that point the teaching lineages of Eastern and Western Tibet merged into one. Thereafter Zu's four sons spread the lineage far and wide.[45]

Lhade, the son of Khore, invited the paṇḍita Subhutiśrīśānti, and together they translated treatises on the Prajñāpāramitā. The first of all the lotsāwas of the latter propagation was the unrivaled translator Rinchen Zangpo, who was made the chaplain of the kingdom of U.

Lhade had three sons: Ode, Zhiwa O, and Jangchub O. The youngest, the monk Jangchub O, aspired to invite paṇḍitas and propagate the Dharma in accordance with the wishes of his uncle, Lha Lama Yeshe O. He sent Nagtso Lotsāwa to India in order to invite the glorious Jowoje Atiśa. Following a prophecy from his yidam deity, Atiśa traveled to Ngari and expounded many deep and profound Dharma teachings to worthy ones like Lha Lama. He composed the treatise called *Bodhipathapradīpa*. Dromton Gyalwai Jungne invited Atiśa to U, where he expounded many Dharma teachings from both the Hīnayāna and Mahāyāna.

Many scholars and adepts who spoke both Tibetan and Sanskrit appeared during this period, including the lotsāwa Rinchen Zangpo, Lha Lama Yeshe O, Podrang Zhiwa O, Nagtso, Ngog Legpai Sherab, Zangskar Pagpa Sherab, Drogmi Śākya Yeshe, Marpa Chokyi Lodro, Go Khugpa Lhetse, Malgyi Lodro Drag, Patsab Nyima Drag, Dro Sherab Drag, Ra Dorje Drag, Ra Chorab, Chag Drachom, Tropu Jampai Pal, and the Dharma lord Sapaṇ. They translated, taught, and practiced a vast number of scriptures from the three scriptural collections and the four classes of the tantras, and caused the precious teachings of the Conqueror to shine like the sun.

In particular, the lotsāwa Tropu Jampai Pal invited the great Kashmiri paṇḍita Śākyaśrī to Tibet. In Gyengong temple in Lower Nyang, Śākyaśrī ordained Sapaṇ, and in the Trogma retreat in Chushul he ordained eleven men, including Kherge Jangchub Pal and Tsangma Dorje Pal, all in a single day. It is well known that the lineage of the vows of the great Sakya Monastery comes from the Dharma lord Sapaṇ, while the Ngorpa lineage of the vows comes from the great scholar Dorje Pal via the transmission of the omniscient Kunga Zangpo and his son. Right up to the present day, this lineage of the vows is the one that has spread everywhere.

An account of the schools of those who upheld the teachings

This is in two parts: a brief account of the Old and New schools, and an extensive account of the traditions of glorious Sakya.[46]

A brief account of the Old and New schools

After the lotsāwas and paṇḍitas of Tibet established the scriptures and treatises by requesting, translating, studying, and teaching them, a great many individual schools appeared. Some were known by the name of their systems of precepts: the Kadampa, the Dzogchenpa, the Kagyupa, and the Zhijepa. Some were known by the names of places, like the Sakyapa, the Jonangpa, the Shangpa, the Drigungpa, and the Gandenpa. And some were known by the names of masters, like the Karmapa and the Bulugpa.[47] Thus the practitioners of specific Dharmas came to be identified as individual schools. The schools do not seem to have been identified according to their philosophical views, as was the case in the noble land of India.

Nyingma

The Nyingma school of the earlier propagation is famed for its accomplished masters, thanks to the kindness of the Dharma king Songtsen Gampo. In the year of the iron tiger 937 years after the ruler of Tibet Nyatri Tsepo passed away, the abbot, the master, and the Dharma king came together in Tibet.[48] A hundred paṇḍitas came to Tibet. The great lotsāwa Bairotsana and the trio of emanational lotsāwas Kawa, Chogro, and Zhang translated all the famous scriptures and commentaries from the noble land of India. A great number of incredibly profound secret tantras were drawn from the secret treasury of the ḍākinīs by masters like the great Orgyen Padmasambhava. An inconceivable number of Padmasambhava's direct students and the descendents in his lineage, such as the great twenty-five disciples, reached high stages of accomplishment.

The secret mantra of the Nyingma is divided into transmitted scripture (*kama*) and treasures (*terma*). The main upholders of the long tradition of the Nyingma transmitted teachings are the three kings of mantra known as So, Zur, and Nub: So Yeshe Wangchug, Zur Śākya Jungne, and Nub Lachen Jangnying. On the treasure side there are said to have been a hundred great treasure revealers (*terton*), including the first source of treasures Nyangral Nyima Ozer, the second source of treasures Guru Chowang, and a thousand minor treasure revealers. They discovered an inconceivable number of treasuries of Dharma, jewels, objects, medicine, and sites that had been hidden by the great Orgyen Padmasambhava for the benefit of later generations of Tibetans. These treasures will continue to bring benefit to beings in the manner best suited to the individual until the teachings come to an end.

The best-known tantras among the Nyingma are (1) the eighteen tantras of mahāyoga, which include the *Guhyasamāja*, the *Māyājāla*, the *Candraguhyatilaka*, and the eight transmitted precepts for great accomplishment,[49] (2) the scriptures of anuyoga such as the *Dupai Do*, and (3) the instructions of the Great Perfection.

Kadam

During the period of the later propagation of the teachings, owing to the work of the nephew of Lha Lama, the matchless Jowoje Atiśa arrived in Tibet in the first water-horse year (1042). Through his teaching of the Hīnayāna and Mahāyāna, Atiśa founded the Kadam teachings, and his student Dromton Gyalwai Jungne established the Kadam tradition. The three brothers Potowa, Chengawa, and Puchungwa spread the Kadam teachings. After that came many great figures who brought with them the seven divine Dharmas, including Khampa Lungpa and the trio of Langtangpa, Sharwapa, and Chekhawa, all of whom spread the teachings widely.[50]

Shangpa Kagyu

The accomplished scholar Khyungpo Naljor was born in the first earth-sheep year (1079).[51] He traveled to India, where he received the treasury of the Dharma as the heart nectar of a hundred and fifty accomplished and learned gurus, including Vajrāsana,[52] Maitrīpa, and the two wisdom ḍākinīs (Sukhasiddhi and Niguma).[53] He studied and practiced a multitude of profound Dharma teachings, including the five tantric cycles of Hevajra, Cakrasaṃvara, Guhyasamāja, Mahāmāyā, and Vajrabhairava.

Khyungpo Naljor's main students were Meu Tonpa, Yarpo Gyamoche, Ngulton Rinwang, Laton Konchog Bar, Mogchogpa Rinchen Tsondru, and Zhangom Choseng. After Mogchogpa came Kyergangpa, then Nyenton, and then Sangye Tonpa. The lineage up to this point is known as the "seven jewels."[54] An inconceivable number of saints followed, and this became known as the Shangpa Kagyu lineage.

Dakpo Kagyu

In the second earth-hare year (1099) the translator Marpa Chokyi Lodro was born.[55] He met many accomplished teachers in India, such as Nārotapa and Maitripa, and studied a multitude of tantras with them, including *Mahāmāyā*, *Buddhakapāla*, *Hevajra*, *Catuḥpīṭha*, and *Guhyasamāja*. Returning to Tibet, he spread these teachings there. His students known as the four great sons of the transmission were Tsurton Wange, Ngogton Chodor, Meton Tsonpo, and the exalted Milarepa. This tradition came to be known as the Marpa Kagyu.

Milarepa had two principal students who were like the sun and the moon. The one like the sun was Dagpo Dao Zhonu, also known as Gampopa.[56] He had three students, the so-called three men of Kham, who were the founders of the precious Kagyu lineage that later became known as the Dagpo Kagyu.[57]

The four great Kagyu schools are: (1) the Tsalpa Kagyu, founded by

Zhang Yudragpa Tsondru Dragpa, a student of Gampopa's nephew Ongom, (2) the Karma Kagyu, founded by the glorious Dusum Khyenpa, also known as Khampa Use, (3) the Pagdru Kagyu, founded by Pagmodrupa Dorje Gyalpo, who was a close disciple of Sachen Kunga Nyingpo and later became a student of Gampopa, and (4) the Barom Kagyu, founded by Barompa Darma Wangchug.[58]

The Karma Kaṃtsang orginated from the rebirth of Dusum Khyenpa, Drubchen Chokyi Lama.[59] There are two branches of the Kaṃtsang: (1) the Zurmang Kagyu was founded by Mase Lodro Rinchen, a close disciple of the Fifth Karmapa, Dezhin Shegpa, who established the monastic seat of Zurmang; (2) the Nedo Kagyu is named after the monastic seat of the teaching lineage of Karma Chagme, a student of the Sixth Zhamarpa, Garwang Chokyi Wangchug, who was one of the principal students of the Ninth Karmapa. These two schools developed independently, both bringing together the two rivers of Kagyu and Nyingma.

Pagmodrupa had eight hundred students, five hundred of whom were known as "lofty parasols." Foremost among them were Drigung Kyobpa and Taglung Tangpa Trashipal, who founded the Drigung and Taglung Kagyu; Gyaltsa Kunden Repa and Lingje Repa, who founded the Tropu and Lingje Kagyu; Marpa Drubtob Sherab Yeshe and Yelpa Drubtob Yeshe Tsegpa, who founded the Marpa and Yelpa Kagyu; Zarwa Kalden Yeshe and Nyame Gyergom Chenpo, who founded the Yamzang and Shugseb Kagyu. These are known as the eight minor Kagyu schools.

Sakya

The long tradition of the Sakya began at the same time as the initial teachings of the Kagyu. This will be explained below in the main part of this history.

Zhije and Cho

Padampa Sangye was born in the second iron-hare year (1091). After his initial visit to Dingri, Padampa traveled to Tibet on five different occasions. On the second visit he taught Zhangzhung Lingkhawa and Trotsang Onpo Druglha. On the fourth visit he taught Ma Chokyi Sherab, Sochungwa, and Kamgom. On the fifth visit he conferred the four yogas of the four gates, foremost among which was the permission for Zhije, the sublime Dharma that pacifies suffering. There are said to have been three sequential teachings of Zhije, though it forms a single continuum of activity for the general benefit of sentient beings through instructing them in dependent origination. Those who maintained the continuum of Zhije, like Dingri Kunpang Chenpo, propagated the teachings far and wide.

On Dampa Sangye's third visit to Tibet, he taught Yarlungpa Mara Serpo and Kyoton Sonam Lama what became known as the male Cho. The wisdom ḍākinī Machig Labkyi Dronma studied it with Kyoton and disseminated what became known as the female Cho, focusing on the precepts of Cho practice. Cho exists in the form of transmitted scriptures, treasure texts, and pure visions.

Ganden (Gelug)

In the sixth fire-bird year (1357) Jamgon Tsongkhapa was born. He studied with the great scholars of the Sakya sūtra teachings Rendawa, Lama Dampa Sonam Gyaltsen, and Sazang Mati Paṇchen. He studied the texts of the causal vehicle, including Madhyamaka, Prajñāpāramitā, Vinaya, Abhidharma, and Pramāṇa. He received the transmission of texts of ripening and liberation including the two kings of tantras, the cycles of Cakrasaṃvara and Yamāntaka. He disseminated the teachings far and wide.

Most importantly he revived the dying embers of the Kadampa teachings, disseminating the long tradition of teaching and meditating that combines the texts of the Kadampas with the mantras and tantras of the New schools. Therefore his school came to be known as the new Kadam (Kadam Sarma). In the seventh earth-ox year (1409) the monastery of Ganden Nampar Gyalwai Ling was established on the elevated plain of Riwoche, and from this monastery the school came to be known as Gandenpa. There have been many saints in this school; the primary disciples who held the lineage were Gyaltsab, Khedrub, Jamyang Choje, Jamchenpa, and Gendun Drubpa.

There have also been other minor traditions such as the Jonang, Bodong, and Bulug that have split off from the Sakya. The long traditions that have been summarized here are each in their own way profound and extensive, and each one is certainly a basis for an inconceivable number of miracles, inclined toward liberation, and flowing into omniscience itself.

People like me, whose lowly intellects have little knowledge or perseverance, may not be capable of such achievements. However, if we consider and analyze the biographies of the three spheres of activity, which praise the conquerors who have come before us in the lineage of sublime saints of the Old and New schools with all their qualities of learning and accomplishment, then it may be possible for us to fathom the cause by seeing the result.[60] In particular it is possible to achieve confident certainty just by considering the wonderful activities of maintaining the nonpartisan (*rime*) teachings—through the dedicated study and dissemination of the precious and profound precepts that came from the traditions of lineages known as the *eight chariots*—carried out by those two great holders of all the teachings of the land of snows, the great saints Khyentse and Kongtrul.

• 2 •

The Sakya Family Lineage

THIS EXTENSIVE ACCOUNT of the traditions of glorious Sakya is in four parts: the lives of the precious family line of Sakyapas, lords of the teachings; an account of the Lamdre, the precious oral instructions that are the essence of the teachings; the nature of the special transmission of the ocean of profound precepts; and the history of how the teachings of the Sakyapas spread the length and breadth of the land of snows.

THE LIVES OF THE PRECIOUS FAMILY LINE OF SAKYAPAS, LORDS OF THE TEACHINGS

The early history of the Khon family line

The biographies of the family lines revered by many in the noble land of India and the family line of the Khon Sakyapas here in the land of snows have been lauded in a single voice by those sublime ones who stand at the gateway to limitless virtue. Following them, I will set down a few words here.

Near to the lofty and bright realm of western Ngari, or perhaps near the northern snowy land of Sheltsa Gyalpo, there were three brothers, all sky gods made of light: Chiring, Yuring, and Use. They were the dance of Mañjuśrī's compassion. The middle brother, Yuring, had seven sons known as the seven brothers Masang. The youngest of the seven was called Masang Chije. His son was Togtsa Pawo Tag. His son was Lutsa Tagpo Ochen. All of the above had superhuman forms and lived in the skies.

The son of Lutsa Tagpo Ochen was Yapang Kye; from him onward this is known as the family line of luminous gods. Yapang Kye defeated a vampire called Kyareng the Bloodless and married his wife, Yadrug Silima. She gave birth to a single son, who was named Khon Barkye because he was born (*kye*) due to a grudge (*khon*) between (*bar*) a vampire and a divinity. From this point onward this lineage is known as the Khon family. The definitive meaning of *khon* is a grudge against ignorance of what is to be adandoned. The Khon family line has this quality rather than the other ways of identifying extraordinary people, like wheels marking the hands and feet, cow-like eyelashes, and blue-black eyes.[61]

The son of Khon Barkye was Khonpa Jegung Tag, who became the interior minister for the Dharma king Trisong Detsen, during which time he greatly increased the prosperity of the religious government in Tibet. For this reason he was acclaimed by all as Khon Palpoche, the "magnificent Khon." His son became one of the precious master Padmasambhava's closest disciples and was also among the first seven men given full ordination by the great abbot Bodhisattva, whereupon he received the name Nāgendrarakṣita, "protected by the lord of the nāgas."[62]

His younger brother was accomplished vidyādhara Dorje Rinchen. His son was Sherab Yonten. His son was Yonten Jungne. His son was Tsultrim Gyalpo. His son was Dorje Tsugtor. His son was Gekyab. His son was Getong. His son was Balpo. His son was Śākya Lodro. His sons were Khon Rog Sherab Tsultrim and Konchog Gyalpo. Before Sherab Tsultrim there was an uninterrupted line of vidyādharas practicing the Nyingma secret mantra, and he achieved the two kinds of accomplishment by means of the yidam deities Viśuddha Heruka and Vajrakīlaya. He also bound to service various Dharma protectors, such as the sister and brother called Karmo Nyida and Dugyal Pawo.[63]

Khon Konchog Gyalpo

The younger brother, the unrivaled scholar and practitioner Konchog Gyalpo, was born in first wood-dog year (1034). The elder brother was saddened by certain people who openly proclaimed the secrets of the Nyingma Dharma and said to the younger, "You should travel to Mangkhar to study the profound secret mantra of the new translations with Drogmi Lotsāwa." Konchog Gyalpo left home and met Khyin Lotsāwa, a student of Drogmi, on the way. In the cemetery of Yalung he studied the *Hevajra Tantra*, but before they could finish, Khyin Lotsāwa died. With his last words he told Konchog Gyalpo, "Now you must continue with your Dharma; ask Drogmi Lotsāwa for this teaching."

Thus Konchog Gyalpo traveled on to Mangkhar, where in the presence of Drogmi, he studied the three tantras of Hevajra and the further cycles of the path.[64] He also studied the *Guhyasamāja* with Go Khugpa, the fivefold cycle of the Tilaka tantras with Prajñāgupta,[65] the paṇḍita from Oḍḍiyāna, and the root *Cakrasaṃvara Tantra* and the cycles of the essence of accomplishment with Mal Lotsāwa.[66] He also studied a great number of texts with Bari Lotsāwa, Lama Gyichuwa, Puhrang Lotsāwa, Namkhaupa, and Kyura Akyab, becoming a master of many Dharmas. Konchog Gyalpo built a small meditation center at Brawolung, where he taught extensively, teaching tantras such as the root *Hevajra Tantra.*

Regarding the founding of the Sakya seat, the *Mañjuśrīmūla Tantra* says:

> From that, the letters *sa* and *ka*
> are the first pure expressions.

The master of the early practices, Padmākara, gave a prophecy naming the place and the people and established stūpas on the hills at each of the four directions of Sakya, like the points for moxibustion on a human body. Also when Jowoje Atiśa, on his way to central Tibet, came across some wild yaks, he prophesied that the two wild yaks on the hillside of Ponpo Hill indicated that in the future two forms of Mahākāla would carry out enlightened activities there. When he came to Chagtsal Ridge, he performed extensive prostrations and offerings toward the white earth on the side of the hill. He said: "Over there is a single *hrīḥ*, seven *dhīḥ*, and a single *hūṃ*. This means that in the future a single emanation of Avalokiteśvara, seven emanations of Mañjuśrī, and a single emanation of Vajrapāṇi will come here and act for the welfare of beings."

When the time came for the prophecy to be fulfilled, it was Khon Konchog Gyalpo himself who, one day when he was still living at Brawolung, went for an outing to the other side of the valley in the middle of the day. He saw many auspicious signs, such as the white and glittering earth on the side of Ponpo Hill and the river flowing down to the right. He thought: "If I established a retreat here it would benefit the Buddha's teachings and a great many beings."

Konchog Gyalpo asked permission from the local official and it was granted. To the local landowner and the four nearby villages of *bandes* he said: "I wish to build a little meditation center here.[67] If you do not obstruct me, I will meet your price." They replied: "We would never ask for a price to be paid. We beg you to build the meditation center." Konchog

Gyalpo, however, replied: "I would like to be sure that this is done properly for the future," and he paid a price principally consisting of a white mare, curtains, women's gowns, a jewel rosary, and a coat of armor. Thus Konchog Gyalpo's line came to rule over the land between the ravines of Mongo and Balmo.[68]

When this great lama reached his fortieth year, in the days of the waxing moon in the first autumnal month of the water-ox year (1073), Konchog Gyalpo established himself in the region of glorious Sakya, building temples like the White Zimchil.[69] Living here in the ethos of taking meditation as the most important thing, he studied the Dharma and taught the Dharma to fortunate students.

Drogmi once said to Seton Kunrig: "That spiritual guide Konchog Gyalpo is the greatest student of my complete tantric transmissions, while you, Seton Kunrig, are the greatest of those who have received the complete instructions. But I am a greater lama than the two of you. So the greatest has bestowed greatness upon the greatest, and because of this great occurance, a great welfare of others will come to pass." Thus it was Konchog Gyalpo who gave the teachings on Drogmi's tantric transmission to Seton Kunrig.

From this point onward the family line became known as the Sakyapas. In this way the lineage is said to be composed of three supreme appellations: the divine lineage, the Khon family, and the Sakyapas. Khon Konchog Gyalpo maintained the seat of glorious Sakya for thirty years. In his sixty-ninth year, on the tenth day of the ninth month of the second water-horse year (1102), he passed into peace.

Sachen Kunga Nyingpo

Khon Konchog Gyalpo's son was Sachen Kunga Nyingpo. His mother, Machig Zhangmola, gave birth to him in the male water-monkey year of the second cycle (1092), when Konchog Gyalpo was fifty-nine.[70] From the first he was pleasing to everyone and possessed the sublime qualities of insight and compassion. Atiśa's student Bodhisattva Jinpa identified Sachen as an emanation of Avalokiteśvara. At the age of eleven he studied many Dharmas. Then his father died, and Bari Lotsāwa Rinchen Drag took over the seat of Sakya, looking after the child with compassion.

In the old temple of Zimkhang, Sachen meditated on Mañjuśrī. When he cleared away all of his external obstructions, he had a vision of Tārā. When he cleared all of his internal obstructions, he had a vision of Acala.

After six months of meditation, he was personally accepted by Mañjuśrī, who said:

> Dear child:
> If are attached to this life, you are not a Dharma practitioner.
> If you are attached to saṃsāra, you do not have renunciation.
> If you are attached to your own welfare, you do not have the awakening mind.
> If grasping arises, you do not have the view.[71]

Having received this wonderful summary of the Dharma, Sachen instantaneously saw all the essential points of the Prajñāpāramitā gathered together. He achieved total recall and an unequaled analytical intellect.

In his twelfth year Sachen went to Rongurmig[72] and studied Asaṅga's *Abhidharmasamuccaya* with Drangti Darma Nyingpo. Then Drangti placed a pebble in Sachen's hand and said, "It's time for me to go." After Drangti died Sachen studied Madhyamaka and Pramāṇa with Drangti's closest student, Khyung Rinchen Drag. Back at the Sakya seat, Sachen studied with Bari Lotsāwa, receiving his entire cycle of Dharma, studying, and putting it into practice. He received the textual tradition of the Prajñāpāramitā, including the Ratnakūṭa sūtras and the *Avataṃsaka Sūtra*. He received the two hundred kriyā and caryā tantras and, in the mahāyoga, the two systems of the *Guhyasamāja Tantra*,[73] the *Kṛṣṇayamāri Tantra*, the three Hevajra tantras, and the root and supplemental explanatory Cakrasaṃvara tantras. He also received Bari's collection of sādhanas.[74] Later he studied with Geshe Melhang Tserwa, receiving the *Pramāṇaviniścaya*, the *Nyāyabindu*, and the treatises of the three eastern Svātantrika Mādhyamikas.[75]

Wanting to learn more about his father's Dharma, Sachen went to see Khon Gyichuwa Dralhabar and studied various scriptural collections and tantras, including the three *Hevajra Tantras* according to the system of Ḍombī Heruka and the eighteen sections on accomplishment.[76] He went on to study the *Guhyasamāja* with his relative, Namkhaur Darma Gyaltsen. With the spiritual guide Ngog Lotsāwa, he studied Vimuktisena's *Pañcaviṃśatisāhasrikāloka*, the great commentary on the *Aṣṭasāhasrikā*, and the *Abhisamayālaṃkāra* root text and commentary.[77] From Puhrang Lochung he received the *Cakrasaṃvara Tantra*.

In Gungtang, with Mal Lotsāwa Lodro Drag, Sachen studied various

Dharmas, including the root *Cakrasaṃvāra Tantra* and its supplement, the three cycles of the *Kṛṣṇayamāri*, the entire instructions of Nārotapa, and the caryā tantras. In particular he received the sādhanas and permissions of Mahākāla. He sent off to Sakya a roll of black silk and a nine-pointed vajra made from sword metal to serve as representations of Mahākāla, and he commanded Mahākāla: "Go and look after the Khon Sakyapas!"

Sachen also studied various Dharmas with Kyura Akyab, the Nepalese paṇḍitas Padmaśrī and Jñānavajra, and the Indian yogin Bhotarāhula. At the age of twenty-nine, in the iron-bird year (1120), Sachen went to Sagtang in Ding to study with Zhangton Chobar, who had reached the age of sixty-eight. Over the course of four years Zhangton kindly bestowed upon Sachen the precious oral instructions of the Lamdre. When Sachen was thirty-two, in the water-hare year (1123), Zhangton gave him a prophecy about his future accomplishments and empowered him to be the master of his Dharma.

At the age of forty-seven, in the earth-horse year (1138),[78] while staying at Gungtang, Sachen was poisoned by a zombie and fell ill for a month.[79] Some time later he found he had forgotten all of the Dharma he had learned. So he practiced solitary meditation in his own quarters, praying to his lama, and recovered some of the words. Then he had a dream of the master of the meditation centers, Zhangton, who expounded the Dharma to him, and after that he remembered everything. Following this the lord of yogins Virūpa came in person and over the course of a month, with no separation of day and night, bestowed a variety of Dharmas upon Sachen, including seventy-two tantras and the four profound Dharmas that do not pass beyond the boundary wall.[80] At the end, Virūpa gave Sachen his blessings. At this time Sachen composed verses of homage to Virūpa beginning "*Alala!*"[81]

Sachen possessed an inconceivable number of qualities. For example, he once taught simultaneously with six representations of his body: he trained around thirty great meditators at Tsarkha, he expounded the Lamdre at Sakya, he acted as an attendant for his lama Mal Lotsāwa at Gungtang, he constructed and consecrated a maṇḍala of the stainless sky at Cham Lhakhang,[82] he expounded the Dharma among the nomads of Zangdong, and he turned the wheel of the Dharma at Shab Gonga.

Thus Lama Sachen spent sixty-seven years working for the welfare of beings through the four means of conversion, without tiring for an instant of the profound two stages.[83] Then on the tenth day of the ninth month in the third earth-tiger year (1158), when he was in Kyawo Kadang Monastery in northern Yeru, he went to the land of bliss. At that moment he displayed four representations of his body, the first in Sukhāvati, the second in Potala, the third in Oḍḍiyāna, and the fourth in the golden realms of the north.

According to the prophecy of Lama Zhang, Sachen would have three supreme disciples who would become adepts before they left their bodies; seven or eleven disciples who would attain forbearance, including Jetsun Rinpoche Dragpa Gyaltsen; fifteen who would abide in the great warmth, including Lobpon Rinpoche Sonam Tsemo; thirty-one who would abide in the medium warmth, including Kyura Akyab; many who would be known by the signs that they abided in the lesser warmth, including Khampa Aseng; and an inconceivable number who would attain accomplishments.[84] This is how the prophecy was related by the omniscient Sonam Senge.[85]

In *A Great Ship for the Ocean of Teachings*, it says:

> Jetsun Tsemo is not ranked among Sachen's students. To dispel doubts arising from this, some scholars say: "The reason that Jetsun Tsemo is not linked with Sachen is that he was of a single essence with that great lama, so they were indivisible."[86]

Sonam Tsemo

Four sons were born to Lama Sachen. The first, Kunga Bar, was the son of Sachen's junior wife Shojo Champurmo. In his youth he traveled to India, where he studied the sciences. He died at the age of twenty-two in Gandhāra,[87] where he was preparing to return to Tibet.

Sachen's senior wife, Machig Odron of the Tsamo Rongpas, had three sons. The eldest was Lobpon Rinpoche Sonam Tsemo. He was born when his father was fifty-one, in the second water-dog year (1142). Immediately, ḍākinīs inscribed letters above the gate to Bodhgaya in India, proclaiming: "An emanation of Mañjuśrī called Sonam Tsemo has been born at Sakya." The baby's body was very beautiful. Bowing twice, he announced: "I am done with childish activities!" Thereafter he always sat with crossed legs.

At the age of three Sonam Tsemo had visions of Hevajra, Mañjuśrī, Tārā, and Acala and was able to recite by heart the tantra trilogy of Hevajra, the root *Cakrasaṃvara Tantra*, and Asaṅga's *Abidharmasamuccaya*.[88]

He remembered having been born as eleven Indian paṇḍitas, including Durjayacandra. When he was seventeen he was able to recite the four classes of tantra by heart and became known throughout India and Tibet as a scholar of the entire Vajrayāna.

At this point Sonam Tsemo had asked his father to confer all of his Vajrayāna Dharma cycles and had then put them into practice. But that year his father died, and the following year his younger brother Dragpa Gyaltsen inherited the seat of Sakya, aged twelve. Sonam Tsemo went to the monastery of Sangpu Neutog, where he studied for eleven years with the great Chapa Chokyi Senge, receiving and learning the entirety of the scriptural collections, including Pramāṇa, Madhyamaka, Prajñāpāramitā, Vinaya, and Abhidharma.

Sonam Tsemo possessed an inconceivable number of qualities showing his accomplishments. Once, while he was teaching the oral instructions of the Lamdre at the Old Utse temple, he appeared to his students Jepa, Zhuje, and Mogton as Mañjuśrī, Virūpa, and Avalokiteśvara among an array of offerings in the sky.

Sonam Tsemo wrote many treatises, including a commentary to the *Saṃpuṭa Tantra*, a commentary on the *Bodhicaryāvatāra*, and *Introduction to the Dharma*. For thirteen years, from the earth-hare (1159) to the iron-hare (1171), he presided over the seat of Sakya. Thereafter his younger brother Dragpa returned to the seat of Sakya, and Sonam Tsemo moved to a lakeside retreat at Chumig, where he concentrated on teaching and practice.[89]

At the age of forty-one, on the eleventh day of the eleventh month in the year of the third water-tiger (1182), seated on a Dharma throne at the center of a congregation of eighty of his students, amid pleasant odors and musical sounds, Sonam Tsemo manifested a radiant body of vajra rainbows. His students included both high lamas and ordinary people.

Dragpa Gyaltsen

The middle son of Sachen's senior wife was Jetsun Rinpoche Dragpa Gyaltsen. He was born among auspicious signs when his father was fifty-six, in the third fire-hare year (1147). From the time he could speak, he enjoyed solitude, had no desires, strove to acquire good qualities, and had no interest in childish activities. When he was eight, Dragpa Gyaltsen received the brahmacarya vows of an upāsaka from Bodhisattva Dawa Gyaltsen.[90]

After being ordained, he acted as a monk, and apart from the gaṇacakra substances, never asked for meat or alcohol.

At the age of ten, Dragpa Gyaltsen received the *Hevajrasādhana* of Saroruha. When he spoke about it at the age of eleven, everyone was impressed by his grasp of the essential points. When he was thirteen, he had a dream about requesting a book of the *Three Continua* and had an experience of the suchness of all phenomena.[91]

When Sachen died, Dragpa Gyaltsen initiated a great turning of the Dharma wheel, teaching the *Hevajra Tantra* to his own students while miracles occurred. Up to this point he had received many Vajrayāna Dharma cycles from his father. After he took up the Sakya seat, Dragpa Gyaltsen received an inconceivable number of Dharmas, comprising the whole of the four classes of tantra and the three scriptural collections, from Lobpon Sonam Tsemo, Nyen Tsugtor Gyalpo, Zhang Tsultrim Drag, Nyen Wangyal, the Nepalese Jāyasena, and Lotsāwa Palchog Dangpo, among others. Every twenty-four hours he performed the deity yoga of seventy maṇḍalas.

Once the great Kashmiri paṇḍita Śākyaśrī published an announcement about a forthcoming eclipse. Jetsun Dragpa prevented the eclipse by stopping the movement of his mind and vital winds in the left and right channels and mingling the white and red inner elements in the central channel. The great paṇḍita said: "In order to show that I am not a liar, I need to go and find out why this old upāsaka is stirring up trouble." When the great paṇḍita arrived, Jetsun Dragpa abruptly stood up and placed his vajra and bell hanging in midair. Faced with a sign of accomplishment like this, quite beyond the intellect, Śākyaśrī exclaimed: "Mahāvajradhara! He is a gathering of secrets!"[92] He honored Jetsun Dragpa as a crown jewel and requested the nectar of his teachings, feeling certain that Jetsun Dragpa was the crown ornament of ten million vajradharas.

When Dragpa Gyaltsen was fifty-six, in the water-dog year (1202), he was staying in the Tsangkha meditation center in Nyemo Rutsam. Once when he was in the state of vast luminosity that is the mind's characteristic nature, Lama Sachen displayed his wisdom body and bestowed special instructions illuminating the symbolic meaning. This is the very close lineage of the Lamdre.

Though Dragpa Gyaltsen had declined several invitations from the ḍākinīs at the ages of twenty-eight and twenty-nine, they still blessed the formative elements of his lifespan over and over again.[93] Dragpa Gyaltsen clarified the teachings of the Sage through exposition, debate, and composition and in particular established his fortunate followers in the supreme liberation by means of the oral instructions of the Lamdre. A prophecy was found that stated that Dragpa Gyaltsen would be reborn with the accoutrements of a wheel-turning emperor and would achieve buddhahood in three rebirths, having traversed all of the grounds and paths.

And thus, in the middle of his seventieth year, having carried out the welfare of countless trainees, Dragpa Gyaltsen passed into bliss on the twelfth day of the waxing moon of the second month of the fourth male fire-mouse year (1216). The majority of the students of Sachen and Sonam Tsemo were also the students of Dragpa Gyaltsen. In particular, his principal students were the Dharma lord Sapaṇ and his brother, who were known as his two closest disciples. Furthermore, there are also said to be four or eight disciples whose names ended in Dragpa, four men who requested the *Ornament for the Vajrapañjara*, and four great ascetics who were vidyādharas.

Sakya Paṇḍita

The youngest son of Sachen was Palchen Onpo, born in the iron-horse year (1150), when his father was fifty-nine. He trained in the Dharmas of his forefathers, in particular learning many religious topics and the medical sciences. Through his compassion he carried out the benefit of a multitude of beings. He passed away joyfully at the age of fifty-four, in the water-pig year (1203).[94] Of his two sons, the eldest was the great Sakya Paṇḍita.

Sakya Paṇḍita was born of Palchen Onpo (his father) and Tra Puma Nyitricham (his mother) on the twentieth day of the second month in the third water-tiger year (1182) amid many miraculous signs. He carried the marks of glorious Siddhārtha, and immediately after being born, pronounced Sanskrit words. He understood, without studying, all of the arts and sciences of India and Tibet. In his previous human lives he had been reborn twenty-five times as a paṇḍita, and he become known as one who has been accepted by Mañjuśrī. According to the definitive meaning, he was an emanation of Mañjuśrī, prophesied by Tārā to the Kashmiri paṇḍita Śākyaśrī, and recognized as such by the scholar Tsang Nagpa and the physician Biji.[95] The reasons for this are explained in Sapaṇ's biographies. According to the provisional meaning, in the course of his life he studied all the inner and outer sciences, fully understanding them after hearing them just once or twice. He thus obtained fearlessness in his powers of speech.

Like the great Jetsun Dragpa before him, Sapaṇ took the brahmacarya vows of an upāsaka and was given the name Kunga Gyaltsen. Thereafter he also received the bodhicitta vows, the complete four empowerments of mahāyoga, and from his father, the empowerment of Hevajra. Thus he came to hold the three vows.

He had limitless qualities. For example, at the age of nineteen, in the state of vast luminosity, he spent one month studying the *Abhidharmakośa* with the scholar Vasubandhu, who appeared in front of his grandmother's tomb. After that he knew the words and meaning by heart. Later, when he received the same text from Śākyaśrī, he declared that it was no different to what he had previously received. Also, one evening he dreamed that he was on the lion throne of the master Dignāga in eastern India, where he got hold of the key to an immeasurable number of books. After that he understood pramāṇa without having to make any effort.[96]

Later he received several transmissions, including the five Dharmas of Maitreya from Zhudon Dorje Kyab. At Kyangdul he received the pramāṇa of the old Tibetan lineage from Maja Jangtson and Tsurton Zhonseng.[97] He received all of the Dharmas of the four philosophical systems known in Tibet from Tsegpa Wangchug Senge. He received all the oral precepts of Zhije, Dzogchen, Cho, and the Kadam from Chiwo Lhepa Jangchub O.

At the age of twenty-three Sapaṇ met the great Kashmiri paṇḍita Śākyaśrī at Chumig in Tsang. The paṇḍita was attended by his disciples Saṅghaśrī, Sugataśrī, and Dānaśīla. With them, Sapaṇ studied the ten areas of science: the five major sciences, such as pramāṇa, and the five minor sciences, such as poetics. Thus they praised Sapaṇ as a paṇḍita.

At the age of twenty-seven Sapaṇ was given full ordination by Śākyaśrī at the Gyengong temple in Lower Nyang. During his thirty-fifth year, he received the complete instructions of the Sakya hearing lineage of sūtra and mantra from Jetsun Rinpoche Dragpa Gyaltsen. When he specially requested the guruyoga of the profound path, he had a vision of Mañjuśrī, the essence of all buddhas. Thereafter he obtained an unerring intellectual understanding of all topics in Dharma and an inconceivable meditative absorption and realization.

Sapaṇ taught continuously, from the age of nine when he taught the *Hevajrasādhana* of Saroruha, eleven when he taught the *Hevajra Tantra* and the *Buddhasamāyoga Tantra*, and twelve when he taught the *Vajrapañjara* and *Saṃpuṭa* tantras, up to the age of seventy. When the lord of philosophers Harinanda came from India with five other teachers looking for a debating contest, Sapaṇ refuted each of them in turn with the logic of the three pramāṇa texts, placing them in the yogic discipline of silence.[98] All of them cut off their hair and in Sapaṇ's presence took the monastic vows. The locks of hair were placed in the ornamental pillar in Sakya Monastery.

Having obtained fearlessness in his powers to explain all subjects of knowledge in this way, Sapaṇ composed many treatises for the benefit of future trainees, including:

- *An Entrance Gate for the Learned: A Treatise on Grammar*
- *A Summary of Grammar* and other such works
- *A Bouquet of Flowers: A Treatise on Composition*
- *A Treasury of Words: An Explanation of Terms*
- *The Joyful Entrance: A Treatise on Drama*
- *A Treasury of Logic: A Treatise on Pramāṇa*, written to conquer the rocky mountain of mistaken notions of the Indians and Tibetans

In the genre of the inner sciences, he wrote *Clarifying the Sage's Intention* on the application of the Prajñāpāramitā. In the genre of Vajrayāna he wrote *Commentary on the Hymn to Nairātmyā* and many other such works.[99] He wrote *Distinguishing the Three Vows* to clear away the grime of misconceptions about the scriptures in general, and he also wrote down many question-and-answer sessions about specific difficult points in these scriptures.[100]

To summarize the essentials of all of the above, he wrote *Letter to the Buddhas of the Ten Directions*, and he wrote many other marvelous treatises, such as the *Precious Treasury of Excellent Sayings*, which distinguishes the right and wrong ways of behaving. Furthermore, he wrote an appendix to the Tengyur and completed many translations.[101] In particular Sapaṇ introduced the tradition of three outer sciences, and it is generally acknowledged that, in Tibet, both the concept and the embodiment of an "expert in the ten sciences" began with him.[102]

The flag of Sapaṇ's famed and unrivaled qualities flew everywhere, and for this reason, at the age of sixty-three, he was invited as an honored guest by Godan Khan, the ruler of Central Asia. At the age of sixty-five he arrived at the Khan's great palace at Liangzhou. In order to test Sapaṇ, the king invited him to an illusory temple by a lake. With his powers of absorption, Sapaṇ blessed the temple to make it real. This temple, known as the "magical temple of the north," became well known in all quarters, and the king and his entourage developed an undivided faith in Sapaṇ.

Up to the age of seventy, Sapaṇ disseminated the teachings of explanation and accomplishment in the land of China. In the end, while residing at the magical emanation temple, he passed away at dawn on the fourteenth day of the eleventh month in the fourth iron-pig year (1251). Having manifested signs of having attained the first bhūmi, with marks of excellence like the crown protusion (*uṣṇīṣa*), he passed into the realm of the vidyādharas with innumerable miraculous emanations. It is well known that his lama and his presiding deity gave a genuine prophecy that he would traverse an abundance of bhūmis and paths and then attain buddhahood as the tathāgata Vimala in the pure land of Abhirati.

From the age of nine—when he expounded the sādhana of Saroruha—until the age of seventy, Sapaṇ opened the lotus petals of the profound truth with the sunbeams of the teaching in the three countries of China, Tibet, and Mongolia. The swarm of bees that were his clear intellect, humming with excellent explanations, pollinated the lotuses of the Sage's teaching. Thus he became the most important teacher for many people, including his younger brother Zangtsa Sonam Gyaltsen; his two noble uncles Sonam Tsemo and Dragpa Gyaltsen; Drub and Tsog, who held the realization lineage; Lho and Mar, who held the instruction lineage; Gyalwa Yang Gonpa, who held the accomplishment lineage; Shar, Nub, and Gung, who held the explanation lineage; thirteen junior and senior vow-holders called Śrībhadra; seven young men whose names ended with Gyaltsen; the four great lotsāwas Lo, Zhang, Rong, and Chag; and four secret yogins. Furthermore, he also taught Tsangnag Pugpa Sherab Ozer, Rabjam Gon, the physician Biji, Khenpo Dragpa Senge, and Lama Ozer Śākya, among others.

Zangtsa Sonam Gyaltsen

Sapaṇ's younger brother Zangtsa Sonam Gyaltsen was born of his mother Nyitricham in the third wood-dragon year (1184), when his father, Palchen Onpo, was thirty-five. From childhood he had a kind heart and was filled with the nectar of compassion. In general, he had a firmly disciplined awareness and great strength of mind. Once, when the master was twenty-seven, a strongman from Upper Nyang called Nyangtsa Dring, whose physical prowess was famous throughout Central Tibet, came to challenge him. Zangtsa told the strongman, "You cannot beat me," but it was no use. So

Zangtsa seized him by the hair and performed physical feats, finally swinging him round seven times before dropping him on the ground. The strongman lay there a while in shame and then fled. There are many miraculous stories like this around.

Zangtsa knew most of the tantra collections, as well as the extensive and medium-length Prajñāpāramitā sūtras. He had an extensive knowledge of the methods of the four classes of secret mantra. As for the teachings on Mahākāla and his consort, he delighted in them as if they were perfume.

The political domain of Sakya was greatly expanded by this lord. For example, he constructed the Old Utse temple and designed the towns of Upper and Lower Drompa, Shab, and Tanag.[103] He instituted regular exorcism rituals and group sādhana practices, and he built the inner and middle boundary walls of Sakya.

Zangtsa had a vision of his yidam deities Hevajra and Mañjughoṣa as one inseparable pure and profound intention. Afterward he said, "After this life I will be born in the south as one who confers empowerment upon certain disciples and practices the profound path through secret yoga." He passed away at the age of fifty-six, on the twenty-second of the twelfth month of the fourth earth-pig year (1239), high on the sacred mountain of Toro.

Chogyal Pagpa

Drogon Chogyal Pagpa was the son of Zangtsa. He was born of his mother Machig Kunchi, accompanied by auspicious signs in the fourth wood-sheep year (1235), when his father was fifty-two. He remembered a number of previous lives, including Saton Riwa and Lang Riwa. When he was three he recited the *Hevajrasādhana* of Saroruha. At eight he recited the stories of the Buddha's previous lives by heart. At nine he recited the *Hevajra Tantra* to a great Dharma assembly convened by the Dharma lord Sakya Paṇḍita. When he taught the *Saṃbhāraparikathā* everyone witnessed miracles. The pride of all the scholars was broken, and they said: "It's impossible for an ordinary person to have an intellect like this; he must be a noble one (*pagpa*)." Because everyone praised him in this way, he became known as Pagpa.

When he was ten, Pagpa traveled to the north as an attendant of Sapaṇ. On the way he took ordination from Sapaṇ in front of the Jowo statue at Lhasa. At Kyormolung, near Lhasa, he undertook the training of a novice (*śrāmaṇera*) with Sherab Pal. Up to the age of seventeen, while in Mongolia, he studied all of the qualities of esoteric secret mantra, put them into practice, and showed the outer signs of mastery.[104] This greatly pleased Sapaṇ, who gave Pagpa his begging bowl and white conch trumpet with a range of two miles. Sapaṇ then entrusted his teachings to Pagpa, saying: "The time has come for you to teach assemblies of students and carry out the benefit of a multitude of beings, so remember your previous vows!" Thereafter the Dharma lord Sapaṇ passed into the pure lands, and Pagpa arranged his funeral service and other affairs.

When he was nineteen Pagpa was summoned by Sechen, the emperor of Mongolia.[105] Pagpa instilled undivided faith in Sechen with his marvelous acts and magical displays, such as when he severed his five extremities with a sharp sword and showed each of them marked with one of the buddhas of the five families. He gave the empowerment of Hevajra to twenty-five people, headed by the emperor and empress, and thereafter was taken as the crown ornament of the Vajrayāna in the kingdom of Mongolia. Sechen conferred the title of imperial preceptor (*dishi*) upon Pagpa and offered him the thirteen myriarchies of Tibet in return for the empowerment.[106]

Thereafter the whole of Tibet gradually came under the rule of the two laws, religious and secular, as admistered by the glorious Sakyapas, and the lamas of Tibet came to accept Pagpa as their ruler. Within Tibet Pagpa displayed great kindness toward the teachings in general, ruling without any diminishment of the Conqueror's teaching and without strife.[107]

At the age of twenty-one, on the border between Mongolia and China, Pagpa was fully ordained by the abbot Nyetangpa Dragpa Senge and the preceptor Joden Sonam. Afterward he received the Prajñāpāramitā from the abbot and the Vinaya from the master. When he was twenty-three, Pagpa traveled to the five-peaked mountain of Wutaishan at the invitation of Dongton, "the blind master." There he received many teachings, including Yamāri. Returning to the emperor's palace, Pagpa convened a Dharma assembly, where he defeated seventeen Daoist teachers with logic and instilled the correct view in them.[108]

At the age of thirty Pagpa traveled to the Sakya seat and convened a major Dharma council, studying the scriptures, precepts, and instructions with scholars of the inner and outer sciences, including Nyen Osung, Drubtob Yontenpal, Chim Namkhadrag, Tsogom Kungapal, Lowo Lotsāwa, and Chiwo Lhepa Jose.[109] Thus he became a great master of the Dharma. Summoned once again by the emperor, Pagpa returned to China at the age of thirty-three, where he was granted the three provinces of Tibet in return for bestowing empowerment. He established thirteen official posts: three attendants responsible for provisions, chambers, and offerings; a triumvirate of steward, secretary, and treasurer; three overseers of cooks, waiters, and utensils; two overseers of horses and crops; and the overseer of cattle and hunting dogs.[110]

At the age of forty-two, Pagpa traveled back to the Sakya seat, and without keeping for himself so much as a grain of the enormous wealth that had come into his hands, he used it all for the teachings and the welfare of sentient beings.[111] He convened a major Dharma council, established the foundations of a Dharma college, set up physical representations of the Buddha's body, speech, and mind, and distributed alms to the poor. Most importantly, Pagpa gave the incomparable alms of the Dharma to the three countries of China, Tibet, and Mongolia, acting as the abbot for 1,450 novices and monks. He gave Vajrayāna empowerments in fourteen different languages, and he ripened and liberated countless disciples through his precepts, instructions, and blessings. He composed many treatises, which are well written and easy to understand, including commentaries on scriptures and treatises, on the stages of practice in the Hīnayāna and Mahāyāna, and question-and-answer sessions.

Then, in his forty-sixth year, on the morning of the twenty-second day of the eleventh month of the fifth iron-dragon year (1280), having ensured the welfare of vast numbers of beings, Pagpa sat with crossed legs while holding his vajra and bell and passed into peace. His passing was heralded by such signs as beautiful sounds, lights and fragrances, and a rain of flowers.[112]

The greatest among his students included his nephew Dharmapāla, his younger brothers Lobpon Yeshe Jungne and Rinchen Gyaltsen, the holders of the transmission of esoteric instructions Zhang Konchog Pal and Gelong Kunlo, the holders of the tantric transmissions Ganden Trashi Pal and Ganden Kunso, the holder of the Mahākāla transmission Dampa Kunga Drag, and two great men: his brother Drogon Chagna and Prince Jinkim.[113] There were also several groups of students, such as the four supervisors of offerings (including Tishi Drago) and the six saints (including Sharpa Dukhorwa Yeshe Rinchen).

Drogon Chagna

Pagpa's brother Chagna was born in the fourth earth-pig year (1239), when his father Zangtsa was fifty-six. When Chagna was seven and Pagpa was ten, they traveled together to Mongolia as attendants of the Dharma lord Sapaṇ.[114] Later on Chagna also traveled to China, as an attendant to Pagpa. He was famed as an emanation of Vajrapāṇi and for his magical powers, which included the power to raise the dead, hanging his robes on a sunbeam, and shooting an arrow into rock to draw out water. In his twenty-eighth year Chagna became the ruler of all Tibet. But when he was twenty-nine, on the first day of the seventh month of the fifth fire-hare year (1267), he passed away blissfully in the library of the Gorum.[115]

Up to this point, in accord with Atiśa's vision, mentioned earlier, the early Sakya family line[116] were emanations of Mahākāla, and Sachen Kunga Nyingpo was an emanation of Avalokiteśvara. Sachen's son Khonton Kunga Bar, as well as Lobpon Rinpoche Sonam Tsemo, Jetsun Rinpoche Dragpa Gyaltsen, Palchen Onpo, his son the Dharma lord Sapaṇ, Zangtsa Sonam Gyaltsen, and his son Drogon Chogyal Pagpa, are known as the seven emanations of Mañjughoṣa. Finally Chagna was an emanation of Vajrapāṇi. From this point onward, every member of the family line has been an emanation of Mañjuśrī.

Lama Sachen once had a dream in which everywhere was filled with an inconceivably vast number of forms of Mañjughoṣa, with seven great forms of Mañjughoṣa ornamented with the signs and marks in the middle. After having had this dream, Sachen said, "This is a sign that there will be many scholars here in Sakya who will be of benefit to the Buddha's teaching, and in particular there will be a lineage of seven Mañjughoṣas." Due to this, out of all the Sakya family line, the seven miraculous ones have been made especially prominent, but all of the others were without doubt emanations of Mañjughoṣa's compassion as well.

Dharmapālarakṣita

Chagna's son Dharmapālarakṣita was born to his mother Yumkha Drobum six months after his father's death, in the fifth earth-dragon year (1268). Dharmapāla received a complete education from Pagpa himself and was made imperial preceptor by Sechen when he was twelve. He built a particularly glorious crystal stūpa holding relics, including those of Chapa Chokyi Senge and the Dharma lord Sapaṇ. He passed away in Tri Maṇḍala at the age of twenty, and his son Ratnabhadra died at the age of eight.[117]

The other descendents of Zangtsa

Zangtsa's son Lobpon Rinchen Gyaltsen was born to his mother Machig Jodro in the fourth earth-dog year (1238). He was made chaplain of the emperor of Mongolia and died in the fifth earth-hare year (1279), at the age of forty-two, in the Flower Courtyard in China.[118]

Zangtsa's illegitimate son Lobpon Yeshe Jungne was born to his mother Machig Dorje Den in the fourth earth-dog year (1238). The emperor of Mongolia, Hukarche, made him imperial preceptor. He passed away at thirty-seven in the Yunnan region in the fifth wood-dog year (1274).[119]

Dagnyi Chenpo Zangpo Pal was born to his mother Machig Khabmema in the fourth water-dog year (1262), when his father Lobpon Yeshe Jungne was twenty-five, in the lower fortress at Mangkhar. In China Zangpo Pal married seven queens, who were like the breaths of Tārā, and by the age of forty-two he had fifteen sons. He received full ordination at the age of forty-three, and he passed away blissfully in his bedroom at Zhitog at the age of sixty-three, in the fifth wood-bird year (1324).[120]

The Four Houses

The eldest of Zangpo Pal's sons, the imperial preceptor Kunga Lodro, established four noble houses (*labrang*) and granted them to his younger brothers.[121] The four noble houses were Zhitog, Rinchen Gang, Lhakhang, and Dungcho.[122]

The House of Zhitog

Many learned and accomplished masters came from the House of Zhitog, from Khetsun Namkha Legpa to Dagchen Lodro Wangchug.[123]

The House of Rinchen Gang

In the House of Rinchen Gang were the three brothers Kunga Nyima, Jamyang Donyo Gyaltsen, and the glorious Lama Dampa Sonam Gyaltsen.[124] Lama Dampa Sonam Gyaltsen brought about a great transformation of beings by turning the wheel of learning and accomplishment. The transmissions he held were like an ocean, and the learned and accomplished ones of Tibet came to touch his lotus-like feet. He had an inconceivable number of disciples; the most important included two great regents of his mantra teachings, eight keepers of the secrets of his instructions, and eleven famous scholars. The survival up to this very day of the unimpaired spoken transmission of the explication for the assembly (*tsogshe*) and the explication for disciples (*lobshe*) is purely thanks to the activities of this master.[125]

Jamyang Donyo Gyaltsen's sons included Lachen Kunga Gyaltsen. His sons included Jamyang Namkha Gyaltsen. His sons were Gyagarpa Sherab Gyaltsen and the treasury of oceans of transmissions, Dagchen Lodro Gyaltsen. Through them the esoteric face-to-face transmission of the extraordinary precepts, such as the greater and lesser Mahākāla, became an unparalleled backbone of the teachings.

The House of Lhakhang

The House of Lhakhang included many who possessed the qualities of a true monk, from the two brothers Ngawang Kunga Legpai Jungne and Kunga Gyaltsen to Chokyi Gyaltsen and Kunga Legpa.[126]

The House of Dungcho

The House of Dungcho is the source of the present-day Sakya family line. Kunga Legpa Zangpo Pal had three sons, including Dagchen Kunga Legjung.[127] His son was Dragpa Gyaltsen. His son was Namse Gyaltsen. His son was Namkha Legpa. His son was Namkha Trashi.[128] His four sons were Sa Lotsāwa Jamyang Kunga Sonam, Ngagi Wangchug, Jampal Dragpa, and Sangye Tseten. The elder son of Sangye Tseten was Dagchen Kunga Samdrub, and the younger was Ngawang Chenpo Kunga Rinchen. The first son took up residence in Tsedong, beginning the family line of Tsedong, which goes up to Ngawang Norbu Gyenpa.

Ngawang Chenpo Kunga Rinchen

The second son of Sangye Tseten, Ngawang Chenpo, was a supreme being and an emanation of the great lotsāwa Bairotsana and Jetsun Dragpa Gyaltsen. Relying on the great Sa Lotsāwa, Konchog Lhundrub, and others, he mastered the ocean-like qualities of realization. This was a period of severe difficulties for the great seat of Sakya, a situation Ngawang Chenpo found impossible to bear. He bound several vajra Dharma protectors to his service, and after they were done, nothing remained of the opponents of the Sakya but their names.

Ngawang Chenpo carried out the three spheres of activity to benefit the temples, the physical representations of the Three Jewels, the saṅgha, the systems of philosophical teaching, the mantra rituals, and the essential practices. Thus he infused the teachings and communities of the Sakyapas with his kindness. Ngawang Chenpo had two sons, Jamyang Sonam Wangpo and Ngagchang Dragpa Lodro. Although the precepts of the spoken transmission had been somewhat diminished, from this point onward they gradually began to spread again.

Jamgon Ame Zhab and his descendents

The son of Ngagchang Dragpa Lodro was Jamgon Ame Zhab Kunga Sonam Wangpo. He received the ocean-like precepts of sūtra and mantra along with the spoken transmission from his relatives as well as from holy lamas like Muchen Sangye Gyaltsen, Dorje Chang Wangchug Rabten, and Khenchen Ngawang Chodrag. He carried the enlightened activity of spreading the teachings and wrote Dharma histories on the cycles of Cakrasaṃvara, Guhyasamāja, Yamāntaka, Hevajra, and Vajrakīlaya, as well as many literary works of exegesis.[129]

Ame Zhab's son was Jamyang Sonam Wangchug, who studied and contemplated with his father and Zhalu Khenchen and built upon his father's enlightened activities in religious government.

Sonam Wangchug's son was Ngawang Kunga Trashi, who requested the nectar of instruction from Ame Zhab, Jampa Ngawang Namgyal, Lhundrub Palden, Jampa Ngawang Lhundrub, Zangpo Gyaltsen, and Mindrol Lochen Dharmaśrī.

Kunga Trashi's son was Jamgon Sonam Rinchen, who studied and contemplated with many tutors, including his father, Chogyepa Khyentse Rabten, Trolungpa Sonam Chopal, Ngorchen Sonam Zangpo, and Tartse Namkha Samdrub. Sonam Rinchen's sons included the two brothers Nyigdu Tenpai Nyima and Jamgon Ngagi Wangpo Kunga Lodro.

Jamgon Kunga Lodro and his descendents

Jamgon Kunga Lodro was born from the play of the magical wisdom net of the noble Padmapāṇi, in a line of pure rebirths including a ruler from the noble land of India called Jetāri (in Tibetan, Drale Namgyal), and in Tibet,

Tsechen Kunga Nyingpo and Dagchen Lodro Gyaltsen. In his own lifetime, he was able to expound clearly on any scripture merely by opening it and saying Mañjuśrī's mantra, *a ra pa tsa na dhīḥ*. Thus he was an open lotus of knowledge and a spreading sunshade of compassion who mastered all of the qualities that are praised by the wise.

Kunga Lodro studied with many tutors, including his own father, Jetsun Khacho Wangmo, Tartse Namkha Samdrub, Dragtsewa Losal Tendzin, and Ngorchen Sangye Yeshe. He received an inconceivable number of empowerments, scriptural transmissions, and instructions from all traditions but primarily from his own Sakya tradition. In particular he received the complete cycle of spoken transmission, including the Lamdre explication for one disciple from Nesarwa Ngawang Kunga Legpai Jungne, and an ocean of profound and extensive transmissions, including the precious Kangyur.

Kunga Lodro constantly meditated upon and recited the mantras of up to thirty personal deities, including performing the service to Hevajra three times a day. Due to this single-minded practice of his commitments, Kunga Lodro was accepted by many personal deities. As the vajra Dharma protectors had promised to carry out his enlightened activities, the oath-bound Putra and his brother and sister, and the Vajrakīlaya protectors Karmo Nyida and Dugyal Pawo carried out his commands like servants.

Whether he was giving empowerments, precepts, or practical instructions, Kunga Lodro taught everything by heart. When he gave the permission for Virūpa's exoteric protection practice during the teaching of the Lamdre explication for disciples, he explained it using paintings, in harmony with the original intention of he who stopped the sun in its tracks.[130] When he commisioned a statue of Virūpa, Kunga Lodro constrained the vital winds of the right-hand channel in the central *dhūti* channel and was blessed as Virūpa in all but form. These are just some of the infinite signs of his accomplishments.

Kunga Lodro maintained the teachings as if they were part of his own life force, commissioning many physical representations of the Three Jewels throughout his life and constantly carrying out enlightened activities to spread the teachings. Furthermore, his writings filled thirty large books. His personal students included his brother and children, Tartse Dorje Chang Namkha Chime, Nesar Chogtrul Namkha Legpa, Chogye Trichen and his brother, Zimwog Tulku Tendzin Trinle, Sakyai Zurchepa Rinchen Gyaltsen, Ngarigpa Kunga Trashi, and the Rikhug tulku Kunga Khedrub

Wangpo. All of them were holy people who truly followed the teachings. The undiminished textual tradition of empowerments, scriptural transmission, instructions, and practice instructions among the venerable Sakyapas would not exist today were it not for the kindness of this master.

Kunga Lodro's sons were Jamgon Wangdu Nyingpo and Kunga Pende Gyatso. They received an ocean of precepts from numerous holy teachers, of whom their own father was the most important. With their enlightened activity in spreading the teachings and gaining accomplishment, they increased the happiness and welfare of beings.

The sons of Jamgon Wangdu Nyingpo were the throne holder Pema Dudul Wangchug (also known as Kunga Trashi), Ngawang Kunga Rinchen, Jamgon Kunga Gyaltsen, and Gonpo Ngodrub Palbar.[131] With their father and the Nenga Rigpai Paṇḍita, Kunga Trashi, they studied mostly the precepts of their own school, contemplated, practiced, and helped spread the teachings.

Pema Dudul Wangchug's son was the throne holder Trashi Rinchen. He received an ocean of Dharma transmissions, primarily in his own tradition, from his father and brother, and Tartse Dorje Chang Jampa Kunga Tendzin.

The son of Ngawang Kunga Rinchen was Jamgon Dorje Rinchen.[132] He received an ocean of profound and extensive precepts from his father, Jamgon Kunga Gyaltsen, and Yongdzin Lodro Gyatso, among others. In his short life Dorje Rinchen performed an inconceivable number of acts worthy of an enlightened sage and a constant stream of enlightened activities that helped spread the teachings.

Dorje Rinchen's sons were the throne holder Kunga Sonam and Palden Chogyi Langpo, whose qualities are said to have been beyond intellectual reckoning.[133]

The sons of Dagchen Trashi Rinchen[134] were the two brothers Kunga Nyingpo (the rebirth of the glorious Tsewa Chenpo) and Sangdag Palchen Onpo (the rebirth of Dropugpa Śākya Senge). They studied and completed the practices of deity yoga with their father and the throne holder Kunga Sonam, thus coming to possess countless qualities of accomplishment.

The son of the throne holder Kunga Sonam was Dzamling Chergu Wangdu, and his sons were the throne holder Ngawang Tutob Wangchug and Tubten Khedrub Gyatso, who both came to possess special qualities of holiness.

Ngawang Tutob Wangchug's son was Jigdral Ngawang Kunga Sonam, the tulku of Ewam Luding Khenchen Gyalse Jamyang Chokyi Nyima. Today he devotes his life to the prosperity of beings and the teachings, and I pray for the stablity and expansion of his life force and buddha activity.[135]

Kunga Nyingpo had four sons. The eldest was Dorje Chang Dragshul Trinle Rinchen. He was undoubtedly the rebirth of Dagchen Trashi Rinchen. He received all of the oral precepts that ripen and liberate from his father, from the queen of the vajra ḍākinīs Jetsun Tamdrin Wangmo, and from Drubwang Ratnabhadra, among others. Thus he came to possess an inconceivable number of the qualities of learning and accomplishment.

Dragshul Trinle Rinchen's sons were the two brothers Ngawang Kunga Rinchen and Kunga Tenpai Gyaltsen. They studied and completed the practices with their father and had an inconceivable number of the qualities of experience, realization, and accomplishment.

His Holiness Sakya Trizin

Ngawang Kunga Rinchen's son was the master of oceans of buddha families and maṇḍalas, the throne holder Ngawang Kunga Tegchen Palbar Trinle Wangi Gyalpo, born in the sixteenth wood-bird year (1945).[136] He was granted the nectar of the precepts for ripening and liberation by his father and by Ewam Khangsar Khenchen Dampa Rinpoche, Lhakhang Khenchen Jampal Zangpo, and others. From the lion of speech Khenpo Yonten Zangpo he studied and contemplated many explanations of the texts of sūtra and mantra, fully opening the lotus of knowledge and becoming a great treasury of the qualities of scriptural knowledge and realization.

As a youth he was reserved and displayed an inherent intelligence and courage. Due to these qualities, he placed his feet upon the high throne of the religious governance of the great seat of Sakya. Today he practices his meditation in India and sends out a great rain of extensive and profound Dharma in the ten directions. With his limitless activities in the three spheres, including establishing monastic communities and schools of philosophy, his unequaled enlightened activities of maintaining and disseminating the precious teachings of the glorious Sakyapas have spread to the ends of the earth, and he has devoted his life to being a sublime guardian of all humanity, including myself. I constantly pray at the lotus feet of the protector of the Rime teachings and of all beings: In the future may you be strengthened by the essence of the three deities of long life, may the white parasol of your precious enlightened activities cover the entire earth, and may you always bestow welfare and happiness upon all humanity.[137]

In short, the members of this family line, who all possessed the three supreme signs of a master of the teachings, have been praised thus by the omniscient Konchog Lhundrub:

> The ignorant, outcast, misfortunate child
> is lifted up by saṃsāra and cast into this world,
> but the sound of a thousand voices proclaiming it an illusion and a waterfall
> makes the world unsteady, so it need not be like this.

As he says, this particular precious family line has its own qualities, such as knowledge and strength, yet they are made available to others. And today, it is obvious that those who take pride in their greatness cannot rival even a fraction of this great family line.

• 3 •

The Lamdre

THIS ACCOUNT of the Lamdre, the precious oral instructions that are the essence of the teachings, is in two parts: its history in India and its history in Tibet.

THE HISTORY OF THE LAMDRE IN INDIA

Virūpa

The glorious *Hevajra Tantra* was expounded by our teacher in the style of a recitation in order to summarize the meaning of the original 100,000 verse *Hevajra Tantra*. As it says:

> First there should be a purification of transgressions (*poṣadha*),
> then they should be taught the ten rules of virtuous conduct,
> then the Vaibhāṣika teachings, and then the Sautrāntika,
> and after that the Yogācāra, and then the Madhyamaka.
> Then when they understand all the methods of mantra,
> they should begin Hevajra.[138]

The great chariot of independent explication of the intended meaning of the three tantras of glorious Hevajra, that ultimate and definitive pinnacle of all sūtras and tantras, is he who was looked after by Nairātmyā herself and who realized the sixth bhūmi, the Indian adept, the lord of yogins Virūpa. It says in the *Mañjuśrīmūla Tantra*:

> The syllable *dha* refers to the ascetic
> famed in the southern regions.
> This ascetic will also accomplish mantras.

Drogmi Lotsāwa considered this to be a prophecy about the lord of yogins, saying:

> There is a complete correspondence: Virūpa was called Dharmapāla, the name that is indicated here. Between his twice reversing the flow of the Ganges and his conversion of Caṇḍikā, he was in the southern regions; thus he became increasingly famous in the south. His teaching activities employed the methods of an ascetic, and when he had been blessed by Nairātmyā, Virūpa fully accomplished the secret mantra. Those who connect this prophecy to the famous Dharmakīrti have some difficulty in making a definitive case for all of its aspects.[139]

In any case, this great sage was born into a royal line 1,020 years after our Teacher passed into nirvāṇa. Casting aside his kingdom like spittle in the dust, he traveled east to the monastery of Somapuri, where he took ordination with the abbot Vinītadeva and the master Jinakīrti.[140] He commissioned physical representations of the Three Jewels and traveled to the monastery of Nālandā. He received full ordination from a Mūlasarvāstivādin abbot called Vijayasena and was given the name Śrī Dharmapāla. He received the empowerment and oral precepts of Cakrasaṃvara from this abbot and engaged in an extensive study and contemplation of the five sciences, eventually completing the study of the ocean of Buddhist and non-Buddhist traditions. After the death of the abbot, Virūpa was appointed abbot of Nālandā.

During the daytime Virūpa carried out his monastic duties of exposition, debate, and composition, while during the night he strove to accomplish Cakrasaṃvara. Yet even after a long time, no definitive signs or accomplishments arose. Then one evening he had a dream in which a river flowed uphill, the sun and moon fell from the sky, and a mountain cracked open. Disheartened, he thought: "I have no connection with the Vajrayāna. From now on I'll just carry out my monastic duties and give up the sādhana of my yidam deity."

So on the twenty-second day of the fourth month, Virūpa threw his rosary into the latrine and did as he pleased all day. That night the exalted Vajra Nairātmyā appeared to him in a dream and said, "This kind of improper behavior is unfitting of you—go and get your rosary! I am the deity with whom you have accumulated karma through your proper sādhana practice and the maintenance of your vows, and you are one who carries my blessings."

Then, on the evening of the twenty-third day, the master had done as instructed, and Vajra Nairātmyā came in person in her fifteen-goddess maṇḍala and bestowed the complete four initiations. Through this Virūpa actualized the wisdom of the path of seeing on the first bhūmi. By upholding that wisdom, he moved up to the next bhūmi on each subsequent day, until on the twenty-ninth day he became a great bodhisattva of the sixth bhūmi.

While Virūpa was upholding his realization in this way, he did a variety of strange things that caused misgivings in all his fellow monks. "I'm wicked," he admitted to them and proceeded to carry out shockingly worldly activities.[141] This brought about his expulsion from his position at Nālandā. Setting off for Vārāṇasī, he said to the River Ganges, "I'm a wicked person whom you shouldn't touch, so open up a way for me!" So the Ganges reversed its flow, and the monks who witnessed this, finally understanding that Virūpa was an adept, asked for his forgiveness.

At Vārāṇasī he spent a long time sitting in the forest in meditative absorption. The king of that region, called Govindacaṇḍa, said to everyone, "Find out if this yogin is good or bad!" But since no one could establish this through external signs, the king had Virūpa pushed into water, dropped into a trench, and pinned down with iron weights. Virūpa returned from these murder attempts to stand unharmed before the king, and the king asked for his forgiveness with great faith. Virūpa established the king and his entourage in the Vajrayāna.

After that Virūpa traveled south to Bhīmeśvara. On the way he came to a ferryman at the banks of the Ganges who said, "If you can't pay the toll, there's no way across."

"Well then I will have to give you this river," said Virūpa, and pointing with his index finger, he reversed the flow of the Ganges. Then he snapped his fingers and the river flowed as before. A strong faith in Virūpa arose in the ferryman, and he became a disciple. This was Ḍombīpa.[142]

Master and disciple traveled to a town in south India called Ḍākinīpata, where they were served beer by a barmaid called Kāmarūpasiddhi. Eventually she asked, "When are you going to pay?" Virūpa drew a line between the sunlight and the shade, and replied, "When the sunlight passes this line." Since the sun remained stuck where it was, Virūpa and Ḍombī finished all the beer, while the sunlight and shade did not move at all. The normal passage of time was disrupted, and as the people were drunk with tiredness they came to know of the power of the lord of yogins. The king asked Virūpa to release the sun and paid the bill for the beer. When the red sun finally set in the west, three days had passed. The fame of the one who had turned back the Ganges twice and held the sun in the middle of the sky spread through every quarter.

Later, in the southern region of Bhīmeśvara, Virūpa split and then restored the statue of the deity Īśvara. He displayed innumerable other magical feats of his yogic discipline, instilling faith in many. After one of these feats, an ascetic with knotted hair became his disciple. This was the easterner Kāṇha.

Master and disciple traveled to see the Khasarpaṇa statue at Devikoṭa.[143] There the noble Avalokiteśvara said: "You have performed great acts for the teachings; however, due to the differing karma of sentient beings, you must use skillful means with compassion."[144] After that Virūpa traveled southward and established the monastic community of Somanātha. There, by prohibiting animal sacrifices, he saved the lives of tens of thousands of sentient beings.

Virūpa revealed the *Raktayamāri Tantra* from the land of Oḍḍiyāna and wrote the unelaborated original text of the Lamdre.[145] Then in accord with the words of the Great Compassionate One, having practiced projection and reabsorption within his yogic discipline, Virūpa dissolved into a stone statue. Others say that he became a stone statue. In any case, as the statue's hand imparted a liquid that could turn anything into gold, Virūpa continued to ensure the welfare of a vast number of beings.

In short, there has been nobody to equal this master, who carried out activities for the teachings through the unworldly methods of yogic discipline. This accords with the famous prophecy that says: "The upholder of the teachings of yogic discipline will be the lord of yogins Virūpa, the upholder of the teachings through debate will be Śrī Dharmakīrti, and the upholder of the teachings of rulership will be the Dharma king Aśoka."

Ḍombī Heruka

Two disciples received the grace of the precious oral instructions of the Lamdre from the lord of transcendent yoga, Virūpa. The first of these was

Ḍombī Heruka, the boatman who witnessed Virūpa turning back the Ganges for the second time. Because he was one of those blessed with instant realization, Ḍombīpa was led along the instantaneous path. With just a single element of the path, he was able become one with realization.

Ḍombīpa practiced in various southern countries. When converting the king of Kaṃkana palace, he rode in on a man-eating tiger that he had harnessed with a serpent. Brandishing the serpent in his hand, he subdued the king. A small part of the rootless Lamdre derives from Ḍombīpa, and today this part of the transmission lineage is taught according to the commentarial method.[146]

Kāṇha

Virūpa's second disciple Kāṇha was one of a group of five hundred ascetics with matted hair from the south of India. Initially he was not a follower of the Buddha's teachings and disputed with those who wanted to follow the teachings. Because Kāṇha had all the signs of someone headed for the lower realms, Virūpa led him through the stages of the genuine teachings after giving him the root text of the Lamdre, the *Vajra Lines*, and he became one with realization.

Kāṇha left the south of India and went to live in eastern India and therefore came to be known as "the easterner Kāṇha." There he destroyed the attachment of a king to his seventy-two queens. This was achieved in the following way. First Kāṇha went into the company of the queens. Then when the queens explained to the king what had happened, the king said: "He must be killed!" When the king's troops arrived, the master went back inside. As soon as the troops went inside, Kāṇha went outside. When inside and out were completely filled by the troops, Kāṇha sent forth magical emanations outnumbering the king's troops. When their number increased to 108, the king realized that Kāṇha was an adept and bowed at his feet.

The Lamdre lineage in India

How did the Lamdre lineage proceed from these three great adepts, these lords of yogins? Virūpa bestowed upon Kāṇha very concise explanations of the tantras and very extensive practices from the hearing lineage of instructions. Kāṇha bestowed these upon Ḍamarupa, a yogin from Magadha. Ḍamarupa was capable of performing activities and playing his hand drum (*ḍamaru*) simultaneously in the thirty-two sites, including the twenty-four sacred places.[147] He passed on the teachings to a king of Magadha called Siṃha Vikrīḍita. This king achieved a high level of realization and spent his time among children, practicing the abandonment of duality. This is how he came to be known as Avadhūti. In addition, he was a genuine example of someone who attained the bhūmis.

Avadhūti bestowed the teachings upon Gayadhara, who came from a family of royal scribes. When he requested empowerment in the maṇḍala of Hevajra, he developed the empowerment wisdom, and cultivating it for three nights, he came to reside at the supreme worldly qualities of the path of application.[148] He possessed numerous qualities, including the unhindered ability to transfer his consciousness into a corpse and the ability to place his hand drum in midair, where it sounded on its own.

Furthermore, Virūpa bestowed upon Ḍombī Heruka very extensive explanations of the tantras and very concise practices from the hearing lineage of instructions. These teachings were then transmitted to Aścaryavajra, then to Vanaprastha, then to Garbharipa, then to Jāyaśrī, then to Durjayacandra, and then to Bhikṣu Vīravajra.

The history of the Lamdre in Tibet

This is in three parts: initially, how it was introduced by Gayadhara, in the middle, how it was disseminated by Drogmi Lotsāwa, and finally, how it was passed on by the Sakyapa masters and disciples.

Initially, how the Lamdre was introduced by Gayadhara

Once when the great lama Drogmi Lotsāwa Śākya Yeshe was studying and teaching at Mugulung in Mangkhar, he had a dream that had never come to him before in which he saw a vast country that he didn't recognize. The morning after, his heart was gladdened by the sound of someone blowing on a conch shell at the gatehouse. He went to the door of his bedroom and saw Gayadhara, who said, "I am a paṇḍita!" in Sanskrit. After further exchanges, Drogmi invited the paṇḍita inside and offered him a meal.[149]

The paṇḍita said: "If you are a suitable vessel, I will bring your qualities of learning and accomplishment to fruition." The lotsāwa felt that this more than fulfilled the prophecies he had received from Avalokiteśvara and Bhikṣu Vīravajra and was greatly pleased.[150] After the meal Drogmi sat down again with the great paṇḍita and had a discussion over tea. Drogmi wanted to study the Mahāyāna in general and the Vajrayāna in particular, and from within the latter the unsurpassed yoga in the system of Virūpa. So he made a maṇḍala of loose tea and several ounces of gold, bowed down and offered it to Gayadhara, placing his head at the paṇḍita's feet and asking to be taken as a disciple. Gayadhara said: "I came to look for you when I received a prophecy from the Great Compassionate One. Do you have much gold?"

Drogmi asked Gayadhara to fulfill his wish to be taken as a disciple. The paṇḍita replied: "Puhrang Lotsāwa Zhonu Sherab has already asked me with great urgency, but I came to find you based on the prophecy of my yidam deity. I agreed to return to him in three months, and a month has already passed. After I have done that I need to go and fetch a book from Nepal, but I will come back in two years at the earliest, three at the latest. In the meantime gather the gold."[151]

The lotsāwa said, "I will perform the offering in accordance with your instructions and give it to you in person. But I'm worried that this auspicious connection will disappear if you bestow a great many empowerments in the meantime. So I would ask you to please stay for just a year, starting right now." The paṇḍita replied: "All right then, I won't go until I receive a summons from Puhrang Lotsāwa."

The next morning Drogmi invited Gayadhara to the caves of Lhatse. There they spent a month teaching and receiving teachings, and examining the connection between master and disciple according to the method of the *Gurupañcāśikā*.[152] After that month Gayadhara began teaching his oral precepts. He offered practical guidance and helped with Drogmi's translations, with the result that Drogmi achieved a certain level of accomplishment.

After six months had passed, Puhrang Lotsāwa Zhonu Sherab came to meet the master and his disciple. Drogmi requested further teachings from Gayadhara, who promised to return in two years and to confer the complete Dharma cycles of Virūpa. In turn Gayadhara made Drogmi promise to come and meet him at Kyirong and bring his complete offering of gold and other valuables. Drogmi offered Gayadhara ten ounces of gold and a full set of clothing as payment for his requests and acted as his escort as far as the border of Barpug.

During this first visit to Tibet, Gayadhara was known as the red paṇḍita.

In his absence Drogmi went to Namtang Karpo in Dringtsam and turned the wheel of the Dharma. Over two years a large amount of gold came into his hands. When Gayadhara returned and was in the area again, he sent a letter to Drogmi asking him to come to Mangyul. Drogmi was delighted and arrived in Mangyul four days later. The lotsāwa and twenty attendants, along with a noble minister with two attendants, came bearing fine gifts and offerings and met Gayadhara at Kyirong. Drogmi pleased his guru with offerings and services, and master and disciple traveled together to Mugulung in Mangkhar.

Drogmi asked his guru for the Dharma and offered a maṇḍala of three ounces of gold for him to begin. Three days later Gayadhara drew the boundaries for a retreat, and for the next three years Drogmi and Gayadhara worked on translations, including the tantra trilogy of Hevajra. Gayadhara also gave teachings, including the Lamdre, and gave practical guidance to Drogmi.

Saying, "Though you don't need this, it is what we do in my tradition," the paṇḍita placed a torma representing Mahākāla of the Tent on top of his head and a picture of the deity behind his back. Then he swore an oath that he had now given Drogmi the complete Dharma cycle of the lord of yogins and all of his other Dharmas.

Drogmi offered five hundred ounces of gold, a thousand measures of musk, and six fathoms-length of white tail-hair.[153] Gayadhara was very pleased and said, "Is there anything else you want?"[154]

The lotsāwa replied, "I am worried that in extreme circumstances I may forget these teachings. Can I put together some small notes as reminders, and may I also be allowed to see a special sign of the path?"

Gayadhara said, "Then I must set the sacred boundaries in another solitary place, not here, and we must perform an uninterrupted feast offering (*gaṇacakra*)." At midnight that night, Gayadhara invited Drogmi to his hermitage, and they did what he had said. Having done these additional things, Gayadhara asked, "Is there anything else you want?"

Drogmi replied, "May I request that you do not give the precious oral instructions of the Lamdre—the textual transmissions you have given me along with the additional things—to anyone else in Tibet?"

The paṇḍita said, "You will pass into the celestial realm of Khecara without leaving your body, and someone will be appointed master of your teachings by your descendants. Your sons will dissipate all of your auspicious connections, so train in the transference of consciousness (*powa*) now and go to Khecara as soon as you leave your body. The sons who are to carry on your precepts must not practice them for thirteen years; otherwise the precepts will not spread. I bind you to this command. You should decide who will be a suitable vessel for the teachings according to their gifts of food and valuables."

Having acceded to Gayadhara's request, Drogmi escorted him to Lesser Totang and did not leave him until they reached Kyirong. This constitutes the paṇḍita's first visit to Tibet.[155] Gayadhara is known to have made three trips to Tibet. The first time he came on the basis of prophecies from his guru and yidam to teach Drogmi the Dharma cycles of Virūpa, including the precious oral instructions of the Lamdre, as stated immediately above. The second time he was invited by Go Lotsāwa to teach the tantra trilogy of Hevajra, the *Guhyasamāja Tantra*, and many other Dharmas.[156] The third time Gyijo Dawai Ozer invited him and requested many Dharmas. During this visit, two of Gyijo's patrons invited Gayadhara to Kharag and gave him considerable offerings and services.[157] Gayadhara said, "Now I am engaged in virtuous practices here in Tibet, where the rivers are clear, the climate remains pleasant and cool, where animals are few yet very nourishing. I will not go back to India. I have no desire for piles of gold, and I have little time left to teach many Dharmas."

Fulfilling an earlier promise, Gayadhara worked on a translation of the *Kālacakra Tantra*.[158] When this was finished he said, "If Drogmi were here, you would see that the father and the son have become equal in their accomplishment, but he has gone to Khecara." Over the next few years, the paṇḍita gave away every offering he had received to virtuous causes and then began to show the signs of dying. He said, "I will not remain here much longer. Accompany me to Tobu; my children are there."[159]

Thus Gayadhara was invited to Tobu in Kharag. There at the paṇḍita's request a feast offering was convened by a group of people whose samaya was unspoiled, and everyone was satisfied with the ritual substances. Gayadhara adopted the meditation posture and crossed his vajra and bell at his heart. He spoke to all of his spiritual children about the importance of meditation and not tiring of their practice, and then said, "I have traveled back and forth between India and Tibet spreading the teachings, and I've had little time to practice with great seriousness. Nevertheless, when a yogin dies, this is how he does it."

The paṇḍita took three breaths, and a globe of light left the Brahmā aperture at the crown of his head. At the center of the globe the body of Heruka appeared very clearly. Various sounds of music, showers of flowers, and limitless rainbows appeared and then disappeared into the southwest. These things are said to have been seen by all the people of Bartang.

Accounts differ as to whether Gayadhara bestowed the oral instructions of the Lamdre during his second and third visits to Tibet. According to Khenchen Ngawang Chodrag:

> It is not clearly stated in Kunga Zangpo's *Sunlight That Spreads the Teachings* whether he agreed or refused to give the oral instructions to Go Lotsāwa at that time. However, there are translations by Go of both the *Vajra Lines* and the *Divisions of the Empowerment*, which proves that Go did receive Gayadhara's oral instructions.

He also says:

> Gayadhara gave Gyijo many Dharmas, including the oral instructions of the Lamdre. Gyijo translated the *Vajra Lines*, and the holders of his lineage disseminated these teachings. Gyijo appears to have written a summary of the teachings and several manuals on the fourteen syllables of the *bhaga* and to have passed the lineage on to Zhu Khormo, Zhu Darma Gyaltsen, Zhu Horma, and so on. Some say that Nyo Lotsāwa Yonten Dragpa definitely received Gayadhara's oral instructions at this time as well. This can be inferred from the fact that the technical term *the path including the result* appears frequently in the thirty-two Rali tantras that were composed by Nyo.[160]

Jamgon Ame Zhab writes:

> There is a well-known story that as well as giving the oral instructions to Drogmi during his first trip to Tibet, the paṇḍita gave them to Go and Gyijo when they invited him to Tibet. This does not appear in any of the histories of the exalted lamas of India and Tibet. In particular, the *Incisive Vajra* written by Marton, the *Miraculous Manifestation* of Lama Dampa, and the Lamdre

> history composed by Chagen Wangchug Gyaltsen all state precisely that Gayadhara did not bestow the Lamdre during his two subsequent visits to Tibet. Since Gayadhara made a vow not to give the oral instructions that he had bestowed on Drogmi to anybody else in Tibet, it seems to me that he would not have taught them during this time.

According to the Dharma history of the vidyādhara Wangchug Rabten, the Zhama and Drom traditions say that Gayadhara did not teach the Lamdre while he was with Gyijo.[161] Yet Gyijo does seem to have possessed the entire oral instructions of the Lamdre, since there exists a translation of the *Vajra Lines* by Gyijo, lineage histories written by his students, and the manuals on the fourteen syllables of the *bhaga*. According to some manuscripts in my possession,[162] Gayadhara did not grant the Lamdre to Go, but since there is a translation by Go of the lord of yogins' *Divisions of the Empowerment*, it seems that he must have given some of the oral instructions to Go. It is important to understand the analysis of the Lamdre masters, but it is difficult to determine which of their positions on whether Gayadhara gave the Lamdre to Go and Gyijo is correct.

In the Middle, How the Lamdre was Disseminated by Drogmi Lotsāwa

In the past at the Drompa Gyang temple in Rulag there lived three brothers known as the Three De of Eastern Tibet or the Three Noble Brothers of Lhatse. They held a formal meeting and sent a request for a chaplain to the two successors to the abbacy of the great lama Gongpa Rabsel, Loton and Tsongtsun, who were living in the Gyengong temple in Lower Nyang.[163] A group of monks was dispatched headed by the two heirs to the abbacy of Loton: Gya Śākya Zhonu and Se Yeshe Tsondru. When they arrived they gave the full ordination to Drogmi Śākya Yeshe, Taglo Zhonu Tsondru, and Leng Yeshe Zhonu, with Gya as the abbot, Se as the preceptor, and Nyang Dorje Gyaltsen as the secret preceptor. In addition a further three hundred people became monks. When they began the threefold training, they felt that they did not have enough of the Buddha's teachings.[164] So the patrons and priests held a meeting and decided to send Drogmi, Taglo, and Leng to train as lotsāwas in India.

The abbot, the preceptor, and the three noble brothers are said to have declared: "Study the Vinaya because it is the root of the teachings, the perfections because they are the heart, and secret mantras because they are the vital essence!" Regarding this speech, Sakya Paṇḍita has said:

> These are words of advice on understanding the basics of the teachings. This is why. The Vinaya is the basis of the teachings; if one does not have renunciation endowed with morality, then even if one has many fantasies of being a yogin, one will be incapable of practicing the authentic teachings. The perfections are the heart; without the perfections one will not be able to fathom bodhicitta, which is the root of the Mahāyāna, or the presentation of the paths and bhūmis. The secret mantra is the vital essence; without relying on the secret mantras with a teacher who brings together all of the profound points of the exoteric and esoteric teachings, one will not attain the ultimate result.

Thereafter the three traveled in stages to Nepal, where they asked four excellent paṇḍitas for the empowerments of Hevajra, Cakrasaṃvara, Guhyasamāja, Vajrabhairava, and Mahāmāyā and became their students.[165] Furthermore, the great lama Drogmi remained for a year to study grammar, mathematics, and the like, attaining the title of lotsāwa. Then since the gurus had granted their instructions, Drogmi traveled to Bodhgaya, where he prostrated and made offerings at the Mahābodhi Temple. In response to his prayers, he received excellent omens.

Then Drogmi traveled to Vikramaśīla, where he stayed for eighteen years in the presence of Śāntipa, the protector of the eastern gate. He studied various Dharmas of the perfections and secret mantra. In particular Drogmi received profound instructions known as the *Unified Meaning of Sūtra and Tantra* from Śāntipa. He received *Illuminating the Recollection of the Innate* from Vāgīśvarakīrti, the guardian of the southern gate. He received *Instructions Guarding Against the Hindrances of External Demons* from Prajñākaragupta, the guardian of the western gate. He received *Purifying the Threefold Suffering* from Nārotapa, the protector of the eastern gate. He received *Instructions Guarding Against Disturbances in the Bodily Elements* from Jñānaśrī, the guardian of the great central pillar. Finally, he received *Esoteric Instructions Guarding Against Hindrances to Mental Concentration* from Ratnavajra, the other guardian of the great central pillar. Today these texts are known as Drogmi's Dharma from the six gates.[166]

Then Drogmi went to pay homage, make offerings, and renounce malice in the presence of the Khasarpaṇa image of the Great Compassionate One, which had been brought from the pure land of Potala by the paṇḍita Ajitamitra.[167] Due to the power of Drogmi's prayers, the Great Compassionate One spoke directly to him, saying: "On the road ahead you will meet a guru. Do what he says. When you are in Tibet once again, a guru will escort you through the gates of Dharma. You will be blessed by myself as well."

Hoping to fulfill the prophecy straight away, Drogmi made further prayers and traveled on. As he traveled, he met the Bhikṣu Vīravajra amid a dense forest.[168] Thinking, "Is this the fulfillment of the prophecy?" Drogmi bowed down at the feet of the monk and asked to be taken as a disciple. Vīravajra declared him a worthy disciple and bestowed the empowerment of Hevajra. Drogmi also received many Dharmas, including an explanation of the tantra trilogy of Hevajra. When it was time to travel on, Drogmi met up again with his two former companions. When they compared what they had learned, Drogmi was found to be the greatest paṇḍita.

On their return to Tibet, Drogmi and his companions were greeted at Kyirong in Mangyul by the patrons and priests, who escorted them back. The abbot, preceptor, and saṅgha requested many Dharmas from Drogmi, while the patrons—the three divine brothers—requested empowerment. Drogmi set up residence in the Lhatse caves, where he practiced deity yoga and wrote several handbooks that had been requested.

After two years had passed, Drogmi traveled once again to India, after accepting marvelous donations from the patrons and priests.[169] In the court of King Canaka he met again with Vīravajra. Drogmi requested empowerment, and the guru granted thirteen empowerments in succession.

Vīravajra said: "I have heard the Dharma cycles of the lineage of the great lord of yogins, the powerful protector, Virūpa. You are a suitable vessel for the whole host of teachings, so let your commitment and diligence grow stronger!" Then he began to teach the tantra trilogy of Hevajra, and over the course of a year supplemented the root and explanatory tantras with esoteric instructions dealing with the difficult topics in the explanatory tradition. It was possible for Vīravajra to teach Drogmi at one and the same time the elaborate versions of all the Dharmas he had previously received. Considering the oral tradition of the paṇḍita Durjayacandra—the ninth in Virūpa's Dharma lineage—to be particularly fine, Drogmi trained in it without becoming distracted for so much as a second.

After four years had passed, the guru arranged an excellent thanksgiving ceremony for the ḍākinīs and Dharma protectors and said to Drogmi: "I have bestowed my Dharmas upon you without leaving anything out, so meditate joyfully! When you return to Tibet, divide your time between practice and teaching. Sometime soon I will completely eliminate elaboration.[170] You yourself will be the master of the Lord of Yogin's Dharma, and another paṇḍita will escort you through the gates of Dharma."

Drogmi then asked for some further transmissions to take to Tibet. Vīravajra replied: "You already know the most important root tantras, explanatory tantras, instructional tantras, additional tantras, and profound shorter tantras of the highest yoga tantra, along with many commentaries. Now that I have given you around eighty tantras along with their commentaries and ṭīkās, many collections of sādhanas, and around fifty sūtras and dhāraṇīs, your knowledge is limitless!" Nevertheless Drogmi asked that Vīravajra bestow, as a parting gift, some of the extraordinary topics of the general perfection stage, such as his rootless Lamdre, the eight further cycles of the path, and his profound oral precepts on the transference of consciousness.

On his return to Tibet Drogmi arrived in the company of envoys who had escorted him from Palmo Paltang onward. The abbot, the master, and the three brothers invited Drogmi to Lhatse and requested a number of empowerments, such as Hevajra and Cakrasaṃvara.

Thereafter Drogmi established the teaching center of Mugulung, which was made possible by the three brothers. His knowledge became famous, and many sages became his students, including Marpa Chokyi Lodro and Go Khugpa Lhetse. Thus in general this great lama, thanks to the compassion of the buddhas and the blessings of his gurus, came to possess an unimaginable number of qualities of renunciation and realization. In particular, he fulfilled the prophecies of his gurus and yidam deities and was satisfied with the ocean of teachings he had heard.

At one time, when Drogmi was considering giving a teaching, a magical emanation of Bhikṣu Vīravajra arrived and stayed with him for a month. Vīravajra resolved some doubts of Drogmi's and helped translate some short texts, including the *Suparigraha*, the *Ratnajvāla*, and the *Stotraviṃśaka*.[171] Then Vīravajra departed on a sunbeam.

A few days later Maitrīpa Advayavajra came to Drogmi's cave.[172] He too stayed for a month, granting several instructions and translating some of the Dharma cycle of Khecarī.[173] Maitrīpa then departed to Śrīparvata. During this time Drogmi had an inconceivable number of experiences and realizations. Furthermore, as discussed above, Drogmi received the complete tantras and instructions of the lord Gayadhara during the latter's second visit to Tibet.

In general, Drogmi was a great paṇḍita learned in the five sciences and possessed great qualities. Since he attained stability in the perfection stage, he was able to emanate two forms of his single body and take useful goods out of the hearth of his fire rituals. Due to his power over the vital winds, he was able to sit cross-legged in midair, and he had the power to read other people's thoughts.

The Nine Cycles of the Path

Sapaṇ writes of "the nine cycles of the path including the Lamdre," and indeed Drogmi possessed nine cycles of the path, the most important of which was the Lamdre:[174]

1. The cycle of the path known as the *Lamdre*, or the *Path Together with Its Result*, written by the lord of yogins Virūpa based on the tantras in general and the tantra trilogy of Hevajra in particular[175]
2. The cycle of the path known as the *Nine Methods of the Profound Development Stage* and the *Perfection Stage Like the Tip of a Flame* by the great adept Saroruhavajra, based on the root *Hevajra Tantra*[176]
3. The cycle of the path known as the *Commentary on Bodhicitta* by the master Nāgārjuna, based on the *Guhyasamāja Tantra*.[177]
4. The cycle of the path known as the *Inconceivable* by the great adept Kuddālapāda, based on the *Saṃpuṭa Tantra*[178]
5. The cycle of the path known as the *Olapati*, or *Drops of Spring*, written by the great adept Caryāvajra, based on the mother tantra *Cakrasaṃvara*[179]
6. The cycle of the path known as *Straightening the Crooked* written by Acyuta Kāṇha, based on all of the mother tantras[180]
7. The cycle of the path known as the *Complete Path of the Consort* written by the great Indrabhūti, the actual student of the Buddha, based the *Jñānatilaka Tantra*[181]

8. The cycle of the path known as the *Innate Accomplishment* written by the great adept Ḍombī Heruka, based on the tantra trilogy of Hevajra[182]
9. The cycle of the path known as the *Letterless Mahāmudrā* written by Vāgīśvarakīrti, based on the *Hevajra Tantra* and the *Guhyasamāja Tantra*[183]

Of these, *Straightening the Crooked* was taken from a few of Kāṇha's profound precepts and is not a complete path. The *Letterless Mahāmudrā* was written based on the *Hevajra Tantra* and the *Guhyasamāja Tantra*, but because its blessings come from the methods of the fifteen goddesses of Nairātmyā, it is included in the Dharma cycle of Hevajra.[184] It and the other six are all complete paths.[185] Although it is different from the instructions in the Lamdre, the *Letterless Mahāmudrā* has been held very dear by the lamas of the past because it was a particularly special precept of Drogmi's and there has been no degeneration of its transmission or practical guidance.[186]

All of these were received by Drogmi, who translated them and disseminated them through teaching. Drogmi received the first six cycles of the path from Bhikṣu Vīravajra and Lord Gayadhara, the next two from the paṇḍita Prajñāgupta, and the final one from the paṇḍita Amoghavajra.[187]

Drogmi's students

Drogmi, as a great lotsāwa, came to have an inconceivable number of students and close disciples in U, Tsang, and Kham. His most important students included those who received all the tantras, those who received all the instructions, and those who gained accomplishments.

According to the histories of exalted lamas of India and Tibet the *Incisive Vajra* of Marton and Lama Dampa's *Miraculous Manifestation*, five students received all the tantras: Khon Konchog Gyalpo, Reton Konchog Gyalpo, Gyijang Ukarwa, Dragtse Senagpa of Shang, and Ngaripa Selwai Nyingpo. One history also includes Zurpoche Śākya Jungne of Nyari, making six. The students who received all the instructions are the same in all sources: Drom Depa Tonchung, Lhatsun Kali, and Seton Kunrig. As for the students who gained accomplishment, according to the histories mentioned above, there were seven in total. Three were men: Tsangmepa Gyergom Sewo, Tanagpa Shengom Rogpo, and Penyulpa Upa Drongpoche. Four were women: Chemo Namkha of Penyul, Mangkhar Topowa Tomo Dorjetso,

Yangkharwa Dremo Kone, and Tsamo Rongpa Shapamo Jocham Gyaltsen. In one history the number of men is increased to five with the addition of Chogro Zhongpa Driche Śāka Tson and the son of Phedrugpa Chagtsang Tongol, making nine students who gained accomplishment. Setting down the biographies of each of these students would require a huge amount of writing, so they will not be elaborated upon here. Those who want to know more can consult the works of previous lamas.[188]

These precious esoteric instructions of the Lamdre in the present day are in the lineage derived from Seton Kunrig, one of the students who received Drogmi's complete instructions. This lama was born into the Chidrumpa Seche family in Dogme. He was a good talker and highly intelligent. Due to the power of his awakened imprints from previous lives, Seton traveled to Mugulung, guiding a herd of about thirty female yaks and their offspring. There he made his offering to Drogmi and requested his esoteric precepts. Drogmi said: "This is not a large offering, but they will be useful for grazing the three upper slopes of the valley."

Drogmi accepted the offering, but apart from a few empowerments, he didn't grant the oral instructions of the Lamdre right away. Seton had to wait a long time, but Drogmi was pleased with his behavior and granted all of the oral precepts. Seton put them into practice and had excellent visionary experiences, mastering in particular the methods for clearing away obstacles.

The students of Seton who received the Lamdre were: the superior recipients, the two Zhangton brothers; the middling recipients, the Zhama brother and sister;[189] and the inferior recipient, Segom Jangye. It was the elder of the Zhangton brothers, Zhangton Chobar, who gave the Lamdre to Lama Sachen. The Zhangton brothers pleased Lama Seton with their offerings and their behavior, and he granted them his complete oral instructions. Thus they became known as "the Zhangton brothers who heard the complete Lamdre." Their lama said to them: "This Dharma of mine is well understood by the two Zhangton brothers. Between the two of them, it is best understood by Zhangton Zijibar."[190]

Zijibar, the younger brother, died young. The elder, Chobar, lived in the style of a secret yogin, staying at home and diligently making practice his main aim. During the day he farmed and taught Dzogchen, maintaining the postmeditation view. After eight years he arrived directly at the intermediate gathering of the essential constituents and attained claivoyance and magical powers. In particular, through his mastery of the four malleable qualities, Zhangton Chobar was able to assume other forms, such as a tiger or a bird.[191] Based on prophecies from the yidams and ḍākinīs, he guided every vessel for the teachings individually, giving them what was appropriate to their mental capacity.

Thus Zhangton Chobar gave his complete guidance on the first gathering of the elements to two of his students, Dome Lingkhawa Aseng and Zhang Olkawa from Drangyul. There were also several secret yogins and yoginīs who gained control of their minds and vital winds. Fifteen of them perfected the transference of consciousness in great secrecy. Zhangton Chobar unraveled the knots in the guiding instructions of Dzogchen through his experiences of the Lamdre. Some say that his two students who mastered Dzogchen went to the lake island of Dhanakośa.[192]

Finally, how the Lamdre was passed on by the Sakyapas from master to disciple

This is in two parts: an account of the eighteen traditions of the Lamdre, and the dissemination of the supreme Sakyapa system.

An account of the eighteen traditions of the Lamdre

A number of different systems developed out of Drogmi's Lamdre lineage. Nowadays there are said to have been eighteen separate oral traditions of the Lamdre, including the Drom system, the Zhama system, the Chegom system, the Jonang system, the Pagdru system, and the greatest of all, the Sakya system. These can be summarized as the lineage of the father and the lineage of the children.

The lineage of the children is divided into the lineage of the sons and the lineage of the students. The lineage of the students comprises the Drom system and the Se system. The Se system is divided into the superior, middling, and inferior systems.

First of all, the superior recipients, the Zhangton brothers, became the Zhang system and the Sakya system. The Sakya system is divided into the close lineage and the distant lineage. The distant lineage is divided into earlier and later. The earlier comprises the Pagdru and Chegom systems. The later comprises the oral lineage and the written lineage.[193] The close lineage comprises the precepts of the extensive, medium, and condensed Lamdre given to the elder brother, Sachen, by the actual presence of Virūpa, and the precepts of the extensive, medium, and condensed versions given by the magical emanation of Sachen to the younger brother, Dragpa Gyaltsen.

The middling recipients, the Zhama brother and sister, became the lineage of the father, the lineage of the mother, and the mixed lineage. The lineage of the father is twofold: the lineage of the students derived from Lord Khumbu and spread by Segom Dragkyab and Lord Malgyo, and the lineage of the son, spread by Lord Khumbu's son Zhama Caṇḍi. The lineage of the mother is threefold, being the three systems that derive from the disciples of Zhama Machig Gyalmo: Nyangomla Monkharwa, Tonchung, and Onpo Shertsul. The mixed lineage comprises initially the three systems of the mother lineage combined, and based on that lineage, all aspects of the teachings in the father lineage. This is further ornamented with various methods, like little knives for removing obstacles, such as the Ocean of Perceiving One's Conceptual Fabrications as the Syllable Ha. It includes the system of Kodragpa Sonam Gyaltsen and all of the profound points of the Zha system.

In addition there are the false systems discussed in the notes taken from the words of Zhangton Chobar:

1. The system of Chagen, who practiced all of the fragmentary special Dharmas taken individually from the eleven commentaries of the Sakyapas and combined them according to his own needs
2. The system of Jonang Kunkhyen Chenpo Pal Mikyo Dorje, who wrote commentaries on systems that had gone before, including a commentary that reorganized the *Vajra Lines* from top to bottom and beginning to end, so that all of the previous Lamdre teachings could be collated into a single system
3. The system of Lato Wangyal, which discussed the subsidiary topics
4. The system of Manglam Zhigpa, combining the *four gates*: the two sons of Drogmi and the two Zhang brothers

These are the eighteen systems of the Lamdre, which is the medium classification. The extensive classification is as follows: There were two diffusions from Drogmi, one of which can be classified into twenty-three subdivisions. If one calculates the number of systems extensively on the basis of the diffusion shown above, the number comes to twenty-four. The condensed classification combines these into twelve systems: Gyijo, Drom, Zhangton, Zhama, Kodragpa, Manglam, Chagen, Jonang, Wangyal, Sakyapa, Tartsawa, and Chegompa.

The Dissemination of the Most Successful System of Lamdre, the Sakyapa

This is in three parts: the long lineage, the short lineage, and the extremely short lineage. The long lineage is in two parts: how the instructions were passed down and how the tantras were passed down.

How the Instructions Were Passed Down

Among the inconceivable number of systems that appeared within the Lamdre tradition, the one that became the most successful was that which was passed down from the great Se Karchungwa to the Zhangton brothers. The elder of the two brothers, Zhangton Chobar, granted the teachings to Sachen Kunga Nyingpo himself. From then onward this became the extraordinary system of the Lamdre.

When Sachen was practicing the ten virtues at Sakya, he was invited by Lama Seton to be the head of a Dharma council in a region known as Ug. When Seton first met Sachen, he pressed his face to Sachen's and expressed his great delight. For a few days they sat with their cushions pushed together, and Seton gave Sachen a brilliant exposition of the inner structure of the teachings, including an elucidation of the root verses of the precious oral instructions of the Lamdre and various subsidiary topics.

Very soon after that, Lama Se left his body. A little later, Lama Gyichuwa also left his body. In his last testament Gyichuwa wished for Sachen to be ordained as a monk. However, Lama Namkhaupa said, "Due to circumstances yet to come I predict that there will be great benefit if you do not take ordination. I have seen the special circumstances in which your sons will spread the stainless lineage of the Dharma."

A little while later Sachen decided to request the oral instructions of the Lamdre from Lama Zhang Chobar. Having received permission from Lama Namkhaupa, he traveled to Ding along with a certain Jose Gyalpo, taking with him a suit of armor worth a thousand ounces of gold.[194] He offered the armor to Zhang Chobar and fervently requested the precious oral precepts. Sachen wrote of his happiness at being granted the teachings in an introduction to them. It was agreed that the teachings would be given in the autumn.

Thus having arrived at the autumn of his twenty-eighth year, Lama Sachen completed four years of teachings in which he received the *Three Continua* of the precious oral instructions of the Lamdre along with the supplementary cycles of the path. Finally, Zhang Chobar gave Sachen a prophecy about what he would accomplish and then displayed various miraculous powers, including displaying various forms, conjuring animals, and sitting cross-legged and covering the whole of the valley of Ding.

Then Zhang Chobar said, "There is no Dharma in the mere understanding of words, so apply yourself to meditation. When you cut through the internal elaborations of meditative experiences, remain in silence without loosening the external knots of words. Don't speak even the name of these teachings until eighteen years have passed. Then whether you teach it or write it down, you will be the master of this Dharma."

Zhang Chobar continued, "If you accomplish these practices you will attain the mahāmudrā without leaving the body. If you concentrate on teaching, you will have three students who attain the accomplishments, seven who attain forbearance, and eighty endowed with realization." This was his prophecy.

How the tantras were passed down

Jetsun Rinpoche Dragpa said:

> The lamas of the four lineages descended from the feet of Anavatapta Jñānapāda are those whose names ended with Gyalpo, Rig, Nyingpo, and Nangwa. From the feet of Rig and Nangwa it passed to two whose names end with Bar. I constantly pay homage to the great lama who held the four lineages.

As he said, after the great Drogmi Lotsāwa came the lineage of the tantras and instructions which is like the four great rivers that include the

Ganges:[195] Khon Konchog Gyalpo, Seton Kunrig, Ngaripa Salwai Nyingpo, and Khyin Lotsāwa Okyi Nyangwa. Drogmi took the great Sakyapa as his closest disciple.

Regarding the two at the beginning and end of this lineage: Khon Konchog Gyalpo received the transmission from both Drogmi and Khyin. Then the great lama Sachen received it from Khon Konchog Gyalpo and accomplished the practices. Regarding the two in the middle of this lineage: Zhangton Chobar received the transmission from Seton, and Gyichuwa Dralhabar received it from Ngaripa. Then Sachen received it from Gyichuwa and accomplished the practices.

The short lineage

When Sachen was in his forty-seventh year, he was poisoned by a zombie at Gungtang and fell ill for a month. Due to this he forgot all of the Dharma he had previously known. Sachen knew that there was nobody he could ask to teach it to him, and even if he went to India, he would be unlikely to find the same teachings again. Feeling sad at heart, he went to practice solitary meditation in the Mañjuśrī cave.[196] Sachen prayed fervently to his lama, and after a while Zhangton Chobar came to him and taught him Dharma in dreams.[197] Gladdened, Sachen continued to pray, and Zhangton appeared in person to teach him the Dharma. After that Sachen remembered clearly and by heart all of the Dharma he had known before.

Thereafter Sachen was greatly heartened and prayed even more strongly. At dawn he beheld the lord of yogins Virūpa sitting cross-legged and making the gesture of turning the wheel of the Dharma. To the right of Virūpa was the easterner Kāṇha, sitting cross-legged and holding a horn trumpet in his right hand and a skullcup full of nectar in his left. To the left of Virūpa was Gayadhara, wearing white clothes and holding a vajra and bell crossed at his heart. Behind Virūpa was Koṭalipa, kneeling and holding up a parasol. In front of Virūpa was Vanaprastha, "the man of the forests," with both hands joined together offering nectar. These five figures sat before a backdrop of the white earth of Sakya, and they covered with their crossed legs the area from Mongo Ravine at one end to Balmo Ravine at the other.

All of these figures came and spoke to Sachen, and at the sight of them an inconceivable nonconceptual absorption was born in him. Afterward, Sachen wrote the verses beginning "*Alala!*"[198] Thereafter Sachen received sustenance from an unknown source and went into retreat for a month. There Virūpa came to him, sometimes with his entourage and sometimes alone, and conferred upon Sachen seventy-two unsurpassed yoga tantras and seventy-two Dharmas, including the initiations connected with the unsurpassed yoga tantras.[199] In particular, he gave Sachen the four profound Dharmas that do not pass beyond the boundary wall.[200]

Lobpon Rinpoche Sonam Tsemo wrote:

> Arising before the eyes, the stainless moon of wisdom
> clarified the qualities of the three scriptural collections.
> Beautiful like a jewel in the depths of the ocean,
> the intelligent will understand this; others will not.

Now to decode the symbolic meaning of this verse. The *moon* is known to be unique, symbolizing that the unique Vajradhara, endowed with the five wisdoms, is the primal ground that is the destination of all lineages. The *eyes* are known to be a pair, symbolizing the second figure in the lineage, Virūpa, teaching the stainless white light of the blessings of the nondual deity and consort. The *scriptural collections* are known to be a triad, symbolizing the third figure in the lineage, the great lama Sachen, who cleansed the jewel-like qualities of thusness. The *oceans* are known to be four, symbolizing the fourth figure in the lineage, Lobpon Sonam Tsemo himself, who entered the ocean of suchness, was *beautiful like an ocean jewel*, and granted all wishes and needs. The meaning of this close lineage will not be realized by those of lesser intellect or fortune. It will be received by those born strong, endowed with pure discernment and fortunate circumstances, who have gained some understanding and striven in their practice. They will be taken as a crowning ornament for the victory banner of teaching and accomplishment. This is the first symbolic commentary.

The second symbolic lines are by Jetsun Dragpa Gyaltsen:

> The unsurpassed (the directions, multiplied by the mountains
> plus the eyes)
> were clarifed by the Vedas and assigned by the hands to the fire.
> There the ocean's illuminating light flowed into the elements.
> If the intelligent understand the meaning of this, let them speak!

The commentary on the symbolic meaning of these lines will be given according to Dagchen Dorje Chang Lodro Gyaltsen. *Unsurpassed* means the unsurpassed lineage, or the Dharma that is connected with the unsurpassed. There are ten directions and seven mountains, which multiplied together make seventy, and two eyes, making seventy-two. The four *Vedas* symbolize the close lineage of the unsurpassed tantras and instructions together, which were *clarified* by means of the four methods of teaching the tantras and the four close lineages of the instructions.[201] The one with two *hands*—the lord of yogins—*assigned* them to the one with three *fires*—the great lama Sachen. The *light* of this enlightened activity *illuminated* all directions. The four treasures from *the ocean flowed into* Lobpon Rinpoche Sonam Tsemo. The five *elements* flowed into Jetsun Dragpa Gyaltsen. This is how the meaning of the second set of symbolic lines is decoded, showing how and when the short lineage began.

How, then, did the great lama Sachen disseminate the oral instructions of the Lamdre? In his fiftieth year Sachen was freed from his vow of secrecy regarding Zhangton's precepts. At the very beginning of his fiftieth year, the one known as Khampa Aseng from Dome requested the Lamdre.[202] Aseng's father, Kyura Akyab, had already instructed Lama Zhang in the first gathering of the essential constituents. When Aseng requested the Lamdre, the auspicious circumstances for ending the vow of secrecy came together. This was the first time Sachen granted the precious oral instructions. The earliest of the explanations of the root text, the *Asengma*, came out of Aseng's request, and this is said to be first time that the Lamdre was set down in writing.

After that Sachen did not teach the Lamdre for four years. Subsequently he taught to one person, to three, to five, to seven, and so on, and later to thirty-seven. Ultimately, the number of people to whom Sachen taught the Lamdre is unknown. As for Sachen's explanations of the root text, he taught two people at the beginning, two in the middle, and two at the end. They practiced four feast offerings, and after that, at the beginning, middle, and end, strengthened their samaya vows. After that he taught two people, or one, or whatever was appropriate. In short, Sachen made the teachings of the precious oral instructions shine like the rising sun.

Regarding the miraculous writings like the explanations of the root text, which arose from the great lama Sachen and his lineage, Zhuje Ngodrub has written:

> You instructed in writing eight male and three female disciples who completely received the profound meaning.

This refers to the ones who were bound to their vows by the great Vajradhara (Sachen): Aseng, Zhu, Log, his wife, his son, Da, Zang, Mang, Ga, Au, and Nyag.

1. The *Asengma* was granted to Aseng.
2. The *Zhujema* was transmitted to Zhuje himself.
3. The *Logkyama* was transmitted to Logkya Jose Chodragpa.
4. Sachen and his first wife, a noblewoman from an aristocratic Tibetan family, had a son called Kunga Bar. When he died, his mother's heart turned to the Dharma, and she received from Sachen the profound meaning of the *Hevajra* and *Cakrasaṃvara Tantras*. Sachen transmitted the development stage based on the *Cakrasaṃvara Tantra* and the perfection stage based on the oral instructions of the Lamdre. The commentary that is connected with the Cakrasaṃvara development stage is the *Yumdonma*.
5. Sachen condensed the meaning of the oral instructions for his sons, the two exalted brothers Sonam Tsemo and Dragpa Gyaltsen. One of Sachen's spiritual sons, known as Nyenpul Jungwa Tsugtor Gyalpo, but whose real name was Sonam Dorje, edited these teachings. The *Sedonma* was transmitted to these three sons.
6. Sachen bestowed the vows of an upāsaka upon Bodhisattva Dawa Gyaltsen, who in turn gave the vows to Sachen's son Dragpa Gyaltsen. The *Dagyalma* was transmitted to Dawa Gyaltsen.
7. The *Zangripugma* was transmitted to Zangri Pugpa.
8. The *Mangchungma* was transmitted to Jomo Magchungma of Mangkhar.
9. The *Gatengma* was transmitted to Zhabchung Zekyog and Gyolwa Khampa Gateng.
10. The *Auma* was transmitted to Jomo Auma of Yalung.
11. The *Nyagma* commentary was transmitted to Nyag Zhirawa Wangchug Gyaltsen.

These are known as the eleven commentaries on the *Vajra Lines*, the root text of the Lamdre. The one that has been taught in uninterrupted succession up to the present day is the *Nyagma*, but it seems that there are others for which a continuous textual transmission still exists, such as the *Sedonma*.[203]

Thus the explanations or commentaries upon the root text that Sachen himself transmitted to his students in person are generally said to be eleven in number. But when all of the explantions of the root text derived from Sachen and his students are added together, there are said to be twenty in total. In addition to the eleven commentaries, there are the ones written by Naro Bande, Togom Jangchub Sherab, Minyag Prajñājvāla, Zhudrag Marwa, Zhangse Marwa, Jarbuwa of Uyug, Pagmodrupa, and others. When the commentary known as the large *Asengma* is included, there are said to be twenty-one.[204]

The extremely short lineage

Forty-four years after the great lama Sachen passed into peace, Jetsun Dragpa Gyaltsen was in his fifty-sixth year and living in the Tsangkha meditation center in the district of Nyemo. There Sachen came to him in a dream and gave him a smooth white pebble inscribed with an eight-petaled lotus. The leaves of the four directions were empty, while the leaves in between them contained the letters *ya*, *ra*, *la*, and *wa*. Sachen spoke the following verses, which summarized the symbols and meaning of this object:

> First take the *ālaya* as your meditation cushion,
> then grasp a handful of the vital winds.
> Directing the flow of *bodhicitta* into the central channel,
> bring earth and the other elements under your power.[205]

Thus he summarized the practice. Sakya Paṇḍita has written on the hidden meaning of these words:

> This clarification of the symbolic meaning of the *Vajra Lines*,
> received in person at the feet of the lord of yogins,
> was granted to the venerable lama in Utsang.
> The meaning of it should be clarified so that doubt is removed.[206]

But if the transmission was received directly, why is it taught in this history that it arose in a dream? It is said that there is no contradiction, because for a holy person there is no difference between dreams and everyday appearances.

Many students upheld Jetsun Dragpa Gyaltsen's oral instructions of the Lamdre, including the four whose names ended in Drag. Of these, the main upholder of the lineage of enlightened activity was the Dharma lord Sakya Paṇḍita himself. Of the Dharma lord's students, the two who were famous for spreading the lineage of the precious oral instructions were known as "Lho and Mar who upheld the lineage of explication." They were Lhopa Kunkhyen Rinpoche Palzang and Mar Chogyal. The lineages of instruction and practice were upheld by the three known as Tsog, Drub, and Won. They were Tsogom Kunga Palzang, Drubtob Yonten Palzang, and Sapaṇ's own nephew Pagpa Lodro Gyaltsen.

The three lineages of Tsog, Drub, and the nephew flowed into a single river in the person of Drubchen Dragpugpa Sonam Pal in the following way: Zhang Konchog Pal obtained the complete oral instructions of the Lamdre from Drubtob Yonten Palzang. He also received the complete oral instructions a second time from Rinchen Gyaltsen and after that from Pagpa Rinpoche as well. Dragpugpa received the oral instructions twice from Zhang Konchog Pal and again from a student of Tsogompa called Nyenchen Sonam, thus collecting all three lineages. There are also many lineages derived from the students of Nyen and Zhang that uphold the lineages of Tsog, Drub, and the nephew.

After this, the teaching of the precious oral instructions of the Lamdre became somewhat weakened. The one prophesied by the Conqueror and known as Ngorchen Dorje Chang Kunga Zangpo became the crown ornament of all the upholders of the teachings among the exalted Sakyapas, sovereigns of the teachings in the land of snows. He and others such as Jodenpa Kunga Namgyal propagated these oral instructions. Their biographies will be given later.

Regarding the explication for disciples—it was the real heart of the profoundest teachings of the Lamdre, taught in secret to a few people down to Muchen Sempa Chenpo Konchog Gyaltsen, the close disciple of Ngorchen Dorje Chang Kunga Zangpo. The explication for disciples was a unique hearing lineage, not to be found in any written works. Muchen's best student, Dagchen Dorje Chang Lodro Gyaltsen, was granted the explication for disciples without secrecy. Thereafter it was spread by Lord Doringpa Kunzang Chokyi Nyima, Tsarchen Losel Gyatso, Lord Ludrub Gyatso, and others.

The Lamdre—the precious oral instructions that are the final intention of the conqueror Vajradhara, the oral tradition of the fearless lord of yogins Virūpa, which fell to the exalted Sachen, sovereign of the teachings in the land of snows—is said to be endowed with eleven great profundities, four authenticities, and four hearing lineages. The eleven great profundities are:[207]

1. The oral precepts in which the path includes the result
2. The oral precepts in which the result includes the path
3. The oral precepts in which knowing one means knowing many
4. The oral precepts in which faults manifest as qualities
5. The oral precepts in which obstacles are taken as accomplishments
6. The oral precepts in which hindrances to contemplation are cleared away by recognizing the state of absorption
7. The oral precepts in which demonic hindrances are cleared away by recognizing obstacles
8. The oral precepts in which faults manifest as qualities and impediments are taken as accomplishments
9. The oral precepts in which one understands without error the true nature of the three scriptural collections
10. The oral precepts that are like an elixir that turns everything into gold
11. The oral precepts that are like a wish-fulfilling jewel, the root text of the *Vajra Lines*

The four authenticities are:[208]

1. The authenticity of the guru
2. The authenticity of the experience
3. The authenticity of the treatise
4. The authenticity of the textual transmission

The four hearing lineages are:

1. The never-declining river of empowerments
2. The never-degenerating lineage of blessings
3. The never-erring basis of oral precepts
4. The genuine mind of devotion

Thus the oral instructions of the Lamdre are superior to all other precepts. There are twenty-four Dharmas that appear in the book of the precious oral instructions in addition to the root text itself.[209] They are:

1. The *Nyagma* commentary on the *Vajra Lines*
2. The *Causal Continuum of the Ālaya*
3. The *Dentsog*
4. The *Physical Maṇḍala in the Twenty Dharmas of the Path*
5. The *Signs of Death in the Context of the Vase Empowerment for the Practice of Dying, Including the Yogic Postures and the Cheating of Death*
6. The *Practice of Dying in Which Appearances Are Transformed in the Vase Empowerment*
7. The *Yoga of the Drop in the Context of the Secret Initiation*
8. The *Characteristics of the Mudrā in the Insight Wisdom Initation*
9. The *Practice of Dying According to the Fourth Initiiation, Including Blocking the Gates with the Syllables in Accordance with the Vase Initiation*
10. The *Oral Precepts on the Four Bardos*
11. *Extensive, Medium, and Condensed Empowerments for the Phase of the Path*
12. The *Four Authenticities*
13. The *Six Oral Precepts*
14. The *Five Dependent Arisings*

15 and 16. The two texts for removing obstacles[210]

17. *Maintaining the Drops*
18. The *Method for Reciting the Hundred Syllables*
19. *Guidance for the Seven Practices of the Vital Winds in the Context of the Worldly Path*
20. The *Fourteen Syllables of the Bhaga*
21. The *Seal of the Cakras in the Context of Secret Initiation on the Transcendental Path*
22. The *Eight Topics of the Lord in the Context of the Fourth Empowerment*
23. The *Realization that Opens up the Thirteenth Bhūmi*
24. The *Verses That Summarize the Whole Meaning*[211]

As it says:[212]

These are the Dharmas taught in isolation to those with good karma:
the inseparability of saṃsāra and nirvāṇa based on the instructions of the four empowerments,
the method of the supreme empowerment, the condensed development stage,
the sādhana of the pills, and the blessings of the consort.[213]

Then the four texts on clearing away hindrances, the three sādhanas for the stream of empowerment,[214]
dispelling the errors of the root downfalls, the feast offering, and the fire ritual.[215]
These are the seventeen instructional Dharmas,
seven of which are to be found elsewhere.

Then there are the medium and concise paths, the four great central pillars,
the unsurpassed profound path of the five Dharmas that produce realization,[216]
the four scriptural connections, and the two histories.[217]
Along with the brief instructions, there are sixty texts in all.

This has been a concise account of the precious oral instructions. For an extensive history, an explanation of how the four actualities and sixty Dharmas were written, and so on, see the history books of the Lamdre written by the lamas of the past.

· 4 ·

The Thirteen Golden Dharmas and the Protectors

THIS ACCOUNT of the spoken transmission of the deep ocean of precepts is in two parts: how the Thirteen Golden Dharmas were passed down, and how the major and minor guardians were passed down.

HOW THE THIRTEEN GOLDEN DHARMAS WERE PASSED DOWN

The exalted Sakyapas, lords of the teachings in the land of snows, received the spoken transmissions of many cycles of precepts connected with the four classes of tantra in lineages derived from four great lotsāwas:

1. The cycle of the tantra trilogy of Hevajra in the lineage of Drogmi Lotsāwa
2. The cycle of Cakrasaṃvara, including the explication for groups and the explication for one disciple, in the lineage of Mal Lotsāwa
3. The yoga cycles and the instructions of the Dharma cycles in the lineage passed on to Dragtengpa and Mal Lotsāwa from Lochen Rinchen Zangpo
4. The Hundred Sādhanas in the lineage of Bari Lotsāwa

Supreme among these is the cycle known as the Thirteen Golden Dharmas, the hearing lineage that never passes beyond the boundary wall, which comes out of the ocean-like oral tradition of the vast and deep precepts connected with the unsurpassable tantras. The first three of the Thirteen Golden Dharmas are known as the three cycles of the Red Lady (Marmo Khorsum), or the three cycles of Khecarī (Khacho Khorsum). They concern the supreme accomplishment (*siddhi*), with the ordinary accomplishments as an addendum. They are:

1. The Khecarī of Nārotapa (Nāro Khacho): sādhanas, aspects of the path, and other texts composed by the exalted Nārotapa on the basis of the *Saṃvara Tantra* and received by Sachen from Malgyowa[218]
2. The Khecarī of the great king Indrabhūti (Indra Khacho): the blessings and collected mantras of the two-faced Vajravārāhī, composed by Indrabhūti based on the same tantra as above and received by Sachen from the Nepalese Jñānavajra
3. The Khecarī of Maitrīpa (Maitri Khacho): the blessings and instructions of the playful Vidyādharī, composed by Maitrīpa on the basis of the *Tārāmūlakalpa Tantra*, and received by Jetsun Dragpa Gyaltsen from Sumpa Lotsāwa

The next three of the Thirteen Golden Dharmas are known as the three red cycles (Marpo Khorsum), or the three major red cycles (Marchen Khorsum). They concern the ordinary accomplishments, with the supreme accomplishment as an addendum. They are:

4. The Dharma cycle of exalted Kurukulle: explicated by the great masters Sahajalilata and Ḍombī Heruka based on the words of the root and explanatory tantras of glorious Hevajra and received by Sachen from Bari Lotsāwa
5. The cycle of Great Red Gaṇapati: explicated by the lord of men Indrabhūti and the master Kāṇha on the basis of the *Saṃvara Vajraḍāka Tantra* and received by Sachen from Mal Lotsāwa
6. The Dharma cycle of the King of Desire Kagchol: explicated by Vajrasāna and others on the basis of tantras like Cakrasaṃvara and received by Sachen from Bari Lotsāwa

The next three of the Thirteen Golden Dharmas are the three deities from the principal empowerments of Nyen Lotsāwa, also known as the three minor red cycles (Marchung Khorsum). They are the profound instructions to vanquish three hundred thousand paṇḍitas, given as permissions to Nyen Lotsāwa by Tārā:

7. Kurukulle Garbhasuvarṇasūtra Śrī
8. Red Vasudhārā
9. The magnetizing goddess Tinuma

These three were received by Sachen from Namkhaupa. The last four of the Thirteen Golden Dharmas are:

10. Blue Siṃhamukha, who arose to quickly and pointedly repel the extremes of outsiders and was taken from under the rocky crag shaped like a yak's corpse north of the vajra seat. This was received by Bari Lotsāwa in the form of a prophecy from the wisdom ḍākinī Siṃhamukha.
11. The two forms of Black Mañjuśrī, praised as the supreme remedy to defilement and disease, received by Sachen from Bari Lotsāwa
12. Sky-Soaring Vajragaruḍa, who pacifies the poisons of the animate and inanimate world, one of the three extraordinary deities taught in the *Kālacakra Tantra*, recieved by Sachen from Mal Lotsāwa
13. The lifeforce practice of Red Jambhala, received by Sachen from Khon Gyichuwa

The lineages for the permissions, textual transmissions, and instructions for these Thirteen Golden Dharmas continue to the present day.

How the Major and Minor Guardians were Passed Down

Among the exalted Sakyapa masters and disciples, all the spoken transmissions of the oral precepts of the many families of Dharma protectors, sharp and swift as swords that protect the teachings, have been passed down. Chief among them are major and minor Dharma protectors known as the major guardian and the minor guardian.[219] The one known as the major Dharma protector, or the major guardian, is the mighty one Vajra Mahākāla himself, the protector assigned to guard the gate of Bodhgaya in the holy land of India. This is explained in the fifteenth chapter of the *Vajrapañjara Tantra*, the extraordinary explanatory tantra of glorious Hevajra, which says:

> Thus Vajra Mahākāla was emitted from the vajra body, speech, and mind of the Bhagavan, born from the wisdom of *hūṃ*.

The *Mahākāla Tantra* expounds the sādhanas for everything from the Two-Armed to the Thousand-Armed Mahākāla, and this form of the Two-

Armed Mahākāla is taught extensively. The *Śmaśānālaṅkāra Tantra* teaches the empowerments in the maṇḍalas of five and twelve deities and the extensive sādhanas. Based on these tantras, the exalted Sakyapas established four spoken transmissions of the guardian.

The first spoken transmission lineage

The oral tradition of the lord of yogins Virūpa was passed as a lineage from the great paṇḍita Gayadhara to Drogmi Lotsāwa. It will not be experienced by anyone who has not obtained the complete oral precepts of the Lamdre. This solitary, heroic guardian, known as the guardian of the Lamdre, is taught in the sādhana in the twenty-fifth chapter of the *Vajrapañjara Tantra* and in the deity-yoga practice in Jetsun Dragpa Gyaltsen's *Ornament for the Vajrapañjara*. He is found in the ritual collections of protection, exorcism, and slaying, and an undiminished oral tradition of permissions and textual transmissions still exists.

The second spoken transmission lineage

The permissions and the sādhana written by the brahman Vararuci for the solitary guardian in the lineage were received by Bari Lotsāwa from the paṇḍita Amoghavajra. The indisputable Sanskrit text of the sādhana can be found in the Hundred Sādhanas of Bari.[220] The table of contents for it is to be found in Jetsun Dragpa Gyaltsen's commentary on the Hundred Sādhanas. The unbroken transmission through to the present day includes the permissions and textual transmissions.

The third spoken transmission lineage

This lineage, passed from the paṇḍita Śraddhākaravarman to Lochen Rinchen Zangpo, Dragtengpa, and Mal Lotsāwa, spread more than any other instruction. Lochen employed these methods to carry out wrathful rituals against many of the Bonpos in Upper Ngari. Ever since then, the lineage descended from the Sakyapa lords from uncle to nephew, and it is the one that has usually been used by the Sakyapas to accomplish wrathful activities. Therefore the actual practice of these ritual activities remains undiminished, and they are endowed with great power. Prior to Lord Sachen, nobody had given even the permission for this lineage unless it was in the presence of the Skin Mask Guardian. It is not given to anyone who has not received the Hevajra empowerment. This transmission is very strict and is the heart essence all of the others; therefore, it is treated as the most important.

The fourth spoken transmission lineage

This lineage was received by Sakya Paṇḍita from the Kashmiri paṇḍita Śākyaśrī. It comes from the original texts of Vararuci, and its instructions are famously known as "the three cycles: the razors of the secret accomplishment." The three are:

1. The instructions on service, which are connected with the powers attained through accomplishing Mahākāla as the exoteric male deity
2. The esoteric accomplishment of liberating known as the *seven black days*, based on the *Lamp* of Drubpa Zhuchen
3. The instructions on slaying known as *knocking enemies to the ground*, based on the ritual known as the *fleshy heart*

These are the four spoken transmissions of the guardian among the Sakyapas, all of which still exist along with their textual transmissions. Three of these spoken transmissions came down through Sachen, and one came through the Dharma lord Sapaṇ. The first two of these and the last do not seem to have spread much apart from a few ritual collections for accomplishing the solitary male deity. The method of practicing the third spoken transmission, Mal Lotsāwa's system, is presented in two parts: the solitary accomplishment and the complete accomplishment.

The solitary accomplishment

This is in three parts: the solitary male deity, the solitary female deity, and the solitary entourage. The first of these includes the instructions and ritual collections for accomplishment in the form of Gaṇapati, accomplishment as the attendant, accomplishment as the yakṣa, and accomplishment as Yama.

The second, accomplishment as the solitary female deity, consists of the accomplishment of the esoteric pacifying deity based on the octameter verses of praise by the brahman Vararuci;[221] the system of practice for the exoteric wrathful secret mantra translated by the master Lokaśrī;[222] and the instructions for the service, accomplishment, and rituals based on these. This deity is clearly to be found in the *Vidyottama Tantra* and in the dhāraṇī of the Black Goddess translated by Bari Lotsāwa. She is the great protector of the teachings explained in the context of the special *torma* offering of four stages.[223] The Ngogpa lamas call her Dhūmāṅgārīdevī and say that the original text translated by Lokaśrī was a sādhana written by Guru Nārotapa.[224]

The third, accomplishment as the solitary entourage, consists of the instructions for the service, accomplishment, and rituals of the exoteric servant, the Naked One Wielding a Copper Knife, and the esoteric servant, the Black-Cloaked One Wielding a Copper Knife. Most importantly, it also includes the service, accomplishment, and rituals of five protectors: Putra and his brother and the Monpa brother and sisters.[225] There are other minor protectors as well, including the servant who holds the banner, a demon slave called Black Yama.

The complete accomplishment

This comprises an inconceivable number of cycles of accomplishment, sharp, swift, and profound. They include: the accomplishment of the complete trio of brother, sister, and deity, the ordinary and extraordinary accomplishment of the complete eight ḍākinī deities, the ordinary and extraordinary accomplishment of the twelve deities, the sacred sealed accomplishment of the complete lord and his retinue, including the ten fearful guardians, and as a supplement, the extremely profound and secret guidance on the eight deities of Mahākāla, made up to nine deities when the Black-Cloaked One Wielding a Copper Knife is added.

The history of this particular oral tradition

The king of Upper Ngari, Lha Lama Yeshe O, and his nephew, Lhatsun Jangchub O, dispatched the lotsāwa Rinchen Zangpo to Kashmir. He was commanded to study the teachings of sūtra and mantra in general, and in particular to bring back to Tibet a special protector of the teachers. During his long stay in the holy land of India, Rinchen Zangpo received and studied many teachings. On his way back to Tibet, Rinchen Zangpo invited Śraddhākaravarman and asked him to grant the permissions and instructions for a special Dharma protector.

Śraddhākaravarman replied: "First come to the temple of the protector of Bodhgaya's northern gate and praise him with a series of songs, including the ones called 'The Form of a Rākṣasa' and 'The Melody of the Tigress.'" When he had done as Śraddhākaravarman suggested, Rinchen Zangpo saw an apparition of the form of Mahākāla, as it is known today, filling the entire world. A blissful absorption arose in his mindsteam, and he heard Mahākāla say: "Go and receive the oral precepts, and then lead me to Tibet, where I will protect the teachings."

Rinchen Zangpo's guru now performed the permission and guarding spell and granted him the relevant instructions. Then Rinchen Zangpo turned toward Tibet again. When he was only one day from the border, Rinchen Zangpo saw the Dharma protector fly away, only to return again later. Rinchen Zangpo thought, "So far, all the auspicious circumstances relating to the king's commandments have come together, but I cannot go on without asking my guru about this." So Rinchen Zangpo returned again and asked his guru for an interpretation.

Śraddhākaravarman said, "That was a sign that the teachings will spread in Tibet. There are disciples in need of this Dharma protector in Tibet. The compassion of the noble ones is being limited by ordinary beings, so lead the protector there." The guru gave Rinchen Zangpo the Skin Mask Wisdom Guardian as a representation of the Buddha's body, a cloak of fine cloth on which the quintessential root mantra of Mahākāla was written in lapis as a representation of the Buddha's speech, a nine-pointed vajra made from sword metal as a representation of the Buddha's mind, and the instructions for the sādhana and rituals inside a leather amulet box as a representation of the Buddha's qualities and enlightened activities.[226]

Rinchen Zangpo returned to Upper Ngari, where he granted the teachings to Dragtengpa Yonten Tsultrim, who in turn granted them to Mal Lotsāwa Lodro Dragpa. Mal Lotsāwa granted the permission and all aspects of the cycles of accomplishment to Lord Sachen in front of the dance mask of the Skin Mask Guardian. When giving the permission, Mal Lotsāwa also bestowed the special representations of the Buddha's body, speech, and mind. When the guarding spell was performed, Mal Lotsāwa raised the dance mask and placed it in Sachen's hands.

Mal Lotsāwa said, "In general, it is important that Dharma practitioners rely upon one of the excellent Dharma protectors. In particular, there are many auspicious signs that this protector will benefit you and your lineage. He will also be of great benefit to the teachings. Due to the blessings of the guru's lineage, the representation of the Buddha's body known as the Flying Black Skin Mask, which belonged to the brahman Vararuci, who was blessed by Vajradhara in person, is under my command. I pass it on to you."

Then he spoke to the dance mask: "Now that I am old, I no longer need you. Follow this prince to Sakya. Carry out the commands of Kunga Nyingpo and his descendents."

From that time onward, the Skin Mask Guardian has acted as the servant of the Sakyapas. However, on occasion he behaves with excessively violent force. For this reason Lama Sachen said, "The forcefulness of Mal's Skin Mask Guardian is unrivaled even in India. However, if you visualize either Vajrapāṇi or Bhūtaḍāmara over his right shoulder, it will be all right." This was put into practice, and it is said to be the reason that nowadays every painting and statue of the Skin Mask Guardian has Bhūtaḍāmara on the shoulder.

Thus Sachen and his disciples brought the dance mask and other representations of Mahākāla to Sakya. While they were traveling a horseman rode up from nearby and began harassing them. When he caught sight of the dance mask, the horseman vomited blood and died. After this incident the fame of this Dharma protector spread in every direction. Ever since then, when such masks are made, they are consecrated in extreme secrecy.

When the dance mask was brought to the White Gorum Zimchil temple at glorious Sakya, it was housed there in a small room where it is still situated today. Sachen had the idea of building a new guardian temple, but the Skin Mask Guardian said, "It is not neccessary to make a new guardian temple. This place where I am residing now is good enough. Since I was the guardian of the northern gate of Bodhgaya, I will subdue your enemies from here at the northern gate. I will liberate the pernicious enemies of the teachings and protect those who uphold the teachings, but I wish to stay in this place."[227]

Upon hearing this pronouncement, Sachen immediately composed the prayer known as "the great wrathful propitiation ritual." He requested Mahākāla to remain at the site of the wish-fulfilling jewel that is the Skin Mask Guardian and then performed the extensive guarding spell and invocation. Due to this the family line of the Sakyapas will not degenerate as long as the teachings of the Sage remain, and auspicious circumstances will naturally come together.

The minor Dharma protector

The minor Dharma protector, or minor guardian, is the extremely fierce extraordinary protector of the second Conqueror, Ngorchen Dorje Chang.

Based on the seventeenth chapter of the *Guhyasamāja Tantra* and the explanatory tantra of Cakrasaṃvara, he is known as Kṣetrapāla (Zhingkyong), the Four-Faced Black Strongman (Tobtrog Nagpo Dongzhi), or the Fierce and Brilliant Lord (Dragpo Ziden Wangchug). This lineage comes from Nyen Lotsāwa.

Exoterically he is accomplished as the Brahman (Dramze). Esoterically he is accomplished as Kṣetrapāla. Secretly he is accomplished as the Strongman. This last includes the four-faced guardian for service, the hawk-faced guardian for accomplishment, and the cruel-faced guardian for rituals.[228] There are also forms for the fathoming ritual, for the determination of the place of death, for the four activities, and for the extraordinary secret accomplishment.

Of these, the guardians of the four activities are the white guardian who increases the lifespan, who has both ordinary and extraordinary forms; the yellow guardian for expanding merit, who has both a nine-deity and a five-deity accomplishment; the red guardian for exerting power over living beings; and the blue guardian for subjugating enemies.[229] The lineages of all of these profound oral precepts remain unbroken.

The history of the minor Dharma protector

In the past, Nyen Lotsāwa Darma Dragpa from Upper Shab went to India to study the Dharma. He received many Dharmas from Guru Sendhepa Ratnakīrti, Vajrasāna, and others. Having gained an understanding of the five topics of science, he returned to Tibet. Just before returning he asked Guru Sendhepa for the empowerment of Guhyasamāja in the tradition of Jñānapāda.

The guru replied, "There is no point in my giving it to you. In a forested valley to the south of Khasarpaṇa my sister, the yoginī Kusālipa, lives and practices Guhyasamāja. Request the empowerment from her. Because you have a karmic connection with her, she will bestow the oral precepts upon you." The phrase "to the south of Khasarpaṇa" was a reference to the Khasarpaṇa image of Avalokiteśvara brought back from the Potala mountain by Mitra Śāntivarman, who traveled there in person. The image was placed in Devikoṭa.[230] Because the valley in question was to the south of there, the guru spoke of it in this way.

In any case, carrying out the command of Guru Sendhepa, Nyen Lotsāwa traveled south. Just as the guru had said, in a forested valley he found a yoginī and her four attendants sitting inside the trunk of a vast tree. Three of the attendants came out one at a time and went to a nearby village. Having found food, they came back and sat down to do the practice. In order to determine whether this was the yoginī prophesied by his guru, the lotsāwa revealed himself and said, "Prove to me that you are yoginīs!" One of the yoginīs cut open her chest and revealed inside it butter lamps as numerous as the deities of the Guhyasamāja maṇḍala. Convinced, Nyen prostrated and offered a maṇḍala to the chief yoginī and then requested the Guhyasamāja empowerment.

"Who gave you a prophecy?" she asked him.

"I requested a prophecy from Guru Sendhepa," Nyen replied. "Since I haven't received the permission from Mañjuvajra, he said that I must stay here for a year before you can give the empowerment."

Nyen asked the yoginī to comply with this. She said, "All right. You will risk encountering dangers like borderland bandits, beasts of prey, and poisonous snakes. In the village of Paki there is a blue-skinned brahman who holds a thighbone flute. Go and see him, and give him the best food and drink. Venerate him, making whatever offerings you can afford. Then I will bless you so that no obstacles arise for you."

Nyen did as the yoginī had said. After a year had passed the yoginī said, "Now I can give you the permission for the deity. Go and find the requisites for a feast offering." Nyen took three *zho* of gold and used one *zho* to buy thirteen *khal* of fruit to make beer, one *zho* to buy meat, and one *zho* for the other neccessities like incense. Then he carried these requisites back to the yoginī and offered them to her as substances for the feast. Once he had set out many seats, the yoginī asked him to invite the guests. He said, "I can't find them on my own."

"Ask that brahman friend of yours," the yoginī replied. So Nyen asked the brahman, who took his thighbone flute out of his hair and played it. Then from the eight cardinal and intermediate directions came an inconceivable number of ḍākas and ḍākinīs and male and female yogins, each distinguished by their individual style of ornamentation, as well as Kṣetrapāla and his attendants. They all sat down in lines and feasted. Then, having been made happy, they granted the complete empowerments to Nyen.

In general, Nyen was granted the extraordinary precepts, the yidam practices of Guhyasamāja and Uṣṇīṣa, the six-branch yoga, the sādhana of Tārā, and the precepts of the Dharma protectors. In particular, Nyen was granted the empowerment of this Dharma protector in person. At the time of empowerment the brahman commanded Kṣetrapala: "You must be a servant to this one, abandoning the discordant and accomplishing the concordant conditions." Then Kṣetrapāla granted the empowerment personally, just as if it were from one man to another. Since this protector is like a wish-fulfilling jewel, the stream of his blessings is unimpeded. Therefore the precepts that bring about the accomplishment of this protector are of incalculable importance.

After receiving these empowerments Nyen Lotsāwa left India and returned to Tibet. He was accompanied by Kṣetrapāla himself as far as Nepal, but as soon as they reached the edge of the Tibetan border, Kṣetrapāla ceased to appear in person. It is said that in a time of great need he will come to Tibet himself. When the great lotsāwa Nyen crossed over from Kashmir into Puhrang, the local leader Tsede thought, "I'm the king here. I am famed throughout Upper Ngari, and no one is more powerful. When a lotsāwa meets me, he should prostrate." Meanwhile Nyen thought, "I'm a great lotsāwa, the student of Indian scholars and adepts. In particular, I hold the lineages of Vajrasāna, Guru Sendhepa Ratnakīrti, and Dipaṃkarabhadra. Shouldn't noblemen prostrate to me and offer me their hospitality?"

When Nyen arrived in the company of several merchants and did not prostrate, the king tried to slander him, saying, "This so-called Nyen Lotsāwa has come here having studied all the evil mantras in India; there is nothing authentic about him." Nyen thought, "It's really true that even a king can be deluded due to the extent of his negative imprints."

The king sent thirty of his ministers who were fearless horsemen to kill the lama. In a dream Nyen saw that these pernicious ministers had been dispatched by the king. He said to the merchants, "Gather together the choicest portions of your goods. Something has occurred to obstruct us, and it is very important that we send a great torma to the Dharma protector." The merchants presented Nyen with spices, grain, and medicines for the construction of the torma. Nyen then prayed and recited mantras to the great Four-Faced Kṣetrapāla. Later the merchants said that they had seen five black-skinned Monpa dancers, two entertainers, two sword-swingers, one lady wearing a petaled cap, and an entourage of many Dharma protectors. A dust storm became a tornado whirling round them. The master and his disciples stepped inside.

When the ministers arrived they saw nothing inside the tornado except the two sword-swingers. Upon their return the king questioned them exhaustively about the master and his disciples. Thinking "This lama has the power to bind a Dharma protector into servitude," the king felt full of remorse. He made a confession to Nyen and placed the lama's feet upon his head. It was only because of this that the king did not die. All of the ministers died, some from vomiting blood, some fainting, some going mad, some suffering paralysis, and some having seizures. After this the power of the Dharma protector became widely known.

The statue of the Dharma protector was brought in stages to Namkhau Kyelhe on the upper slopes of glorious Sakya. A temple was built for the Dharma protector, and homage was paid to him. When the entrustment ritual was performed for the Dharma protector, the temple blazed with light, which is why it became known as the Temple of Blazing Light (Menbar Tsuglakhang).

The great Nyen Lotsāwa granted his complete precepts, including the permission for this Dharma protector, to Namkhaupa Chokyi Gyaltsen. When Namkhaupa quarreled with a Bonpo settlement in the mountains near Khau, he used the collected rituals of this Dharma protector to bring about the deaths of a hundred Bonpo men and women, causing a town to be abandoned. Because this was all due to the power of the Dharma protector, its swiftness and severity became well known.

A little while after this, Nyen Lotsāwa passed into nirvāṇa. At the moment of his passing, Nyen spoke to the Dharma protector, who had emanated the form of a young monk. He said, "Since I am going to nirvāṇa, my own supreme son Namkhaupa from the mountain fortress of Khau should be known as my Dharma regent. Go before him and act as his servant, just as you have done for me. When he passes into nirvāṇa, go back to India."

Following these commands, the Dharma protector went to Namkhau to act as the attendant for Lama Nam. Some time later, due to the auspicious circumstances of this great Dharma protector being the protector of the teachings in the snowy land of Tibet, a great snowstorm blew up for a single day. The Dharma protector reached out with his long arm from the window at the top of the Khau fortress and took the ladle for scooping up water for offerings that had been left beside the river at the foot of the mountain. Seeing this, Lama Nam said, "Your power is greater than any other's, and you are able to display a multitude of emanations. In particular, the way that you magically retrieved that ladle just now is truly a miraculous emanational power. Please show yourself in person."

In response to this request, the Dharma protector said, "Please do not speak in this way. It is improper for the two of us to speak. If you make that request again, I will be bound by samaya to protect you. Previously I looked after Nyen in accordance with the command of the yoginī of the valley. Now in accordance with the command of Nyen I have come to look after you, after which I am to return to India."

When Lama Nam made the request again, the Dharma protector said, "Lama, please do not ask for even a slightly fearsome manifestation." Then the Dharma protector emanated his full four-faced form, filling the whole sky. At this brilliant display even the lama fell briefly into a state of unconsciousness. When he awoke from that state, he found that the vision had given him a minor nosebleed and the protector was once again in the form of a statue. The nosebleed, dripping onto a cotton cloth, had created an exact depiction of the body of the Dharma protector, red on the right side and white on the left. The form seen in his vision dissolved in rainbow lights into the rocky overhang above Lama Nam's meditation cave. It is said that he resides above the entrance to the cave to this day. The depiction of the Dharma protector known as the "vision of Lama Nam" is still to be found inside the entrance to the cave.

The Dharma protectors received by Sachen

The profound precepts of the strict and powerful Dharma protector Kṣetrapāla were received by Lama Sachen from the two lamas Nyen and Namkhau. In addition, Jetsun Sachen received the Begtse brother and sister (the red pair in the group known as the black and red butcher servants), chief among the attendants of the lordly strongman Kṣetrapāla. Sachen received this, along with the cycles of accomplishment for many deities, from Namkhau.

Sachen also received the permission for the Lord of the Charnel Grounds and his consort (the protectors of glorious Cakrasaṃvara), along with the relevant tantra and the sādhana written by Vairocana. In addition, the complete cycles of the face-to-face precepts of service, accomplishment, and ritual along with various miscellaneous instructions were offered to glorious Sachen in the same manner that Go Lotsāwa had received them from Vairocana.[231]

The instructions for Viśuddha and Vajrakīlaya, along with the sister and brother protectors called Karmo Nyida and Dugyal Pawo and the twelve oath-bound Kīla protectors, were granted to Khon Nāgendrarakṣita and his younger brother Dorje Rinchen by Padmasambhava during the earlier propagation of the teachings. From then onward each member of the precious Sakya family line has acted as the source of the oaths of Viśuddha and Vajrakīlaya and has cultivated Karmo Nyida, Dugyal Pawo, and the twelve oath-bound protectors.

Finally, the lineages received by Sachen from Mal Lotsāwa, comprising various oral traditions of Dharma cycles such as that of the goddess Magzorma, have been passed down without hindrance to the present day. This is how the lineages of numerous profound precepts passed from Bari Lotsāwa and Malgyo Lotsāwa to Jetsun Sachen.

Bari Lotsāwa Rinchen Dragpa

Bari Lotsāwa's birthplace was Yermo Tangpa in Dokham. He was born into the Lingkhawa line, one of the four Bari families. As a little boy he used to recite the six-syllable mantra, and due to a blessing from Avalokiteśvara, he received a prophecy from a ḍākinī, who assured him that he would go to central Tibet at the age of nineteen. Before that, he saw a vision of the three forms of Tārā, one large, one small, and one thumb-sized, all smiling and surrounded by limitless light. They bestowed prophecies and offered him protection from fear of robbers.

Bari Lotsāwa traveled to Uruto, where he was ordained by the abbot Kusulupa Zhang Yonten Rinchen and the master Tenchigpa Tsondru Drag.[232] He received the name Rinchen Drag. He met numerous learned and upright spiritual guides and listened and contemplated extensively.[233] Then one night after he had performed a hundred thousand circumambulations of the Jowo at Lhasa, Bari had a dream in which he saw the eleven-faced Avalokiteśvara, not large in size, situated to the right of the Jowo. Avalokiteśvara said to him, "Go to India, carrying as much as you need. You will fulfill many extraordinary needs and benefit sentient beings."

Based on this prophecy, Bari Lotsāwa decided to go to India. He traveled the route from Kyirong through Nepal. He asked the Nepalese paṇḍita Yerangpa for his precepts, including the empowerments and sādhanas of Saṃvara, Vajrayoginī, and the Vajracatuḥpīṭha, as well as for the perfection-stage tantras. Having become proficient in these subjects through study,

Bari left for India. The first person he met in India was Guru Mahāyogin, from whom he requested the oral precepts and blessings of Vajravārāhī.

One evening, during a feast offering, the guru asked Bari if he could see Vajravārāhī in the sky. Looking up, he saw Vajravārāhī with her five attendants. Many doors to absorption opened up in his mind. Around that time Bari met the younger Vajrāsana, who was undisputed and universally famed throughout India. He received many secret mantra empowerments, tantras, and sādhanas from Vajrāsana. He also received teachings on the *Avataṃsaka*, *Ratnakūṭa*, and *Samādhirāja Sūtras*, among others.

Furthermore, from the elder Vajrāsana, the paṇḍita Amoghavajra, and others, Bari received 1,008 sādhanas of yidam deities. From among these he collected together the best and most profound, which were translated by the lotsāwa and the paṇḍita. These two gurus were of equal realization; each of them clarified the different sādhanas for Bari, and each gave him the teaching transmissions, the transmissions of blessings, the recitation transmissions, and the vow transmissions for every sādhana. Thus he received each of these four kinds of transmissions twice. Having found these teachings and practices, Bari propagated them widely. In addition Guru Vajrāsana granted instructions for repelling the harmful work of non-Buddhists, the great torma ritual of Jvālamukhī, and the fire rituals from the wrathful instructions for Bhayanāsa.[234]

While traveling back to Tibet, Bari rested for a while near the border. He heard the weeping of many hungry ghosts. "Why are you weeping?" he asked. "If you stay here," they replied, "you will give us many torma, and we will never go hungry. But if you go to Tibet, there will be nobody who knows how to offer torma, and we will suffer hunger and thirst." To this end, Bari bought forty loads of fruit and set up a great series of torma, placing each on a base made from nine ounces of gold.

Then Bari arrived in Nepal. Several merchants who had come from Tibet to accompany him were staying at an inn where the landlord took half of their merchandise and denied that the other half had any value. Because they were likely to suffer indignities like receiving the king's punishment for the slightest misbehavior, having nowhere to recover when ill, and being thrown out of doors, Bari purchased a city square on one side of the "upper jaw" of Kathmandu, which became known as the Tibetan square. The Tibetans constructed several small dwellings and shelters there and were allowed to remain. Previous accusations were forgotten, and the companions were allowed to trade with their merchandise as they wished. Also, in order to protect them from the heat, Bari made an excellent and spacious wooden house without walls, which was called Chopari. He told them he had left a great deal of money with the innkeeper with the instruction to rebuild the house if it was destroyed.

Bari stayed in Nepal for nine years before returning to Tibet at the age of forty-three. At first the Lungtengpa geshe Konchog Kyab offered Bari an excellent welcome and attended upon him for a long time. With his many students he turned a vast wheel of Dharma, empowerments, tantras, and sādhanas. Then Lama Konchog Gyalpo invited Bari to Sakya and studied many Dharmas with him. Bari granted a certain amount of Dharma to his devoted students after they had attended upon him for a long time.

When Bari Lotsāwa was sixty-three, Lama Konchog Gyalpo passed away. Since at that time Lama Sachen was still in his infancy, Bari was asked to sit on the Sakya throne. Bari acted as the throne holder for eight years, giving many lectures on the Dharma to his students. He erected an Uṣṇīṣavijayā stūpa as a physical representation of his yidam, placing inside it three million Uṣṇīṣavijayā dhāraṇīs, seventy thousand tsatsas, and many beautiful physical representations from India and Tibet. To consecrate the stūpa he wrote two thousand copies of the ritual manual of Uṣṇīṣavijayā, and when he scattered flowers on the eighth day of the month, the stūpa vessels radiated a yellow light the color of refined gold that filled the earth and sky as far as the eye could see, and everyone was astonished to hear the sound of bells and a voice repeating quietly, four times, "All is well." From then onward an inconceivable number of auspicious signs constantly appeared around Bari, though he maintained the appearance of an ordinary person.[235]

Bari Lotsāwa built the temple of Yukharmo for the purpose of drawing out sentient beings trapped in the copper pots of hell. He also erected many stūpas, established many bridges, and built many guesthouses. After working for the benefit of beings in these and other ways, Bari at the age of seventy-one entrusted the Sakya throne to Sachen. He went to live in a hermitage in Barpug Rong to concentrate on his yidam.

Two years later, at the age of seventy-three, Bari Lotsāwa was granted an audience with Sachen on the fourteenth day of the ninth month. He said, "I have gone from happiness to happiness. At any time I can look upon the faces of my yidams Mañjuśrī, Vajravidaraṇa, Acalā, Avalokiteśvara, Tārā, and Uṣṇīṣavijayā whenever I wish. In particular, I have looked upon the face of the Great Compassionate One uninterrupted for seven days and nights in Sakya, Lato Jangyab, and Yeru Khato. He is my supreme deity, and I am under his care. I am happy, and I have no regrets. You, noble son, belong to the lineage of the Mahāyāna. Abandon any entanglement with selfish desires that do not involve the teachings of the Buddha or the benefit of sentient beings. Then whatever you do will go toward the Dharma."

Having given this and other advice, Bari Lotsāwa assumed the bodily postures and passed into bliss. Subsequently Lama Sachen himself arranged extensive funerary activities, including the recitation of prayers, the creation of representations of his form, both indoors and outdoors, and the regular practice of making offerings.

Malgyo Lotsāwa Lodro Dragpa

In general, Mal Lotsāwa studied the whole of the Vajrayāna. In particular, he received the whole of the Dharma cycle of Cakrasaṃvara from the Pamtingpa brothers and Lokya Sherab Tseg. When he received the root tantra of Cakrasaṃvara in seventy-three chapters, Mal Lotsāwa requested one feast offering for each of the chapters. He achieved stability in the perfection stage and an unhindered accomplishment of the ritual collection of Saptākṣara. Mal Lotsāwa received the cycles of the Dharma protectors from Dragtengpa and Lobpon Chen Chenpo. Striving for accomplishment, he never waned in his practice of yoga in four sessions. When he passed away his body was dressed in bone ornaments, and his passing was accompanied by sounds, lights, and dancing in the sky.

• 5 •

The Ngor Tradition

THE HISTORY OF how the teachings of the Sakyapas spread the length and breadth of the land of snows is in five parts: the succession of the great monastic seat of Ewampa, the biographies of the great scholars, the lives of those who upheld the Tsarpa tradition's spoken transmission, a list of the Dharmas that were taught and practiced, and the spread of the teachings of the eight chariots of the lineage of accomplished ones.[236]

THE SUCCESSION OF THE GREAT MONASTIC SEAT OF EWAMPA

Ngorchen Kunga Zangpo

Supreme among the regents of the Sage here in Jambudvīpa, the activities of this Sakya master and his disciples in the snowy land of Tibet was like the unparalleled chariot that pulls the sun through the sky of the four continents. His famed biography covers the whole earth, and he was greatly praised by the Conqueror himself with the sixty aspects of Brahma's melodious speech.

Just by hearing the name of the second Conqueror of this degenerate age, Dorje Chang Kunga Zangpo, the seeds of liberation will grow into a sublime tree of merit for all beings. From his time onward the succession of abbots who have protected the succession of throne holders have disseminated the traditions of the venerable Sakyapas throughout the snowy land of Tibet by means of explanation, accomplishment, and ritual. They have been praised in the scriptures of the Conqueror too. From the *Kuśalamūlaparigrāhabodhisattvapiṭaka Sūtra*:[237]

> When an emanation of Lokeśvara is emanated,
> then the monk Ānandabhadra (Kunga Zangpo) will appear.

He will be a noble being pervaded by merit,
noble in his learning and his practice of the perfections.
He will train thoroughly in means and wisdom,
and these Dharmas will never be absent from his mind.
He will always keep company with noble beings
and have the qualities of a hero.
Although learned, he will not reach the final goal,
but remaining a hero, he will bear that name.
Any woman who hears this name,
will henceforth cease to be a woman in truth.
Thus even the name of this man, who is like a medicinal essence,
is enough to bring about the actions of a buddha.
When he is praised throughout the ten directions,
whoever hears the name of this hero
will have their karma transformed by that name.
If this is true of a woman who never comes into contact with him,
how much more so someone who sees and pays reverence to him?
Because of the activities of this monk emanated by the Conqueror
and known as Ānandabhadra,
the Conqueror has praised him in these words.
All who reside in enlightenment pay respect to him.
When the name of Ānandabhadra Varmavīra
is praised throughout the world,
those outside of the Dharma will become monks.
Other monks who are rude, angry, and abusive
will argue with him,
saying, "This Dharma was not taught by the Conqueror."
Such mistaken worldly beings should turn to Ānanda.
Then in this degenerate age,
they will arrive in the buddha realms at the same time as me.
When they attain this supreme enlightenment of mine,
they will no longer be regarded as sentient beings.[238]
In the future, in times of great fear
he will give up his life and others will think, "I should do the same."
He will disseminate my supreme Dharma and hold fast to it.
What are Ānandabhadrapāla, Ratnasambhava,

Ratnākara, or Captain Bhadra
compared with his hidden qualities?
Anyone who sees Ānanda
or hears his name
will always be fearless toward enlightenment,
will never fall into error,
will, by striving in everything, gain the accumulation of merit,
will, by understanding everything, transform it into the
accumulation of wisdom.[239]

From the *Saddharmapuṇḍarīka*:[240]

I announce to you, the saṅgha of monks,
that Ānandabhadra (Kunga Zangpo), upholder of my Dharma,
will, having worshiped 600 million sugatas,
in the future become a conqueror.

His name will be Sāgarabuddhidhārī Abhijñaprāpta;
thus will he be known
in the pure land, beautiful to behold,
of Anonatāyāṃ Dhvajavaijayantyām.

As many bodhisattvas as the sands of the Ganges
will be brought to full ripeness there.
As a conqueror, he will have great magical power,
and his voice will resound throughout the worlds of the ten
directions.

His lifespan will be measureless;
he will benefit the world and remain there out of kindness;
after this protector has passed into parinirvāṇa,
his true Dharma will remain for twice as long as mine.

After that, its reflection will last twice as long again;
such will be the teaching of this conqueror.
Then beings as numerous as the sands of the Ganges
will develop the seeds that give rise to buddhahood.

Ngorchen Dorje Chang Kunga Zangpo, the great saint who has been described in this way in the scriptures of the Conqueror, was born into the Chogro family. This is the same family as Chogro Lui Gyaltsen, the maternal uncle of Tibet's Dharma king Trisong Detsen. His father, Drubpa Yonten, was an attendant at the Sakya assembly, the person responsible for the tea offerings for Dagchen Zhitogpa Kunga Rinchen.[241] According to some biographies, he was the son of the Dagchen himself. His mother, Paldren, was the daughter of the ruler of Shab.

Ngorchen was born at Sakya in the water-dog year of the sixth cycle (1382), with the marks and signs of a buddha's body. From when he was small, he was beyond childish activities. He received the grace of the three vows from Sharchen Yeshe Gyaltsen. At the age of nine he was granted ordination and a feast of teachings. Up until the age of twenty-five he honored Sharchen as his primary teacher, receiving from him the profound nectar of the tantras and instructions. He also received and fully assimilated the teachings of sūtra, mantra, and science from others including Sazang Pagpa Zhonu Lodro, Trashi Rinchen (from the Dharma lineage of Zhaluwa), and Khenchen Yagpa.

When Ngorchen was twenty-five, Sharchenpa passed into peace. Ngorchen was greatly upset that he had not asked Sharchen for the essential oral instructions of the Lamdre. Then at the meditation center of Shang Chokor, he met Lochen Kyabchog Pal and received many Dharma scriptures from him, most importantly the Vinaya. The mind of the lama and the mind of the disciple mixed together as one, but Ngorchen harbored no expectations of receiving any practices apart from the *Three Perceptions* of the Lamdre.[242]

While staying there in Shang Chokor, in the luminous appearances of a dream, Ngorchen had indications of receiving the Lamdre from the great adept Buddhaśrī in Zhegon. Later he traveled to Zhegon, and everything that had occurred in the dream came to pass, which filled his mind with devotion. He asked to be satiated with the nectar of the precious oral instructions.

Devoting himself to viewing and understanding the libraries at the Sakya Gorum temple, Ngorchen mastered the Dharma in general and the philosophical precepts of the Sakyapas in particular, concentrating on the experiential practice of Lamdre and the six yogas, among other systems.[243] Making himself a seat of limestone, Ngorchen stayed in solitude, far from moral transgressions. He saw the faces of the five Sakya patriarchs again and again, and his auspicious connections came together. He received prophecies about sacred sites from Uṣṇīṣavijayā and the Guardian of the Tent, and his lifespan and activities increased.

Ngorchen was also appointed the throne holder of the Sazang Ganden temple, where he listened to teachings and increased his enlightened activities. He also spent time at Sakya teaching and practicing at Śākya Zangpo's thousand-image stūpa. He was always humble and focused on Dharma. Monks from all quarters said, "Lama Sazangpa Kunga Zangpo gives the gift of Dharma without expecting material goods. Let's go and request his teachings!" And they gathered around him like clouds.

He was very strict about granting the full ordination only to those whom he was sure had maintained the vows and precepts. After he saw the faces of the great adept Buddhaśrī and the Dharma lord Sharchen Yeshe Gyaltsen in the state of luminosity, whoever received full ordination from Lama Ngorchen Kunga Zangpo went on to become an exceptional trainee. Then Avalokiteśvara appeared to Ngorchen and told him that he was being too strict. After that he granted ordination to many, spreading the Kashmiri paṇḍita Śākyaśrī's lineage of the vows to over twelve thousand monks. Even today it remains an excellent lineage.

He granted many complete Dharma collections, including the Tsar transmission of the Lamdre eighty-three times and the Vajramālā empowerments over sixty times. Spreading the teachings with these enlightened activities, he acted as a second Teacher of the Conqueror's teaching. There are four books of his writings that deal primarily with mantra. He wrote on all the four classes but was particularly gracious toward the teachings of the kriyā and caryā tantras.

Ngorchen traveled twice to U. The first time he dedicated himself to teaching, studying, and visiting holy places. In addition he made offerings of gold, water, and butter lamps and made extensive aspirational prayers. He went to the Sang, De, and Tsurpu monasteries, and visited Sera and Riwo Ganden. On the subsequent trip, he was invited by the great patriarch Dragpa Jungne and greatly benefited the beings of the Yarlung region. He received invitations from all over Kham and Ngari but resolved to concentrate on teaching and studying. Nevertheless, due to commitments that made it necessary to go to Ngari, he traveled there three times, acting for the good of beings on a vast scale.

Ngorchen's intention of teaching and studying in a solitary place with no belongings, for the benefit of humble pupils, arose at the luminous mountain retreat of Ewam Choden. Uṣṇīṣavijayā said to him, "Your temple will be indicated by Dondrub." Just as she had said, a little later a Geshe Dondrub praised the qualities of that site. Thus the auspicious circumstances of the excellent path all came together, and the temple of Ewam Choden, the second Akaniṣṭha, was founded in the seventh earth-bird year (1429), when Ngorchen was forty-eight.

Furthermore a new saṅgha was established, a Dharma community comprised of a thousand monastics right from the outset. A group of five hundred came from Chudu, two hundred from Tingkham, two hundred from Guge, and so on. These thousand followers of the oral instructions of the Lamdre gathered together in Ewam and soon grew to become an unmatched assembly of monastics practicing in accordance with the three vows. Then at the age of seventy-five, having fulfilled the needs of the trainees of this world for a while, he who had brought so much benefit to the teachings passed into the pure lands on the twenty-fifth day of the fourth month of the eighth fire-month year (1456).

An immeasurable assembly of students came to this master. Even counting only those who definitely spread the teachings of sūtra and mantra, nobody had more students than Buton Rinpoche and Ngorchen. The best among them were his closest student, Muchen Sempa Chenpo Konchog Gyaltsen; his nephew, Gyaltsab Dampa Kunga Wangchug; and Je Konchog Pal. All three touched the feet of this master.

There were also: Jamyang Sherab Gyatso, Khedrub Palden Dorje, Guge Paṇḍita Dragpa Gyaltsen (also known as Guge Paṇchen), Cho Pal Zangpo, Gungru Sherab Zangpo, Dagpo Trashi Namgyal, Zangchen Chogle Namgyal, Markhampa Dragpa Zangpo, Marton Gyaltsen Ozer, Paṇchen Śākya Chogden, Zhalu Kuzhang Khyenrab Choje, Jamchen Rabjampa Sangye Pal, Jamyang Kunga Chozang, Palbumtrag Sumpa Jampa Cho Dondrub, Jangchub Sempa Zhonu Gyalchog, Drubchog Konchog Lodro, the omniscient Gowo Rabjampa Sonam Senge, Nyagre Palgyi Gyaltsen, Yonten Ozer, Dragpa Rinchen Dondrub, Denma Drung Kunga Rinchen, Sepa Kunlo, Khedrub Dawa Zangpo, Chudu Khetsunpa, Dragkar Sempa Chenpo, the adept Tangtong Gyalpo, Ngonga Chodei Khenpo Palden Sangye, and Lama Palden Gyalpo. These saints upheld the teachings of a mind enriched with realization, scripture, and qualities. Due to them, the Dharma community that maintained the activities of the master Ngorchen

Kunga Zangpo spread immeasurably from Ngari in the west to the Chinese border in the east.

The throne holders of Ewam Choden

After Ngorchen Dorje Chang Kunga Zangpo passed into peace, Muchen Sempa Chenpo Konchog Gyaltsen, an emanation of Cakrasaṃvara in saffron robes, took the seat of Ewam Choden. Muchen was born into the Mu Tagmoling Kyarzhang family. He completed the practices of listening, contemplating, and meditating, relying on forty tutors including Rongton and Dorje Chang. After the death of Dorje Chang he took over his seat for three years, arranging and extending his writings.[244] Among his personal students there were Lamdre lineage holders of the explication for the assembly (including the all-knowing Sonam Senge) and of the explication for disciples (including Dagchen Dorje Chang). Thus this very master is the source of the explication for the assembly and the explication for disciples.

Eventually Muchen passed on to the bhūmi on which one accomplishes and fulfills one's commitments within contemplation. After his passing at the age of eighty-three, the following held the seat of Ewam Choden:[245]

3. Garton Jamyang Sherab Gyatso from Tsang Chumig[246]
4. Gyaltsab Dampa Kunga Wangchug, the nephew of Ngorchen and an emanation of the great adept Virūpa[247]
5. Khedrub Palden Dorje
6. Gowo Rabjampa Kunkhyen Sonam Senge[248]

All of the above were close disciples of Ngorchen Dorje Chang.

7. Yongdzin Konchog Pel, in the nephew line[249] of Ngorchen[250]
8. Khedrub Chenpo Sangye Rinchen, in the nephew line of Muchen[251]
9. Gyalwa Lhachog Senge, in the nephew line of Ngorchen, who was looked over by Lobpon Sonam Tsemo
10. Jamyang Konchog Lhundrub, a maternal nephew of Yongdzin Konchog Pal Rinpoche and a genuine omniscient[252]
11. Dongag Rabjam Mawa Jamyang Sangye Senge, in the nephew line of Ngorchen, an emanation of the Dharma king Pagpa Rinpoche
12. Tsungme Konchog Palden, a paternal nephew of Konchog Lhundrub who attained both scholarship and accomplishments[253]
13. Mahāpaṇḍita Tartse Namkha Palzang, an expert in the five topics, born into the family of Drangti Khepa[254]

14. Jampa Kunga Trashi, born into the family of his maternal uncle Dagchen Sharpa of glorious Sakya
15. Jamyang Kunga Sonam Lhundrub, also the throne holder of Tsedong at glorious Sakya
16. Drubkhangpa Palden Dondrub, a master of scholarship and accomplishment[255]
17. Drangti Khenchen Drubpai Wangchug Namkha Sangye
18. Sharchen Sherab Jungne, an emanation of the glorious Atiśa whose knowledge and enlightened activities were limitless
19. Drangti Khenchen Namkha Rinchen
20. Dagpo Gyaltsewa Jangpa Ngawang Sonam Gyaltsen, who upheld the lineages of both Ngor and Tsar
21. Nartang Paljor Lingpa Khangsar Khenchen Sonam Gyatso
22. Khenchen Jamyang Palchog Gyaltsen, in the nephew line of Drubkhang[256]
23. Drenchog Namkha Palzang, born into a Mongolian family close to Sechen[257]
24. Jamgon Lhundrub Palden, the teacher from Shar Minyag
25. Khenchen Jampaiyang Sangye Puntsog of eastern Ngari, the sun of the teachings in this degenerate age
26. Jangchub Sempa Chenpo Sangye Tendzin, born into the family of Dagchen Sharpa
27. Shabto Dzilungpa Khenchen Jampa Sheja Zangpo, maternal nephew of Tartse
28. Jampa Tsultrim Palzang, the creative display of Mañjuśrī in saffron robes
29. Tsangchug Zhungpel Kyawa Tsungme Sonam Palden[258]
30. Khangsarwa Drubpai Wangchug Jamgon Jampa Sonam Zangpo
31. Tsang Dokharwa Khenchen Trashi Lhundrub, an emanation of Buddha Dīpaṃkara
32. Jampa Tsultrim Lhundrub, born into the family of Dartsedo, a lord of limitless knowledge
33. Drangti Khenchen Drubpai Wangchug Jampa Namkha Samdrub
34. Khenchen Dorje Chang Palden Chokyong, an emanation of the lord of yogins

35. Tsungme Kheshing Drubpa Jamgon Sangye Palzang
36. Khangsarwa Khenchen Jampa Sonam Lhundrub
37. Sharchen Rinchen Mingyur Gyaltsen[259]
38. Jamyang Chokyi Lama Sangye Yeshe, in the nephew line of Khenchen Trashi Lhundrub
39. Jamyang Chokyi Je Konchog Dragpa
40. Khangsarwa Ngawang Chokyong Zangpo
41. Khedrub Sangye Dragpa
42. Tsungme Puntsog Dondrub
43. Khedrub Chenpo Jampa Kunga Sonam
44. Drangti Khenchen Tamche Khyenpa Jampa Namkha Chime
45. Rabjam Sheja Kunzig Khedrub Ngawang Damcho
46. Mawai Wangchug Khenchen Sonam Paljor
47. Jampa Kunga Tendzin, born into the family of Drangti Khepa
48. Khangsarwa Ngawang Lodro Zangpo
49. Yongdzin Paṇḍita Palden Chokyi Gyaltsen, born in Gartar in the family of Shar Minyag Seu Gyalpo
50. Jampa Palden Zangpo, an emanation of Rinchen Chogdrub, the nephew line of Penkhang Khenchen Palden Chokyong
51. Drangti Khenchen Jangchub Sempa Rigyai Khyabdag Naljor Jampal Zangpo
52. Khangsar Khenchen Tsungme Ngawang Lodro Tendzin
53. Khenchen Kunga Tenpai Lodro, in the nephew line of Penkhang and an emanation of Rinchen Chodze
54. Drangti Khenchen Tamche Khyenpa Jampa Kunga Tenpai Gyaltsen
55. Khangsar Khenchen Ngawang Sonam Gyaltsen
56. Jamyang Sherab Gyatso, a nephew of the family and an emanation of Khen Ngawang Lodro Zangpo
57. Penkhang Khenchen Palden Lodro Gyaltsen, a nephew of Jampa Palden Zangpo
58. Jamyang Rinchen Dorje, born into the family of Drangti Khepa
59. Khangsar Khenchen Dorje Chang Ngawang Lodro Nyingpo, a secret treasury of an ocean of profound secret tantras
60. Khenchen Ngawang Khyenrab Jampal Nyingpo
61. Penkhang Ngawang Kunga Tenpai Gyaltsen
62. Jampa Palden Chodze[260]

63. Tartse Jamyang Kunzang Tenpai Gyaltsen
64. Penkhang Jamyang Kunzang Tubten Chokyi Gyaltsen
65. The lord of accomplished monks Khangsar Khenchen Dorje Chang Ngawang Lodro Zhenpen Nyingpo, of the Nub clan
66. Luding Gyalse Jamyang Chokyi Nyima
67. Tartse Jamyang Kunzang Tubten Chokyi Gyaltsen, the rebirth of Jamyang Rinchen Dorje
68. Penkhang Ngawang Lodro Tegchog Tenpai Gyaltsen, the rebirth of Palden Lodro Gyaltsen
69. Khangsar Ngawang Yonten Gyatso, the rebirth of Chetsun Ngawang Sonam Gyaltsen
70. Penkhang Ngawang Khedrub Gyatso, the rebirth of Jampa Palden Chodze
71. Tartse Jampa Namkha Kunzang Tenpai Gyaltsen, of the Che clan
72. Luding Jamyang Tubten Lungtog Gyaltsen, of the Lang clan
73. Khangsar Ngawang Khyentse Tubten Nyingpo
74. Tartse Jamyang Kunga Tenpai Gyaltsen
75. Luding Jamyang Tenpai Nyima, of the Lang clan

These successive seventy-four abbots have taught the Lamdre and conferred the monastic vows without interruption over all the years that have passed since Ngorchen Dorje Chang was on the throne. They greatly expanded the teachings with their wealth and reputation. In addition to the five hundred monastics in permanent residence, there were many residential colleges composed of people visiting from all directions to hear the Lamdre teachings.

• 6 •

Biographies of Great Scholars

Dzongpa Kunga Gyaltsen

DZONGPA KUNGA GYALTSEN was the same age as Ngorchen. He was born the son of Onpo Norpel, in the family line of Lotsāwa Zhang Yeshe Dorje, at the Tongmon House of Sakya. He became a close disciple of Tegchen Choje Kunga Trashi, who was himself a student of Lama Dampa. He was given the ordination name Jamyang Dragpai Pal.

Ngorchen and this master Dzongpa together met Sharchen Yeshe Gyaltsen and Kunkhyen Yagpa. The pair, known as Ngor and Dzong, wrote primarily on the rituals of Ngorpa and Sharpa. Since Dzongpa made his residence at the Dzongchungwa House, these two have been known as "Ngor and Dzong, upholders of the Sakya teachings" and the "two Kungas skilled in mantra."

Dzongpa was guided by the Ngamring Khenpo and Yoga Choding, among others, and saw the faces of the five patriarchs. He composed the hymn that begins, "A gift from a Conqueror's son placed before the Conqueror." His students included Jang Dagchen Palden Chokyong, Sempa Chenpo Zhonu Gyalchog, and Khedrub Geleg Palzang. He passed away on the twenty-eighth day of the eighth month of the fire-dragon year (1436) at the age of fifty-five.

Tuton Kunga Namgyal

Chief among those who upheld the Dzongpa traditions was Tuton Kunga Namgyal, a close disciple of Dragtog Sonam Zangpo, himself a student of Tegchen Choje. He is said to have been an emanation of the vidyādhara Śrī Siṃha and Nanam Dorje Dudjom. He was born in the seventh water-mouse year (1432) into the wondrous family line of Tumi Sambhoṭa. His father was Gyalwa Sherab and his mother was Palden Dorje Dema. Because he came from the Tumi family line, he was known as *Tuton*. In his youth he was famed as the king of the five textual systems.[261] He studied with Dragtogpa among others and received his full ordination from Je Jampa Lingpa.

At the age of thirty-three, in the eighth wood-monkey year (1464), Tuton established the Dharma community of Gongkar Dorje Den in U. There he established regular practices, including ritual dances and the rites of several maṇḍalas from the four classes of tantra. Thus he became an upholder of the teachings, using his strength to raise up the teachings of Sakya in the region of U. When he was thirty-five, in the fire-dog year (1466), Tuton returned to Sakya. Because he was an upholder of the teachings, he was given an immense welcome with a procession, music, songs, and a ceremonial scarf.

Tuton possessed an inconceivable number of methods for accomplishing the activities of the Dharma protectors and was famous for his powers. He also wrote many literary works. His practice of offerings that combines the Dzong and Buton traditions has been constantly maintained, and the stream of ripening and liberation has continued undiminished to the present day. Tuton passed into peace on the twenty-fourth day of the third month of the eighth fire-dragon year (1496) at the age of sixty-five.

Yagton Sangye Pal

The great scholar Yagton Sangye Pal is often known as one of a pair of upholders of the Sakya teachings and scholars of the sūtras, either Yag and Zhon, or Yag and Rong.[262] He was born at the so-called Sakya Pass in the sixth earth-mouse year (1348). He was the son of Jangchub Rinchen, a great man of Tsetang. He was treated like a son by an attendant of his father called Yagyu, the "turquoise yak," and thus came to be known as Yagtru, the "baby yak."

Yagton studied and trained at glorious Sakya, Tsetang, and elsewhere. For his sūtric training he relied mainly on Yagyal Khepai Wangchug Tsondru Pal, one of the two great Sakya scholars known as Nya and Tson. He received the oral instructions of the Lamdre from Gonjo Yeshe Pal. He mastered the 1.8 million scriptural teachings. The students of Bu and Dol were Nya and Tson. The students of Nya and Tson were Yag and Zhon. So these became sacred syllables of the teachings.[263]

Yagton lived in Central Tibet. He was one of the very few students able to name the places of origin of every one of the scholars and adepts of the past. He prolonged the flow of explanation, and an inconceivable number of students upheld his lineage, including Rongton Mawai Senge and Sempa

Chenpo Zhonu Gyalchog. He passed into Tuṣita in the wood-horse year (1414), when Muchen Sempa Chenpo was twenty-seven.

Rendawa Zhonu Lodro

Rendawa Zhonu Lodro was born in the sixth earth-ox year (1349), at the castle of Renda, situated near the great seat of glorious Sakya. His family line was that of the minister Gar Tongtsen.[264] His father was Trashi Gyaltsen and his mother was Wangchug Kyi. He studied with Mati Paṇchen among others. Through praying to the Three Jewels, and with his own analytical reasoning, he achieved certainty in the essential points of the Madhyamaka Prāsaṅgika.

He said, "When I was first studying, I had a book on Madhyamaka, and I didn't make any major errors. Now I have taught this method of analysis, my work is done." Karma Konchog Zhonu said of him, "Nowadays every deluded scholar has a different kind of Madhyamaka that they call Madhyamaka, and this is why Rendawa is so gracious." He was particularly gracious toward both Guhyasamāja and Madhyamaka, and with these two he united teaching and practice.[265]

Rendawa spent twelve years in the retreat at Bulerong. He wrote many works, including the *Four Great Textual Traditions: The Supreme Ornaments Decorating Jambudvīpa*.[266] His students included Kunkhyen Shero and Tsongkhapa Lozang Dragpa. He passed away at the age of sixty-four, on the twenty-ninth day of the twelfth month of the seventh water-dragon year (1412).

Rongton Sheja Kunrig

The great Kunkhyen Rongton Sheja Kunrig was born in the sixth fire-sheep year (1367) in eastern Gyalmorong in the royal line of Tragi Sita. As an emanation of Maitreya, he accomplished the texts of logic through reasoning. His previous incarnations included many paṇḍitas of India and Tibet, and he directly remembered having been Kamalaśīla in particular. Up until the age of eighteen, Rongton practiced exposition, composition, and debate within the Bon tradition. Then at the age of eighteen he went to Sangpu Neutog, where he relied upon the explanations of Lingtopa Rinchen Namgyal, Kongpo Lodro Wangchug, and Kazhipa, abbot of Kyormolung.[267] There he became an expert in the five topics and a great and accomplished master.

Rongton received full ordination from the great abbot of Dro, Kunga Gyaltsen. He composed a commentary on Dharmottara's *Pramāṇaviniś-caya*. From the age of twenty-two he accepted teaching responsibilities, and he spent the whole of the rest of his life in the three activities of a scholar.[268] At the age of twenty-seven, in the water-bird year (1393),[269] he met the great abbot Yagpa Sangye Pal and received from him the traditional explanation of the sūtric teachings according to the Sakya tradition. He also received the profound meaning of mantra from Tegchen Choje and others. He maintained the teaching traditions of Sa and Ngog. He also maintained the teaching lineages of Chapa Chokyi Senge, Chomden Rigral, and Kunkhyen Shero, and it is said that there was no greater source of students who upheld the teachings.

Rongton went to Tsang three times. The first time was when he was twenty-seven. He acted as a servant to the great abbot, doing nothing but speaking on the profound meaning of the sūtras and making offerings of elegant sayings. The second time was when he was forty-eight. Then, when Rongton was fifty, the great abbot passed away, and Rongton traveled to Dingri and Mu, where he did nothing but explain the profound meaning of mantra and spread the enlightened activities taught in the sūtras. The third time was when he was seventy, in the seventh fire-snake year (1437), when he established the great and glorious Dharma college of Nalendra at Penpo.[270] There he acted for the welfare of others for fourteen years. While touring Central Tibet Rongton wrote only ten volumes. However, there are also said to be sixty-four books of notes taken from his advice to others and forty other books of teachings he composed himself. Rongton also received the profound meaning from Senge Gyaltsen, Lochen Kyabchog, Kunkhyen Shero, Nyan Nganpa Jamyang Khache, and Mu Namkhai Naljor.

The consciousness of Kamalaśīla was transferred into the body of Dampa Sangye; this is proof that Rongton was a rebirth of both. Rongton gave elegant explications of Dampa's Zhije and Kamalaśīla's *Bhāvanākrama*. In particular, this omniscient being was exceptionally kind to the teachings of the Prajñāpāramitā and the Svātantrika Madhyamaka. He possessed the signs of realization of one who has attained the sixth bhūmi as they are taught in the scriptures. For example, he performed magic such as flying like a bird to the Glittering Lake in Yardrog, he had the five eyes of clairvoyance, and at death he manifested the signs of one who has seen the truth of reality itself.[271]

At the age of eighty-four Rongton went to the Tuṣita heaven, fulfilling a promise he had made. His physical remains turned into jewels and precious stones and can still be seen today. Thus, from the age of twenty-two to eighty-four, his teachings and analysis based on the four kinds of correct reasoning were renowned as an unceasing flow of melodious, elegant explanation, pleasing to scholars. His students, scholarly and accomplished upholders of the teachings, are enumerated as follows: his early children, the four great pillars who held up the teachings; his middle children, the eight ornaments beautifying the land of snows; the two supreme ones; the three children with the harmonious conduct of a buddha's body, speech, and mind; his later children, the sixteen illuminators of the teachings; and his further children, the four famous ones. Of these, the four first children were:

- Sempa Chenpo Zhonu Gyalchog
- Sempa Chenpo Pema Zangpo
- Zepa Lodro Gyatso
- Chenga Tsultrim Darma

The eight middle children were:

- Markhampa Dragpa Zangpo, Gewa Gyaltsen, Gungru Gyaltsen Zangpo, and Rongchung Sherab Pal (these were the four Khampas)
- Cholung Kachupa Choje Palzang, Khewang Ratnaśrībhadra, Nartangpa Sherab Senge, and Zangden Kachupa (these were the four Tsangpas)[272]

The two supreme ones were:

- Upa Marton Gyatso Rinchen
- Tsangpa Sempa Chenpo Konchog Gyaltsen

The three with harmonious conduct were:

- Dokhampa Palden Tose
- Gomde Trahrel
- Zhonu Senge from Sakya

The sixteen later children were the four great paṇḍitas:

- Nartang Lotsāwa Saṅghaśrī
- Yargyab Onpo Paṇchen Sonam Namgyal

- Pobdarwa Lochen Zhonu Pal
- Dagpo Onpo Paṇchen Trashi Namgyal

And the twelve scholars who upheld the tradition of elegant speech:

- Sherab Dorje and Rinchen Lodro (two teachers from Lhadri in Kham)
- Namgyal and Khedrub Donyo Palwa (two from Zochen in U)
- Nyangtopa Sherab Legpa
- Ngamringpa Sangye Samdrub
- Jamyang Sherab Gyatso from Ngari
- Zhudon Sonam Rinchen from Ngeme
- Paṇḍita Namkha Tenpa from Sangpu
- Kar Śākya Drag from Tsangrong Jamchen
- Gonjo Jinzang and Gazi Lodro Senge from Kham

The four further children were:

- Dratonpa Yonten Gyatso from Sangpu and Chenpo Paljor Gyatso from Tsetang (the first pair)
- Gowo Rabjampa Sherab Pal from Kham and Jamchen Rabjampa Sangye Pal from Tsang (the second pair)

Furthermore, six thousand upholders of the scriptural collections were students of Rongton's main disciples.

Jamchen Rabjampa Sangye Pal

Yagyal Khepai Wangpo Jamchen Rabjampa Sangye Pal, one of the four further children of the great Kunkhyen Rongton, was born in Dorpe in the seventh water-dragon year (1412). He received the gracious gift of the three vows from Ngorchen Dorje Chang and studied with many scholars and adepts, including the great Rongton. The use of the title *rabjampa* began with this master.[273]

When Jamchen Rabjampa considered whether to concentrate single-pointedly on accomplishment or to teach and study, the importance of teaching and studying dawned on him. Thus from the age of eighteen to the age of seventy-five, he elucidated the teachings through explanation, debate, and composition, becoming the grandfather of all philosophers. In the eighth earth-snake year (1449) he established the Dharma college of Dreyul Kyetsal, which became a great source of scholars. Jamchen Rabjampa died on the first day of the fifth month of the fire-horse year (1486), at the age of seventy-five.[274] Subsequently his close disciple, Jamyang Kunga Chozang, took over the monastic seat.

Jamchen Rabjampa produced many students who could recite the Dharma of the entire three scriptural collections, including Sungkye Tendzin Gyalse Khedrub Tensal, Tsetang Sanglhun, Bum Rabjampa Cho Dondrub, Gowo Rabjampa Sonam Senge, and Jamyang Kunga Chozang. The stream of Jamchen Rabjampa's miraculous activity continued. The great colleges of Tanag Tubten Nampar Gyalwai Ling emerged out of Kyetsal itself, founded by Jamchen Rabjampa's close disciple Gorampa Kunkhyen Sonam Senge.[275] The college of Je Tubten Yangpachen was founded by Gorampa's student Mu Tugje Palzang and maintained by Khenchen Wangchug Palzang and Paṇchen Ngawang Chodrag. Nyenyo Jago Shong was founded by Jamchen Rabjampa's personal student, Paṇḍita Bumtragsum.[276] Chokor Lhunpo was founded by Zhungya Ngodrub Palbar, a student of Jamyang Kunga Chozang. Paṇchen Lhawang Lodro founded Zheri Kyetsal Ogma. Together these great philosophical colleges are known as the six branches of Kyetsal temple.[277] Many other monastic communities developed from them to beautify the precious teachings.

Gorampa Sonam Senge

Gowo Rabjampa Kunkhyen Sangye Pal was one of the two great scholars of glorious Sakya famed as "Go and Shā, the scholars of sūtra and mantra." He emerged in the stainless tradition of Jamgon Sakya Paṇḍita, with great waves of enlightened activity, performing the three deeds of a scholar, epitomizing the explication of the teachings with an unparalleled kindness, like one who prolongs the life force at the moment of death. He was born in earth-bird year (1429) in the Dokham region, in the area above Bom known as Bom Lungda. His father was called Rutsa Zhangkyab and his mother Gyalwa Men. He was said to be an emanation of Jetsun Dragpa Gyaltsen.

At the age of ten, he asked for ordination from Jangchub Sempa Kunga Bum and received the name Sonam Senge. After that he began his studies with this master. He also received many vast and profound Dharmas from Gowo Rabjampa Sherab Pal and Kachupa Jinzang. Because of his acute intelligence, he came to be known by the name Gowo Rabjampa at this early stage.

At the age of twenty, Gorampa traveled to central Tibet. At Nalendra he sat at the feet of the omniscient Rongton and tasted the nectar of his teaching. Since this was close to the time of Rongton's passing, it seems that Gorampa would not have had long to study the Dharma with him. Then at the age of twenty-two Gorampa went to the Dharma college of Dreyul Kyetsal to study with the lord of scholars, Sangye Pal. He studied whatever books were being taught, whether Prajñāpāramitā, Pramāṇa, Vinaya, or Abhidharma. His intellectual acuity and his skill in debate increased like a mountain lake in the summer. He became known by all teachers and their students as a holy being who has arisen through purification in previous lives.

At the age of twenty-five, Gorampa went to Ewam Choden. Over the next four years he studied with Ngorchen Dorje Chang Kunga Zangpo, receiving the Lamdre twice, the empowerments of practice manuals for Saṃvara, Hevajra, Guhyasamāja, and Raktayamāri, and an inconceivable number of profound precepts, including the Hundred Sādhanas of Bari.

At the age of twenty-nine Gorampa was made a master of the teachings, with Je Kunga Zangpo acting as the abbot, Sempa Chenpo Konchog Gyaltsen as the ceremonial preceptor, and Domtson Sangye Paldrub as the secret preceptor. He received the pure vows for his full ordination in an assembly with more than a full complement of the saṅgha. He took on the responsibility of the vows with the earnest intention never to stain them with the slightest transgression.

From Sempa Chenpo Konchog Gyaltsen, Gorampa received the transmission for the collected tantras and many empowerments, including Akṣobhya in the Guhyasamāja maṇḍala. In addition, he received many vast and profound Dharmas from Khenchen Khachar and Gungru Sherab Zangpo.

After Dorje Chang Kunga Zangpo passed into peace in the fire-mouse year (1456), Gorampa continued to receive transmissions from Muchen Sempa Chenpo, including the Lamdre; empowerments of Saṃvara, Guhyasamāja, and Vajrabhairava; explanations of the tantras; and transmissions of the collected works of the five venerable patriarchs, Gyalse Togmepa, Ngorchen, and Sempa Chenpo Konchog Gyaltsen. There is not enough space here for an extensive account of the teachings he received.

When he was thirty-two, Gorampa decided to return to Kham. On the way he stopped at Dreyul Kyetsal. Since Jamchen Rabjampa was currently the only teacher there, he strongly urged Gorampa to stay and teach. So he stayed on for four years, during which time he practiced Hevajra, the preliminaries, basic services, and so on. Initially he acted as the assistant teacher at the Dharma college. Then, after Jamchen Rabjampa went to Mu, Gorampa was made abbot in his absence. He taught in the style of Kunkhyen Sangye Pal, drawing from the great books of the scriptural collections, including Prajñāpāramitā, Pramāṇa, Vinaya, and Abhidharma, and striking the perfect balance between summarization and full explication of the texts. Due to this, Gorampa became hugely successful at fostering the intellects of college students, and his fame as a scholar spread among the people of the land of snows.

Later on, at the age of thirty-seven, Gorampa went to Mu, drawn there by Muchen's lasso of compassion. He received many profound Dharmas from Muchen, including the Dharma cycle of Cakrasaṃvara. At the age of thirty-eight, Gorampa accompanied Muchen to Jang Ngamring at the invitation of the Dharma king Namgyal Dragpa and his son. While there he conferred elegant explanations upon some bright minds. That year there were forty clever and diligent students.

Provided with resources by Rinpung Nangso Dondrub Dorje Ponlon, Gorampa established the Dharma college of Tanag Serling. Over the next eight years, up to the age of forty-five, he spread out a feast of teachings just for the diligent and intelligent few. When he reached forty-five, in the eighth water-snake year (1473), Gorampa established the Dharma college of Tubten Namgyal. Studying and teaching sūtra and mantra, he illuminated the teachings like the sun.

These are the scriptural texts that Gorampa taught:

- The *Ratnaguṇasaṃcayagāthā*
- The five Dharmas of Maitreya, along with *Illuminating the Meaning*, a commentary on the *Abhisamayālaṃkāra*[278]
- Vasubandhu's *Abhidharmakośa*
- Asaṅga's *Abhidharmasamuccaya*
- All five of Nāgārjuna's analytical works that were translated into Tibetan, including the *Mūlamadhyamakakārikā*
- Āryadeva's *Catuḥśataka*
- Candrakīrti's *Madhyamakāvatāra*
- Śāntideva's *Bodhicaryāvatāra*
- Dharmakīrti's *Pramāṇavārttika*

- Sapaṇ's *Treasury of Logic*
- Sapaṇ's *Distinguishing the Three Vows*

He was able to expound these texts by heart, along with their commentaries. Additionally, he gave the reading permission (*lung*) and explanation of countless texts, including Asaṅga's *Bodhisattvabhūmi* and Śāntideva's *Śikṣāsamuccaya*.

These are the mantra texts that Gorampa taught over and over again:

- The *Hevajra Tantra*, along with Chogyal Pagpa's commentary *Endowed with Purity*
- The *Vajrapañjara Tantra*, along with Jetsun Dragpa Gyaltsen's commentary *Ornament for the Vajrapañjara*
- The *Saṃpuṭa Tantra*, along with Gorampa's own commentary *Illuminating the Topics*
- The main *Saṃvara Tantra*, on the basis of Sachen's commentary *Garland of Pearls*
- The *Vajrabhairavakalpa Tantra*, on the basis of Sachen's commentary[279]
- The root *Guhyasamāja Tantra*, on the basis of Buton's commentary *Bright Lamp Illuminating the Six Divisions*
- The *Sarvadurgatipariśodhana Tantra*, on the basis of Gorampa's own commentary[280]

From the age of fifty-four, for the four years between the water-rabbit year (1483) and the fire-horse year (1486), Gorampa held the throne of Ngor Ewam Choden. There he fulfilled the intentions of Ngorchen Dorje Chang and his lineage, turning a great wheel of Dharma teachings, including the oral instructions of the Lamdre. Later he empowered Yongdzin Konchog Pel as his regent. After this period Gorampa went to Tubten Nampar Gyalwa, where he expounded an inconceivable number of sūtra and mantra teachings to the fortunate few. The flow of his activities to spread the teachings never ceased. In between teaching and studying he gave empowerments, permissions, consecrations, and fire rituals whenever appropriate.

Furthermore, by the force of the great waves of his intelligence, both innate and learned, his wondrous arguments and his way of expressing them robbed all scholars of their mental faculties. He wrote numerous treatises that skillfully extracted the intention of the discourses of the exalted patriarchs of glorious Sakya.[281]

His collected works on the three scriptural collections include:

- *Illuminating the Meaning of the Mother*, a textbook on the Prajñāpāramitā
- A commentary on the difficult points of the Prajñāpāramitā[282]
- An explanation of the above, elucidating all aspects in detail[283]
- *Illuminating the Supreme Sages*, a presentation of the twenty varieties of the saṅgha
- *Illuminating Those Who Entered Absorption*, a treatise on those who crossed over to absorption in the cessation of thought and form
- *Illuminating Saṃsāra and Nirvāṇa*, a textbook on dependent origination
- An unfinished commentary on Maitreya's *Uttaratantraśāstra*[284]
- *Samantabhadra's Sun*, an extensive commentary on Dharmakīrti's *Pramāṇavārttika*
- An extensive textbook that is a commentary associated with the above[285]
- An elucidation of Sakya Paṇḍita's *Treasury of Logic*[286]
- A topical outline and lessons on the Guṇaprabha's *Vinaya Sūtra*[287]
- *Threefold Miracle*, an unfinished commentary on Vasubandhu's *Abhidharmakośa*[288]
- A presentation of the aggregates, constituents, and sense bases[289]
- A commentary on Nāgārjuna's *Mūlamadhyamakakārikā*, from chapter 24 to the end[290]
- A commentary on the difficult points of Candrakīrti's *Madhyamakāvatāra*[291]
- The larger and smaller treatises on the main points of the Madhyamaka[292]
- A summary of Nāgārjuna's *Ratnāvalī* and his other four logical works[293]
- A textbook on Sakya Paṇḍita's *Distinguishing the Three Vows*[294]
- Answers to questions about *Distinguishing the Three Vows*[295]
- A supplement to *Distinguishing the Three Vows*[296]
- A commentary on the *Guide to Signs*[297]

His collected works on the four classes of tantra include:

- A response to objections about the *Guhyasamāja*[298]
- *Conquering the Obstacles to the Benefit of Others*, a response to objections about Sarvavid Vairocana
- *Illuminating the Topics*, a response to objections about the *Candrikāprabhāsa*
- *Benefit of Others Permeating Everything*, a commentary on the *Saṃpuṭa Tantra*
- A supplement to the Lamdre history begun by Ngorchen Dorje Chang[299]
- An explanation of the stream of empowerment in the *Hevajra Tantra*[300]
- The *Essential Nectar of Great Bliss*, an explanation of the body maṇḍala of Hevajra.
- A history, manuals, explanations, sādhanas, and maṇḍala rituals connected with the two systems of Guhyasamāja[301]
- An explanation of the *Vajrabhairavakalpa Tantra*[302]

These cycles of teachings and others were brought together through the valiant efforts of the great spiritual guide of Yong, Gapa Lama Jamyang Gyaltsen. They were printed and published in fifteen volumes at the Dharma college of Derge Lhundrub Teng.

In short, this master became a great lion of faultless speech for the Sakya tradition. Toward the teachings he was the kindest of lamas, repairing and reviving the sacred texts in general and the study of the vows in particular. Although he had clear comprehension of the ordinary, extraordinary, and inner teachings, Gorampa received Dharma in a visionary state from the master Muchen, and when he was composing treatises he saw clearly in his dreams signs that the four-faced guardian was carrying out enlightened activities for him. Gorampa practiced the yogic discipline of extreme secrecy, even though he certainly resided on the great bhūmi of accomplishments; he was, for instance, granted prophecies on many occasions through clear visions of the future.

At the age of sixty-one, on the twenty-first day of the first month of the eighth earth-bird year (1489), Gorampa passed into the realm of Sukhāvati while on the road at Ngonmo Dzong, having just set out a feast of Dharma at Sakya.[303] Thereafter his close disciple Kongton Wangchug Drub accepted the throne at Tanag; the line of masterful scholars that followed maintained Gorampa's tradition of enlightened activity.

The students of Gorampa who upheld the teachings through explanation and accomplishment included the following: Sonam Gyaltsen Palzangpo, Dagchen of glorious Sakya; Kongton Wangchug Drub; Choje Gonpo Wangchugpa; all the senior Sakyapa teachers of Jangamring, headed by Khenpo Jangsempa; Yongdzin Konchog Pel, the abbot of Ewam; Choje Tugje Palsang; Choje Kunga Paljor; Choje Sangrinpa; Choje Śākya Lodropa and his disciples; Rabjampa Lhawang Lodro; his younger nephew Legpa Gyaltsen; and Kachupa Sherab Senge. In total, there was an inconceivably vast assembly of students who spread explanation, accomplishment, and enlightened activity in the eight directions.

Śākya Chogden

The great paṇḍita Śākya Chogden Drime Legpai Lodro can be shown through scripture and reasoning to have been the rebirth of the undifferentiated master-and-disciple pair, Mapam Namtrul Khenchen Yagton Zhab and Bagton Śākya Ozer.[304] In particular Bagton said in his last testament that his rebirth would be born in Sangda Bangrim near Sangpu, and both mother and son would bear the name Śākya.[305]

In accord with that, Śākya Chogden was born to his mother, Śākya Zangmo, in the seventh earth-monkey year (1428) at Sangda Bangrim, near Sangpu. At the age of ten he met the great Rongton for the first time. He renounced the world and entered the gates of the teaching. He received the name Śākya Chogden, "Supreme One of the Śākyas," and was granted the ritual permission of White Acala. Due to the prophecy indicating that Śākya Chogden was a rebirth of Bagton, he was entrusted to the care of Khedrub Donyo Palwa, a student of Rongton. Śākya Chogden first studied the cycles of Prajñāpāramitā, Pramāṇa, and Madhyamaka at Nalendra under the tutelage of the great Rongton at the age of eleven. From then until Rongton passed away at the age of eighty-four in the iron-sheep year (1451), Śākya Chogden received a vast number of teachings on countless scriptural collections from him.[306]

At the age of thirteen Śākya Chogden was made a novice monk in Nalendra by the great Rongton, and the name Drime Legpai Lodro ("stainless, excellent intellect") was added to his existing name. In this period Śākya Chogden studied with numerous masterful scholars, including Je Donyo

Palwa, the master Gakhangpa Sonam Tsultrim, and Khenchen Chokyab Palzang at the great Dharma colleges of Sangpu Neutog and Kyormolung, among others. He received many of the principal texts, the most important of which were the cycles of the Vinaya, Vasubandhu's *Abhidharmakośa*, Asaṅga's *Abhidharmasamuccaya*, and Sakya Paṇḍita's *Treasury of Logic*.

Because of the sectarian attitude of the Neudzong ruler, Śākya Chogden had to go to Chokor Ling, where Chogyal Namgyalwa taught him the commentaries on Nāgārjuna's *Mūlamadhayamakakārikā* and Candrakīrti's *Madhyamakāvatāra* written by Je Tsongkhapa in order to change his mind. It happened in earlier times that Dharmakīrti received an elucidation of the words of Dignāga and then the secret texts of the non-Buddhists by Kumārila in order to refute them. Similarly, later on Śākya Chogden would write down arguments in the larger and smaller versions of his *Overview of the Madhyamaka* that established that all of the main points made in the teaching lineage of the new Mañjuśrī are unfounded.[307]

Regarding the vast tradition of the principal texts, from the age of eighteen on, Śākya Chogden mastered an ocean of the tenets of his own and other schools. Due to this he was made an assistant teacher at Sangpu, and his eloquent expressions broke down the arrogance of every scholar. At the age of nineteen he was appointed head teacher at Donyo Palwa's seat, the Nego college of Sangpu. At the age of twenty he studied at Nyetang Chodzong with Paṇchen Loten Zhipa (also known as Nyetang Lotsāwa), from whom he received and studied all of the aspects of linguistic sciences, including the *Nighaṇṭu*, the Sanskrit grammatical systems of Śarvavarman's *Kalāpa*, Daṇḍin's *Kāvyādarśa*, and Ratnākaraśānti's *Chandoratnākara*.

At the age of twenty-four, Śākya Chogden visited the recently established Ngor Monastery. There in the presence of the lord of Dharma, Ngorchen Dorje Chang Kunga Zangpo, he received numerous empowerments and practical guidance, including the empowerments for the Lamdre, Akṣobhya from the *Guhyasamāja Tantra*, the fifteen Nairātmyā goddesses, the Cakrasaṃvara of the Luipa system, and guidance in the Thirteen Golden Dharmas and the central channel practices of the yoginī tradition. Later he received guidance in Sachen's *Parting From the Four Attachments* and many empowerments and guidance in the Hundred Sādhanas of Bari.

At the age of twenty-five, Śākya Chogden received full ordination and was presented with the articles of a fully ordained monk. The abbot was Ngorchen Dorje Chang Kunga Zangpo, the ceremonial preceptor was Khachar Jangchub Sempa Sonam Gyaltsen, the secret preceptor was Muchen Sempa Chenpo Konchog Gyaltsen, the timekeeper was Jamyang Sherab Dragpa Pal, the assistant was Gyaltsab Dampa Kunga Wangchug, while Gendun Sempa Chenpo Legpai Sherab helped make up the full complement.

From Duzhabpa Chenpo Rinchen Trashi he received the *Kālacakra Tantra*, the *Vajramālā Tantra*, and the forty-five associated empowerments of the *Kriyāsamuccaya*.[308] From Lodro Chokyong, a disciple of Tegchen Choje, he received explanations of the *Vajrapañjara*, *Hevajra*, and *Saṃpuṭa* tantras in Tegchenpa's lineage. He also received the four transmissions of Hevajra;[309] twenty associated teachings of unsurpassed yoga including the cycles of Saṃvara, Guhyasamāja, and Yamāntaka; empowerments including Sarvavid Vairocana; and explanations such as the three cycles of benefit to others.[310]

Śākya Chogden also received many vast and profound Dharmas from Rongton, Loten Zhipa, Paṇḍita Vanaratna, the master Khachar Jangchub Sempa, Muchen Sempa Chenpo, Gewa Gyaltsen, and Dagchen Lodro Wangchug. At Nenang, Lobpon Dragpa Ozer gave him many empowerments and transmissions in the Karma Kagyu tradition, a great many explanations including the trio of the *Profound Inner Meaning*, the *Hevajra Tantra*, and Maitreya's *Uttaratantraśāstra*,[311] and many mantric instructions including practical instructions in the trio of dancing, drawing maṇḍalas, and chanting.

When he was twenty-three, Śākya Chogden received the *Vajrapañjara Tantra* from Lodro Chokyongwa. Because he was able to distinguish the significance of the Sanskrit in the *Vajrapañjara* and the Prakrit in, for example, the *Śmaśāna Tantra*, Lodro Chokyongwa was overjoyed and called him "paṇḍita" again and again. After that, the name Paṇchen stuck.

In accordance with a suggestion made by Ngorchen Dorje Chang Kunga Zangpo, Śākya Chogden, at the age of twenty-eight,[312] established a study program of the great textual systems at glorious Sakya suitable as exemplary models for the teachings. Therefore he added the following texts to the eighteen texts of great renown, as they are known within Sakya:[313]

- The extensive, medium, and concise versions of the Prajñāpāramitā
- The *Mahāyānasaṃgraha* of Asaṅga
- The *Triṃśikā* and *Viṃśatikā* of Vasubandhu
- The *Pañcaskandhaprakaraṇa* of Vasubandhu

Because of Ngor's loyalty to the Sakyapas, the following texts authored by Sakya Paṇḍita were also expounded:

- *Clarifying the Sage's Intention*
- *Entrance Gate for the Learned*
- *Summary of Grammar*
- *Treatise on Medicine*[314]
- *Bouquet of Flowers*
- *Treasury of Words*
- *Scholar's Mouthwash*
- *Joyful Entrance*
- *Precious Treasury of Excellent Sayings*

Śākya Chogden taught these works in their entirety, from head to toe, using the method of aphoristic expression. As background material, he taught the following:

- Śarvavarman's *Kalāpa* on Sanskrit grammar
- Daṇḍin's *Kāvyādarśa*
- Ratnākaraśānti's *Chandoratnākara*
- Amarasiṃha *Amarakośa* on synonymy
- Harśadeva's dramatic play *Nāgānanda*
- Vāgbhaṭa's *Vaidyāṣṭāṅga*
- Tumi Sambhoṭa's *Basic Grammar in Thirty Verses* and *Guide to Signs*
- The *Vacanamukhāyudhopama* of Smṛtijñānakīrti
- Sonam Tsemo's *Easy Introduction for Children*

Śākya Chogden also expounded the proportions of statues as taught in the *Kālacakra* and *Samvarodaya* tantras. To introduce the tantras to a general audience he developed an extensive presentation for ordinary people, backed up with the *Classes of Tantra* and *Introduction to the Dharma*.[315] Later, at Zhitog itself, in the center of an array of masters of esotericism consisting only of Sakya nobles, he granted secret mantra texts including the tantra trilogy of Hevajra, the bodhisattva trilogy of commentaries,[316] the *Mañjuśrīnāmasaṃgīti*, Sakya Paṇḍita's *Advice of Mañjuśrī*, Vibhūticandra's *Piṇḍīkṛtasādhana*, the *Graded Presentation of the Sūtras*, and Āryadeva's *Caryāmelāpakapradīpa*. He also gave a bundle of explanations on these texts and ended with an extensive explanation of the *Supratiṣṭha Tantra*.

The excellence of Śākya Chogden's study program for ordinary people, taken by the likes of his attendant Tsalpa Ringyal, and his methods of teaching logic in particular became more and more famous. As the feast of explanation that Śākya Chogden had laid out—teaching countless systems of sūtra, mantra, and the sciences—was greater than anything previously known, everyone became certain that he was a fearless master of speech unmatched anywhere in the world. Later, when he returned to Ngor, the Dharma lord Dorje Chang presented him with a number of precious religious objects as a gift during a tea ceremony in honor of the study program.[317]

In the iron-hare year (1471), when he was forty-four, Śākya Chogden went to Je Donyo Pal's monastic seat at Zilung at the command of Dagchen Lodro Gyaltsen. He gave that monastery the name Serdogchen. He established the practice of the three foundations,[318] and he drew up a monastic charter that ordered the undeclining practice of the lineage of the all-knowing Rongton (in the sūtra context) and Ngorchen Dorje Chang (in the mantra context). He helped the monastery expand through the three spheres of activity, such as setting up a new statue of Maitreya.

At the age of forty-five, Śākya Chogden went to Ngari to be the chaplain of Chogyal Trashi Gon, whereupon he began turning a vast Dharma wheel of sūtra and mantra at Lowo. Furthermore, in his own monastic seat, as well as in Gyama, Langtang, Nalendra, Jago Pungpo, and Sheldrong, he turned an inconceivable number of Dharma wheels at various times, including in the sūtra context the eighteen texts of great renown, and in the mantra context the Lamdre (many times), the Vajramālā empowerments, and explanations of the tantras.

Having attained a fearless courage regarding the subjects of knowledge, he engaged in composition. The following eighteen great books of elegant explanation—which are like suns illuminating the teachings and have captivated the minds of scholars—are just a sample.

The Prajñāpāramitā cycle, including:

- *Garland of Ocean Waves: A Traditional Commentary on the Prajñāpāramitā*
- Three introductory commentaries on the Prajñāpāramitā[319]
- The larger and smaller commentaries on general principles[320]

The Pramāṇa cycle, including:

- *Great Verification of Pramāṇa*

- *Samantabhadra's Cosmic Ocean: An Explanation of Pramāṇa*, generally known as the *Śāk Ṭīk*
- *Illumination of Logic: A Commentary on the Difficult Points of the Pramāṇavārttikakārikā*
- *A Cosmic Ocean Discoursing on Dharmakīrti's Seven Treatises: A Commentary on the Treasury of Logic*

The Vinaya cycle, including:

- *Chariot of the Sun: A Commentary on the Difficult Points of the Vinaya Sūtra*
- *Explanation of the Karmaśataka*
- Works on moral training[321]
- *Cosmic Ocean of Nectar: Rituals for the Three Foundations*

The Abhidharma cycle, including:

- *Ocean of Explanation: A Detailed Outline of the Abhidharmakośa*
- *Commentary on the Difficult Points of the Abhidharmasamuccaya*

The Madhyamaka cycle, including:

- *Harbor for the Fortunate: An Explanation of the Mūlamadhyamakakārikā*
- *Key to the Essential Points of the Definitive Meaning: An Explanation of the Madhyamakāvatāra*
- The larger and smaller *Overview of the Madhyamaka*

The tantric cycle, including:

- *Hundred Gates to Liberation: A Commentary on the Guhyasamāja Tantra*
- *Commentary on the Saṃvara Tantra*

In addition, when he was forty-eight, Śākya Chogden wrote down 108 questions on *Distinguishing the Three Vows*. He sent them in a sealed letter to Kunkhyen Sangye Pal, saying: "This work is the grandfather of today's teachings." Later, when he was fifty-six, Śākya Chogden composed his *Golden Spoon of Elegant Explanations: Questions and Answers*. Regarding this, the *Detailed Biography of the Great Paṇḍita Śākya Chogden* says:

> When evaluating the essential points (questioning the essential points and explaining the essential points),
> he comprehended his own approach (toward our own texts and everything's own nature);
> without mixing them with anything other (others' words and others' approaches),
> he accomplished the essence of the teachings (explaining the teachings in accordance with the teachings).[322]

In between studying, contemplating, teaching, and composing, he did whatever was most useful, including performing extensive service to Bhairava, Hevajra, and Acala. Because he shone with luminosity, he read books continuously even at night, without distinguishing the night from the day, and at Vulture's Peak he passed his hand through a tree without obstruction. Many things happened to him that were in accord with the signs of accomplishment. For example, one time in Lowo he placed his daily torma offering in the direction of an army, and a magical emanation of Four-Faced Mahākāla himself appeared and defeated the army.[323]

And thus, having brought great waves of benefit to beings and the teachings, Śākya Chogden merged his mind with the space of reality on the fifth day of the waxing moon in the sixth month of the ninth fire-hare year (1507), having reached the age of eighty.[324] Among those students born of his instruction were: Tsalpa Rinchen Gyaltsen, Trapuwa Sangye Zangpo, Khartse Chang Rawa Lodro Zangpo, Nyangto Tsechenpa Dorje Gyaltsen, Naljorpa Unyon, Kunga Zangpo, Mupa Tugje Palwa, Murampa Konchog Dragpa, Doring Kunpang Chenpo, and Khondung Śākya Gyaltsen. These and many other scholars and practitioners carried out extensive activities on behalf of the teachings.

Tagtsang Lotsāwa

Regarding the famous trio known as the great scholars Go Śāk Tag: these days, among the great talkers of the land of snows, even the herds of philosophical cattle are thrown into doubt when they hear the mere names of these lion-like lords of speech. The last of these three masters was Tsang Tagtsang Lotsāwa Drapa Sherab Rinchen.

He was born around the same time as Gorampa and Śākya Chogden. He was the disciple of Jamyang Kunga Chozang, who was himself a student of

Kunkhyen Sangye Pal. In general, he studied the topics of the inner and outer sciences. In particular, he became a great lotsāwa, a speaker of two languages. He founded several meditation centers including Tsang Tobgyal Chokor Gang and Tsedong Rinchen Gang. The great Sakyapa Namkha Trashi Gyaltsen relied on Tagtsang Lotsāwa as his lama.

Tagtsang Lotsāwa's writings included the treatises *Knowing All the Philosophical Systems*, *Knowing All the Sūtra Sets*, and *Knowing All the Tantra Sets*. In the field of Vinaya, he wrote commentaries on the *Prātimokṣa Sūtra*, Guṇaprabha's *Vinaya Sūtra*, and the *Karmavibhaṅga*. He also wrote commentaries on Vasubandhu's *Abhidharmakośa* and Asaṅga's *Abhidharmasamuccaya*, the five Dharmas of Maitreya, Nāgārjuna's *Sūtrasamuccaya*, Dharmakīrti's *Pramāṇavārttika*, and Sakya Paṇḍita's *Distinguishing the Three Vows*. He also wrote a textbook on the *Kālacakra Tantra*, an extensive commentary on Śarvavarman's *Kalāpa*, and a brief commentary on Ratnākaraśānti's *Candoratnākara*. These are found in his sixteen-volume collected works.

Zhuchen Tsultrim Rinchen

These six ornaments of the snowy land, great scholars from the previous generations of glorious Sakyapas, gave rise to an unbroken line of innumerable learned and accomplished saints who upheld the Great One's teachings. Among later generations of Sakyapa upholders of the teachings, one was a second Daṇḍin who spoke poetry in the land of snows. He was Zhuchen Tsultrim Rinchen, mahāpaṇḍita of the definitive meaning. Zhuchen Tsultrim Rinchen clarified to a great extent the legacy achieved by the three spheres of activity and precious teachings of the all-knowing Ewampa Chenpo. Therefore, remembering his kindness, I will faithfully elaborate upon his autobiography.

This lord of scholarship was born in the country of Denma, which is part of the region of Zemogang in Dokham. His birthplace was in the vicinity of a meditation center called Densa Kar Samdrub Ling, which was founded by the great Sakyapa Dagchen Jamyang Rinchen. He came from a family line that included many sages skilled in the arts, crafts, writing, and astrological calculation. His father was Legshe Kunga Pel and his mother was Buchog Nyi. He was born in the twelfth fire-ox year (1697).

From the age of seven, Zhuchen learned to read from the doctor Tsoje Lhagon. He acted as an assistant, assembling and distributing bags of medicine, and he read the books of the medicinal tantras again and again. Thus he opened the door to understanding the medicinal sciences from the very beginning. He quickly learned to read and write the Lañtsa script from observation alone.

When he was eleven, he received the brahmacarya vows of an upāsaka from Kunga Gyatso, and he requested the name Kunga Sonam. He learned religious painting from his father and elder brother and understood how to do it without difficulty. He also trained, learned, and practiced the ordinary sciences. He received the drawing manual for religious painting from the master Sangye Chopel. He learned the science of black astrology and white astrology from the latter, as well as from Sera Rabjampa Trashi Gyaltsen and Lab Lama Dogyu Gyatso. He also received Tumi's *Basic Grammar in Thirty Verses* from the Sera Rabjampa. He was instructed in drawing and coloring maṇḍalas by the chant leader of the Shugra meditation center, Sangye Tendzin, and in the science of medicine by Tsoje Karma Ngawang. From Tse Bhrūṃ Choje Karma Tutobpa he received instruction and enlightenment in Śarvavarman's *Kalāpa*, Daṇḍin's *Kāvyādarśa*, Ratnākaraśānti's *Chandoratnākara*, Tumi's *Thirty Verses*, and in the calligraphy of several scripts, including Lañtsa and Vartu.

This master did not engage in formal study of the main texts of the causal vehicle, but he innately possessed a miraculous understanding of them that was sharp, swift, and profound. Because his great diligence never slackened, he was able to achieve a detailed understanding of any sūtra or mantra text by reading it on his own. Thus he absorbed the fundamental principles correctly, and he captivated the minds even of those who were trained in the methods of teaching and composition. As a writer, his rhetoric was eloquent and his poetics beautiful. His writings are pleasingly replete with scriptural citation and rational analysis.

Even more, at that time in the land of snows, those who were skilled in classical poetry (*kāvya*) and those who were entirely ignorant of it praised Zhuchen unanimously. He mastered many qualities such as memorization and inspired speech without ever needing to rely on others. These qualities are displayed in his biographies of extraordinary saints who completely transcended the ways of ordinary people. These sublime ones also reveal the limitless previous training of Zhuchen, as he was prophesied to be an emanation of Lobpon Jamyang Dragpa and the great abbot Śāntarakṣita.

He himself had innumerable inner qualities; for example, in a dream he saw Sarasvatī and asked her about the signs of receiving accomplishments.

At the age of twenty-nine, Zhuchen traveled to a number of colleges. First he made a devotional visit to Sakya in order to make heartfelt prayers. Then he went to Ewam Choden, where he accepted the possessions of a fully ordained monk from Khenchen Tsultrim Lhundrub by receiving the three stages of ordination. He stayed at Ngor for three years, during which time he received the oral Dharma instructions of the Lamdre three times.

He received transmissions from Khangsar Khenchen Jampa Sonam Zangpo, Morchen Ngawang Kunga Lhundrub, Khenchen Trashi Lhundrub, Jamyang Sangye Palzang, Nesarwa Ngawang Kunga Legpai Jungne, Je Namkha Palzang, Sharchen Rinchen Mingyur Gyaltsen, and Wangla Kunga Tendzin. These transmissions included the empowerment manuals for Saṃvara, Guhyasamāja, Vajrabhairava, Kālacakra, the Vajrakīlaya of the Sakya tradition, Sarvavid Vairocana; the permissions, manuals, esoteric instructions, and whispered transmissions of the Hundred Sādhanas of Bari, the Ocean of Sādhanas, the Thirteen Golden Dharmas, and the major and minor protectors; and the collected works of the five Sakya forefathers and Ngorchen Dorje Chang. Furthermore, by training others in the ritual manuals of Sakya, Ngor, and Tsar, he brought them to enlightenment.

Zhuchen received the transmission of the sādhana *Excellent Vase for the Wish-Fulfilling Cow* from Zechen Rabjampa Pema Sangag Tendzin; the transmission of many profound Dharmas from the Nyingma transmitted (*kama*) and treasure (*terma*) teachings such as Black Mañjuśrī, the Lord of Life, from Lama Sonam Lhundrub; and the reading transmission of the complete Kangyur from Choje Sonam Lodro. These are just a few examples. His own two-volume record of the teachings he received, *Cosmic Ocean of Confidence and Endeavor*, shows that he received a huge number.

Many of the teachings Zhuchen received, and not just the oral instructions of the Lamdre, he received two or three times. He developed further than ever before the excellent traditions of the arts and sciences by composing manuals for students on topics like grammar, classical poetics, and poetic composition for ordinary and outstanding students, including Jamyang Sangye Palzang, Khenchen Trashi Lhundrub, Khangsar Khenchen Jampa Sonam Zangpo, Chagra Tulku Ngawang Trinle Palzang, Denma Rabjampa Sangye Lhundrub, and Kui Won Ngawang Geleg Lhundrub.

The Derge Dharma king Jangchub Sempa Tenpa Tsering commissioned a complete set of master copies for the printing blocks of the collected works of the five Sakya forefathers in sixteen volumes and of the complete Tengyur. Later, during the rule of his son and heir, Sakyong Lama Kunga Trinle Gyatso, an order was issued by Khenchen Trashi Lhundrub along with the great Dharma king and his chaplain that resulted in Zhuchen being placed at the head of the editorial team. Because Zhuchen fully understood Tibetan orthography and terminology and had analyzed all the intended meanings of the sūtras and tantras without error, he managed the editorial team so that all of the words and their meanings in the texts were free from mistakes. Thanks to his kindness, today this Derge edition has come to be regarded as the most reliable of all the master copies of the Tengyur.

After the printing blocks had been made, Zhuchen composed a marvelous array of works clarifying an extensive range of subjects, including a catalog called *New Moon That Increases the Miraculous Ocean*, a Dharma history of Tibet, and a chronicle of the Derge royal family.[325] Because Zhuchen acted as editor in chief for the carving of new printing blocks for sacred writings like these, the new official title of Zhudag Lama ("editor lama") was given to him.

He turned an unceasing and vast wheel of activities. For example, whenever it was necessary he gave personal advice and practical instructions on subjects like the techniques for carving and painting new sacred images. In addition, in the spaces between these activities, he practiced primarily the basic yoga of Hevajra and the full yoga of Vajrabhairava, the protector Dragzongma, and Sarvavid Vairocana. Furthermore, when he was on retreat, his practice of yoga was accompanied by the signs that are spoken of in the tantras, both in real experiences and in dreams. Throughout his life Zhuchen spent all his time engaged in the ten religious activities.[326] His innumerable miracles were beyond the realms of ordinary peoples' activities. Such was his nature.

There are twelve volumes of this great master's compositions, which include the following:

- Many catalogs of temple holdings, including his Tengyur catalog
- Official regulations for Dharma communities
- Empowerment ritual manuals
- Textbooks for empowerments and ritual permissions
- Maṇḍala ritual manuals

- Compilations of liturgies for fire rituals
- A cycle of practice manuals
- Many verses for requests, dedications, and aspirational prayers
- Many sections on smoke offerings for all deity families
- Letters of request
- A collection of hymns
- A record of teachings received
- Answers to questions
- Official correspondence
- Biographies of the sixteen elders

At the age of seventy-eight, having brought so many enlightened activities to completion in his lifetime, Zhuchen showed the way to merge one's mind with the space of reality. Sitting in equipoise in the Vajradhara posture, he passed away at daybreak in the tiger hour, on the fifteenth day of the seventh month of the thirteenth wood-horse year (1774).

• 7 •

The Tsar Tradition

THE HISTORY OF the Tsarpa tradition is in two parts: the spread of the Tsar tradition and the succession of the monastic seat of Nalendra.

THE SPREAD OF THE TSAR TRADITION

The Tsarpas were lords of the Dharma and keepers of the treasury containing an ocean of the hearing lineages of the glorious Sakyapas. The central part of this tradition, the precious oral instructions of the Lamdre, was passed as a single-disciple lineage from Ngorchen Dorje Chang to Muchen Sempa Chenpo and then to Dagchen Dorje Chang. In total three lineage traditions came down to Dagchen Dorje Chang, including also that of his father Jamyang Choje. Other lineages, including the Thirteen Golden Dharmas and the major and minor protectors, were passed down as single-disciple transmissions from the Dharma lord Lama Dampa to Yarlung and Lupa. These teachings and more came down to Dagchen Lodro Gyaltsen, that magical emanation of benevolence, the crown of scholars, the crown ornament of adepts, the ocean of vast and profound precepts.

Jetsun Doringpa

Among the innumerable students who personally received the ambrosia of Dagchen Lodro Gyaltsen's teachings, the one who was given the full vase of the precepts of the extraordinary hearing lineage was Jetsun Doringpa Kunpang Kunzang Chokyi Nyima Loden Sherab Gyaltsen Palzangpo. He was a buddha here in this world who came from a succession of rebirths, a garland of scholars and adepts. This master learned the teachings of the Old and New schools without partiality, studying with seventy-two scholars and adepts including the spiritual sons of Ngorchen Kunga Zangpo. Using scripture and reasoning based on an ocean of precepts of sūtra and mantra, he cut through all misapprehensions.

In particular, Jetsun Doringpa attended upon Dagchen Dorje Chang with the three kinds of delight.[327] He studied all the precepts of the hearing lineage endowed with the four authenticities, exemplified by the precious oral instructions of the Lamdre, contemplating them through and through. He accomplished them all, up to and including even the most minor practices. He spent his life in solitude among the mountains, living in retreats like Khau Dragzong Nagpo. Since he never missed the four sessions of yoga, he reached a high stage of accomplishment, and he became as famous as the lion's roar for his profundity. Spreading the precepts of the profound hearing lineage to the edges of existence, he founded many lineages of what became known as the Khaupa tradition.

Tsarchen Losel Gyatso

Among the many students of Jetsun Doringpa, the closest was Tsarchen Losel Gyatso. He came at the end of a succession of rebirths like a rosary of *mandāra* flowers, including scholars and adepts like Virūpa in India and Buton, the Omniscient One of this age of strife, in Tibet. He came from a family line of divine beings at Nordzingyi Tigle near Mangkhar Mugulung. His father was called Rinchen Palzang and his mother Trashi. When he was born on the tenth day of the third month of the eighth water-dog year (1502), the first flowering of the marks and signs and the qualities of learning, diligence, and goodness naturally awoke within him. He possessed many miraculous qualities. For example, he accomplished enlightened activities with a variety of emanations from the vajra Dharma protectors, and he clearly saw the three vajra thrones of the maṇḍala.[328]

Tsarchen received ordination from the omniscient Gendun Gyatso and studied the analytical vehicle at Trashi Lhunpo and broke the battle standards of scholarly pride of the resident proponents of scripture and reasoning.[329] As the aspirations of his previous lives awoke within him, he developed an unshakeable faith in the Sakya tradition and in Doringpa, supreme among adepts. When the auspicious conditions were brought together by an actual statement from Vajrayoginī, Tsarchen traveled to the mountain retreat of Khau Dragzong, the second Oḍḍiyāna of snowy retreats. There he received an inconceivable number of profound precepts from the great Doringpa, exemplified by the hearing lineage endowed with the four authenticities and the explication for disciples, not meant for the ears of every Sakyapa.

During the many years of his studying these practices, he thought about even the most minor of them and cut through all his doubts. Through his experiences in meditation, he manifested the signs of meditative heat, he saw the coemergent wisdom of reality, all his perceptions of phenomena arose as the deities' maṇḍalas, and the Dharma protectors acted as his servants. In particular, when he placed his lotus feet upon the throne of the omniscient Buton Rinpoche, he received the vajra samaya on the crown of his head from Yamāntaka, the Lord of Death. Then everyone with intelligence became certain that Tsarchen was the creative display of the dance of the wrathful Mañjuśrī in saffron robes.

Furthermore, since Tsarchen relied on sixty-three sublime teachers without sectarian bias, he received all of the profound precepts leading to the supreme and ordinary accomplishments and thus became a second Vajradhara for this degenerate age. During his time in places like Dar Drangmoche, Mankhar Tubten Gepel, and Chalung Dorje Dragzong, Tsarchen wrote in order to further his teaching and practice.[330] Swarms of honeybees—fortunate sublime beings of all schools—gathered like clouds to taste the sweet honey of this flowering lotus pool—Tsarchen's learning and accomplishment. Through pouring out the nectar of the profound hearing lineage, Tsarchen created great waves of benefit for beings and the teachings.

At the age of sixty-five, on the fifteenth day of the seventh month of the ninth fire-tiger year (1566), while at Dar Ladrang, Tsarchen showed the way to merge the manifestation of the rūpakāya into the space of reality.

Jamyang Khyentse Wangchug

Tsarchen Losal Gyatso had a vast number of students who, drinking the nectar of his speech, became rich in the tantras of ultimate realization. The most important among them, those who grasped the secret significance of his speech, were connected with him as master and disciple for many lifetimes. However, in this lifetime the one who is indicated by the phrase "Tsarchen and his son," the one who became his single closest disciple, was Nesarwa Jamyang Khyentse Wangchug. This sublime being was born in an Azha family lineage in the ninth wood-monkey year (1524). He studied with numerous scholars and adepts of the Old and New schools. He was the close disciple of Dagchen and Doringpa, and later Jetsun Gorumpa Kunga Legpa and Je Tsarchen became his most important teachers.

On the side of the New schools, he received 116 major empowerments, 64 blessings, 178 associated permissions, and over 121 guidance manuals. On the side of the Old school (Nyingma), he received 171 major empowerments, 31 minor empowerments, 38 guidance manuals, and more. He also received hundreds of books as background material. Studying and contemplating these, he cut through all his doubts.

Jamyang Khyentse Wangchug understood without any confusion even the most minor practices, from making books and tangkas to constructing tormas and the different ways of holding the vajra and bell. His enlightened activities of practice and scholarship in an ocean of scriptural traditions of sūtra and mantra were like the sky, and he was made the throne holder at the seat of Buton Rinpoche. Moreover, he completed the triad of hearing, contemplating, and meditating upon the cycles of the hearing lineage endowed with the four authenticities. Writings based on clear recollections of his conversations were given out to many, so that they became the single eye of wisdom for the holders of Jamyang Khyentse Wangchug's lineage.[331]

In short, he delighted the learned with his qualities of knowledge, compassion, and power, and accomplished sages became certain that he was the only person worthy of veneration throughout the land. Furthermore, because he was blessed by Jamgon Sakya Paṇḍita, his intelligence became unbounded. He was the jewel in the crown of those who discussed the sciences. His closest students were the following four:

- Yangchen Drinpar Chagpa Pal Mangdu Topa Ludrub Gyatso, the great abbot (Khenchen) of Nyenyo Jago Shong[332]
- The emanation of the hidden yogin of Nyenyo
- Nedong Tsetsog Khenchen Yolwa Zhonu Lodro, whose qualities of learning, discipline, and accomplishment were unmatched
- Bokharwa Maitri Dondrub Gyaltsen the Fourth, who was a master of the hearing lineage and lord of magical potency

In addition there were limitless students of the father and son, including Khenchen Labsum Gyaltsen and Dorje Chang Wangchug Gyaltsen.[333] Yolwa Dorje Chang Zhonu Lodro passed this lineage on to Yarlung Trashi Chode. Later it was maintained by the nephew and rebirth lines of Nesar, such as Kangyurwa Gonpo Sonam Chogden.

The Tsarpa lineage

Among the many students who came to Jamyang Khyentse Wangchug, his lineage was passed down in stages by the following three:

- Bodong Khenchen Ngamding Mawa Labsum Gyaltsen
- His own nephew Nesarwa Dorje Chang Wangchug Rabten
- The powerful lord Dru Sibui Ngagchang Gonsarwa Sonam Chopel

Those students who came in the middle, including personal students and rebirths, caused the teachings of the extraordinary explication for disciples to shine like the sun. They were:

- Khyabdag Kangyurwa Chenpo Nesarwa Won Rinpoche Gonpo Sonam Chogden, an emanation of Tsarchen Rinpoche
- Zhalu Khen Rinpoche Sonam Chogden, master of an ocean of tantras
- Chetsun Khyenrab Jampa Ngawang Lhundrub, the Chogyepa abbot of Nalendra
- Morchen Ngawang Kunga Lhundrub, a sun illuminating this degenerate age and a master of exposition of sūtra and mantra
- Nesarwa Ngawang Kunga Legpai Jungne, an emanation of Khyabdag Kangyurwa
- Jamgon Kunga Lodro, the great Sakyapa
- Yarlung Chogtrul Rinpoche Namkha Legpa Lhundrub, an emanation of Nesarwa

Furthermore, since a few Dharma transmissions were also received by Sakyapa Jamyang Sonam Wangpo from the powerful lord Yolwa Zhonu Lodro, the auspicious connections were brought together for propagating the father's Dharma at the great monastic seat of Sakya. The lineage passed from Khenchen Ngawang Chodrag (a student of both Mangto Ludrub Gyatso and Ngagchang Sonam Chopel) to the glorious Sakyapa Jamgon Ame Zhab on the Sakya side, and to Gyaltsewa Ngawang Sonam Gyaltsen and others on the Ngor Ewampa side.

Since Bokharwa graciously accepted Gyalwang Sonam Gyatso, the sun of the teachings of the Yellow Hats, the gate to his enlightened activity was opened in Riwo Ganden as well.[334] The Great Fifth Dalai Lama received the complete cycles of the path of the extremely detailed explanation of the hearing lineage of the explication for disciples from Khyabdag Kangyurwa

Gonpo Sonam Chogden. Thus the Great Fifth made him chief among his tutors and became a great benefactor of the teachings of the explication for disciples, publishing via dictation supplementary notes on the great Lamdre explication for disciples guidance manual and biographies of four lamas of the Tsar tradition.

The nectar of this profound Dharma was also passed on by Morchen to the monastery of Dorje Drag via Rigdzin Pema Trinle and Rigdzin Terdag Lingpa. Thus the lotus of faith opened in the hearts of the great upholders of the teaching in the Nyingma school too.

Furthermore, Jamgon Kunga Lodro received the entire hearing lineage from Nesarwa Ngawang Kunga Legpai Jungne. Therefore the great monastic seat of Sakya became the primary source of this lineage, like a wellspring of the teachings of the explication for disciples in U, Tsang, and Kham. Also, Jamgon Kunga Lodro, his nephew Khyentse Rabten, Tsedong Trichen Khyenrab Tendzin Lhundrub, Dzongshar Bodrugpa Choje Losel Puntsog (the personal disciple of Nesarwa), his personal disciple Chobgye Trichen Ngawang Kunga Khyenrab, Tsedong Trichen Gendun Trashi Paljor (the personal disciple of Jamgon Kunga Lodro), and Zimwogpa Ngawang Tendzin Trinle all spread the nectar of the explication for disciples to glorious Tsedong and Nalendra.

Due to the enlightened activities of Khyabdag Kangyurwa, Zhalu Khenchen, and Morchen Dorje Chang, the monasteries of glorious Zhalu, Dorje Den, and Tubten Rawame came to uphold the lineage of the explication for disciples. Tartse Khenchen Namkha Chime opened up a new tradition of the profound explication for disciples in Ewam Choden, Derge Lhundrub Teng, and elsewhere. Due to the work of his two nephews, there appeared limitless upholders of the teachings of the hearing lineage endowed with the four authenticities.

In short, the enlightened activities of the Dharma king Tsarchen embraced most systems of practice from this school and others, and in this degenerate age he carried out the activities of a second conqueror in the tradition of the teachings in general and the Vajrayāna in particular.

The succession of the monastic seat of Nalendra

The Dharma college of Nalendra in Penyul was a great source of the teachings of sūtra and mantra. After it was first established by the omniscient Rongton, it was maintained by generations of throne holders through study, practice, and ritual. In particular, since the sixteenth throne-holding abbot, Chetsun Khyen Rabjampa Ngawang Lhundrub (a personal student of Jamyang Khyentse Wangchug), a garland of virtuous monks from the noble Che family known as the Chogyepas, along with the garland of generations of the Zimwog family, have proclaimed a great lion's roar of the profound and secret explication for disciples. They have spread far and wide the teachings of the hearing lineage that came from Tsarchen and his son, and Nalendra has been highly esteemed as a great Tsarpa college.

Initially, during the great Rongton's lifetime, Nalendra consisted of the large assembly temple connected with Rongton's own residence, the four colleges of Tongmon, Ducho, Tsegye, and Tsezhi, and various halls of residence and monastic cells—forty-five buildings in all. After he established the monastic seat, Rongton acted as abbot for eight years. Subsequently the second throne holder was Rongton's disciple Kunkhyen Trashi Namgyal, the third was Rigpai Wangchug Gewa Gyaltsen, the fourth was Gungru Sherab Zangpo, and the fifth was Lopa Choje Chenga Kunga Dorje. These abbots held the throne over a twenty-year period, during which time Nalendra expanded very quickly to two or three thousand monks, and day and night there was the constant sound of Dharma.

The sixth abbot was Khyenrab Trinle Zangpo and the seventh was Khenpo Lozang Namgyal. During these two abbacies a great many setbacks occurred, leading to an unacceptable decline. When rumors of this reached Sakya, Dagchen Dorje Chang came to oversee the running of the monastary and restored the monastic rituals. He invited his own maternal uncle, the Zhalu abbot Chetsun Khyenrab Choje Rinpoche, who came from the luminous divine lineage of the likes of Lotsāwa Che Khyidrug. Reminding Choje Rinpoche of his samaya commitment to Ngorchen, Dagchen Dorje Chang appointed him the eighth abbot of Nalendra. After this the number of monks never fell below four thousand, at times reaching as high as seven thousand, and the study and practice of sūtra and mantra never ceased.

Choje Rinpoche passed into peace at the age of sixty-two, on the eighteenth day of the twelfth month of the eighth fire-snake year (1557). Right up to the present day, those who are responsible for the offerings on holy days at Nalendra have been called Choje Chogyepa.[335] The ninth abbot was Choje's nephew, Chetsun Nyamtogkyi Dagnyi Sonam Chogdrub. After his tenure, the abbacy overseeing the general assembly at Nalendra split in two.

On the earthen throne to the right were:

- Muchen Sangye Rinchen
- Salo Jampal Dorje
- Jamyang Ngagi Wangpo
- Sakya Chenpo Jamyang Namkha Gyaltsen
- Lopa Chenga Konchog Dragpa
- Jamyang Damcho Gyaltsen
- Sakyapa Ngagchang Chenpo Kunga Rinchen
- Tongra Kunga Legdrub
- Sheu Lotsāwa Kunga Chodrag
- Sakyapa Jamyang Sonam Wangpo
- Tsedong Trichen Kunga Sonam Lhundrub
- Sonam Tendzin Wangpo

All of them remained in permanent residence after they came to the throne, apart from when they had to make personal visits. Subsequently, during the time of the Great Fifth, the abbatial estate, which included land bringing in an income, was taken from the monastic community and donated to the central government. In the subsequent stages of the lineage, those who came to the throne were not chosen from the inheritors of this estate, which was instead passed like a stone from hand to hand between the likes of Dorje Gyaltsen, who was a personal attendent of the Dalai Lama, and Ngawang Lhundrub, an associate teacher from the Jangtse college of Ganden.[336]

On the wooden throne to the left:

- The tenth abbot was Śākya Dondrub.
- The eleventh abbot was Chetsun Jamyang Donyo Gyaltsen. He was honored by the Chinese emperor, who gave him the official golden hat and robes, an imperial edict, and a golden seal.
- The twelfth abbot was Lhatsun Sonam Lhundrub.
- The thirteenth abbot was Drenchog Chogleg Dorje.

- The fourteenth abbot was Khedrub Sempa Chenpo Chetsun Tendzin Zangpo. He spent his efforts primarily in meditation, and his enlightened activities pervaded as far as Dartsedo.
- The fifteenth abbot was Dogyal Namtrul Chetsun Khyenrab Tendzin Lhundrub.
- The sixteenth abbot was Chetsun Khyenrab Jampa Ngawang Lhundrub, a contemporary of the Great Fifth and an emanation of Jetsun Jampa. He was unrivaled in his learning and understanding of sūtra and mantra. He was granted the Lamdre thirty times and the Vajramālā empowerments fifteen times. His students, from Ngari in the west to Mongolia in the east, were like grains of sand too numerous to count. He was venerated by over two hundred incarnate abbots and lamas of every school and became a life-staff of the teachings, both the Dharma of the Conqueror in general and the hearing lineage in particular.
- The seventeenth abbot was Chetsun Khyentse Rabten, the nephew of the previous abbot and an emanation of Nesar Khyentse Wangchug. He mastered an ocean of sūtra and mantra and saw the faces of deities and lamas. His autobiography, which contains nothing but accounts of his meditative experiences and realizations, exists in six parts. He was truly an ornament of the teachings, and his enlightened activities in the three spheres, including establishing many temples in the Kham district such as Dezhung Monastery, were widespread.
- The eighteenth abbot was Chetsun Gachen Khyabdag Nyingpo, the rebirth of Khyentse Rabten. Due to his wish to see the sights of India and Tibet, he left his temple for Lhasa, where he received permission to travel. At the age of twenty he ended his wanderings.
- The nineteenth abbot was Chetsun Ngawang Kunkhyen. He spread the activities of study, practice, and teaching through all of Central Tibet. He performed countless recitation practices and spent three years training in the essential view of the inseparability of saṃsāra and nirvāṇa. He built a stūpa with a hidden panel containing a wish-granting jewel said to have been given to him by the gods and nāgas.
- The twentieth abbot was Chetsun Tenpai Wangchug Chogdrub, the nephew of the previous abbot. He granted the Lamdre many

times. In a dream he saw the rising sun transform into Mañjuśrī and then dissolve into his body. At this, his wisdom burst forth.

- The twenty-first abbot was Chetsun Gendun Trashi Paljor. He was recognized as the Tsedong rebirth. He sent forth great waves of activity for the teachings, such as granting the Lamdre.
- The twenty-second abbot was the Zimwog rebirth Chetsun Tendzin Nyendrag. He was made throne-holding abbot for three years. He established a teaching center at the Tongmon Monastery. He was appointed master of science at the highest level of the central government.[337] He traveled to Kham three times, granted the Lamdre many times, and acted for the teachings in many other ways as well.
- The twenty-third abbot was Khyenrab Ngedon Zangpo, the younger brother of the previous abbot.
- The twenty-fourth abbot was Chetsun Rinchen Khyentse Wangpo. He accepted the request to come to Nalendra because he wanted to spread the teachings of Rongton in this degenerate age. He was recognized as a rebirth of Rongton Śākya Gyaltsen—who was prophesied by Machig Labdron, the great instructor in the practice of Cho, as "an emanation of Maitreya with the name Gyal"—and of his three emanations with the name Khyen: Khyenrab Choje, Khyenrab Jampa, and Rinchen Khyentse. He received oral instruction in the Lamdre three times, the Vajramālā empowerments four times, and the reading transmission of the Kangyur three times. His activities were vast and included the establishment of a large ceremonial throne at the temple and a request for the return of the abbatial seat from the central government.
- The twenty-fifth abbot was Chetsun Trichen Ngawang Khyenrab Tubten Legshe Gyatso Chog. He performed extensive activities of receiving, studying, and meditating upon sūtra, mantra, and the sciences. He possessed marvelous qualities of excellent learning and discipline. In recent times he constructed a new monastery at the Lumbinī grove, the birthplace of our Teacher.[338] In connection with that, he established a meditation center for the practice of the cycles of the hearing lineage, especially the Lamdre explication for disciples. There he lived, looking after the upholders of the teaching in the Sakya practice lineage with great kindness. I pray that his feet may be firmly placed in the essence of limitless life and that

his activities, which are of great benefit to the teachings, go from strength to strength.[339]

The Zimwog garland of rebirths

Zhabdrung Ngawang Norbu, who was the nephew of the sixteenth abbot of Nalendra, Khyenrab Jampa Ngawang Lhundrub, and an emanation of the omniscient Rongton and his disciples as well, established a monastic college at Zimwog Tongmon. The Zimwog garland of rebirths appeared when the expanded monastic college was passed on to a successor. The origin of the name Zimwog comes from when the second abbot of Nalendra, Kunkhyen Trashi Namgyal, built a new home for Rongton; at that time Rongton's previous home became known as Zimwog, meaning "previous residence."

The rebirth of Zhabdrung Ngawang Norbu, the second in the garland of rebirths, was Jampa Ngawang Sangye Tendzin. The third in the garland of rebirths was Jampa Ngawang Tendzin Trinle.[340] The fourth in the garland of rebirths was Jampa Ngawang Tendzin Nyendrag.[341] The fifth in the garland of rebirths was Dorje Chang Jampa Ngawang Kunga Tendzin Trinle. All of the above possessed the qualities of learning and accomplishment and were all sages of great kindness who upheld the Tsarpa hearing lineage tradition of Sakya. The sixth in the garland of rebirths was the supreme nirmāṇakāya Datse Sarpa Ngawang Tendzin Norbu. The system of study and practice today is still implemented according to his teachings. By stages he perfected every aspect of the qualities of scripture and realization. He was a guide who spread far and wide the ocean-like teachings of the hearing lineage and who granted the wishes of the great upholders of the teaching who came after him.

• 8 •

The Essential Sakya Teachings

THIS IS A presentation of the Dharmas that have brought about learning and accomplishment for the upholders of the Sakya teachings, continuing to the present day. This presentation begins with the entrance gate to the precious Dharma and goes on to the subjects to be learned and contemplated once one has entered the Dharma. The vow lineages of the *Prātimokṣa Sūtra*, transmitted along with their ceremonies, are the lineage from Paṇchen Śākyaśrī to Jamyang Sapaṇ and so on (the vow lineage of the great Sakya Lhakhang) and the lineage from Khenchen Dorje Pal among others to the omniscient Ngorchen Kunga Zangpo and his disciples (the Ngorpa vow lineage). Now, the subjects to be learned and contemplated can be divided into the causal vehicle and the secret mantra, the vehicle of the result.

THE CAUSAL VEHICLE

When we distinguish the different kinds of entrance gates for beginners, it is said:

> The six great topics propounded by the Sakyapas are Prajñāpāramitā, Pramāṇa, Vinaya, Abhidharma, Madhyamaka, and the three vows.

And in more detail:

- The Vinaya cycle: the *Prātimokṣa Sūtra* and Guṇaprabha's *Vinaya Sūtra*
- The Pramāṇa cycle: Dignāga's *Pramāṇasamuccaya*, Dharmakīrti's *Pramāṇavārttika*, and Dharmottara's *Pramāṇaviniścaya*

- The Abhidharma cycle: Asaṅga's *Abhidharmasamuccaya* and Vasubandhu's *Abhidharmakośa*
- The Prajñāpāramitā cycle: the five Dharmas of Maitreya and Śāntideva's *Bodhicaryāvatāra*
- The Madhyamaka cycle: the great trio of Nāgārjuna's *Mūlamadhyamakakārikā*, Āryadeva's *Catuḥśataka*, and Candrakīrti's *Madhyamakāvatāra*
- The cycle of Sapaṇ's *Treasury of Logic*, the commentary on Dharmakīrti's *Seven Treatises*
- Sapaṇ's *Distinguishing the Three Vows*, the general commentary on the scriptural collections and the classes of tantra

These are known as the eighteen texts of great renown. The tradition of teaching the six great topics in this way spread far, including to the great Sakya Tubten Lhakhang, Tanag Tubten Namgyal, Upper and Lower Kyetsal, Tubten Rabme, Namrab Dagpo Dratsang, and Dhīpu Monastery in Amdo. Traditionally the qualifications received for completing the study and contemplation of these texts are Kazhipa, Kazhupa, and Rabjampa. In more recent times, the study and teaching of the eighteen texts of great renown has become very popular at several monastic colleges, including the teaching center in Derge and Ga Kyegu Dondrub.

Finally, there are the practice cycles, the transmitted texts that are exemplified by the two systems of generating bodhicitta: *Parting From the Four Attachments* and the *Seven Points of Mind Training*.[342]

The vehicle of the result

This will be discussed in three parts: in general, the cycles of the four classes of tantra; in particular, cycles of the explication for disciples and the Thirteen Golden Dharmas; and in addition, the related works of the lamas.

The cycles of the four classes of tantra

In the category of general transmissions are the permissions of: the Vajramālā empowerments, the Hundred Sādhanas of Bari, the Ocean of Sādhanas, and the Nartang Hundred.[343] The specific transmissions will be discussed in four parts: kriyā tantra, caryā tantra, yoga tantra, and unsurpassed yoga tantra.

Kriyā tantra

For the whole of this class of tantras there is the empowerment of the three buddha families.[344] Then from the individual kriyā tantras:

The Tathāgata family

- The principal deity of the family: Śākyamuni with the sixteen elders; also Viśuddhaprabhā (Ozer Drime), Bhaiṣajyaguru (Menla), and Nāgendrarāja (Luwang Gyalpo) and so on
- The lord of the family: Mañjuśrī, in the tradition of Mati, including the cycles of Pūrṇamati (Gangloma), Prajñācakra (Sherab Khorlo), and Vādisiṃha (Senge Mawa)
- The consorts of the family: the empowerments of the Pañcarakṣā goddesses (Sungma Lhanga), Mārīcī (Ozerchen), Grahamātṛkā (Zayum), Uṣṇīṣasitātapatrā (Tsugtor Dugkarpo) in maṇḍalas of seventeen and twenty-seven goddesses, and Vimaloṣṇīṣa (Tsugtor Drime) and so on
- The wrathful deities of the family: the cycles of the white and blue Acala

The Lotus family

- The principal deity of the family: the nine-deity maṇḍala of Amitāyus (Tsepagme); also the *Drum of Immortality* dhāraṇī, White Amitāyus of the Mitrayogin tradition, and the dhāraṇī of Kurava (Draminyen)
- The lord of the family: the empowerment of the thirty-seven goddess maṇḍala of Avalokiteśvara (Chenrezig) in the Nāgārjuna tradition; also the permissions and esoteric instructions of Ekādaśamukha in Gelongma Palmo's tradition;[345] Mahākaruṇika in the tradition of Kyergangpa Chokyi Rinchen; the union of Mahākaruṇika and mahāmudrā in the Sakya tradition and the principal deity with a twofold entourage, the five-deity maṇḍala of Amoghapāśa, and Siṃhanāda
- The consort of the family: the nine transmission lineages of White

Tārā (Drolma); also the combined permissions, profound guidance manuals, and esoteric instructions of six forms of Mārīcī; the permissions of the solitary Khadiravaṇī Tārā (Sengdeng Nagdrol), the twenty-one Tārās of Jowo Atiśa's tradition—Tārā who clears away all obstacles, Red Tārā, and so on; the esoteric instructions of the four maṇḍalas; and the cycle of Śramaṇa Devī (Lhamo Śramaṇa)

- The wrathful deity of the family: the permissions and esoteric instructions of Hayagrīva (Tamdrin) in the traditions of Bodhisattva Dawa Gyaltsen and Machig Drubpai Gyalmo, and Yellow Parṇaśabarī (Ritroma)

The Vajra family

- The principal deity of the family: the empowerment of the nine-deity maṇḍala of Akṣobhya (Mitrugpa)
- The lord of the family: Vajrapāṇi (Chagna Dorje) in Drozang Nyingpo's tradition and Vajravidāraṇā (Namjom) in Bari's tradition
- The messenger of the family: Bhurukuṃkūṭa (Metseg) in the traditions of Sakya and Jowo Atiśa, along with the esoteric instructions; also the female messenger Bhurukuṃkūṭī (Metsegma), and so on

The Jewel family

- Seventeen permissions from different families, of various higher and lower classes of tantra, including Yellow Jambhala and Black Jambhala in the Bari tradition, White Jambhala "Dragon Youth" in Jowo Atiśa's tradition along with the esoteric instructions, and Great Yellow Vaiśravaṇa. Also included are the textual transmissions for a great many esoteric instructions.

Caryā tantra

This consists of the empowerment of the five-deity maṇḍala of Arapacana Mañjuśrī (Jamyang Arapatsana), lord of the family, and the permission of the main deity alone.

Yoga tantra

This consists of the twelve essential tantric practices and Sarvavid Vairocana, Vajrapāṇi "Overpowering Death," the textual transmissions for many manuals including the three cycles of benefit to others, and the texts of Sarvavid (Kunrig).

Unsurpassed yoga tantra

This is in three parts: father, mother, and nondual tantras.

The father tantras

- The transmissions and empowerments of Guhyasamāja in the maṇḍalas of Akṣobhya, Mañjuvajra, and Avalokiteśvara
- The empowerment of the five-deity maṇḍala of Red Yamāri along with the profound guidance manual
- The empowerments of the thirteen-deity maṇḍala of Black Yamāntaka (Dranag), the cycles of Bhairava in the Sakya tradition, and the eight Vetālī in Ra Lotsāwa's tradition
- The guidance manuals for Kyo Ojung's tradition of focusing the mind on the horn tips of Bhairava, the whispered tradition of the ḍākinī in Ra Lotsāwa's tradition, and the transmission of four volumes of background material
- The permissions for the extensive Mahāmayūrī "Overcoming the Poisons" (Dugwang Maja), the solitary Bhairava, and Karmayama (Leshin) including the four families, along with the four volumes of background material for these

The mother tantras

- Contained in the Heruka family from the *Ṣaṇmukhīdhāraṇī*: the empowerment of Saṃvara arranged according to the *Kālacakra Tantra* and that arranged according to the *Ḍākinīsaṃvara Tantra* and the ultimate secret yoga in the traditions of Luipa, Kṛṣṇācārya, and Vajraghaṇṭa;[346] the empowerment of the donkey-faced Cakrasaṃvara (Bongzhalchen); the blessings of the Vajravārāhī cycle in the Chal tradition; and the White Vajravārāhī "Illuminating Insight"[347]
- Included in the family of Padmanarteśvara: the empowerment of

the five-deity maṇḍala of Kurukulle, the blessings of Amitāyus in the Machig Drubpai Gyalmo lineage (this is included in the Heruka family of tantras), the guidance manual of Mahākaruṇika "Vase of Immortality" in the Tsembupa tradition[348] (this is also said to be a father tantra), and the permission for the twenty-one Tārās in the Sūryavajra tradition

The nondual tantras

- The seven empowerments in the four spoken transmissions that are included within Hevajra, the essence of body, speech, and mind: the esoteric instruction tradition, the commentarial tradition, the Saroruhavajra tradition, and the Kṛṣṇa tradition[349]
- The empowerments of the fifteen-deity maṇḍala of Nairātmyā (Dagme Lhamo), the explanatory tantra *Vajrapañjara*, and the associated tantra *Saṃpuṭa*
- The permissions of the three deities from the *Vajrapañjara* who carry out the activity of expansion: Vajrapāṇi Overcoming the Demons, White Prajñāpāramitā (Sherchin Karmo),[350] and White Pratisarā (Sordrang Karmo)
- The complete empowerment for the body, speech, and mind of the *Kālacakra Tantra*
- The permissions for the three deities from that tantra who carry out the activity of expansion: Vajravega (Dorje Shug), Śabala Garuḍa (Dorje Khyungtra), and Viśvamātṛ (Natsog Yum)

Specific transmissions

These are the cycles of (1) the extraordinary hearing lineage of the Lamdre, (2) the Thirteen Golden Dharmas, and (3) the protectors.

The precious oral instructions of the Lamdre

The main teachings[351]

- The causal empowerments of the esoteric instruction tradition of the glorious Hevajra[352]
- The recitation transmission for the Aṣṭa prayer

- The path empowerments
- The recitation transmission for the hundred-syllable mantra
- The outer and inner profound path of guru devotion
- The Guru Ratnasambhava (Lama Rinjung)
- The triple cycle of breathing
- The outer and inner protection practices of Virūpa
- Nairātmyā
- The teaching on the secret path
- The illumination of the symbolic meaning[353]
- The ordinary and extraordinary exclusive lineages of the symbol
- The summation of the path and prediction of accomplishment[354]
- Sealing the ten secrets
- Virūpa's system of Vajravidāraṇā
- The blessings of the auspicious protectors (Tendrel Sungwa)
- The solitary guardian (Gonkyang) of the Lamdre tradition
- The experiential guidance manuals for the Lamdre explication for the assembly and explication for disciples
- The practices of physical training and yogic exercise

The background material passed down in stages through textual transmissions

- Several volumes containing the biographies of individual masters of the explication for the assembly and explication for disciples
- The *Yellow Book* of the Lamdre, including the nine cycles of the path, by Jetsun Dragpa Gyaltsen
- The *Little Red Book* by Ngorchen Kunga Zangpo
- The *Black Book* by Lama Dampa Sonam Gyaltsen
- The *Blue Book* by Tongrawa
- *Sedonma*, the explanation of the fundamental verses of the Lamdre
- Tsarchen's *Sunlight of Explanation*
- The guidance manuals of Khyentse Wangchug and others
- The textual transmissions for a great many works of later lamas, such as Ludrub Gyatso, Paṇchen Ngawang Chodrag, and Ngawang Tendor

The Thirteen Golden Dharmas

Within the Thirteen Golden Dharmas, the hearing lineage that does not pass beyond the boundary wall, the first three are known as the three cycles of the Red Lady (Marmo Khorsum), or the three cycles of Khecarī (Khacho Khorsum). They concern the supreme accomplishment, with the ordinary accomplishments as an addendum. They are:

1. The Khecarī of Nārotapa (Nāro Khacho): including the individual blessings of the Ngor and Tsar traditions, the experiential guidance manual for the development and perfection stages, the blessings for showing the genuine state of reality, and the guidance manual for the great central channel

2–3. The blessings of the Khecarī of Indrabhūti (Indra Khacho) and the Khecarī of Maitrīpa (Maitri Khacho) with three volumes of background material

The next three of the Thirteen Golden Dharmas are known as the three red cycles (Marpo Khorsum). They concern the ordinary accomplishments, with the supreme accomplishment as an addendum. They are:

4. Kurukulle: the ordinary and extraordinary permissions of the Ngor tradition (the outer accomplishment), the ordinary and extraordinary permissions of the Tsar tradition (the inner accomplishment), the blessings of the five-deity secret accomplishment of the Dombi tradition, and one volume of textual transmissions
5. The Great Red Gaṇapati (Tsogdag Marchen). There are five permissions: the extraordinary Great Red Gaṇapati of the Ngor tradition, the extraordinary twelve-handed Great Red of the Tsar tradition, the special Great Red, the White Gaṇapati of the Jo tradition (also known as Rāgavajra), and the four-armed Gaṇapati. There is also one volume of textual transmissions.
6. The wrathful Kagchol Kāmarāja (Dopai Gyalpo): the extraordinary permission of the God of Desire in the Ngor tradition and the permission of the Secret Mantra Roar, plus one volume of textual transmissions

There is also a lineage of direct practical instructions on these practices.

The next three of the Thirteen Golden Dharmas are known as the three minor red cycles (Marchung Khorsum), or the three deities from the empowerments of Nyen Lotsāwa. This is comprised of the permissions along with the transmissions for the esoteric instructions of:

7. Kurukulle Garbhasuvarṇasūtra Śrī (Palmo Sergyi Nying Tagchen)
8. Red Vasudhārā (Norgyunma Marpo)
9. The goddess Tinuma (Lhamo Tinuma)

The remaining four of the Thirteen Golden Dharmas are the permissions and the transmissions for the respective esoteric instructions for:

10. Blue Siṃhamukha (Senge Dongchen Ngonmo)
11. Black Mañjuśrī (Jampal Nagpo)
12. Sky-Soaring Vajragaruḍa (Dorje Khyungtra)
13. The lifeforce practice of Red Jambhala (Dzambhala Marpo)

In addition to the Thirteen Golden Dharmas there is also the permission and textual transmission of Siṃhanāda the Protector and Liberator, which is known as "the Fourteenth Golden Dharma of Lupa." Also added to the Golden Dharmas are:

- The permission for Amitāyus Nirmāṇakāya
- The meditation instructions for the three Jambhalas in one, which is the Golden Dharma of Nyen Lotsāwa
- The textual transmission of the esoteric instructions for the Three Lhamo Yugu Sisters

The Dharma protectors

The Guardian of the Tent

An ocean of Dharma protectors, who act as the vajra sword that protects the teachings, has been passed down as a spoken transmission from master to disciple among the glorious Sakyapas. The main deity among them is the two-faced Mahākāla Guardian of the Tent (Gurgyi Gonpo). There are four spoken transmissions of the Guardian of the Tent cycle, comprising the permissions and the textual transmission of the esoteric instructions for:

1. The solitary guardian of the Lamdre tradition—the Gayadhara lineage

2. The solitary protector of the Bari tradition, drawn from the Hundred Sādhanas of Bari

And also:

3. The textual transmissions for the three cycles of the razor—the lineage from the Kashmiri Paṇḍita Śākyaśrī
4. The cycle of the Lama Mal lineage—the most profound and widespread of these

This last includes extensive background material for ripening and liberating:

1. The night transmission of the empowerments and the night transmission of the permissions. The first of these comprises the empowerments for:
   - The hearing lineage tradition of the five, eight, eleven, and seven-deity maṇḍalas of the guardian
   - The five-deity maṇḍala of the curved blade (this lineage is from Gayadhara)

   The second comprises the permissions for:
   - Mahākāla and his sisters in a three-deity maṇḍala, the ordinary and extraordinary eight-deity maṇḍalas, the eight-deity maṇḍala of the Ngor tradition, and the ordinary and extraordinary twelve-deity maṇḍalas
   - The exoteric guidance manual of the ten wrathful ones and the secret guidance manual of the nine wrathful ones
   - The exoteric and secret sādhanas for accomplishment as the secondary solitary goddess Dhūmāṅgārīdevī (Dusol Lhamo)
   - The Naked One Wielding a Copper Knife (Cherbu Zangrichen)
   - The Black-Cloaked One Wielding a Copper Knife (Bernag Zangrichen)
   - The ordinary and extraordinary Putra
2. The exoteric and secret guidance manuals and the lifeforce guidance for the secondary white guardian
3. The *Book of Blazing Fire*, with its supplements and hearing lineage. The further supplement contains the writings of the later holders of the hearing lineage, and there are two large supplementary volumes arranged by Kyoda Sonam Wangchug: the *Book of Gyijang* and the *Book of Dhūmāṅgārī*.[355]

The Four-Faced Kṣetrapāla

The cycle of the Four-Faced Kṣetrapāla (Zhingkyong) consists of:

- The ordinary guardian for the phase of service
- The ordinary guardian for the phase of accomplishment
- The extraordinary versions of the above
- The cruel-faced guardian
- The permission for the preliminary secret guidance manuals
- The ordinary white extender of the lifespan
- The extraordinary version of the above
- The yellow guardian for bringing about prosperity
- The red guardian for conquest
- The blue guardian for overcoming obstacles
- The nine deities for creating wealth
- The guardian for invocation[356]
- The garuḍa-faced guardian
- The guardian who shows the site of death
- The brahman who takes commands
- The wisdom guardian, Black Siṃhamukha (Senge Nagpo)
- The six cycles of Black Brahman, "the butcher" (Dramnag Shenpa)

In the Ngor tradition, for the phase of service, there is the permission of the three-deity maṇḍala of the protectors Begtse and his sister and their numerous entourage, along with the guidance manual for the phase of secret personal guidance. These are listed in the *Necklace of Jewels* catalog, with the ordinary protectors in one volume, another volume on the extraordinary protectors, the exclusive lineage of the black Hala mother and child, and another volume on Begtse. Furthermore, there are the permissions of the white guardian, of Magzorma, and of the lord and lady of the charnel grounds. There are books of esoteric instructions for each of them. There are other permissions including the tiger-riding guardian from the Nub tradition and the three victorious brothers (from the kriyā tantras).

The Cycles of Collected Works

This comprises a deep Dharma lake of sūtra and mantra, exemplified by the following:

- Fifteen volumes of the collected works of the five Sakya patriarchs

- A single volume of the collected works of Gyalse Togme
- Four volumes of the collected works of Ngorchen Dorje Chang
- One volume of Muchen
- Fifteen volumes of the collected works of the omniscient Sonam Senge
- Four volumes of Konchog Lhundrub
- One volume of Drubkhangpa Palden Dondrub
- Ten volumes of Zhuchen Paṇḍita
- Various collected works by Tsarchen and his disciples Ngawang Chodrag, Sangye Puntsog, Morchen, and Jamgon Kunga Lodro
- Thirteen volumes of the collected works of Jamyang Khyentse Wangpo

In addition, the monastic complexes that uphold the traditions of Sakya, Ngor, and Tsar contain various cycles that bring learning and practice to their fullness, exemplified by the following:[357]

- Kriyā tantra: the nine-deity maṇḍala of Amitāyus, Mañjuśrī "Thunderous Drumbeat," Akṣobhya, Uṣṇīṣavijayā, Vajravidāraṇā, and White Tārā
- Yoga tantra: Sarvavid Vairocana and Vajrapāṇi "Overpowering Death"
- Unsurpassed yoga tantra, the father tantras: Guhyasamāja Akṣobhya and Mañjuvajra; the mother tantras: Cakrasaṃvara in the Luipa and Vajraghaṇṭa traditions; the nondual tantras: Hevajra in the esoteric instruction tradition, Vajrapañjara, and Saṃpuṭa. These are known as the seven maṇḍalas of the Ngor tradition.
- Also, extensive sādhanas including the five-deity maṇḍala of Nairātmyā, the triad of the red and black Yamāntakas and Bhairava, the thirteen-deity maṇḍala of Bhairava, the ocean of ḍākinīs, the duo of Viśuddha and Vajrakīlāya, and glorious Kālacakra
- Also, torma exorcism rituals including Bhagavan Vajrabhairava and Vajramahākāla

• 9 •

Masters of the Nineteenth and Twentieth Centuries

Jamyang Khyentse Wangpo

THE WAY OF the Sage, the complete Dharma transmission of sūtra and mantra, was well established in the land of snows thanks to the translation, teaching, and meditation of lotsāwas, paṇḍitas, scholars, and practitioners.[358] The spoken transmissions of the profound precepts of the eight chariots of the practice lineage are as follows:

1. Nyingma
2. Kadam
3. Sakya
4. Marpa Kagyu
5. Shangpa Kagyu
6. The six yogas of Kālacakra
7. Zhije and Choyul
8. Orgyenpa's deity yoga of three vajras[359]

There was one person who was able to completely elucidate all of these teachings with his miraculous and unparalleled activities of teaching, practice, and ritual. He was a venerable wheel of the teachings clad in red robes, the crown ornament of every upholder of the teachings in the land of snows, the Dharma king of the three realms. He was raised to the pinnacle of the three worldly realms and celebrated under the name of Jamyang Khyentse Wangpo Kunga Tenpai Gyaltsen.

This saint was born at midday on the fifth day of the sixth month of the fourteenth iron-dragon year (1820) in a village called Sakhul Terlung Dilgo in the Derge area of Dokham. His father was Drungche Rinchen Wangyal of the Nyo family, and his mother was Sonam Tso of the Mugpodong family. He was born among numerous signs of virtue. Among the inner signs, he was born with the placenta wrapped around him like a Dharma robe and some kusha grass fashioned into a belt. He was born with lustrous reddish-brown hair. The outer signs attending his birth included a predawn light like the rising sun appearing in the house on the night before his birth, all the water in the house turning into milk, and miraculous rainbow-hued clouds appearing in the sky. That year the fruits of virtue became evident, including good living, pleasant times, and increasing wealth. The baby was given the name Tsering Dondrub, "long-lived and successful."

As a young child Khyentse Rinpoche saw that he was always under the protection of the Six-Armed Guardian and the Protectress of Mantra. He possessed the imprints of holiness, like great compassion, delighting in solitude, and playing at giving empowerments and teaching the Dharma. At the age of five he learned writing from his mother, and from his father he learned calligraphy and the black and white forms of astrology. With the medical scholar Tsewang Paljor, he completed the study of the medical tantras along with the esoteric instructions and practices. During the period in which he was allowed to practice medical science, he was so clearly of more benefit than any other doctor that it was said he had been blessed by Yutog Yonten Gonpo.[360]

Just before Ngor Tartse Khenchen Jampa Namkha Chime passed into nirvāṇa, while the prayers were being recited for his rebirth, he had said: "This Drung Rinchen Wangyal has a good character, so these prayers may be effective. If I were reborn as a child of his, it might be of some lasting benefit to the teaching and living beings." Later, when Khyentse Rinpoche was five he met Khenchen Jampa Kunga Tendzin at the family estate and acted as if he had known him for a long time. Based on this, Jampa Kunga Tendzin's nephew Khenchen Naljor Jampal Zangpo recognized Khyentse Rinpoche as the rebirth of the previous Ngor Tartse Khenchen and offered him the title and rank of abbatial candidate when he reached the age of twelve. Khenchen Kunga Tendzin gave him the name Jamyang Khyentse Wangpo Kunga Tenpai Gyaltsen, "Mañjuśrī, Lordly Pinnacle of Understanding, Blissful One, Victory Banner of the Teachings."[361]

At the age of seventeen Khyentse Rinpoche studied the three Sanskrit grammars *Kalāpa*, *Candra*, and *Sarasvatī*, as well as synonymy, poetics, and classical poetry with Zhechen Mahāpaṇḍita Gyurme Tutop Namgyal.[362] For his total understanding of etymology he was given the title Tsangse Gyepai Loden Dongdrug Gawai Langtso, "Happy Intelligent One, Joyful Youth of Six Faces."[363]

At the age of twenty, Khyentse Rinpoche traveled to Central Tibet to visit Ngor Monastery, where he received the precious oral instructions of the Lamdre explication for the assembly from the throne holder of Ngor, Naljor Jampal Zangpo. At the age of twenty-one, he went to Mindroling Monastery, where he was given full ordination, receiving the three vows in the presence of Khenchen Rigdzin Zangpo, thus becoming a fully ordained monk.

He then went on a pilgrimage as an itinerant mendicant, with just a single attendant, not just to all of the major and minor pilgrimage sites of Central Tibet, but as far as the borders of India and Bhutan as well. At the sacred meditation sites he practiced deity yoga and performed the associated feast offerings. During this pilgrimage Khyentse Rinpoche received Dharma teachings from many holy sages. He expended great effort in looking for rare and important textual transmissions, searching for the sacred objects of each particular place and replacing those that were missing. Thus he wandered, scorning hardship and weariness, for about three and a half years.

At the age of twenty-four he returned to Kham, where he went into retreat, practicing deity yoga, especially the root yogas of kriyā and caryā, Sarvavid Vairocana, and the basic service of glorious Hevajra.

At the age of twenty-seven he returned to Central Tibet again, spending about three years receiving Dharma teachings, primarily from his own Sakya tradition, and teaching extensively. During this period he also received again and again the vows of the two traditions of developing bodhicitta from Sakyapa Jamgon Dorje Rinchen, Khenchen Naljor Jampal Zangpo, Zhalupa Rinchen Losal Tenkyong, Zimwog Jampa Tendzin Nyendrag, Minling Trichen Sangye Kunga, and Jamgon Kongtrul Lodro Taye. At this time he received the name Lodro Gyatso Drima Mepai O, "Ocean of Intelligence, Stainless Light."

From Zimwogpa and Litang Geshe Jampa Puntsog, among others, he received the textual traditions of the philosophical vehicle, including the eighteen texts of great renown and the five books of virtuous scripture.[364]

He received the transmitted scriptures (*kama*) and treasures (*terma*) of the Nyingma early translations from the Minling Trichen, Zhechen Gyurme Tutop Namgyal, Khuwo Jigdral Choying Dorje, Jigme Gyalwai Nyugu, and Jamgon Kongtrul, among others.

He received the old and new Dharma cycles of the Kadam from Amdo

Dragom Zhabdrung Konchog Tenpa Rabgye, Sogpo Lhatsun Yeshe Dondrub, and others.

He received the complete empowerments, guidance manuals, and textual transmissions in all the classes of tantra found in Sakya, Ngor, and Tsar from Tartse Khenchen Dorje Chang Jampa Kunga Tendzin and his brother and from Zhalu Losal Tenkyong, Zimwog Jampa Tendzin Nyendrag, Ponlob Ngawang Legdrub, and others.

He received all of the extant lineages for the oral precepts for ripening and liberation in the four major and eight minor Kagyu schools from Karmapa Tegchog Dorje, Situ Pema Nyinje Wangpo, Jamgon Kongtrul, and others.

In particular, because he obtained the spoken transmissions of the eight great chariots—the lineages of accomplishment in Tibet—he was accepted as a disciple by the masters of all these Dharmas.

In short Khyentse Rinpoche received the reading transmissions for seven hundred volumes, when one adds together the various works of the different religious systems of Tibet, including the precious Kangyur of the Conqueror, the Collected Tantras of the Nyingma, the transmission lineages from the Tengyur, and the collected works of the great saints of the Old and New schools. He relied on five hundred tutors from U, Tsang, and Kham: vajra-wielding teachers, spiritual guides, and experts in the fields of science. Thus he spent thirteen human years dedicated to searching for texts. He received most of the traditions of the famed "ten great transmissions that support the teaching tradition,"[365] becoming a great holder of the vajra endowed with the three kinds of vow.

Doing nothing but studying day and night, he continually read and understood the entirety of the profound and extensive ways of the Dharma. He studied—without mixing them up—all of the individual traditions of religious systems, and in particular, the methods of deity meditation, the activities of the practical instructions, the secret topics of the esoteric instructions, the assertions of the philosophical systems, and the presentations of the basis, path, and fruit. He found the confidence that has no fear of the points of dispute and doubt, truly becoming a great spiritual guide.

At the age of thirty-three, in the iron-pig year (1851), he traveled to Dome and finally settled in Trashi Chime Drubpai Gatsal, where he had his own meditation cell. There he stayed on his meditation cushion. On the side of the New schools, he practiced Kālacakra, Saṃvara, and the

Khecarī of Nārotapa, all of which he had previously been granted. On the side of the Nyingma, he practiced the cycles of transmitted scriptures, primarily sūtra, illusion, mind, and space,[366] and the revealed treasures of the two supreme treasure revealers, primarily the trio of lama, perfection, and compassion.[367]

Beginning when he was very young, Jamyang Khyentse spent short periods, one after another, in retreat, amounting to a total of thirteen years. During these times, amid his practice, he studied the traditions of the eight chariots of the practice lineages—the fundamental texts of the development and perfection stages—along with a graduated study of key points of the complete corpus of the *Hundred Instructions* of Jetsun Drolchog Zhab, which gathers them all together, and he meditated to connect with the actual meaning of these teachings.[368] Thus he completed his study, contemplation, and meditation.

Most of the Dharma systems that he studied he then proceeded to teach several times. No matter how many times he had taught something, he never stopped and always treated it as a gift of the Dharma, meeting the needs of everyone, high and low, without having any self-interest about it. He placed most value on gathering together the scriptures and associated texts in order that none of the great Dharma treasures for striving and accomplishment should be lost to the hundreds of potential difficulties. In addition he rendered each sādhana complete by producing the appropriate handbooks and empowerment implements.

At the time when Khyentse Rinpoche had been appointed to the offical department that sat with the governer general of Derge, Gyalse Zhenpen Taye gathered together the transmitted teachings of the Nyingma and gave a copy of them to him. Then because Khyentse Rinpoche spread these teachings in the region of Palyul, they were disseminated there once again.[369] Then, thanks to the great efforts of Jamgon Kongtrul Pema Garwang in protecting and propagating the treasures, the Treasury of Precious Terma came into being, this collection, with the catalog, comprising exactly fifteen volumes.

As for the New schools, he collected together all of the pure lineages for the traditions connected with the four classes of tantra, the permissions and sādhanas, the textual transmissions for meditation and recitation, the blessings, the entrustments of mantras, and more. He put together eleven volumes, which became the "Compendium of Sādhanas: A Bountiful Source of Precious Accomplishments." He had copies of the volumes made to give away and taught them at least four times, thus spreading them far and wide. Later his close disciple Jamyang Loter Wangpo compiled a supplement of three volumes, resulting in an edition of fourteen volumes.

His close disciple, the Tartse abbot Jampa Kunga Tenpai Gyaltsen, formed the aspiration to compile a collection of the traditions of the great tantras of the kriyā, caryā, yoga, and unsurpassed yoga classes. He was supported in this by Ponlob Jamyang Loter Wangpo. They printed more than thirty volumes, based on oral advice and study notes connected with over seventy empowerment traditions of the great tantras, which were given to them by Khyentse Rinpoche himself.[370]

This venerable lama, through his powers of clairvoyance, received a message on the first month of the water-dragon year that it was important for him to spread the teachings. This became a major cause of his propagating the original teachings without the merest pause. As a gift of the Dharma he wrote the seven great volumes that are the heart of the twenty volumes compiled by Jamgon Kongtrul Lodro Taye. These cover the stages of instruction in the precepts of the eight chariots of the practice lineage.[371] These two noble lamas granted each other teachings many times, preserving the life-force of the teachings.

Among the sūtras, he looked throughout Kham, U, and Tsang for extant copies of original scriptures and commentaries by authenticated scholars and had them printed. These were then disseminated by his own students, scholars who were upholders of the scriptural collections. Thus the way that Khyentse Rinpoche left his imprint on the teachings for study and practice is truly unequaled.

Even more, he collected many volumes of whatever original scriptures he could gather, even in the field of ordinary sciences, and had them printed. It was thanks to this master that the college for the study of the sciences was established at Ngor, and he produced a number of brilliant textbooks for teaching the students there. In addition he collated into five small volumes the works, songs, and face-to-face precepts of learned and accomplished sublime sages from the Old and New schools without partiality. As this shows, he gathered together many different lineages. He made some minor corrections to the sūtra and tantra sections of the Derge Dharma king's printing blocks of the precious Kangyur.

His kindness in making it his sole intention to protect every surviving text of the whole of the teachings made it possible for those in search of the Dharma to receive whatever they wanted. For example, he kindly engaged in discussions—which were put down in writing—about adding new discoveries to the existing sections of the Collected Tantras of the Nyingma and the precious Tengyur.

As an auspicious outcome of his preserving and disseminating the fundamental teachings by means of observing the rules of the Vinaya, this master was appointed abbot of Ngor Monastery in the monkey year, having accepted this appointment the previous summer. He gave teachings on the texts of the three vows and later established a tradition of regular observance of the three foundations, as well as the study of the general and specific texts of the three vows, at numerous groups of monasteries, including his own, Dzongsar Trashi Lhatse.

He never ever collected donations through improper ways of making a living, like the village rituals that are practiced in the name of benefiting those who are to be trained. However, because he came to have the qualities of the three blazes and the three gatherings, he received material goods, even though he never strove for them.[372] With all of this, he never let even the slightest bit go to waste. As representations of the Buddha's body, he had two thousand statues made entirely from gold and copper. As representations of the Buddha's speech, he had nearly forty volumes printed, and if one adds together the manuscripts and the printed works, it comes to two thousand books. As representations of the Buddha's mind, he made over a hundred stūpas, including the great stūpa at Derge Lhundrub Teng. He built thirteen beautifully situated temples of various sizes in the same places and instituted regular offerings there.

Later, at those monasteries that had declined due to local problems, Khyentse Rinpoche gave over three thousand gifts of tea. Also, by entreating some of the great benefactors of the teachings, such as the royal ministers of the Dharma king of Derge, he had new repairs made to certain sites that had previously been restored, and he made donations to the endowments of monasteries. Through personal advice, he granted the kindness of spreading and propagating the Dharma to people to live in accord with the proper way of life. He made offerings to support the annual dedication of dhāraṇīs and mantras at these Dharma centers, donating a total of four thousand bricks of tea over the years.

In general, he attained stability in the two kinds of precious awakened mind. Specifically, he had a clear understanding of every philosophical system and an expansive devotion. Furthermore, since he never had any partiality or held any erroneous opinions, he was a great sage and an upholder of the Gelug, Sakya, Kagyu, and Nyingma schools. His countless students were completely nonsectarian, and included monks, hermits, those with little experience of Buddhism, and upholders of the Yungdrung Bon tradition.

From the age of thirty-three to seventy-three, thinking only of helping the teachings and sentient beings, Khyentse Rinpoche made a vow never to cross the threshold of his meditation room except for a few trips to other places. In that way he benefited the teachings and beings in inconceivable ways indistinguishable from the enlightened activities of a conqueror. At the age of seventy-three, on the morning of the twenty-first day of the first month of the fifteenth water-dragon year (1892), he spoke many auspicious words while scattering flowers, and then as he assumed the meditation posture, his bodily form was gathered into the mind-space of Vimalamitra. Furthermore, as it was prophesied, he simultaneously manifested five supreme emanations from the source of emanations at Wutaishan. This is how he performs, and continues to perform, an inconceivable number of activities to benefit the teachings and sentient beings.[373]

Loter Wangpo

Many students came to the great lama Jamyang Khyentse Wangpo. Among those who continued his enlightened work and aspirations in great waves, the best was Jamyang Loter Wangpo, a lord of secrets and a great vajra master who possessed an ocean of tantric teachings. He was born on a great estate at Samdrub Tse in the left horn of Tsang into the family line of the Minyag Siu kings. His father was Sangye Norbu, a relative of Yongdzin Paṇḍita Khenchen Palden Chokyi Gyaltsen, and his mother was Tsering Kyi. He was born amid wonderous omens at sunrise on the third day of the eleventh month of the fifteenth fire-sheep year (1847). With his karmic imprints activated, he made sacred gestures as if holding a vajra and bell.

From his sixth year Loter Wangpo was taught to write and understood it without any difficulty. In his ninth year he went to glorious Ewam Choden, the pure land of Akaniṣṭha on this earth. He had an audience with the Tartse Khenchen Jampa Kunga Tendzin and, offering a lock of his hair, received the complete vows of an upāsaka. He was given the name Tsultrim Gyatso, "Ocean of Moral Conduct."

After that, Loter Wangpo studied, was tested, and received the highest marks on the following works:

- The Ngor liturgical collections
- The "four smaller tantric texts"—the *Hevajra Tantra*, the *Little Tree*, the *Three Means*, and the *Three Vows*
- The "seven texts necessary for all"—the *Three Perceptions*, the *Three Continua*, the *Jewel Tree*, the *Classes of Tantra*, the *Tantra Fragments*, the *Overview*, and the *Commentary on the Hymn to Nairātmyā*[374]

When he was studying the great *Jewel Tree*, Loter Wangpo met with Jetsun Dragpa Gyaltsen in a dream and received a prophecy that he was under his special care.

When he came of age, Loter Wangpo had an audience with the all-knowing great abbot of Tartse, Jampa Kunga Tenpai Gyaltsen. From the abbot, with his paternal uncle Ponlop Namkha Gyaltsen acting as the ritual master, he received ordination in the full vows of a monk amid the whole monastic community. In addition the abbot himself gave Loter Wangpo a second special transmission, granting him the vows for generating supreme bodhicitta in line with both ritual methods: that of the Madhyamaka and that of the Cittamātra. He received the name Jamyang Loter Wangpo, "Mañjuśrī, lordly treasure of intellect," as well as the name Lodro Chokyi Nyima, "intelligent one, sun of the Dharma."

When Loter Wangpo received the ripening and liberating empowerment of the great sand maṇḍala of Hevajra endowed with the eight realizations, he swore to take great care of the three vows and always did so with great diligence.[375] He received most of the major texts from the scriptural collections from the all-knowing great abbot and from Khuna Sherab Gyatso, Jigme Palden, Jamgon Kontrul Rinpoche Yonten Gyatso, Mipam Senge Rabgye (the abbot of Tanak Tubten Namgyal), Tubten Chokyi Drakpa, and Jamgon Mipam Namgyal. These included:

- The three Sanskrit grammars: *Kalāpa*, *Candra*, and *Sarasvatī*
- Epistemology
- Formal logic
- Dharmakīrti's *Pramāṇavārttika*
- Sakya Paṇḍita's *Treasury of Logic* and *Distinguishing the Three Vows*
- Śāntideva's *Bodhicaryāvatāra*
- The five Dharmas of Maitreya

- Candrakīrti's *Madhyamakāvatāra*
- Śāntarakṣita's *Madhyamakālaṃkāra*

By studying these, he completely cut through all of his doubts. He relied on fourteen teachers, all of whom were vidyādharas, but the best were the three great beings unmatched in the snowy land of Tibet at that time: the all-knowing great abbot Jampa Kunga Tenpai Gyaltsen, the perfect buddha Lama Jamyang Khyentse Wangpo, and his student Jamgon Kongtrul Lodro Taye.

He crossed an ocean of learning in the tantras of the New schools, including the cycle of 315 empowerment transmissions, main and ancillary combined, of the vast and profound tantras. He received 150 guidance manuals, including the twenty-five great manuals of the Lamdre explication for the assembly and explication for disciples, and the hundred manuals of Jetsun Drolchog. For background, he received the complete Kangyur and Tengyur, as well as the collected works of many of the great Tibetan scholars and adepts, comprising 280 volumes of sūtra and tantra. He also received over a thousand permissions, main and ancillary combined, of which the most important was the Compendium of Sādhanas. He received the complete empowerments, guidance manuals, and textual transmissions of the Treasury of Precious Termas well as numerous transmissions of commentary on tantras including the *Kālacakra* and *Hevajra*. Meditating on the true meaning of what he had studied, he took it to heart.

When he reached his fifteenth year he received the experiential guidance for the Lamdre explication for disciples in the presence of the all-knowing great abbot over a period of six months. During the preliminaries—the *Three Appearances*—he cut through his conceptual elaborations. During the main practice—the *Three Continua*—he fully realized the view of the inseparability of saṃsāra and nirvāṇa. From that time onward, whether meditating or not, he no longer moved from the natural state. He also gained experience in the yoga of the channels and winds. In order to maintain the continuity of his practice, he undertook an eight-month retreat on Hevajra.

He practiced recitation texts such as Sarvavid Vairocana, Bhūtaḍāmara, the *Dragzongma*, and the three red cycles (*marpo korsum*) in a hundred different places. After he went to Kham he stayed in places like Dzongsar, Gagu, and Karmo Ritro, practicing the roots of the four classes of tantra, including:

- The outer, inner, and secret *Dragzongma* practice
- The preliminary Acala from the empowerment of the great class of tantra
- Amitāyus from the tradition of Machig Drubpai Gyalmo
- The general three families of kriyā tantra
- Viśuddhaprabhā
- Mahākaruṇika in the Nāgārjuna tradition
- Vairocana Abhisaṃbodhi
- Vajradhātu from the yoga tantra
- The two traditions of Guhyasamāja from the father unsurpassed yoga tantra
- Bhairava with thirteen attendants
- Saṃvara in the three traditions of Luipa, Kṛṣṇācārya, and Vajraghaṇṭa.
- The Khecarī of Nārotapa from the ultimate secret yoga (*Cakrasaṃvara Tantra*)
- The five tantra classes of the Shang tradition incorporating all buddha families
- Kālacakra from the nondual unsurpassed yoga tantras

And he also performed a strict retreat for the service of certain special deities from the Compendium of Sādhanas. He had many signs of attainment, such as seeing a vision of Tārā, being unharmed after he was struck by lightning, and possessing clairvoyance.

At the age of twenty-three, Loter Wangpo became the vajra master of the assembly at glorious Ewam Choden. In this role he behaved in a way suitable to an exemplar of the teachings. In general, he always behaved in accord with the three vows of the textual tradition and with the intention of the rules established by Ngorchen Dorje Chang and Muchen Konchog Gyaltsen. In particular, he arranged the rules for all of the detailed practices of the ritual manuals, especially the group sādhana practice.[376] Because he was always at either Sakya or Ngor monasteries, he established a new tradition of teaching the Dharma in the summer. He increased both the community of monks and the religious wealth of Ngor, causing the teachings to spread far and wide.

At one time Tartse Khenchen Jampa Kunga Tenpai Gyaltsen called this master into his presence and conferred on him the monastic regulations and guidance and also suggested that it would be good if he were to take on the responsibility of arranging the empowerment rituals. The abbot himself had previously composed a work called the *Hundred Empowerments: A Beautiful Garland of Jewels*, a catalog bringing together all of the extant lineages connected with the eight great chariots that came to Tibet from India.

Tartse Khenchen said that he had received various symbolic indications that he would not be granted a long life and therefore it was important that Loter Wangpo rely on someone with qualities like those of Jamyang Khyentse.[377] He also graced and honored Loter Wangpo with a prophecy that he would be a compiler of the Buddha's words in the precious tantras. Bestowing the great gift of the Buddha's words, the abbot entrusted Loter Wangpo through empowerments with the vajra treasury of the great secret.

When he was twenty-eight, Loter Wangpo was appointed abbatial candidate of the Tartse residence. He undertook the task of traveling to Kham to take responsibility for Lhundrub Teng Monastery, which had been a gift to the Sakyapas from the great Dharma king of Derge.[378] He traveled the northern route by way of Nangchen and then arrived at Ga Kyegu Dondrup Ling, where he introduced the practice of the three ceremonies to most of the monasteries in the region. He satisfied monks and laypeople alike by gifts of the Dharma, such as a detailed explanation of the *Bodhicaryāvatāra*.

On an auspicious day of the third month of the water-pig year (1863), Loter Wangpo arrived at the royal palace of Lhundrub Teng in Derge. After that he traveled to Ringmin Dzongsar Trashi Lhatse, where he met the great lama Jamyang Khyentse Wangpo. At once a fierce feeling of devotion arose within Loter Wangpo, and he requested the bestowal of ripening and liberation. Jamyang Khyentse Wangpo accepted Loter Wangpo from the depths of his heart. He established an auspicious connection by initially giving teachings like the permissions of the three white ones.[379]

After that Loter Wangpo traveled on to Derge Lhundrub Teng, where he was made abbot and established anew the practice of the three foundations. Every fortnight during the summer he alternated between teaching first Guṇaprabha's *Vinaya Sūtra* and then Maitreya's *Abhisamayālaṃkāra* to the monks who stayed there for the summer. Then at the behest of his lama he traveled on to Tromtar. At the meditation center there he wrote a new ritual manual for the three foundations, and for four months he taught a crowd of a thousand people the experiential guidance for the explication for disciples. Such was the extent of the great waves of his enlightened activity. He acted as a doctor for beings and the teachings, for example giving the reading transmission for the Kangyur at the Dzingpo Dzong meditation center.

One of the most important achievements of this master was his collection of the scriptures of the precious tantras. This is how he did it. When he received the empowerment of the seven maṇḍalas of the Ngor tradition at the feet of Jamyang Khyentse Wangpo, he saw that the monastic community of lamas who were responsible for these sādhana practices had a great need for such a collection. So he began, feeling as if he were fulfilling a prophecy.

He made excellent offerings, like representations of the body, speech, and mind of the Buddha to those lined up to receive the empowerments, and he said: "In the recent past this meditation center has had excellent auspicious connections for receiving the empowerments. As a next step, it is important to copy each and every ritual manual for the empowerments of the Ngor tradition in clearly legible writing."

"Has the time now come," he wondered, "to implement the wishes of Tartse Khenchen?" He decided that it had and applied himself earnestly to the task. He thought, "When I first looked upon the catalog called the *Hundred Empowerments: A Beautiful Garland of Jewels*, I was filled with the greatest joy. If I compiled a catalog like this one, gathering together in one place all of the tantras drawn from the traditions of the eight chariots, it would fulfill the intentions of the lama. As well as being extremely valuable for the general and specific teachings of the Conqueror, it would more especially be a fulfillment of a prophecy, like taking hold of the vase of the enlightened mind."

Loter Wangpo made polite requests to those who had previously received the empowerments of these tantras, and as a result, in the water-sheep year (1883) he was kindly granted the forty great empowerment cycles connected with the four classes of tantra. This was the beginning. At subsequent occasions he was granted other empowerments, so that altogether he received seventy tantras, vast and profound and miraculous in their rarity. In the presence of Jamgon Kongrul Rinpoche, Loter Wangpo was granted, to his great joy, all of the tantras he needed from the traditions of Marpa, Ngog, Jonang, and others.

Later, since Loter Wangpo had still not finished the work on the actual collection, he made an offering of all the volumes he had gathered to the image of Dzing Namgyal Gonpo Yeshepa that was erected by the Dharma lord and nephew, after which he reached a new peak of productivity. Such things gave him a steadfast courage and the confidence to complete his work. There was also the force of the strict injunctions from those who had encouraged him in his work like Tartse Khenchen, and the marvelous fact of the relationship—which was like the connection of the sun with the moon—between Loter Wangpo and his lord, Lama Jamyang Khyentse Wangpo, the great source of answers to which he put questions about topics of which he was in doubt.

Thanks to excellent opportunities like these, whatever difficulties arose, his deep feeling that the lama and his personal deity were one and the same was the inspiration that turned those difficulties around, and he would think, "This is just my own uncertainty." Wanting to protect the profound secrets of the tantras from the proud and arrogant who rashly disputed them, he combined the armor of a steadfast attitude with the strength of a warrior, and in the year of the iron-horse (1870) he began the actual editing of the collection.

Another excellent circumstance was provided by the Tripiṭaka master Tubten Legshe Zangpo, who wrote a compilation of ritual manuals based on the glorious Vajradhātu maṇḍala. Loter Wangpo arranged the liturgies in just the same way that the great founders of the tantric traditions had done. Though there was nothing important that this master's understanding could not penetrate, he was still in doubt about some minor points. When he enquired about these to the lord Jamyang Khyentse Wangpo and Kongtrul Lodro Taye, they gave him confidence.[380] The fact that he did not renege on his original promise to compile this collection is due to the nature of these two sublime sages.

In this way he constantly maintained the strength of his painstaking efforts, his kindness and wisdom that could not be interrupted by any external force, a support that was like a host of troops, and within five years he had finished the majority of the sādhanas, maṇḍalas, empowerments, and ritual manuals. Furthermore, the lamas said that it was important to be sure that each of these guidance manuals, most importantly the Lamdre, was put in its proper place. When they bestowed upon Loter Wangpo the guidance manuals and textbooks in succession, he arranged them in the same order.

When Loter Wangpo understood from his venerable lama Khyentse Wangpo that he was the rebirth of Tartse Paṇchen, he gave a vase of immortality, which is the same as a long-life empowerment, to Khyentse Wangpo, saying that he wanted to create the auspicious connections for him to live to the same age as Paṇchen Namkha Palzang, who had lived to the age of seventy-five.[381] Throughout his life he performed enlightened activities like these. In particular he wanted to create great waves of teachings on the tantras, and so when he was granted the extraordinary blessings he needed for the accomplishment of power and expansion, he made a vow of kindness to arrange for those texts to be printed.

He tended this aspiration little by little, traveling wherever he needed to. Thus this master naturally accumulated all of the prerequisites of a teacher, such as the qualities of learning, discipline, and excellence, the auspicious condition of being free from attachment to material things, and the activity of protecting the teachings. Every material donation, great and small, was filtered through his vow, and he used them for whatever was needed for the achievement of the first printing of his great Dharma gift of the precious tantras.

In the ten years between the bird year and the horse year (1873–82), he funded the production of thirty volumes, spending, without any sense of loss, five thousand ounces of silver. He achieved this, a great treasury of Dharma acting as a lamp in this dark age equal to the abundance provided by the vidyādharas of past times, without hindrance. He also commissioned 315 maṇḍala paintings, with the figures and backgrounds elaborately designed according to the specific customs of each of these empowerments, mounted on the finest silk, along with the necessary ritual implements, made to a high standard from 1,500 ounces of silver.

In the iron-hare year (1891) he went to a meditation center and committed himself to performing further recitation practices from the tantras. After practicing recitation throughout the year, the noble lama, beginning on the twenty-fifth day of the first month of the water-dragon year (1892), decided that he needed to expand his teachings on ripening and liberation in the tantras. Motivated by the fact that he had not studied the yogatantra cycles, he committed himself to the practice of the appropriate scriptures containing indirect teachings like physical deportment, protective prayers, and aspirations. As he completed the recitations very quickly, he also performed the supplementary practices correctly, including the fire ritual.

Then, staying focused on the essence of the teachings, in the waxing-moon period of the first month, he traveled to his lama's seat, the monastery of Dzongsar Trashi Lhatse. As his precious lama was unwell at that time, he offered to perform all the appropriate prayers for long life, but Khyentse Rinpoche would not accept this and, on the twenty-first of that month, withdrew from his visible body. With great devotion Loter Wangpo paid reverence to the precious remains, including the cremated remains that were offered to vajra students.

Later that year, in the waning-moon cycle, starting on the holy day of the gathering of the ḍākinīs, he made the beginning virtuous by giving thirty major empowerments of the precious tantras starting with the three families that are the most important part of the virtuous kriya tantras. He made the middle virtuous by giving an extensive teaching on the *Hevajra Tantra* based on the four modes.[382] And he made the end virtuous with the empowerment of the supreme deities of immortality.[383] The final ornament was his teaching on the three types of life enhancement.

He bestowed these upon a constant stream of upholders of the Sakya and Ngorpa teachings, endowed with qualities of learning and realization, from the districts of Gato, Dragyab, Chamdo, Trehor, Litang, and Derge, including the head tutor of glorious Sakya, Nangchen Tsangda Purpa Lama Rinpoche. Thus, by the holy day of the descent of the divine ruler, everything was done without the slightest problem from the point of view of the five auspicious circumstances.[384]

When Khenchen Jamyang Rinchen Dorje had come to visit Jamyang Khyentse Wangpo in the previous year, the latter had instructed him to come back to Dzongsar in the first month of the following year. In accord with this, Jamyang Rinchen Dorje arrived while the funeral service was taking place. So, while Loter Wangpo was practicing the funeral rituals and teaching the yogatantra cycles, this Khenchen granted Loter Wangpo the empowerments in stages. This had clearly been the intention behind Jamyang Khyentse Wangpo's instructions. This kind of thing shows that he received his learning and special realization from Mañjuśrī himself.

In this way, through the kindness of his teacher, Loter Wangpo ensured that precious teachings on the Vajrayāna secret mantra that were close to disappearing in this degenerate age would remain for a long time hence. Following the wishes and intentions of his lamas, he acted with concentration, clarity, and thoroughness, purely for the benefit of the precious teachings. Fulfilling the teachings that were given to him, he was an ideal disciple. He cleared away all hardships with the small waves of his understanding, was faultless in all aspects of ritual practice, and was a gateway for many who entered the mantra path. Just one thing was inscribed in his heart: the needs of the teachings and sentient beings. Through his compassion he liberated those who had faith in him, preventing them from falling into the abyss of broken vows.

The way that he went about creating the precious Compendium of All Tantras is comparable to the work of the great Jonang Jetsun Kunga Drolchog, the precious Toyon Lhatsun Dondrub Gyaltsen, and the omniscient Drangti Khenchen Jampa Kunga Tenpai Gyaltsen. Beginning with the maṇḍalas of the three families of the kriyā tantras, he took the maṇḍala rituals that were spread far and wide by the five learned and accomplished patriarchs and essentialized them beautifully for daily practice, clarifying anything that was unclear. Where the order of a practice was disrupted, he studied it and restored the order.

With the master of the scriptures Tubten Legshe Zangpo, Kyoda Drula Ngawang Chodzin, and the teacher of Nangchen Tsanda, Khedrub Gyatso, he appointed scribes and organized the printing boards and model pages. With the learned Zhuchen Lhagsam Tenpai Gyaltsen (who had been an attendant of the noble lama), Jamyang Legpai Lodro, the intelligent and lucid Konchog Gyaltsen, Puntsog Gyaltsen, and the lord of scholars Dragyab Dongkam Trichen Ngawang Damcho Gyatso, he carried out an editing project comparable with that of Tumi Sambhoṭa, one of the great chariots of the Dharma in the land of snows.

In his last testament, the venerable lama Jamyang Khyentse had advised that it was important for his students and others to convene a council for augmenting the collection of the precious Compendium of Sādhanas. In the earth-pig year (1899), Jamgon Kongtrul Lodro Taye and Loter Wangpo met for a discussion. Agreeing on the need for a supplement to the collection, Loter Wangpo began with the liturgical arrangements. Jamgon Kongtrul arranged these into a supplement in fifteen sections, and Loter Wangpo added an appendix in sixty sections. These were combined with some other works by the venerable master Jamyang Khyentse Wangpo and arranged in a set of five volumes. In accordance with the wishes of Jamyang Khyentse, they then commissioned a fourteen-volume manuscript copy of the complete Compendium of Sādhanas.

Furthermore, Loter Wangpo aided the flow of the teachings immensely by commissioning printing blocks of the Lamdre explication for one disciple, including a new method for teaching it, collected into fourteen volumes. On the sūtra side, he composed interlinear commentaries on Madhyamaka, Prajñāpāramitā, Sapaṇ's *Treasury of Logic*, and Vasubandhu's *Abidharmakośa*, which are known as the "four lamps." Thus the rain of Dharma fell everywhere. In various places, such as Kyegu Dondrub Ling, he taught the precious Compendium of All Tantras five times, the precious Compendium of Sādhanas four times, and the secret Lamdre explication for disciples four times. In short, his range of activities was almost inconceivable, as if the spheres of study, renunciation, and action were vying with each other for victory. His was a life of marvels, of upholding, protecting, and propagating the teachings of the precious Sakyapas, the masters of the teachings in the land of snows.

This then is how this master accomplished vast benefit for the teachings and sentient beings. Having helped those who had the good fortune to be his students, it was time to go on to other things. The flow of his teaching came to an end. After sitting in the meditation posture for two days, calm and smiling, he showed how one establishes the rūpakāya, passing into the space of great peace, the immaculate empty sky. It was the second month of the wood-tiger year (1914), and he was in his sixty-eighth year.

At this time everyone who was present witnessed things like the sky being filled with rainbows and a pervasive fine fragrance. After five days had elapsed, the remains naturally dissolved into relics, which were placed in a *kaṭora*, without anything being left over.[385] When it was placed on the pyre, it glowed like fire, and only a small amount of kindling was needed.

Loter Wangpo had students beyond count. Among the best of them were: Ngor Ewampa Pankhang Khenchen Jampa Palden Chodze, the regent of the excellent lama Tubwang Dorje Chang; Tartse Khenchen Jamyang Kunzang Tenpai Gyaltsen; Khangsar Khenchen Dorje Chang Ngawang Lodro Zhenpen Nyingpo; the supreme emanation Trinle Nampar Rolpa Jamyang Chokyi Lodro; Dulwa Dzinpa Chenpo Jamyang Gyaltsen, a mass of qualities of learning and realization; Jetsunma Pema Trinle Wangmo, from the noble Khon lineage; Litang Betsang Choje Khyenrab Gyatso; Kaḥtog Mahāpāṇḍita Situ Chokyi Gyatso; the logician Jamyang Khyenrab Taye; the great scholar and adept Dezhung Chogtrul Rinpoche Kunga Gyaltsen; the strong and powerful lord Khenpo Samten Lodro.

The all-knowing lama Jamyang Khyentse Wangpo and the master of the ocean of tantras Jamyang Loter Wangpo were like father and son, and their kindness was beyond imagining. It was due to this factor alone that the empowerments, permissions, and instructions from the systems of the eight great chariots, the lineages of accomplishment in Tibet, could all be taught to devoted students in a single place, at a single time, by a single teacher. It was the dawn of a new golden age. Since that time, among the students of these two masters who held the lineages of an ocean of scriptures and the students of those students, there has been an uncountable number of great sages upholding the teachings.

Gaton Ngawang Legpa

One of the close students who studied at the feet of Jamyang Khyentse Wangpo was the great lama Gaton Dorje Chang Ngawang Legpa Rinpoche, one of the great upholders of the teaching of the glorious Sakyapas and the crown ornament of all the upholders of the hearing lineage. He was accepted as the rebirth of Kar Śākya Drag, Drungchen Tsultrim Gyaltsen (the rebirth of the paṇḍita and adept Smṛtijñāna and student of Ga Rabjampa Chokyi Gyalpo Kunga Yeshe), Khyabdag Gorumpa Kunga Legpai Jungne, Sangye Palzang (the great abbot of Ngor Ewam), and Jamyang Ngawang Legdrub (the vajra preceptor of Ngor Ewam). According to a prophecy of Chime Dorje, a treasure revealer from Litang Yonru, he was also an emanation of Jamgon Sakya Paṇḍita; this information about the lama was conveyed to me by Tulku Anjam Rinpoche.[386]

Gaton Ngawang Legpa was born in a town called Game Dzinda, in the Drida Zalmogang region of Dokham, in the fourteenth male wood-mouse year (1864). While he was still being nurtured in his mother's lap, unable to crawl, visions illuminated his mind. This is said to be the result of cultivating śamatha in previous lives. When he was a child, he awoke to the lineage of sublime beings. In the presence of Ngawang Shedrub Gyatso, a great being who had renounced everything, he learned to read and received various empowerments and instructions.

When he reached age nine, he offered a lock of hair from the crown of his head to the abbot of Ngor Pende. He was given the religious name Tsultrim Gyaltsen, "victory banner of morality," which he said seemed particularly apt. He obtained the causal empowerment of the estoeric instruction tradition of glorious Hevajra, which he said was the beginning of his spiritual maturity.[387] In his eleventh year he received the recitation practice of Vajrapāṇi "Overcoming the Demons" along with the fire ritual.

In his sixteenth year he received the blessing of the Khecarī of Nārotapa, the cycle of empowerments, blessings, and permissions for Vajra Mahākāla Guardian of the Tent, and the complete set of outer, inner, and secret instruction manuals from Jampal Tendzin Trinle. When he was being given the recitation practice for Dragzongma from the Vajra Guardian of the Tent cycle, the torma that he left for the tutelary deity grew black hair like yak's hair, many spans in length, and when he looked at the sun's rays, they became five-colored rainbow lights. He said that the book of the Black Strongman teaches that these are signs of the unlimited accomplishment of all the four kinds of activity by means of this female protector.

In his eighteenth year he traveled to central Tibet. At Ngor Ewam Choden, in the presence of Chetsun Dorje Chang Ngawang Lodro Nyingpo, the fifty-eighth abbot and regent of the great Dorje Chang Kunga Zangpo, he received the complete ripening and liberating empowerments for the oral instructions of the Lamdre explication for the assembly. When he was nineteen he took up the full monastic vows, receiving the three stages of ordination one at a time. Following that, his tongue never touched meat or alcohol, he would not accept food after noon, and he was never without his three Dharma vestments, sitting mat, and water sieve. In this way he flawlessly practiced the behavior prescribed in the Vinaya.

That year he stayed in Ngor Monastery, putting off returning to his homeland. Over the summer the abbot bestowed on him the complete set of empowerments for the forty-five maṇḍalas of the Vajramālā, the empowerments for the four spoken transmissions of Hevajra, and the ripening empowerment of Vajrabhairava, among others. The lord of scholars Khuna Chogtrul Jamyang Sherab Gyatso gave him various empowerments, blessings, permissions, and instruction manuals for the development and perfection stages of the Lamdre and cut through his doubts like moonbeams and sunrays. He spoke of the great kindness of this teacher, as the one who established his understanding of the oral instructions of the Lamdre.

Then he went to Sakya, where he met the great throne-holder Jigme Wangyal along with his family and disciples. He studied Guṇaprabha's *Vinaya Sūtra* with the great abbot of the Tubten Lakhang, Jampa Cho Trashi, and Rabjam Sherab Chopel taught him *Three Vows: The Ornament of the Guru's Intention*. On the way back to his homeland, he stopped in Lhasa to see for the first time the religious objects there, especially the Jowo Śākyamuni statue, which is like a wish-granting jewel.

As Gaton's mind was absorbed with the thought of studying with the famous Khyentse Wangpo, Mañjuśrī in person, he went to Derge on two separate occasions, carrying his baggage on his back. In the presence of that master, he twice obtained the vow for developing bodhicitta from the lineages of the profound view and vast activity.[388] He also obtained the blessing of Vajrayoginī, the Khecarī of Nārotapa, and several complete collections of profound instruction manuals for the development and perfection stages. At various points he also received a total of ninety-five empowerments, blessings, and entrustments of knowledge from Jamgon Kongtrul Lodro Taye.

He studied Tumi's *Basic Grammar in Thirty Verses* and *Guide to Signs* with Jamyang Legpai Lodro, Kamalaśīla's *Madhyamakāloka* with Minyag Khepa Norbu Tendzin, and Śāntideva's *Bodhicaryāvatāra* with the abbot of Dzongsar Monastery, Yonten Lhundrub. He received the complete Compendium of Sādhanas, excluding the supplementary volumes from the Dharma master of Ngari, Kunga Jamyang.

At various times, when he was living in his homeland, he studied the complete *Kalāpa* system, three chapters of Daṇḍin's *Kāvyādarśa*, and Ratnākaraśānti's *Chandoratnākara* with the upholder of the tradition of Ganden, Odzong Geshe Lozang Jinpa. At Kyegu Monastery in Ga, in the presence of Tartse Khenchen Jamyang Rinchen Dorje, he received the precious oral instructions of the Lamdre explication for disciples. And he received many profound teachings from Dezhung Tulku Nyendrag Lungrig Nyima, Drubtson Kunga Cholha (a practitioner of Khecarī from Tridu Kalzang Monastery), Khetsun Chodrag Gyatso, and others. In the intervals between receiving teachings, he propitiated many yidams, including Hevajra, Khecarī, and White Tārā.

From the year of the iron-mouse (1900), when he was thirty-seven, he took a vow of seclusion to spend fifteen full years in retreat. He remained in silence, took donations of food and drink through a window, and used all of the butter given by his family for offerings rather than putting any of it in his mouth. With such hardships he spent three years practicing the *Three Perceptions*, the prelimary practices of the oral instructions of the Lamdre. After that he meditated on impermanence for twelve months and spent twelve years practicing the *Three Continua*, the main practices of the Lamdre.

He used to say that the preliminary practices were even more profound than the main practices. In accord with that, he took refuge 2.4 million times, recited the hundred-syllable mantra 1.8 million times, and offered the seven-heap maṇḍala one million times. In particular, he sat in front of a life-size painting of Sakya Paṇḍita that he had commissioned, and with this supreme focus for his practice of generating compassion and aspiration, he recited the *Shejama* verse 41 million times, prostrating himself with each verse.[389]

He was taken into the care of the great lama Sakya Paṇḍita in his wisdom body (*jñānakāya*), and visions of other well-known figures came to him in his waking experience and in dreams: the lord of yogins Virūpa, Jetsun Dragpa Gyaltsen, Ngor Dorje Chang, and the Guardian of the Tent. In particular, the great Vajra Mahākāla always protected him with compassion and accomplished enlightened activities for him. He recited the seven-syllable heart mantra of the Guardian of the Tent over 800,000 times, the *śāsana* root mantra 2.2 million times, the ten-syllable mantra of White Tārā a million times, the longer mantra of Tārā 8 million times, and the *maṇi* mantra 10 million times.

At the age of fifty-two, in the year of the wood-rabbit, he left his retreat to confer the Compendium of Sādhanas at the monastic seat of Tarlam. At the age of fifty-four he completed one recitation of the complete oral instructions of the explication for disciples and then traveled to Dezhung Monastery in Litang, where he arranged a feast of Dharma, with the explication for disciples at its center. All in all, he went to Dezhung four times and Derge three times. Because he had been invited to Trehor Nyadrag Monastery and the monasteries of Minyag, he traveled to Ngor, breaking his journey at Dartsedo, where he conferred the precious explication for disciples three times as well as empowerments, blessings, permissions, and manuals for numerous sādhanas.

He forged a Dharma connection with tens of thousands of ordinary male and female householders, showing them how to rouse themselves to virtue by promising to recite the six syllables more than 500 million times—thus planting the seed of liberation in the mindstreams of many beings. In order that the gifts that he received from disciples and benefactors did not go to waste, he established a new garden in the great temple of Tubten Dongag Cho at the monastic seat of Tarlam Ganden Sazang Ling.

He commissioned three richly ornamented interior statues of the supreme teachers Śākyamuni, Sapaṇ, and Ngorchen. They were skillfully and beautifully made, graceful in appearance and pleasing to the eye. Gaton carried out an auspicious consecration ceremony with aspiration prayers. At this monastery he continuously performed the sādhanas of the seven maṇḍalas of the Ngor tradition. In the protectors' chapel, he practiced the recitation of Hevajra during the four periods between dawn and dusk, and in the intervals, he performed two rituals of amendment. Three times during this period he bestowed bountiful ceremonial offerings upon the monks. Such were the ways that in his great kindness, he took care of both Dharma and material needs.

Among his students, the two peerless sons of his heart and supreme upholders of the teachings were Jamyang Chokyi Lodro Rime Tenpai Gyaltsen Palzangpo (the rebirth of Jamyang Khyentse Wangpo) and the master of learning and accomplishment, Dezhung Chogtrul Anjam Rinpoche. There were also many accomplished monks and nuns, learned and accomplished spiritual guides who obtained the whole of the precious oral instructions of the Lamdre, foremost among whom were the two holders of the post of Ngor Ewam Tartse Khenchen as well as the abbot of Dzongsar college Khyenrab Chokyi Ozer, Khenpo Lodro Gyaltsen, Khenpo Jamyang Kunga Namgyal, and from Kyegu Monastery Khenpo Ngaga and Trinle Chopel. Also several abbots, including the great abbot of Ngor Khangsar, Dorje Chang Ngawang Lodro Zhenpen Nyingpo, as well as Ngawang Khedrub Gyatso (the great abbot of Pende) and Ngawang Yonten Gyatso (the great abbot of Khangsar).

His students came from the three realms of U, Tsang, and Kham and included most of the upholders of the Sakya teachings of those times, such as the precious abbot of the great temple at Derge, Ngawang Samten Lodro, and the unparalleled lama Jamyang Gyaltsen. Also included were upholders of the Kagyu teachings, such as Palpung Situ Rinpoche Pema Wangchog Gyalpo, Gyalse Khyentse Ozer (the rebirth of the great Kongtrul), and Karma Chokyi Senge (the rebirth of Minyang Dugkar). Upholders of the long tradition of the early translations, the Nyingma, were also included, such as the great illuminator of the teachings Khenchen Zhenpen Chokyi Nangwa and Sekhar Chodrag. Also among his students were upholders of the teachings of Ganden, including Ngarig Khyenpa Odzong Geshe Lozang Jinpa and the great Geshe Lozang Chokyi Gawa.

Thus, having carried out the three activities of an accomplished teacher, in the sixteenth year of the iron-snake (1941) at the age of seventy-eight, on the afternoon of the twenty-ninth day of the third month, Gaton Ngawang Legpa went amid miraculous signs to the land of bliss like someone fulfilling a promise made long ago. His close students and patrons made donations toward erecting a monument to his achievements.

Khenchen Dampa

Our own sublime root lama was the great abbot of glorious Ewam Khangsar, Ngawang Lodro Zhenpen Nyingpo, a close disciple who sat at the feet of Lord Loter Wangpo. He was truly the conqueror Vajradhara endowed with the three characteristics in the form of a saffron-robed monk. He came from the important clan of Nub, the source of many accomplished mantrins, and was born in Rong Mentang in the fifteenth year of the fire rat (1876). He was enthroned as the abbatial candidate of the Khangsar residence at Ngor Ewam Choden, where he completed the memorization of the seven texts that were required of everyone in the Ewam tradition and practiced the ritual manuals. He received the three vows by the kindness of the great abbot of Khangsar, Ngawang Lodro Nyingpo, and became his close disciple.

Due to the strength of the renunciation and precious bodhicitta that he had possessed from the time he was a small boy, all of his activities were similar to the accounts of those of the noble ones who reside on the great bhūmis. As this was clear to everyone, he came to be known as Zhabdrung Dampa Rinpoche, "the sublime and precious abbatial candidate." By this time he was truly a noble one, and among the upholders of the teachings of Sakya and Ngor he was like a moon among the stars.

Among the class of miscellaneous writings by this master, there is a kind of supplication prayer that seems to be unfinished and lacks a colophon. Since it contains supplications to Virūpa, Kukkuripa, Dampa Sangye, Sachen Kunga Nyingpo, and Tangtong Gyalpo, I am certain that he was an emanation of all of these great sages.

When he was a young man, the Khangsar residence was extremely short of funds, so he had to travel on horseback around Kham in order to collect offerings. During this period he met Dzogchen Khenpo Zhenga Rinpoche, and during his visit they talked about the views and practices of the Sakyapas. Since the master had not had any spare time to study the textual traditions since he was a boy, he was unable to offer precise replies to Khenpo Zhenga's questions, and this made him unhappy.[390]

He thought that, whether or not he could carry out his duties to the

Khangsar residence, the most important thing was to practice in accordance with the precious teachings of the Conqueror, having previously heard and contemplated them. Thus he decided that it was imperative that he become a student of this lord of scholars and asked to be accepted as his disciple.

Khenpo Zhenga said, "Since you were sent by your residence to gather offerings, go and gather offerings. You wouldn't be able to endure the hard work and asceticism of hearing and contemplating." Nevertheless, Khenchen Dampa earnestly made his request again, and finally Khenpo Zhenga gave his consent. Then Khenchen Dampa asked his two brothers, the abbatial candidate at Ling Gotse and Dragra Dorje Chang, for permission to study, giving them the reasons for this wish. The brothers replied, "If you study while you are still young in years, it is entirely feasible. We will organize whatever provisions you need. It will be no problem to send you the residence's yearly offering, whether it's large or small." At this, Khenchen Dampa's heart filled with joy. He made his preparations, including the necessary religious provisions, and with an entourage of a few servants and horses, left for Dzogchen.

Meanwhile Khenpo Zhenga had been teaching his students in the rocky cliffs above Dzogchen Monastery. The night before Khenchen Dampa's arrival, Khenpo Zhenga Rinpoche had a dream. He saw five women all of different colors, ornamented with jewels and holding vases in their hands. With one voice they said:

> The three vehicles and the four philosophical schools,
> the four classes of tantra and their subdivisions,
> all phenomena without exception, identical with reality itself:
> this is the sphere of activity of a great noble one who resides on
> the great bhūmi.

The next morning he said, "The signs in my dream are not about me. Today someone will come to me as a new student. He will certainly be a noble one who resides on the great bhūmi." Just so, Khenchen Dampa did arrive at Dzogchen, where he met Khenpo Zhenga Rinpoche. Later, when Khenchen Dampa had become the throne-holding abbot of Ewam Choden, he allowed a long-life prayer to be composed for him by Zhenga Rinpoche based on these prophetic vajra verses of the ḍākinīs.

Khenchen Dampa himself said:

> Before my horse had reached the cliffs, three pack animals and a guide came to meet me from Dzogchen meditation center as if it had been previously arranged. When I saw smoke rising from the extremely high cliffs, the guide said, "Lama Zhenga and his students are staying at that gap between the rocks." When we had gone a little farther, I heard a sound like a thighbone trumpet. They were using the horn of a *kṛṣṇasāra* deer, which they used instead of a conch shell for the incense procession in which the lama grants monk robes to a disciple and for Dharma lectures. This was the sound with which they welcomed me, and as soon as I met them, I felt an undivided devotion toward the lama and his students, and I was inconceivably happy.

He also said:

> When I read books, I read as much I could with great enthusiasm. At night I used to read books by lamplight, and when the light became too dim to see by, I just looked in the direction of the book until daybreak. I had that experience many times. I reflected upon each verse of Sapaṇ's *Treasury of Logic* for seven days. Such was my training.

Dezhung Chogtrul Anjam Rinpoche, Gapa Lama Jamyang Gyaltsen, Kunga Lodro, and his own brother all advised Khenchen Dampa to study Pramāṇa with great diligence.[391]

Zhenga Rinpoche had a little amulet made of ivory. One of his personal students, called Serkhar Chodrag, once asked him, "You have gathered so many students from Ngari in the west to Dartsedo in the east—do you have some kind of magical charm inside that precious amulet?" Lama Zhenga, who always called Khenchen Dampa by the name "Kusho Rinpoche," replied, "If you were to say that Kusho Rinpoche has acted as a magical charm, you wouldn't be wrong. Apart from his coming here, I haven't any magical charms."[392]

Not long after the Khamje college Shedrub Dargyeling was founded by Jamyang Khyentse Chokyi Lodro, there was a time when all sorts of obstacles arose for the students there. Khenchen Dampa prayed to the four-faced guardian, saying, "Let there be no obstacles at the college." Immediately after this every sort of obstacle was pacified, and the practices of study and teaching increased immensely. When Dezhung Chogtrul Anjam Rinpoche asked, "What is the name of that master?" Jamyang Khyentse Chokyi Lodro placed his hand on Khenchen Dampa's head and said, "This is the great adept Dampa Rinpoche."

Both within and without, Khenchen Dampa's house was always pervaded by the sweet fragrance of moral conduct, and wherever he had been, a sweet fragrance was noticed for a long time afterward. Many such signs of his holiness became generally known. Throughout his life, he possessed an unhindered clairvoyance and gave unerring prophecies.

From masters such as Jamyang Loter Wangpo and Dragra Jamyang Chokyi Nyima he received and meditated upon many empowerments, textual transmissions, and guidance manuals, primarily those of the oral instructions of the Lamdre explication for disciples. At the great seat of Sakya he taught the Compendium of All Tantras, and at the lower seat of Tsedong Sisum Namgyal he taught the oral instructions of the explication for disciples. At Tanag Tubten Namgyal he taught the oral instructions of the explication for disciples, the Compendium of Sādhanas and the Compendium of All Tantras. He also taught the oral instructions of the explication for disciples at the Mutagmo meditation center.

During his office as the abbot of Ngor Ewam Choden, Khenchen Dampa taught the oral instructions of the explication for the assembly many times. Later, toward the end of his life, he taught the oral instructions of the explication for disciples along with further teachings at the Khangsar residence. At Gyantse he granted extensive teachings to the nomads, including the seven maṇḍalas of the Ngor tradition. These were his main teachings, but throughout his life he mixed teaching with practice so that one cannot hope to fully enumerate the number of extensive teachings that he gave.

All of the goods that he was offered by those who had faith in him, he gave away to religious institutions. Even so, he was able to commission one-story images of the Teacher and his two main attendants and a one-story statue of Akṣobhya for the newly built temple at the Khangsar residence. He also commissioned many volumes, exemplified by the Lamdre scriptures, the Compendium of All Tantras, and the Compendium of Sādhanas, asking that each book be given covers of red and yellow. Such was his exceeding respect for books. He offered a hundred thousand butter lamps at Lhasa and elsewhere. Every day he offered a hundred butter lamps, and every day he performed the twenty-one praises and prostrations to Tārā twenty-five times without interruption. Even his performances of meritorious offerings were miracles transcending the intellect.

Thus by the time this sublime sage had reached the age of seventy-seven, he had completed acts of boundless benefit to the teachings and living beings. He passed away peacefully at the Ewam Khangsar residence, on the twelfth day of the fourth month of the sixteenth water-dragon year (1952). Among his personal students were many who possessed splendid learning and discipline, such as: the throne-holder of glorious Sakya from the Drolma Palace, Ngawang Kunga Tegchen Palbar Trinle Wangi Gyalpo; the abbot of Ngor Penkhang, Ngawang Khedrub Gyatso; the abbot of Luding, Jamyang Tubten Lungtog Gyaltsen; the Chogye Trichen of Nalendra, Tubten Legshe Gyatso; and the great abbot of Sakya temple, Palzangpo.

Dezhung Anjam Rinpoche

The disciple of Jamgon Ngawang Legpa known as Dezhung Chogtrul Rinpoche Jamyang Kunga Tenpai Gyaltsen, or Yongdrag Anjam Rinpoche, possessing unsurpassed qualities of learning, discipline, and accomplishment, was born on the fifteenth wood-bird year (1885) into the family of the ruler lord of Dezhung in Litang.[393] He awoke to the spiritual life at a very young age and was recognized as an incarnation of Zimwog Chogtrul Jampa Tendzin Wangdrub. He received and studied several texts with his uncle Tulku Lungrig Nyima, the Dezhung Dargyeling abbot Geshe Tendzin Wangdrub, and Jamyang Nyendrag.

When he reached adulthood, he stayed with Jamyang Loter Wangpo at the meditation center of Derge Lhundrub Teng and inherited the wealth of the ocean of transmissions for ripening and liberation, primarily the oral instructions of the Lamdre, the Compendium of All Tantras, and the Compendium of Sādhanas.

At Dzogchen Monastery in Rudam he studied under Khenchen Zhenpen Chokyi Nangwa. He received twenty-eight texts of sūtra and mantra, including the thirteen great classics, Sapaṇ's *Distinguishing the Three Vows* and *Treasury of Logic*, Sonam Tsemo's *Classes of Tantra*, Dragpa Gyaltsen's *Jewel Tree*, and the *Hevajra Tantra*. When he completed the study of these, his wisdom overflowed. Among the personal students of Khenchen Zhenga Rinpoche, it was generally agreed that Dezhung Tulku was unsurpassed on the Sakya side and Minyag Serkhar Chodrag was unsurpassed on the Nyingma side.

He received many Dharma cycles from the Nyingma tradition of the early translations, including the Longchenpa's *Fourfold Heart Essence Cycle* from Adzom Drugpa Drodul Pawo Dorje. He received many other Dharma transmissions from teachers such as Pende Khenchen Palden Lodro Gyaltsen, Dzongsar Khyentse Trinle Chogtrul Rinpoche Jamyang Chokyi Lodro, Yonru Betsang Choje Khedrub Gyatso, Gaton Naljor Wangchug Kunga Nyima, and Derge Pewar Lama Lodro.

In particular his root lama, surpassing every other, was Gaton Dorje Chang Ngawang Legpa Rinpoche. Since he had already made many such requests, when Anjam Rinpoche invited his root lama to the Dezhung area four times, he agreed to come. Then Anjam Rinpoche pleased his lama by performing an auspicious offering of the four kinds of beneficial object.

Gaton Ngawang Legpa kindly bestowed the three vows upon Anjam Rinpoche. He gave spoken instructions for ripening and liberation on the precious oral instructions of the Lamdre, on Khecarī, and on the outer, inner, and secret forms of the guardian, all of which the lama had already memorized and practiced himself. Thus, like filling a vase, the lama taught Anjam Rinpoche the complete hearing lineage of the glorious Sakyapas, endowed with the four tests of authenticity. Then, when the lama traveled to Derge, Trehor, and Minyag in order to look after his disciples, Anjam Rinpoche went with him.

Anjam Rinpoche also traveled many times to the lama's own seat in Tarlam Monastery in order to meet him there. When he stayed there for a long time, he asked for Dharma teachings and cleared up his uncertainties about his experiences and realizations. Thus he became the supreme heart disciple of Ngawang Legpa, and their minds became mixed as one.

From childhood he took no pleasure in the high status of lamas or officials, donations, or village rituals for collecting offerings. Along with Chodrag Lama Lodro Puntsog, he lived in rocky mountains far from human habitation in the style of a humble monk. In the latter part of his life he made a place to sleep in the rocky woodlands of an area called Rongkog Zhagpa and lived there.

Rolling into one the practices of the unsurpassed profound path, the main path of the secret mantra, he recited the prayer beginning "Encompassing all refuges" 750,000 times along with a supplication prayer to

Ngawang Legpa Rinpoche.[394] He also accumulated 600,000 recitations of the single verse of the Lord of Speech (Mañjuśrī). In addition he practiced the preliminary accumulations and purifications, the development and the perfection stages, and made great efforts in the mind-training practices of the Mahāyāna.

The great lama Legpa Rinpoche said again and again, "Dezhung Tulku Anjam Rinpoche prayed with the devotion that sees the lama as a true buddha. Because of this, all of the realization of the Sakyapas' Lamdre that exists in my mind was transferred to his, like the printing of a book." Anjam Tulku Rinpoche himself said:

> My lamas were four adepts: Loter Je and Legpa Dorje Chang on the Sakya side, and Zhenga Rinpoche and Adzom Drugpa on the Nyingma side. Although they were all equal in quality, an excellent understanding of the extraordinary view and practice of the Sakyapas has been established in my own mind, and this has come from Gaton Dorje Chang. Therefore I offered him these verses:
>
> I have been cared for by many lamas
> whose learning and accomplishment is like a true buddha's.
> But no other kindness is equal to yours,
> exalted one, great treasure of compassion.
>
> There was not a hair's breadth of difference between my devotion for our compassionate teacher Śākyamuni and this precious lama. It is said that it is very difficult for us to have extraordinary, fully reasoned devotion toward the compassionate teacher Śākyamuni, and even more difficult to have it toward one's lama. People of sharp faculties are liberated through faith in the lama.

Because signs of this faith were all present in Dezhung Anjam Rinpoche, the essence of all sacred biographies is contained here. For example, when he sat and performed many supplications to Red Sarasvatī, numerous miraculous signs appeared. Lama Legpa Rinpoche said that Anjam Rinpoche was cared for by Sarasvatī. He also possessed numerous signs of being cared for by the protector of the teachings known as the Vajra Guardian of the Tent.

Once in Jamyang Khyentse's empowerment room at Dzongsar Monastery, the holy lama Gaton Ngawang Legpa bestowed the permission for the ten wrathful protectors upon several worthy recipients, including Khyentse Chogtrul Rinpoche and Tulku Anjam Rinpoche. After the main part of the permission ceremony had been completed and the wisdom was about to descend, the holy lama saw Tulku Anjam Rinpoche himself actually transform into the Guardian of the Tent.

In response to the insistent commands from his lama, Ngawang Legpa, and direct requests from disciples, in the latter part of his life he gave extensive teachings on several textual systems and granted many empowerments and oral precepts. In particular he told Thrinle Chopel—the abbot of Ga Kyegu Monastery who stayed with him for many years as an abbatial candidate—that teaching all of the twenty-eight texts that he had received from Lama Zhenga Rinpoche was an offering that fulfilled the intention of that sublime lama. His success in granting the complete course of teaching and study in all of these texts was very fortunate. Many wonderful treatises written by him remain, including:

- A compilation of hymns to lamas and meditation deities[395]
- A commentary on the *Profound Path*[396]
- *Drops of Nectar*, a commentary on the phases of the path
- An aspirational prayer for the Lamdre[397]
- *Recognizing the Ground of All*
- The profound key points of the inseparability of saṃsāra and nirvāṇa[398]
- *Lamp for the Precious Daily Practice of the Vinaya*
- A biography of Jamgon Ngawang Legpa called *Rosary of Wonderful Jewels*
- Collections of oral teachings
- Songs of yogic experience and of yearning for the lama

At Dezhung temple, having received many encouragements and contributions, he established a funerary stūpa for Gaton Dorje Chang along with a statue and temple. He also burned the hair from the period that Gaton Dorje Chang stayed for fifteen years in a sealed retreat and with the ashes made several thousand images of Sapaṇ. Afterward he established several stūpas in the places where Gaton had lived.

He carried out virtuous acts far and wide—such as purchasing many books of scriptures, mainly the precious teachings of the Conqueror. In the midst of this activity, he passed into peace on the twenty-second day of the eleventh month of the sixteenth water-dragon year (1952), at the age of sixty-eight. Offerings were made in accordance with his wishes, and the final activities, such as constructing a funerary stūpa, were carried out properly by the chief of Dezhungma and the monastic community.

Jamyang Khyentse Chokyi Lodro

Our unparalleled guide Jamyang Chokyi Lodro Rime Tenpai Gyaltsen Palzangpo, the heart disciple of the lords Loter Wangpo and Jamgon Ngawang Legpa, was indistinguishable from Mañjuśrī himself. The way he accomplished the activities of a second Buddha in this degenerate age is unmatched by any of the sages in the land of snows. He was an impartial master of the Buddha's teachings. He was one of the emanations of the play of the body, speech, mind, qualities, and activities of the all-seeing lama Jamyang Khyentse Wangpo himself that were predicted in a famous vajra prophecy. Specifically, he was prophesied by the unobscured wisdom sight of the omniscient Lochen Jamyang Lodro Taye as an emanation of the wheel of unceasing enlightened activity.

This master was born in the fifteenth water-snake year (1893) in the area known as Sangan Sa Dupa, one of the four areas called Dupa—one for each of the four elements—in Dome. His father was Dorje Dzinpa Chenpo Tsewang Gyatso, from the family line of the great treasure revealer Dudul Dorje, and his mother was Tsultrim Tso. When he reached seven years of age, in accordance with Jamgon Kongtrul's prophecy, he was invited to the vajra seat of Kaḥtog by Kaḥtog Situ Paṇḍita Orgyen Chokyi Gyatso.[399] A lock of his hair was cut, and he was given the name Jamyang Khyentse Chokyi Lodro Tsuglag Lungrig Mawai Senge, "Mañjuśrī, pinnacle of understanding, intelligent in Dharma, lion of speech in scripture, reasoning, and science." He was taught to read and write by Yongdzin Khenchen Tubten Rigdzin Gyatso, the teacher of Situ Rinpoche himself. He also understood the liturgical texts and the systems of interpretation without any difficulty.

He was taught by numerous great scholars and practitioners, including Situ Paṇchen Chokyi Gyatso, Zhechen Gyaltsab, Adzom Drugpa Natsog Rangdrol, Dodrubchen Jigme Tenpai Nyima, Terchen Lerab Lingpa, the Fifth Dzogchen Rinpoche, and Khenchen Kunzang Palden from the Nyingma secret mantra tradition; Tartse Ponlop Rinpoche Jamyang Loter Wangpo,

Zhabdrung Rinpoche Trashi Gyatso, Gaton Dorje Chang Ngawang Legpa, Khenpo Samten Lodro, and Dezhung Chogtrul Kunga Gyaltsen from the Sakya school; Jamgon Situ Rinpoche Pema Wangchog Gyalpo, Karse Jamgon Chogtrul, Khewang Trashi Chopel, and the two Zurmang tulkus, Ter and Drung, from the Kagyu school;[400] the religious and secular leader the Thirteenth Dalai Lama Gyalchog Tamche Khyenpa Tubten Gyatso and the lord of scholars Geshe Jampal Rolpai Lodro from the Gelug school.

He insatiably gathered treasuries of the Dharma, including the major and minor topics of the ten sciences, the scriptures and treatises, the transmitted teachings of the early translation period, everything that remained of the stream of hidden treasure teachings, the empowerments and oral precepts of the four major and eight minor Kagyu lineages, the Sakya oral instructions of the Lamdre, the Compendium of All Tantras and Compendium of Sādhanas, the old and new Dharma cycles of the Kadam, the Kālacakra according to the Jonang and Zhalu traditions, and the Five Great Treasuries of Jamgon Kongtrul.

He memorized these without mixing up any of the presentations of view, tenets, and practices, and so when he taught the Dharma, he taught each individual in accord with the specific situation of student and teacher, just like a second Buddha. Without bias or attachment, he spread every little-known teaching that he found. Throughout his life he spent his time teaching and studying the Dharma. Having worked primarily to accomplish the essence of liberation, he then performed countless recitation practices of the major and minor tantras of the transmitted teachings and treasures, and the general and specific practices of the three roots.[401]

Khyentse Chokyi Lodro never had the haughtiness that comes from the eight worldly concerns and never flattered others for the sake of good food and clothes. He was a great lord of yoga, a destroyer of delusion who grasped from the depths the yoga of the inner tantras. He was taken under the care of his yidam deity and was always experiencing visions, including prophecies from the awareness-holding ḍākinīs. He opened up sacred vajra sites as places of pilgrimage and retreat, and during these times he received many profound treasure transmissions.

In the place known as Jematang, in the area below Trashi Lhatse, the Dzongsar seat, he established a new teaching center called Shedrub Dargyeling. There he expanded the teaching and study of the five sciences, principally the eighteen texts of great renown. Thus the place became a root for the propagation of the Buddha's teachings in general and the supreme textual system of Sakya in particular, as well as a source of countless exegetes of the five sciences.[402]

In addition he ordered the establishment of centers for teaching and meditation in every monastery, great and small, and set up endowments for them. These included a meditation center in Rong Me Karmo Tagtsang with eight tutors bringing together eight chariots of the practice lineages; a meditation center in Drama Ridge in the foothills of Derge Lhundrub Teng, the royal seat of Derge, with fifty monks practicing the Dharma cycle of the glorious Sakyapas' hearing lineage; and he repaired and expanded the tantric college and meditation centers at Kaḥtog.

Khyentse Chokyi Nyima continually turned the wheel of the Dharma, giving the empowerments and reading transmissions for the entire Treasury of Precious Terma, the Compendium of Sādhanas (three times), the Compendium of All Tantras (though he did not teach this all together at one time, if one counts all of the major empowerments he granted, he did teach most of the collection), the Collection of Oral Precepts, the Lamdre explication for the assembly and explication for disciples (four times), the earlier and later Heart Essence,[403] the terma teachings of Mindroling,[404] and the terma teachings of Chogyur Lingpa (four times).

His closest disciples included rulers and great sages from the east, west, and middle of Tibet, such as Yongdzog Tenpai Ngadag (he and his son are now the heads of the two houses of Sakya), all of the abbots of Ngor, the Sixteenth Gyalwang Karmapa, Tai Situ Pema Wangchen, the Eighth Dokham Dongyu Chokyi Nyima,[405] the elder and younger Mindroling abbots, Dung Rinpoche and his brother Dilgo Khyentse Rinpoche Trashi Paljor, and the tulkus of the Kaḥtog, Patrul, Zhechen, and Dzogchen lines. In short, the great and the ordinary all bowed at his feet, and once they had obtained the nectar of ripening and liberation, limitless students of this degenerate time were established on the level of emancipation.

He also established numerous religious objects. At Dzongsar Tse Lhakhang he commissioned a series of statues with Mañjuśrī as the main figure, Guru Rinpoche on the left, Atiśa on the right, and the five Sakya patriarchs. Each statue was life size, made of pure gilt copper, and very beautiful. In addition he commissioned more than a hundred statues of the deities of the old and new tantras. The main deities were an arrow's length, the retinue were a cubit's length, and the secondary retinue were a hand span's length. He also made countless bas-relief images. At the newly established Rigsum Trulpai Lhakhang he established an image of Maitreya the height of thirty-two of his own hands, made of gilt copper and studded with precious jewels. At Kaḥtog he produced an image of our Teacher, the Buddha, made from gilt copper, more than three stories high.

He also had many tankas painted, including the wish-fulfilling tree of our Teacher's previous lives, a series of the noble Dharma kings, and the previous lives of Jamyang Khyentse Wangpo. He had printing blocks made in Gonchen, Kaḥtog, Zhechen, and Dzongsar for thirteen volumes of Jamyang Khyentse's collected works, two volumes of Mipham's works, and three volumes of the *Khecarī Collection*.[406] He placed copies of these works in the monastic college at Bamje and the meditation center at Tagtsang. Thus he turned a vast Dharma wheel of good works.

In the latter part of his life Khyentse Chokyi Lodro constantly went on pilgrimages in central Tibet, India, and Nepal, making offerings, aspirational prayers, and gifts of the Dharma. Having thus spontaneously fulfilled the benefit of self and others, on the sixth day of the fifth month of the sixteenth earth-pig year (1959), at the Gangtok temple—which was the seat of Chogyal Puntsog Namgyal (1604–70) and where his previous rebirth Lhatsun Namkha Jigme had opened up a secret site—his body displayed the appearance of being gathered into the space of reality.

This great treasury of Dharma texts—all of the cycles of practice and their ancillary texts, including the teachings of the translators, paṇḍitas, scholars, and adepts of the land of snows; the empowerments and instruction manuals of the very best of the transmissions from the oral traditions of the eight chariots of the practice lineage; sādhanas, permissions, and Indic scriptures, and the personal instructions on all of these—is an excellent tradition of teaching the great secret, the like of which had never before been seen in a single place, at a single time, and in a single vajra master. It could not be outshone by a hundred thousand precious jewels.

In the beginning, the all-knowing master, Mañjuśrī in person, the great Khyentse, focused his powers only on kindness and enlightened activity. In the middle, his son, the lord of secrets, Vajradhara in person, the great Loter, sustained and continued the enlightened activity of his master and bestowed a fine tradition by spreading the teachings for ripening, liberating, and supporting in the precious Compendium of All Tantras. In the end, the teachings of the Compendium of All Tantras, the Compendium of Sādhanas, and the Lamdre explication for disciples were spread many times by Dragra Trashi Gyatso, Khangsar Khenchen Dorje Chang Ngawang Lodro Zhenpen Nyingpo, Khenpo Samten Lodro, Jamyang Chokyi Lodro, and others.

Together they spread the precious teachings of the Vajrayāna to an ever-greater extent in the snowy lands. Their nature never waned but multiplied into a hundred thousand rays of light, the results of their activities of explaining and practicing without bias all that has been taught by the glorious Sakyapas. Throughout the three times, there are no upholders of the teachings who have been, or are yet to come, who could equal them. This is not an exaggerated turn of phrase; the truth of it is evident to all.

• 10 •

Conclusion

I HAVE FAITHFULLY narrated something of the histories of the upholders of the glorious Sakya tradition. Now I will briefly summarize the essence of them all. Jetsun Rinpoche Dragpa Gyaltsen says:

> The White Earth (*sa dkar*) is like a lion's face;
> the Gray Earth (*sa skya*) is the lion's body.
> This is the dwelling of Vajradhara,
> he who fulfills the wishes of all beings.

As he says, the name of the place is like a melodious appellation given to a person and refers to the precious teachings that have been proclaimed from the center of an immense land. This supreme kindness began with teachings of the later translations of the secret mantra at the time of Khon Konchog Gyalpo. By his great kindness, the tradition was established. By his noble descendants, it was propagated and expanded. In the time of the nephew, the Dharma lord Pagpa, the whole of the snowy land was brought under the shade of the white parasol of Sakya rule. As it extended farther and farther, the continuity of the teachings was upheld by the trio of Shar, Nub, and Gung, while the continuity of practice was upheld by the trio of Tsog, Nyan, and Zhang.[407] The Dharma lord Lama Dampa embodied the spoken transmission of all teachings and practices.

After him there was the expert in the sūtras, Yagton Sangye Pal. He and Kunkhyen Rongton Sheja Kungrig are known as the pair Yag and Rong, or he and Rendawa Zhonu Lodro, as the pair Yag and Zhon. The experts in mantra, Ngorchen Dorje Chang Kunga Zangpo and Dzongpa Kunga Gyaltsen, are known as the two Kungas. Another pair—Go Rabjampa Sonam Senge and Serdog Paṇchen Śākya Chogden—are known as Go and Śāk. These upholders of the teachings of the Sakyapas, six ornaments who beautified the land of snows, spread a feast of teaching and practice throughout the eight directions.

There were also an uncountable number of others, such as Nyawon Kunga Pal and the great abbot Tsondru Pal (the pair Nya and Tson), Sempa Chenpo Zhonu Gyaltsen, Jamchen Rabjampa Sangye Pal, Markhampa Dragpa Zangpo, Kunkhyen Namkha Sonam, Rongton Donyo Pal, Jamyang Kunga Chozang, Mu Rabjampa Jampa Tugje Palzang, Bum Rabjampa Cho Dondrub, Zhungya Ngodrub Palbar, Ngaripa Lhawang Lodro, Tag Chagpa Kunga Paljor, Sheldrag Paṇchen Lodro Chokyi Gyalpo, Gazi Kachu Śākya Lodro, Mangto Ludrub Gyatso, Khenchen Ngawang Chodrag, and Ngawang Tenpai Dorje.

After them the oral tradition that characterizes the Sakyapas, exemplified by the six great books, was established through explanation, debate, and composition, and many great religious colleges were set up for upholding correct teaching and practice.[408] In particular, on the side of mantra, throughout the monastic seats of Sakya, we have had the great kindness of Tegchen Choje Kunga Trashi, Gyagarwa Sherab Gyaltsen, Dagchen Lodro Gyaltsen, Salo Kunga Sonam, the lineage from Ngagchang Kunga Rinchen to Ngagi Wangpo Kunga Lodro and the throne-holder Sonam Lhundrub.

In particular, in the oral tradition of the great Ngorchen Dorje Chang, there have been accomplished scholars without equal: Muchen Konchog Gyaltsen, Kunkhyen Sonam Senge, the all-knowing Konchog Lhundrub, Paṇchen Namkha Palzang, Drubkhangpa Khedrub Palden Dondrub, Jamgon Sangye Puntsog, and Zhuchen Mahāpaṇḍita Tsultrim Rinchen. Also there have been many others of vast understanding and enlightened activity, such as Khenchen Trashi Lhundrub, Dorje Chang Palden Chokyong, and Rinchen Mingyur Gyaltsen. In the oral tradition of Dzongpa, there have been Kunkhyen Dorje Denpa Kunga Namgyal and other upholders of the lineage accomplished in teaching and practice.

In the tradition of the Dharma masters of the Tsar, masters of the ocean of the hearing lineage, there is the lineage of the root texts of the explication for disciples from Jamyang Khyentse Wangchug and Khenchen Labsum Gyaltsen to Nesarwa Ngawang Kunga Legpai Jungne and his rebirths. It was also spread by Mangto Ludrub Gyatso, Bokarwa Maitri Dondrub Gyaltsen, Gonsarwa Sonam Chopel, Khenchen Ngawang Chodrag, the Precious Fifth Ngawang Losang Gyatso, and Drubchen Sangye Gyatso.

Later, great kindness toward the teachings of Sakya, Ngor, and Tsar was shown by the all-seeing Jamyang Khyentse Wangpo and his rebirths, Khenchen Dampa Rinpoche, Jamgon Ngawang Legpa and his students, Loter Wangpo, and many others. The cycle of the Golden Dharmas, including the Khecarī of Nārotapa, in the lineage of the Tsarpa masters was passed from Morchen Ngawang Kunga Lhundrub to Jamyang Dewai Dorje, Tagpuwa Losang Tengyen, Changkya Rolpai Dorje, Tukwan Losang Chokyi Nyima, Tagpuwa Chokyi Wangchug, and so on. And from Nesarwa Ngawang Kunga Legpai Jungne, it was passed to Zhiwalha Geleg Gyaltsen, who spread it among the Gelugpa school, after which many textbooks were composed.

These are the extensive biographies of the upholders of the Sakya lineages:

- Konchog Lhundrub's history of the teachings in general called *Great Ship for Entering the Ocean of the Teachings*, and a supplement written by Jamgon Sangye Puntsog[409]
- The *Chronology* by Mangto Ludrub
- *Setting of Beautiful Jewels: A Lecture on the Six Great Topics* by Khenchen Ngawang Chodrag
- A few lectures on Dharma history by Tubtenpa Cho Namgyal entitled *Necklace of Fresh Flowers*
- The *Family History of Sakya* written in verse by Konchog Lhundrub
- The major family history written by Ame Zhab entitled *Treasury of Miracles* and the supplement written by Jamgon Kunga Lodro
- From the great Salo Ngagchang Kunga Rinchen we have biographies of Jamgon Kunga Lodro and his students
- The extensive biography in three volumes of the abbatial succession and oral teachings from Virūpa to Khenchen Trashi Lhundrub and, subsequent to these, the biographies of Palcho, Mingyur Gyaltsen, Chokyong Zangpo, and others[410]
- The abbatial succession of Ngor written by Khenchen Sangye Puntsog entitled *A Garland of Gems*, along with the supplements written by Palcho and others, which contain brief biographies of the succession down to Konchog Dragpa
- Five volumes of biographies of the lineage of lamas in the Tsar tradition from Dagchen Dorje Chang to Nesarwa Legpai Jungne,[411] and as supplement, a brief account of the explication for disciples written by Jamyang Khyentse[412]

- The major *Lamdre History* written by Jamgon Ame Zhab, as well as his Dharma histories of Cakrasaṃvara, Guhyasamāja, Yamāntaka, and Mahākāla, and the first history of the teachings on Vajrakīlāya[413]
- Dharma histories of Mahākāla written by Tsarchen, Khenchen Ngawang Chodrag, and others[414]
- Histories of the Lamdre, Cakrasaṃvara, Yamāntaka, and others by Ngawang Chodrag[415]
- A history of the three cycles of Raktayamāri drawn from various books
- A history of the lineage of lamas of Vajrayoginī by Tukwan Chokyi Nyima

Now for an extremely brief account of the essence of these authentic sages who upheld the teachings. As the great Sakya Paṇḍita says:

> In the beginning, learn everything there is to know,
> in the middle, teach well this accumulated knowledge,
> in the end, meditate assiduously on the meaning of your
> knowledge;
> this is the approach of all the conquerors of the three times.

On the basis of their pure moral conduct, the paṇḍitas and lotsāwas translated and set down the scriptures, while the scholars were judged to be authentic by intelligent people due to their teaching and practice and achieved a breadth of learning in the scriptural systems of sūtra and mantra comparable to an ocean. In their skill in literary composition, commentary on the meaning of texts, and the practice of rituals, they distinguished between real and imputed, basis and purpose, and the tenets of their own and others' schools, smashing to dust the exaggerations of purely intellectual knowledge.

Their instruction of others and composition of treatises was based in scripture and reason. Maintaining the esoteric instructions of the lineage of lamas without error, come what may, they did not speculate about other systems or adulterate them with subtle contaminants of their own devising. They transmitted the profound path in general and in particular the uninterrupted transmission of scholars and adepts beginning with Lord

Vajradhara and Virūpa, and they practiced the precious oral instructions, the unfading speech from the mouths of the ḍākinīs.

In the beginning, they brought about ripening through the causal empowerments. In the middle, they maintained four sessions of practice in an undiminishing flow through the path empowerments, cultivating the four paths in the two stages of development and perfection. Thus at the end, through the result empowerments, they surpassed all other paths in the supreme accomplishment of the true mahāmudrā. Ordinary accomplishments also appeared alongside the supreme one, and with these ordinary accomplishments they passed on profound and extensive precepts, thus helping others to apply themselves to the two kinds of accomplishment, temporal and ultimate.

While maintaining the tenets of their own tradition without error, they didn't follow other traditions; however, apart from a little analysis with scripture and reason, they did not act with attachment or aversion toward any system of tenets either. Though internally they possessed extensive accomplishments such as experience, realization, and foreknowledge, they kept these secret. The glorious *Guhyasamāja* says:

> Externally, maintain the lifestyle of a *śrāvaka*.
> Internally, delight in the truth of the assembly.

This is how they practiced. In so doing, the paṇḍitas who explicated the teaching traditions of the great chariots of the vast Indian and Tibetan textual traditions, including sūtra, mantra, and science, and the meditators on the unerring path that is spoken of in the tantras, became adepts with an inconceivable mastery of yoga, with the qualities of the paths and bhūmis and the wisdom of the mahāmudrā.

The activities of these sages who upheld the Sakya teachings—these masters of good counsel, guardians of custom, possessors of the ten strengths of a true guide—were supported by the monasteries. In the region of Central Tibet there was the great seat, glorious Sakya; the seat of Ngor, glorious Ewam Choden; and in Phenyul, glorious Nalendra. These are the three great monastic seats that are known everywhere as the trio of Sa, Ngor, and Tsar. As for the monasteries that upheld the good customs of teaching sūtra and mantra, the practical experience of meditation, and the practice of ritual, the lower seat of Tsedong Sisum Namgyal was established by Jamyang Namkha Trashi of the Dungcho Palace of glorious Sakya in the eighth earth-bird year (1477). There are also many great and small meditation centers, such as Gongkar Dorje Den, upholding the Dzong tradition, and the six branches of Kyetsal temple, arising from the enlightened activities of Jamchen Rabjampa.

In Gato, in the Kham region, Kyegu Dondrub Ling was established by the great Gyagarpa Sherab Gyaltsen. After Denma Drung Kunga Rinchen established the first meditation hall of Tarlam Sazang Namgyaling in the seventh wood-horse year (1414), it was expanded by Ga Rabjampa Kunga Yeshe in the earth-sheep year (1499). It is the most important of the thirteen meditation centers in the region.

Then there is the great meditation center of Lhundrub Teng at Derge. It was started by the adept Tangtong Gyalpo. Because this great adept was a student of Ngorchen Dorje Chang, this was an auspicious circumstance for maintaining the flow of enlightened activities of the Dharma masters of Ngor. Later Sharchen Kunga Trashi visited there. After that Lachen Jampa Puntsog invited Drubkhangpa Palchog Gyaltsen, and he refuted false versions of the Dharma, explained scripture and reasoning, talked about the essential experiences, and differentiated the ritual practices of the tradition of the great Ngorchen Dorje Chang.

After that many of the Ngor abbots came to Derge Lhundrub Teng, one after the other, including Khenchen Sangye Puntsog, Jamgon Trashi Lhundrub, Dorje Chang Palden Chokyong, Sharchen Mingyur Gyaltsen, Jamyang Sangye Yeshe, Ngawang Chokyong Zangpo, Drangti Namkha Chime, his nephews and close disciples Kunga Tendzin and Naljor Jampal Zangpo, Kunga Tenpai Lodro, Ngawang Sonam Gyaltsen, Jamyang Rinchen Dorje, and Palden Lodro Gyaltsen.

Also, the tradition of the Ngor Ewampas was augmented by Jamgon Trashi Palden, Khedrub Sangye Palzang, Khetsun Kunga Chopel, Lama Trashi Wangchug, Zhuchen Mahāpaṇḍita Tsultrim Rinchen, the casket of excellent Dharma along with the inner and outer sciences Ponlop Jampaiyang Ngawang Legdrub, the master of the ocean of tantras Ponlop Jamyang Loter Wangpo, the master of power and strength Khenpo Samten Lodro, and other saints. The profound teachings of the hearing lineage of the Tsar tradition were spread far and wide by Nesarwa Ngawang Kunga Legpai Jungne, the abbot of Tanag Tubten Namgyal; Zangpo Gyaltsen, the student of

Morchen; Khedrub Sangye Gyatso; the earlier and later Nesarwa Chogtruls, and others.

Encouraged by Khenchen Trashi Lhundrub, Palden Chokyong, and others, the Derge Dharma king Jangchub Sempa Tenpa Tsering commissioned a set of printing blocks. The last part of the Tengyur was overseen by his son Sakyong Lama Kunga Trinle Gyatso. Many other printing blocks were commissioned too, including the works of the five patriarchs and Ngorchen Dorje Chang, creating a great treasury of sublime Dharma.

Additionally, in Mesho, there is Dzongsar Trashi Lhatse, which was established by Drogon Chogyal Pagpa. Here, throughout his life, the all-seeing Jamyang Khyentse Wangpo upheld, protected, and propagated the precious teachings of the Conqueror without partiality, through his teaching, meditation, and good deeds. Since this was the sublime seat and base that nourished these unmatched enlightened activities, it is the chief center for more than thirty monasteries. It has been repaired many times, by Trichen Sangye Tenpa, the Dharma king Tenpa Tsering, and others.

Also, in Drogsa, there is the monastery of Trom Dokog, established by Trom Gyalwa Jangchub. In Amdo, the Dharma lord Chodrag Zangpo established the monastery of Dhīḥ Pu Choje, a great college combining mantra with philosophy. Thus the large and small Dharma establishments of the Sakya, along with all the mountain hermitages, extend without a break from Ladakh in the west to Gyatsam in the east, and to speak of them all and their histories would be endless.

Furthermore, there is a multitude of different philosophical systems here in this country surrounded by a garland of snowy mountains. However, the majority of these, from the point of view of their contents and their lineage, derive from the Sakya tradition. There are many with claims to greatness in the family lineages of So, Zur, and Nub in the Nyingma Secret Mantra, as well as many sages of transmitted teachings and hidden treasures, such as the reborn treasure revealer Guru Chokyi Wangchug.

Among the Kadam there are Jayulwa, Dokongwa, Namkabum, Chim Namkha Drag, and Chomden Rigpai Raldri, for example. However, all of them received the words of the uncle and nephew lords of the Dharma. The holders of the lineage of the great Ngog Lotsāwa, regents of the Buddha in Tibet, lords of reasoning, were Chapa Chenpo and Nyangdran Chokyi Seng. Both received ripening and liberation through the profound instructions of Kyura Aseng, one of the students of Sachen.

The Kagyu is like the source of a thousand rivers. Pagmodrupa sat at the feet of Sachen, relying upon him for twelve years, asking him to teach the Lamdre system. Later he also asked Jetsun Dragpa for the nectar of the oral teachings, and the lotus of his experience and realization blossomed. Pagmodrupa is also famous as the student of Dagpo Rinpoche and holder of his lineage, and most of the Kagyu—including Drigung, Taglung, Tropu, Lingre, and Drugpa—derive from him. Furthermore, the founder of the Kamtsang Kagyu, Karmpa Dusum Khyenpa, received the Lamdre from the glorious Go Lotsāwa, one of the main students of Sachen, as well as from Khampa Aseng and Shen Dorseng. The great adept of the Shangpa Kagyu, Mogchogpa, received the profound teachings including the Lamdre from Khampa Aseng and Nyenton Bepai Naljor after spending a long time at the lotus feet of Jetsun Dragpa.

The all-knowing Buton Rinpoche received all of his tantric lineages and most of his philosophical lineages from Sakya before showing his powers of teaching, debate, and composition. He was also guided by the wisdom body of Jetsun Dragpa. The Jonangpa Kunkhyen Choku Ozer was a student born from the oral instructions of Sapaṇ. Dolpopa Sherab Gyaltsen also trained in philosophy at Sakya, and in later life he often said that it was thanks to the blessings of Sakya Paṇḍita that the view was born in his mind.

Everyone from Shangton Lotsāwa Dorje Gyaltsen up to Bodong Chogle Namgyal had virtuous guides from Sakya, and Chogle Namgyal adopted the Sakya system of tenets, as is made clear in his biography. And Gyalse Thogme also heard uncountable instructions in the Sakya tradition from the Dharma lord Lama Dampa and others.

In the Riwo Ganden school, the students of the great Sakya lama Rendawa Zhonu Lodro included seven with the degree of lecturer in philosophy. Supreme among his sons was Tsongkhapa Lozang Dragpa, and the best in debate was Gyaltsab Darma Rinchen. There were also ten lecturers in the ten topics, including Khedrub Geleg Palzang. Furthermore, Je Rinpoche studied many vast and profound teachings with the all-knowing Nyawon Kunga Pal, Lama Dampa, and Sazang Mati Paṇchen, among others.

As it says in the biography of Jamgon Lama Tsongkhapa, his teaching style was primarily based on the Sakya for philosophy and the Bulug for tantra. Also it is well known that in the teaching traditions of the five great commentaries, the hearing lineages of Sakya and Gelug philosophers begin from the same sources: Yagton for the Prajñāpāramitā, Rendawa for Madhyamaka, Nyawon for logic, Ja Duldzin for Vinaya, and Drangti Darma Nyingpo or Chim Namkha Drag for Abhidharma. All of these virtuous guides upheld the Dharma lineage of Sakya. It is said:

> Among students who uphold the Dharma lineage of Sakya,
> the victory banner of the Sage in Jambudvīpa,
> a great many have been accepted
> as upholders of the teachings.

This aphorism gets to the heart of the matter. The scholar able to refute the traditions of glorious Sakya does not exist. However, some Gelugpas, such as Khedrub Geleg Palzang as well as the all-knowing Buton Rinpoche, Bodong Chogle Namgyal, and others, made some criticisms that were refuted by Ngorchen Dorje Chang and the all-knowing Sonam Senge, while Paṇchen Śākya Chogden addressed their doubts and questions. Also, the all-knowing Pema Karpo made a few criticisms based on the three vows and questioned teachers of the *Hevajra Tantra*. He was answered sequentially by Kunkhyen Rinpoche, Lowo Khenchen, Mangto Ludrub Gyatso, Khenchen Ngawang Chodrag, and others. When the Dharma lord Ngorpa was criticized by Dzonglungpa, the latter was answered by the all-knowing Konchog Lhundrub and Ngawang Tenpai Dorje. When the secret tradition of the explication for disciples was insulted by the Jonangpas and others, profound and extensive responses were given by Mangto Ludrub and Khenchen Ngawang Chodrag. Once they had opened the eye of intelligence and been freed from the stains of erroneous concepts, and once they had fully understood the situation, they achieved an undivided faith.

On the Duration of the Teachings

According to the *Bhadrakalpika Sūtra*, the root texts of the Vinaya, and the *Abhidharmakośabhāṣya*, the teachings will last for a millennium. The *Karuṇāpuṇḍarīka Sūtra* and others say one and a half millennia. The *Candragarbha Sūtra* and others say two millennia. The commentary to the *Vajracchedikā* says two and a half millennia. Vasubandhu's commentary to the *Śatasāhasrikā* and Abhayākaragupta's *Munimatālaṃkāra* say five millennia. Gawai Shenyen's historical works say five and half millennia.[416]

Furthermore, the *Sūtra on Repaying Kindness* says that the teachings decreased by half a millennium because Śākyamuni's aunt took ordination. Thus it says that the duration will be between five and six millennia. Since this statement is of the definitive meaning, and this is literally true, there will be four half-millennia (2,000 years) for the fruition of the intention of the highest of sages, three times three half-millennia (4,500 years) for scripture and accomplishment, and ten half-millennia (5,000 years) for the pure teaching. Because Śākyamuni's aunt took ordination, the period of fruition was decreased by half a millennium. Since this is merely a symbolic period, the pure teaching is nine half-millennia (4,500 years), and the mere image of the teaching is half a millennium, making the duration of the Sage's teaching five millennia in this system.

Moreover in the first three of these ten half-millennia there are many successive arhats who will never return, who attain the result of entering the stream. Therefore these three half-millennia are known as the period of fruition. In this period the teaching of fruition abides. After that, during the next three half-millennia there are many who abide in perfect training, especially in insight, meditation, and morality. Therefore these three half-millennia are known as the period of accomplishment. In this period the teaching of realization abides. After that, during the next three half-millennia there are many who expound the collections of Abhidharma, Sūtra, and Vinaya. Therefore these three half-millennia are known as the period of transmission. In this period the teaching of transmission abides. In the following half a millennium there will be grasping at mere signs and therefore there will be no genuine teaching. Therefore this half a millennium is known as the period of grasping at mere signs.

There are other statements on the duration of the teachings, some of which are from scriptures of provisional or indirect meaning.[417] These are all based in the Buddha's original intention. Thus when it is said that the teachings will last for 2,500 years, this is intended only for the phase of accomplishing the result. When it is said that the teachings will last as long as they increase, this is intended only for relics and books. The Buddha's motive for saying that the teachings will not remain beyond 2,500 years is to spur on those trainees who have become weary, and the motive for saying that they will last as long as they increase is to encourage those who have become very despondent. The logical inconsistency of this account of the duration of the teachings is shown in the *Sūtra of the Prophecy of Vimaladevī*, which contains a prophecy saying, "Two thousand five hundred years after I have passed into parinirvāṇa, the true Dharma will come to the land of the red-faced people."[418]

Furthermore, there are many differences in what is said about the dates of birth and passing of the Lord of Sages.[419] There are the traditions of Atiśa and the Kadampas, of the Kashmiri Paṇḍita Śākyaśrī, of the *Kālacakra Tantra*, and the tradition of the Jetsun Sakyapas. Now we have established that the definitive meaning is that the teachings will last 5,000 years. In Atiśa's tradition the Teacher entered the womb in a male wood-bird year and was born in a female wood-tiger year. He achieved buddhahood in a female earth-pig year, and at the age of eighty, on the eighth day of the waxing-moon phase of the last month of the male wood-monkey year (2136 B.C.E.), he passed away. Therefore, between the current wood-hare year (1975) and the passing of the Teacher, 4,111 years have passed. The Kashmiri paṇḍita takes a fire-snake year as the starting point of the chronology, meaning that 2,518 years have passed between then and the current wood-hare year.

In the Kālacakra tradition, the Teacher entered the womb on the full moon of the *vaiśākha* month of a male fire-horse year, and he was born after tenth months (including the special *āṣāḍha* month) on the full moon of the *māgha* month of a female fire-sheep year. He achieved buddhahood in his thirty-seventh year, on the full moon of the *vaiśākha* month of a male water-horse year, and he passed into parinirvāṇa on the full moon of the *vaiśākha* month of a male fire-tiger year (834 B.C.E.). Thus up to the current female wood-hare year (1975), 2,809 years have passed.

In addition there is the tradition of the *Oral Transmission of the Karuṇāpuṇḍarīka* by Norzang Gyatso and Pugpa Lhundrub. Here the Teacher entered the womb on the full moon of the *āṣāḍha* month of a female earth-sheep year and was born on the seventh day of the *vaiśākha* month of an iron-monkey year. He achieved buddhahood on the full moon of the *vaiśākha* month of a male wood-horse year, and he passed into parinirvāṇa on the full moon of the *vaiśākha* month of a male iron-dragon year (880 B.C.E.). Thus between the current female wood-hare year (1975) and the passing of the Teacher, 2,855 years have passed. This and other traditions differ from the Kālacakra tradition.

The tradition of the Jetsun Sakyapas is epitomized by Sakya Paṇḍita's writings on chronology in his *Biography of the Great Lama Jetsun*. The cycle of the Lord of Sages is as follows. Entering the womb happened at midnight in the *vaiśākha* month of a female fire-hare year, or the year of arising. The birth happened on the full moon of the *phālguna* month of a male earth-dragon year, or the year of abundance. He achieved complete buddhahood on the fifteenth day of the year of the male water-tiger, also known as the virtuous year. He passed into parinirvāṇa at the point which marks the completion of the year of the female fire-pig, also known as the all-subduing year, and the beginning of the year of the male earth-rat, also known as the all-holding year.[420] From the same biography:

> In the male fire-rat year (1216), when the great Jetsun was residing in Sakya Monastery at Upper Drompa in Tsang, he passed away to Sukhāvatī. Learned monks were invited from afar, there was a turning of the great wheel of the Dharma, and a monastic school for teachings and discussion was established. There was a gathering of more than a thousand monks during the period for purifying misdeeds, on the fifteenth day of the *pauṣa* month of the male fire-rat year, when a great festival was held for the writing down of the entire canon. Among them, the copies of the *Bhadrakalpika Sūtra* and the *Prātimokṣa Sūtra* written by the follower of Śākyamuni called Kunga Gyaltsen Palzangpo, were singled out as particularly fine. When we calculate the time of this bringing-together of the Buddha's teaching, then 3,350 years have passed from the parinirvāṇa of the Tathāgata up to this male fire-rat year.

As he says, up to that point 3,349 years had passed, and the 3,350th year was definitely the male fire-rat year (1216). So 219 years later, in the male fire-dragon year of the seventh cycle (1436), was when the divine ruler of Guge took ordination, and by Ngorchen Dorje Chang Kunga Zangpo's calculation, 3,569 years had passed between that date and the parinirvāṇa.[421] From that date until now, 539 years have gone by, and the 540th will be the present female wood-hare year (1975). By this reasoning, the time from the passing of the Lord of Sages to this female wood-hare year can be calculated as 4,107 years (2132 B.C.E.).

Now, if we apply this to the ten half-millennia discussed earlier, up to the present the three half-millennia of the period of fruition and the three half-millennia of the period of accomplishment—that is, three thousand years—have passed, and we are clearly in the three half-millennia of the period of transmission. Also, 107 years have passed since the two half-millennia of the period of the Sūtras and the half-millennium period of the Vinaya. This brings us to the 108th year, the year of insects, the female wood-hare year.[422]

Going forward from the present date, from this female wood-hare year, for the remaining 393 years of the period of Vinaya there will be genuine teaching, and then in the final five hundred years counterfeit forms of the Dharma will appear. When these are added together with the five hundred years of grasping at mere signs, the remaining duration of the teachings will be 893 years.

Now, the above-mentioned three thousand years after the male earth-rat year in which our Teacher passed away was the 159th male earth-rat year (868), and this is the beginning of the period of the transmission of the Abhidharma teachings. The present female wood-hare year is 1,107 years after that earth rat year. The above-mentioned 3,500 years after the passing is the male earth-monkey year of the first cycle (1368). This is the beginning of the period of the Sūtras. A further 607 years after that male earth-monkey year brings us to the present female wood-hare year. The above-mentioned 4,000 years after the passing brings us to the male earth-dragon year of the fifteenth cycle (1868), and this is the beginning of the period of Vinaya. A further 107 years after that earth-dragon year brings us to the present female wood-hare year.

Colophon

I have related something here, expanding and condensing where appropriate, of the history of the supreme protectors of living beings, the lords of the teachings in the land of snows. There are many texts of histories of the Dharma composed by previous great scholars, upholders of the Sakya teachings, and this is not a new Dharma history that surpasses them by addressing different topics or by being written in an excellent style. Beings of little merit like us are destitute of the proper internal qualities, constantly frenzied by the phantasmagoria of this life, and with feeble mental energy. As for external qualities, due to the inexorable passage of time, there is a tower of great books written in the past, now rare and difficult to find, while a scholar who has listened to a complete exposition of a single authentic historical text has become a rare thing indeed.

Still, those of little intelligence start by collating a Dharma history of few words, and based on that alone, develop faith, energy, and intelligence;

by the path of gradually hearing, contemplating, and meditating, they are led to the highest stage. Motivated by that thought I composed this, rousing myself to great efforts in spite of the difficulty of the work. Avoiding approximations, fabrications, and indiscriminately collating whatever people said, I used original sources, those genuine discourses that are like eyes to living beings. I drew with faith from the following learned works:

- Ngorchen Konchog Lhundrub's *Great Ship for Entering the Ocean of Teachings, A History of the Dharma*, with a supplement by Khechen Sangye Puntsog
- Khenchen Ngawang Chodrag's *A Blossoming Lotus Grove: A Setting for the Lamdre*
- Jamgon Ame Zhab's *Miraculous Shower of Blessings: The Biography of Muchen Sangye Gyaltsen*. Also, his *Lamdre History: An Ocean of Excellent Explanation* and his *Dharma History of Demchog and the Protector*
- The all-seeing Jamyang Khyentse Wangpo's *Garden of Miraculous Flowers*, which is an account of the lineages of old and new traditions of secret mantra in Tibet
- Dragyab Dongkam Trichen Ngawang's *Key to a Thousand Doors of Profound Meaning: A Catalog of the Profound Ocean of Dharma, the Compendium of All Tantras*
- From the Compendium of Sādhanas, the section on the practice of the permissions and the sections on the works of the great Gorampa and Zhuchen Tsultrim Rinchen
- Chogye Trichen Legshe Gyatso's *Condensed Dharma History of Sakya*[423]

I also took some short extracts from Kongton's biography of Gorampa and Kunga Drolchog's biography of Śākya Chogden. The *Clarifying Explanation of the Hearing Lineage of the Nalendra Abbatial Succession* of Chogye Trichen Rinpoche was a great help. *Mass of Qualities of Learning and Realization: A Biography of Gaton Dorje Chang and His Students* by the Tarlam Dezhung Lungrig Tulku, Jampa Tenpai Nyima, was also a great help, as was his new version of the biography of Khangsar Khenchen Dampa Dorje Chang and his new additions to the *Sakya Lineage History* and the *Succession to the Throne of Ewam* that take them up to the present.

Finally, I have heard oral historical accounts of the Jamgon Sakyapas from the illuminator of the teachings Chogye Trichen Rinpoche and the learned abbot of Tarlam, Jamyang Sherab, among others, whose conversations are jewels of evidential truth. As I have put this together without falling into the two extremes of excessive length or brevity, it is my hope that it will be accepted with trust as a reliable source.

Melodious, melodious is the melody of the all-pervading and ever-
present bright acclaim of the three supreme ones.
Profound, profound, are the profound precepts of the precious oral
instructions, the nectar of all the sūtras and tantras.
Many, many, are the many scholars and adepts who have upheld the
teachings, explained hundreds of texts, and actualized the two stages.
Excellent, excellent, is the excellent and unerring tradition of the glorious Sakyapas.

This conch shell's melody about the way the supreme tradition
of Sakya arose, following the tracks of countless scholars and adepts:
even to hear it sows the seeds of liberation;
so strive to hear it, and then consider its meaning.

The merit arising from this, like the great Ganges River,
dissolves into the roots of the excellent forest of the teachings of Kunga,
and is liberated in the leaves of enlightened teaching and practice,
where the fruits of altruism satisfy the needs of all living beings.

With this *Sweet Harmonies for Infinite Realms: The History of the Precious Teachings of the Glorious Sakyapas, the Regents of the Sage in the North*, I take the toenails of the great sages of impartial speech—primarily the genuine vidyādhara, great abbot of Ewam Khangsar, the omniscient Ngawang Lodro Zhenpen Nyingpo, and he who is inseparable from Mañjuśrī, Jamyang Chokyi Lodro—and place them on the crown of my head as jeweled ornaments. By tasting the nectar of their words, great good fortune is accomplished.

Born in Lower Trehor, Kham, Tibet, at the Dharma center of Dhongthog Chode Rigdrol Puntsog Ling, which upholds the tradition of the Ewampas, I was crowned with the title of the Fifth Dhongthog ("original face") Tulku, in the same way that the last holder of the tulku lineage of Mapam Namtrul Shar Dzamtang Gyalwa Senge is known as Senge ("lion"). In fact my true name is Chome Mongzug Ngawang Tegchog Tenpai Gyaltsen ("ugly in form and lacking in Dharma, the victory banner of the Great Vehicle, lord of speech"). With an attitude of single-pointed faith and attachment to the precious teachings of the glorious Sakyapas, the supreme expression of the oral tradition of general and special teachings, in the Tibetan year 2102, in the sixteenth female wood-hare year known as "the year of insects," on the fourteenth day of the waxing moon of the eleventh month, having taught in the style of bringing everything into the space-like intention of the great Sakya Paṇḍita, the sole ornament of all the scholars of Jambudvīpa (in its true meaning), I completed this in New Delhi, India, on the day of a great festival. May this supreme tradition of the Sakyapas, the general and special teachings of the Conqueror, come to protect living beings throughout the three realms and spread throughout all places and times.

Sarva maṅgalam

By the excellent printing of this history of Sakya,
compiled by the scholarly method,
may the excellent tradition of Kunga spread in a hundred directions,
and may we attain enlightenment with a mind like the sky.

Notes

1. The phrase "root lama" (*rtsa ba'i bla ma*) usually refers to one's primary teacher. In this case it seems that Dhongthog Rinpoche is using the term in a metaphorical sense, expressing devotion to Sakya Paṇḍita. Dhongthog Rinpoche names his two main lamas in the closing words of this book as Ngawang Lodro Zhenpen Nyingpo and Jamyang Chokyi Lodro.
2. In this verse the *Buddha Ewampa* is Ngorchen Kunga Zangpo, and the *father and sons* are Ngorchen and his two students Jamyang Khyentse Wangchug and Mangto Ludrub Gyatso. The *spoken transmission* is the Lamdre explication for disciples.
3. This is a previous Śākyamuni: see Obermiller 1986, 2:102 and n922.
4. Devoted conduct (*mos spyod*) equates to the paths of accumulation (*tshogs lam*) and application (*sbyor lam*).
5. The *yojana* (*dpag tshad*) is traditionally equivalent to between five and nine miles.
6. *Byang chub kyi snying po*, Skt. *bodhimaṇḍa*.
7. These are (1) absorption endowed with concepts and analysis, (2) absorption without concepts but with analysis, (3) absorption with attention devoid of concepts and analysis, and (4) absorption with joy and attention.
8. These are (1) knowledge of the past lives of oneself and others, (2) supernatural insight into future mortal conditions, and (3) knowledge that one has overcome all afflictions and that this is one's final birth.
9. Translation adapted from Dudjom 1991, 427.
10. This is the *Cakrasaṃvarasyapañjikāśūramanojñā* (Q2121).
11. Probably in the *Hevajrasya-pañjikā-vajrapadoddharaṇa* (Q2322).
12. Translation adapted from Dudjom 1991, 428.
13. Interpolations based on the list of misdemeanors in Suzuki 1904.
14. These are (1) Dīrghāgama, (2) Madhyamāgama, (3) Saṃyuktāgama, and (4) Ekottarāgama.
15. *Dran pa nye bar gzhag pa bzhi* (Skt. *catvārismṛtyupasthānāni*): the four foundations of mindfulness, being the recollection of the body (*lus*), feelings (*tshor ba*), the mind (*sems*), and phenomena (*chos*).
16. On this list of patriarchs, see Chattopadhyaya and Chimpa 1970, 226–32 and 771–73. This list is the one transmitted in the Mūlasarvāstivāda Vinaya, although the version cited by Lamotte, from the Chinese (Taisho 1451), inserts Madhyāntika/Madhyāhnika between Ānanda and Śāṇavāsa. Dudjom (1991, 437) notes and rejects the inclusion of Madhyāhnika in some lists.
17. An interpretation of this list from the *Vinayakṣudrāgama* can be found in Dudjom

1991, 429. An extensive discussion of each of the ten can also be found in Obermiller 1986, 2:92.
18. Translation based on Dudjom 1991, 429.
19. Vinītadeva wrote the *Nikāyabhedopadarśanasaṃgraha* (Q5641), quoted in Obermiller 1986, 2:99.
20. Tibetan text has *dzā landhara ri*.
21. Based on translation in Dudjom 1991, 430.
22. This may be the commentary by Padmavajra (Q2136).
23. This may be the commentary by Śuraṃgavajra (Q3513).
24. Some of the names in the list in this text seem to be corrupted. There are certain differences from the forms of the names found in other sources (Roerich 1996, 22; Obermiller 1936, 2:109). In particular, this list has *Vasunanda* which I have emended to *Vasubandhu*. Note that *Dhṛṭaka* should be distinguished from *Dhītika*, one of the first seven successors listed earlier in the text.
25. Kalyāṇavarman (*Dge ba'i go cha*) in Obermiller 1986, 2:161.
26. *Bhu su ku'i spyod pa*. For a discussion of this term, see Chattopadhyaya and Chimpa 1970, 217n55.
27. These are: *Yogācāryabhūmi*, *Nirṇayasaṃgraha*, *Vastusaṃgraha*, *Paryāyasaṃgraha*, and *Vivaraṇasaṃgraha*.
28. These seven early works are the *Vijñānakāya*, *Dhātukāya*, *Dharmaskandha*, *Prakaraṇapāda*, *Jñānaprasthāna*, *Saṃgītiparyāya*, and *Prajñaptiśāstra*.
29. The *Prajñāpāramitā in a Hundred Thousand Verses*.
30. The eight dissertations (*prakāraṇa*) are the *Sūtralaṃkāravṛtti*, *Madhyāntavibhaṅgavṛtti*, *Dharmadharmatāvibhaṅgavṛtti*, *Vyākhyāyukti*, *Karmasiddhiprakaraṇa*, *Pañcaskandhaprakaraṇa*, *Viṃśatikā*, and *Triṃśikā*.
31. The seven treatises: cf. Q5709–5716 (eight texts).
32. These might be, respectively, *Abhisamayālaṃkāravṛtti* (Q5185) and *Abhisamayālaṃkārakārikāvārttika* (Q5186). Ruegg (2004, 41) distinguishes two Vimuktisenas. Obermiller (1986, 2:156n1078) mentions that Tsongkhapa expressed doubt regarding the authorship of the latter work.
33. This appears to be a reference to the *Abhisamayālaṃkārāloka* (Q5189) and *Abhisamayālaṃkārakārikāśāstravivṛti* (Q5191).
34. On the stories of the gate guardians of Vikramaśīla, see Chattopadhyaya and Chimpa 1970, 294–303. Note that here, and throughout the translation, the name Nārotapa is used instead of Nāropa. In general, Nārotapa is more commonly used to refer to this figure in the Sakya literature.
35. See Chattopadhyaya and Chimpa 1970, 290 and 427.
36. Though these lines attributed to the *Vimaladevīvyākaraṇa* (*Lha mo dri ma med pa lung bstan pa*) are often quoted in Tibetan histories, no text of this title appears in the Tibetan canon. There is a text called the *Enquiry of Vimalaprabhā* (Q835: *Dri ma med pa'i 'od kyis zhus pa*, Skt. **Vimalaprabhāparipṛcchā*). Given that in this text the Vimalaprabhā of the title is a goddess, it seems that the two titles may refer to the same text. The *Enquiry of Vimalaprabhā* has many prophecies, some of which do speak of the red-faced ones, but none of them is exactly the same as the prophecy quoted above.

37. This is a paraphrase of the passage in Nelpa Paṇḍita's *Garland of Flowers* (7a4–7b3 in the edition in Uebach 1987).
38. See Wangdu and Diemberger 2000, 45–46.
39. This statement appears in the Fifth Dalai Lama Ngawang Lozang Gyatso's *Song of the Spring Queen*, 60–61.
40. See the discussion of the disagreements about this matter in Uebach 1987, 31, and van Schaik 2011, 46–48.
41. The more commonly found name of the inventor of the Tibetan script is Tonmi (*thon mi*) Sambhoṭa. Tumi (*thu mi*) is equally valid though cited in fewer historical sources. See Sørensen 1994, 167n462.
42. The trio are Kawa Paltseg, Chogro Lui Gyaltsen, and Zhang Yeshe De.
43. Dhongthog Rinpoche's note (hereafter, DR): In some books *Dmu gzugs la 'bar* is written *Mu zu gsal 'bar*.
44. See Davidson 2005 and van Schaik and Galambos 2012 for more about this period.
45. As implied here, there are two versions of the western Vinaya lineage of Dharmapāla; see Martin 2013.
46. The second part of this twofold division comprises the main body of the present work: in the present translation, chapters 2 through 9 and the first half of chapter 10.
47. The Bulugpa school, which no longer exists, was based on the teaching lineage of Buton Rinchen Drub (1290–1364).
48. "The abbot, the master, and the Dharma king" are Śāntarakṣita, Padmasambhava, and Trisong Detsen.
49. These are the texts of the following eight deities: (1) Shinje (Yamāntaka), (2) Tamdrin (Hayagrīva), (3) Pal Heruka (Śrī Heruka), (4) Dutsi Chemchog, (5) Dorje Purba (Vajrakīlaya), (6) Mamo Botong, (7) Jigten Choto, and (8) Mopa Drangag.
50. The seven divine Dharmas of the Kadam (*bka' gdams lha chos bdun*) are (1) Śākyamuni, (2) Avalokiteśvara, (3) Tārā, (4) Acala, and (5–7) the three scriptural systems (*tripiṭaka*).
51. Roerich 1996, 729, has the year as 1086.
52. This teacher is also known as the elder Vajrāsana.
53. See Roerich 1996, 729–31.
54. The *seven jewels of the Shangpa* are (1) Vajradhara, (2) Niguma, (3) Khyungpo Naljor, (4) Mogchogpa, (5) Kyergangpa, (6) Nyenton, and (7) Sangye Tonpa. See Smith 2001, 54.
55. This is the latest of the dates usually given for Marpa's birth. The date 1012 is more generally accepted (see Davidson 2005, 142–43).
56. The student likened to the moon was Rechungpa.
57. These are: (1) Pagmodrupa, (2) Dusum Khyenpa, and (3) Saltong Shogom.
58. The Barom Kagyu is missing from the Tibetan text.
59. This is an epithet of the Second Karmapa, Karma Pakshi.
60. The three spheres of activity are usually (1) the sphere of reading, studying, and pondering (*klog pa thos bsam gyi 'khor lo*), (2) the sphere of renunciation and contemplation (*spong ba bsam gtan gyi 'khor lo*), and (3) the sphere of action (*bya ba las kyi 'khor lo'o*).
61. These are among the traditional thirty-two signs of a saint (*skyes chen*).
62. The Tibetan version of this name is Lui Wangpo Sung (*Klu'i dbang po srung*).

63. These two protectors are associated with Vajrakīlaya. Their full names are Karmo Nyida (White Lady of the Sun and Moon) and Dugyal Pawo Totrengchen (Skull-Garlanded Hero, King of the Demons). See Nebesky-Wojkowitz 1956, 87, Stearns 2001, 230n104, and Smith 2001, 106 and 299n326.
64. The eight further cycles of the path (*lam skor phyi ma*) are the nine cycles excluding the Lamdre; they are discussed at length in Davidson 2005, 194–204. See also Stearns 2001, 210n30. When the Lamdre is added, these are known as the nine cycles of the path (*lam skor dgu*).
65. Davidson (2005, 429n107) suggests that the five Tilaka tantras are as follows: (1) *Saṃpuṭatilaka* (Q27), (2) *Mahāmudrātilaka* (Q12), (3) *Jñānatilaka* (Q14), (4) *Candraguhyatilaka* (Q111), and (5) *Guhyamaṇitilaka* (Q125). Prajñāgupta was also known as the "red master" (*slob dpon dmar po*) and has sometimes been confused with Gayadhara due to the latter's being known as the "red ācārya" (*ā tsa rya dmar po*). This is discussed in Stearns 2001, 52–53. For more on Prajñāgupta see Davidson 2005, 202 and 413n160, which provides further references.
66. Presumably the six cycles of the essence (*snying po skor drug*) discussed in Stearns 2001, 217n51.
67. In eleventh-century Tibet, the *bandes* appear to have been Buddhists who wore the monastic robes but lived as householders and who upheld some of the older Buddhist traditions (see Davidson 2005, 15–17 and 106–7).
68. The Mongo and Balmo ravines (*grog po*) form the eastern and western borders of Sakya. See the map in Schoening 1990, 23.
69. The White Zimchil, also known as the White Gorum Zimchil, and sometimes simply the Gorum, is the original Sakya temple. It later housed the Skin Mask statue of Mahākāla. See Schoening 1990, 13–14 and map 5.
70. The circumstances of Sachen's conception and birth, which were facilitated by Namkhaupa, are given in detail in Ame Zhab's history of the Sakya family. See Stearns 2001, 61, and Davidson 2005, 293–95.
71. This verse is known in the Sakya tradition as *Parting from the Four Attachments* (*Zhen pa bzhi bral*) and has been the subject of numerous commentaries.
72. According to Stearns 2001, 135, Rong Ngurmig is not a place but another name for Drangti Darma Nyingpo.
73. This refers to the two systems of *Guhyasamāja* exegesis derived from the works of Buddhajñānapāda and Nāgārjuna.
74. This is the collection known as the Hundred Sādhanas of Bari (*Ba ri brgya rtsa*).
75. The *Pramāṇaviniścaya* and the *Nyāyabindu* are pramāṇa treatises by Dharmottara and Dharmakīrti, respectively. The three eastern Svātantrika Mādhyamikas (*dbu ma rang rgyud shar gsum*) are Jñānagarbha, Śāntarakṣita (a student of Jñānagarbha), and Kamalaśīla (a student of Śāntarakṣita). The main treatises associated with them are, respectively, the *Satyadvāyavibhaṅgha*, the *Madhyamakālaṃkāra*, and the *Madhyamakāloka*. See Ruegg 1981, 68–71, 82–86, and 93–99.
76. This unidentified collection (*Grub pa sde bco brgyad*) may be a misrendering of *Grub pa sde brgyad* (Skt. *Aṣṭasiddhi*), a collection of eight Indic texts (written communication from Cyrus Stearns, 2007).

77. The commentaries on the *Aṣṭasāhasrikā* and *Abhisamayālaṃkāra* mentioned here would probably have been Haribhadra's (Q5184 and Q5191, respectively).
78. Tibetan text has the year of the male-earth *tiger*, but this would be 1158, when Sachen was sixty-seven.
79. Stearns (2001 254n232) discusses the early sources for this story in the works of Dragpa Gyaltsen and Sakya Paṇḍita.
80. On the identity of these seventy-two tantras, see Stearns 2001, 255n234. The "boundary wall" (*lcags ri*) symbolically represents the outer limit of the maṇḍala. Here, the meaning is probably that the four profound Dharmas were not transmitted outside of Sakya (written communication from Cyrus Stearns, 2007). In the Lamdre section of this work, the four are said to be (1) the *Teaching on the Secret Path*, (2) the *Profound Path*, (3) *Virūpa's Protectors*, and (4) *Virūpa's System of Vajravidāraṇā*. Three of these texts are mentioned in the same context in the *Incisive Vajra* (Stearns 2001, 153). Sachen's vision and the texts associated with it are the subject of a skeptical treatment in Davidson 2005, 315–21.
81. This is the *Hymn to Glorious Virūpa*. See the translation in Davidson 2005, 50–52. See also Sachen's *Hymn to Zhangton, Possessing the Supreme Qualities*.
82. This event is mentioned in Stearns 2001, 155, where the maṇḍala is that of Jampal Drime (*'Jam dpal dri med*) rather than Namkha Drime.
83. The four means are (1) generosity (*sbyin*), (2) pleasant speech (*snyan par smra ba*), (3) meaningful conduct (*don spyod pa*), and (4) giving appropriate teachings (*don mthun pa*). The two stages are development (*skyes rim*) and perfection (*rdzogs rim*).
84. The path of preparation (*sbyor lam*), the second of the five paths of the bodhisattva, comprises warmth (*drod pa*), peak (*rtse mo*), forbearance (*bzod pa*), and supreme worldly qualities (*chos mchog*).
85. A different form of the prophecy appears in earlier sources. According to Davidson 2005, 303: "He was also told that if he should only practice, he would receive the accomplishment of the Great Seal. But if Sachen were to teach, then he would have an unlimited number of students, including three who would attain the highest accomplishment of the Great Seal, seven who would achieve the 'patience' of a bodhisattva on the mundane path, and eighty who would achieve realization."
86. The issue of the status of Sonam Tsemo is mentioned in Davidson 2005, 337–38, with further references to Tibetan discussions of the topic.
87. Davidson 2005, 338, has Maghada.
88. The tantra trilogy of Hevajra, often referred to merely as "the tantra trilogy" (*rgyud gsum*), comprises the *Hevajra Tantra*, the *Vajrapañjara Tantra*, and the *Saṃpuṭa Tantra*.
89. The lakeside retreat (*rdzing kha*) of Chumig was in the far western part of the Sakya establishment (see Schoening 1990, 44).
90. These are the eight *brahmacarya* (*tshangs par spyod pa*) vows usually given to young ordinands.
91. The *Three Continua* (*rgyud gsum*) are the texts comprising the main practices of the Lamdre. The term refers to the continuum of the universal basis or *ālaya* (*kun gzhi*), which is the cause, the continuum of the body (*lus*), which is the path, and the continuum of the mahāmudrā (*phyag rgya chen po*), which is the result.
92. "Gathering of secrets" (*gsang ba 'dus pa*) is also the name of the *Guhyasamāja Tantra*.

93. This statement indicates that Dragpa Gyaltsen came close to death during his late twenties yet lived to a healthy old age.
94. The Tibetan text has fifty-nine (*nga dgu*), which does not agree with the years given for the birth and death of Palchen Onpo.
95. Tsang Nagpa Tsondru Senge was a student of Chapa Chokyi Senge at Sangpu Monastery. There were many doctors with the epithet Biji (*Lha rje Bi ji*).
96. These two visions are recounted in Sapaṇ's earliest biography in Stearns 2001, 161.
97. Note Stearns 2001, 163–65, has Kyangthur (*rkyang thur*).
98. The three pramāṇa texts (*tshad ma gsum*) are Dignāga's *Pramāṇasamuccaya*, Dharmakīrti's *Pramāṇavārttika*, and Dharmottara's *Pramāṇaviniścaya*.
99. The original hymn was written by Dragpa Gyaltsen and can be found at SKB 7:475–81.
100. For an English translation of *Distinguishing the Three Vows*, see Rhoton 2002. Various question-and-answer sessions (*dris lan* or *zhus lan*) can be found in SKB 12.
101. For an English translation of the *Precious Treasury of Excellent Sayings*, see Davenport 2000. On Sapaṇ's translations, see Jackson 1987, 2:112–13, and Stearns 2001, 258n256.
102. An "expert in the ten sciences" is a synonym in the Sakya tradition for a *paṇḍita* (written communication from David Jackson, 2007).
103. The Old Utse temple was built immediately to the south of the White Gorum Zimchil. According to Schoening it was constructed by Sachen, while Zangtsa and Dragpa Gyaltsen constructed a much larger extension to the south (the New Utse temple) along with a lama residence built over the Old Utse. They also gave the temple a gold roof (Schoening 1990, 14 and map 9).
104. The Tibetan sentence implies that Pagpa arrived in Mongolia at the age of seventeen, but this is in contradiction with the usual date (also given in the section on Sapaṇ) of Sapaṇ and Pagpa's arrival in Liangzhou in 1246, when Pagpa was twelve.
105. The emperor Sechen is Kubilai Khan. Tibetan and Mongolian writers usually use this honorific title (Mongolian *Sečen*) when referring to Kubilai.
106. On the office of imperial preceptor (*dishi*) see Petech 1990, 36–37. According to Petech, Pagpa received the position of national preceptor (*guoshi*) in 1261 and the office of imperial preceptor in 1269 or 1270.
107. For an account of the struggles that occurred within Tibet between the supporters of different Mongol powers, and Pagpa's part in them, see Everding 2002. See also Shoju Inaba 1963 for a translation of a Tibetan account written in the fourteenth century.
108. Pagpa wrote a brief poem on this achievement, entitled *Verses on the Defeat of the Daoist Teachers*, dating the event to the twenty-third day of the middle summer month of the male earth-horse year (1258).
109. At this point, in 1265, Pagpa took the office of throne holder, which had been held by a regent since the death of Sapaṇ (Petech 1990, 22).
110. *Gsol gzim mchod gsum*: three attendants responsible for provisions (*gsol dpon*), chambers (*gzim dpon*), and offerings (*mchod dpon*). These posts continued to exist in the household and goverment of the Dalai Lamas. *Mjal yig mdzod gsum*: a triumvirate of steward (*mgron gnyer*), secretary (*drung yig*), and treasurer (*phyag mdzod*). These posts continued in labrangs and aristocratic residences. *Thab 'dren gdan gsum*: three overseers

of cooks, servers, and seating. *Rta skya gnyis*: two overseers of horses and crops. *Mdzo khyi*: the overseer of cattle and hunting dogs.

111. Before returning to Tibet Pagpa had given up the office of imperial preceptor, which was passed on to Lobpon Rinchen Gyaltsen, another of Zangtsa's sons (Petech 1990, 23).

112. According to the chronicles of the Fifth Dalai Lama, translated in Tucci 1949, 2:627, some people said that Pagpa was murdered by a treacherous attendant.

113. This is Kubilai's heir-apparent Jĭngim. The treatise written by Pagpa for Jĭngim is translated in Hoog 1983, which states that Jĭngim accompanied Pagpa for part of his journey back to Tibet in 1275 (Hoog 1983, 5).

114. The Tibetan text has Pagpa's age as eleven, but this contradicts the account in the previous section.

115. This is the White Gorum Zimchil, the original Sakya temple founded by Khon Konchog Gyalpo.

116. Literally, the "three classes" (*rigs gsum*), taken here to refer to the three classes of being in the early Sakya family line: the divine lineage, the Khon family, and the Sakyapas.

117. Tri (or Tre) Maṇḍala is also known as Chuwo and is situated west of Kardze. Dharmapāla died there in 1287, while making the journey back to Sakya, having given up the office of imperial preceptor in the previous year. See Petech 1990, 26.

118. The Flower Courtyard (Metog Rawa) was the Sakya residence in the Mongol Palace where Pagpa had lived. As mentioned above, Petech (1990, 23) says Rinchen Gyaltsen actually took the office of imperial preceptor after Pagpa had vacated it in 1274.

119. Hukarche is the Tibetan transcription of the name of Kubilai's fifth son Ḣugeči, who was appointed provincial governor in 1267 and died four years later of poisoning. According to some sources, Yeshe Jungne died in Kham, not China (Petech 1990, 72).

120. Zangpo Pal was summoned to the Mongol court at the age of twenty-one (1282) and then exiled to an island in South China. The issue seems to have been doubts cast over his legitimacy. He returned to the court at thirty-seven (1298) and became the Sakya throne holder at the age of forty-five (1306). In the period between the deaths of Dharmapāla and Ratnabhadra and Zangpo Pal's coming to the Sakya seat, it was held by Sharpa Jamyang Rinchen Gyaltsen. Furthermore, after Dharmapāla the post of imperial preceptor was held by a succession of members of the Sharpa and Khangsar clans until Zangpo Pal's son Kunga Lodro took the position in 1315. Thus the Khon clan was in danger of being entirely marginalized during this period, and its continued relevance depended on Zangpo Pal's return to favor and his production of many sons (Petech 1990, 71–78; Tucci 1949, 2:627, 683n78).

121. According to the *Blue Annals*, Zangpo Pal's first son was Sonam Zangpo, who was born at the imperial court and died on the way back to Tibet (Roerich 1996, 213).

122. According to Petech, the Zhitog labrang was already the residence of the Sakya throne holder and continued to be through to the twentieth century. Rinchen Gang was to the northeast of Zhitog and had been built by Kunga Zangpo. Dungcho was to the southeast of Zhitog. See Petech 1990, 81.

123. Khetsun Namkha Legpa was the third son of the imperial preceptor Kunga Lodro. He became the Sakya throne holder. Dagchen Lodro Wangchug was his great-grandson.

124. These three brothers were sons of the imperial preceptor Kunga Lodro. Lama Dampa was also the Sakya throne holder between 1344 and 1347.

125. The explication for the assembly (*tshogs bshad*) and the explication for disciples (*slob bshad*) are two methods of transmitting the Lamdre. The transmission of the explication for disciples is discussed in chapters 5 and 7. For more historical details see Stearns 2001, 39–45.

126. Ngawang Kunga Legpai Jungne and Kunga Gyaltsen were also sons of the imperial preceptor Kunga Lodro. The former became imperial preceptor in 1327 and died in the Flower Courtyard in 1330 or 1339 (see Petech 1990, 83). Kunga Legpa was the great-great-great-grandson of one of the two brothers.

127. Kunga Legpa Zangpo Pal was one of the sons of the imperial preceptor Kunga Lodro. He should not be confused with his grandfather Dagchen Zangpo Pal. He is also not the Kunga Legpa mentioned immediately above in the description of the House of Lhakhang.

128. Note that up to this point in the Dungcho line there are several differences between this account and the genealogy chart in Amipa 1976.

129. Ame Zhab wrote some of the most influential historical works on the Sakya school, some of which are sources for the present work (see the author's colophon in the conclusion).

130. Virūpa's protection practice (*bir srung*), which has an exoteric and esoteric version, is one of the daily practices of the Lamdre.

131. DR's note: The first two sons were the origin of the Drolma Palace and the Puntsog Palace, respectively.

132. According to the genealogy chart in Amipa 1976, Dorje Rinchen was the son of both Pema Dudul Wangchug and Ngawang Kunga Rinchen, by a joint marriage to a single wife.

133. According to the genealogy chart in Amipa 1976, these two brothers were the sons of Ngawang Kunga Rinchen by a second wife.

134. This is the throne holder Trashi Rinchen mentioned three paragraphs above.

135. The family history of Jigdral Ngawang Kunga Sonam (respectfully known as Dagchen Rinpoche) is recounted in detail in Jackson 2003. Dagchen Rinpoche has five children: Minzuvajra, Anivajra, Mativajra, Zayavajra, and Sadhuvajra.

136. According to the genealogy chart in Amipa 1976, he was born of a joint marriage by the brothers Ngawang Kunga Rinchen and Kunga Tenpai Gyaltsen to a single wife.

137. His Holiness Sakya Trizin has two sons, Ratnavajra and Gyanavajra.

138. *Hevajra Tantra* II.viii.9–10. Translation based on Snellgrove 1959, 1:116. This passage in Snellgrove's critical edition is in 2:91. The passage is spoken in reply to a query about how to instruct unworthy beings who are hard to train.

139. This last sentence is a reference to the fact that it was more common to link this prophecy with the great logician Dharmakīrti.

140. Stearns 2006 has Vinayadeva and Jayakīrti.

141. The word translated here as "wicked" is *virūpa* in Sanskrit (literally, "misshapen" or "ugly").

142. Ḍombīpa is also known as Ḍombī Heruka. His biography is given immediately below.

143. The Khasarpaṇa statue of Avalokiteśvara, which also features in the biographies of Drogmi and Nyen Lotsāwa below, is discussed in Stearns 2001, 209–10n25.

144. In the longer version of this prophecy, Avalokiteśvara specifically commands Virūpa to subdue others through skillful means rather than frightening them with feats of yogic discipline. See Stearns 2006, 148–49.

145. On the tantras revealed by Virūpa and the texts attributed to him, see Chattopadhyaya and Chimpa 1970, 245 and 404. The "unelaborated original text of the Lamdre" is the *Vajra Lines* (*Rdo rje tshig rkang*). On this text and its commentaries, see Stearns 2006.

146. Because Ḍombīpa did not receive the root text of the Lamdre, the lineage of the transmissions he received from Virūpa is known as the *rootless Lamdre*. It is also referred to as the *commentarial method* (*'grel pa lugs*). The rootless Lamdre tradition is sometimes identified with Ḍombī Heruka's text *Innate Accomplishment*, one of the nine cycles of the path (see Davidson 2005, 197).

147. The twenty-four sacred places (*pīṭha*) are sacred sites in India associated with twenty-four parts of the sacred body, as enumerated in the *Cakrasaṃvara Tantra*. The thirty-two sites are these twenty-four along with the eight famous charnel grounds. See Davidson 2002, 206–10.

148. Supreme wordly qualities (*chos mchog*) is the highest stage of the path of application (*sbyor lam*), the second of the five paths of the bodhisattva.

149. The rest of this conversation, involving Drogmi's inadvertently insulting Gayadhara in Sanskrit, is recounted in Ame Zhab's *Lamdre History* (329–30) and is retold in Stearns 2001, 51.

150. On these prophecies, see the section on Drogmi below.

151. The *Lamdre History* of Ame Zhab (131) contains a passage omitted here in which Gayadhara asks for five hundred ounces of gold as a price for his teachings.

152. The *Gurupañcāśikā* (*Fifty Verses on the Guru*) was written by the Indian master Bhavideva (although authorship is sometimes attributed to an Aśvaghoṣa) as a treatise on the correct relationship between master and disciple in the context of the Vajrayāna. It is often taught in the Sakya tradition along with the commentary by Tsarchen Losal Gyatso.

153. A fathom (*'dom*) is about six feet, the measurement of between two outstretched arms, from fingertip to fingertip.

154. Here the text omits Ame Zhab's account of Drogmi's request to Zurpoche Śākya Junge to give him enough gold to make up the complete offering of five hundred ounces and Gayadhara's disbelief when presented with the full five hundred ounces. See Stearns 2001, 90–93, and Davidson 2005, 180–81.

155. Although this was actually Gayadhara's second trip, the first two trips are counted as one by Ame Zhab to harmonize this narrative with earlier accounts stating that Gayadhara made only three trips to Tibet. See Stearns 2001, 51–53.

156. Here the text omits several pages from Ame Zhab's *Lamdre History* (135–38) concerning Gayadhara's relationship with Go Lotsāwa; the stories here generally cast Go Lotsāwa in a poor light in comparison to Drogmi. See Stearns 2001, 92–97.

157. One of these patron students was Nyo Lotsāwa. See Stearns 2001, 96–97.

158. Gyijo Dawai Ozer is usually credited with making an early translation of the *Kālacakra*

Tantra and fixing the new Tibetan calendar based on it. According to Sakya sources this was done with Gayadhara, but other sources mention another Indian master, Bhadrabodhi. See Stearns 2001, 219n60. The Kangyur and Tengyur contain a number of tantras and ritual manuals translated by the team of Gayadhara and Gyijo.

159. Those whom Gayadhara referred to as his children were Drogmi's disciples, especially Seton Kunrig and Shengom Rogpo (Ame Zhab, *Lamdre History*, 138). See also Davidson 2005, 182–83.

160. The Rali tantras comprise a group of texts that are considered part of the Cakrasaṃvara cycle, found in the Kangyur (for a list see Obermiller 1986, 2:216n1605). Although Buton attributes their translation to Drogmi, the opinion of the author cited here, as well as certain other Sakya scholars, is that they were fabricated by Nyo Lotsāwa. See Stearns 2001, 220n60, for a discussion of this issue.

161. Wangchug Rabten was a teacher of Ame Zhab (see earlier in this work), nephew of Jamyang Khyentse Wangchug, and abbot of Zhalu Monastery. He is also known as Tsewang Lhundrub Rabten.

162. Here *zin bris* may refer to manuscripts or personal notes, so Ame Zhab may be saying: "according to my personal notes."

163. Loton Dorje Wangchug and Tsongtsun Sherab Senge were two disciples of Gongpa Rabsel who came from Tsang to take ordination in the Amdo region. They returned to Tsang and were significant figures in the revitalization of Buddhism in Central Tibet, founding the Gyengong temple among others. See Sørensen 1994, 448–49nn1633–34; see also Davidson 2005, 92–98.

164. The three trainings are (1) morality (*tshul khrims*), (2) concentration (*ting nge 'dzin*), and (3) insight (*shes rab*).

165. The four paṇḍitas were the Pamtingpa brothers. The brothers were based at a sacred site in the Kathmandu Valley known today as Pharping. They seem to have taught many other Tibetan translators, including Marpa Lotsāwa. See Stearns 2001, 206–7n15, and Davidson 2005, 143.

166. These texts are all found in the *Sa skya Lam 'bras Literature Series* 13:395–410. See Stearns 2001, 208–9n22. On the stories of the gate guardians of Vikramaśīla, see Chattopadhyaya and Chimpa 1970, 294–303.

167. Ajitamitra was also known as Ajitaguptamitra and Mitrayogin. On this figure and his teachings, see Roerich 1996, 1030–43.

168. Bhikṣu Vīravajra was a disciple of Durjayacandra in Ḍombī Heruka's lineage of Virūpa's teachings. He was also known by the name Prajñendraruci.

169. According to Jamyang Khyentse Wangchug's history of the Lamdre, on his second trip to India Drogmi was accompanied by his consort, Lhachig Dzeden Ochag. See Stearns 2006, 173–74. On the differing versions of Drogmi's time with Vīravajra, see Stearns 2001, 210–12n33.

170. Vīravajra here is referring to his own death.

171. Of these three texts, the first two are sādhanas and the third is a stotra, or hymn. They were composed by Durjayacandra, Prajñendraruci, and Ratnavajra respectively.

172. As well as the names Maitrīpa and Advayavajra, this adept is known as Maitrigupta, Maitripāda, and Avadhūtipāda. Maitrīpa is not usually identified with the Avadhūtipa

of the Lamdre lineage, but see Stearns 2001, 189n221. For a study of Maitrīpa see Tatz 1987. The mahāmudrā teachings and lineage of Maitrīpa are discussed in *The Blue Annals* (Roerich 1996, 839–66). See also Stearns 2001, 217n51.

173. Khecarī (*mkha' spyod ma*) is a form of the deity Vajrayoginī. See the section below on the Thirteen Golden Dharmas for an enumeration of the Sakya Khecarī practices, which include the Khecarī of Maitrīpa.

174. The list of nine texts here is taken from the compilation edited by Dragpa Gyaltsen known as the *Yellow Book* (*Pod ser*). The compilation contains texts translated from Sanskrit and texts based on the instructions of Indian teachers written in Tibetan by Sachen Kunga Nyingpo and Jetsun Dragpa Gyaltsen. See Stearns 2001, 34–35, and Davidson 2005, 194–204 and 356–59.

175. This refers to Virūpa's *Vajra Lines*, the root text of the Lamdre.

176. According to Davidson 2005, 199, the actual author of this text is Dragpa Gyaltsen.

177. In the *Yellow Book* this *Commentary on Bodhicitta* is given four other titles including *Received Before a Stūpa* (*Mchod rten drung thob*, SLL 11:400–406). Davidson 2005, 197–98, states that the text was written by Dragpa Gyaltsen based on Sachen Kunga Nyingpo's teachings. The actual *Commentary on Bodhicitta* (Skt. *Bodhicittavivaraṇa*) ascribed to Nāgārjuna serves as the basis for these instructions by Dragpa Gyaltsen.

178. Unlike the other texts in this list, the original Sanskrit text for this one, the *Acintyādvayakramopadeśa*, is still extant; see Davidson 2005, 411n120.

179. Caryāvajra here refers to the author Kāṇha (also known as Kṛṣṇa Paṇḍitā). The *Olapati* is identified by Davidson 2005, 200, as the canonical text the *Four Stages* (*Rim pa bzhi pa*, Q2168). However, the present text appears to identify the *Olapati* with the *Drops of Spring* (*Dpyid kyi thig le*, Skt. *Vasantatilaka*, Q2166). Another complication is that the name of the text by Kāṇha (Caryāvajra) that usually forms part of the nine cycles of the path is the *Complete Path of Inner Heat* (*Gtum mo lam rdzogs*, SLL 11:445–57). According to Dragpa Gyaltsen, the *Complete Path of Inner Heat* represents the oral instructions of the *Olapati* (Davidson 2005, 200), so here the name *Olapati* may be considered to refer to the *Complete Path of Inner Heat* by extension. The meaning of the name Olapati is not clear, but it may be equivalent to the Tibetan *rim pa bzhi*, "the four stages." Davidson (2005, 200–201) states that *ola* survives in another canonical title meaning a stage (*rim pa*). Note also that an *Olipati Tantra* (*sic*) is mentioned in the Dunhuang manuscript Pelliot tibétain 849.

180. Acyuta Kāṇha is the same as Caryāvajra/Kāṇha of the previous text. According to Davidson 2005, 201, the text here was actually written by either Sachen Kunga Nyingpo or Dragpa Gyaltsen.

181. The Sakya tradition distinguishes three historical figures with the name Indrabhūti, known as great, medium, and lesser based on their antiquity. Thus the great Indrabhūti, said to be a disciple of the Buddha himself, is the earliest. This is discussed at the end of this text itself. See Davidson 2005, 202.

182. Though a text of this name survives in Sanskrit, the text in the *Yellow Book* is a different one, apparently an instruction based on the former. See Davidson 2005, 196.

183. According to Davidson 2005, 198–99, this text was written by Dragpa Gyaltsen, based on a teaching of Vāgīśvarakīrti transmitted by Drogmi.

184. The Nairātmyā text in question is the *Nairātmyāyoginīsādhana* (Q2436) by Ḍombī Heruka (Davidson 2005, 198).

185. Here "the other six" refers to the above list excluding the *Vajra Lines.*

186. For a detailed treatment of the nine cycles of the path, see Davidson 2005, 194–204.

187. On Prajñāgupta and Amoghavajra see Stearns 2001, 52–53 and 193n255. Amoghavajra is also known as the younger Vajrāsana.

188. Detailed accounts of all of these students can be found in Jamyang Khyentse Wangchug's history of the Lamdre, translated in Stearns 2006.

189. The names of the Zhama brother and sister were Lord Khumbu and Machig Gyalmo. Their lineages are discussed in the following section.

190. Here "understanding" (*go ba*) refers specifically to intellectual understanding. It is usually said that Zhangton Chobar studied the texts less than his younger brother but engaged in meditation more.

191. Here the translations "essential constituents" (*khams 'dus*) and "malleable qualities" (*mnyen lcug*) are informed by Cyrus Stearns; see Stearns 2006, 635n58 and 647n243.

192. This is the legendary birthplace of Padmasambhava, located in Oḍḍiyāna.

193. DR's note: The oral lineage was later augmented by the writings of Jetsun Dragpa Gyaltsen. The written lineage comprises the eleven commentaries written by Sachen for individual petitioners.

194. Sachen's companion is a rather mysterious figure. In Jamyang Khyentse Wangchug's history of the Lamdre, he is called Apo Gyalpo (Stearns 2006, 220).

195. The four great rivers of India are the Ganges (Gaṅgā), Sindhu, Sitā, and Pakṣu.

196. Note this differs from the earlier account, which says that Sachen practiced in his own quarters. The Mañjuśrī cave is where Sachen received the teachings known as *Parting from the Four Attachments* from Mañjuśrī.

197. In this passage Zhangton Chobar is referred to as *Lord Gonpawa* (*Rje Dgon pa ba*).

198. This is the *Hymn to Glorious Virūpa.*

199. On the identity of these seventy-two tantras, see Stearns 2001, 255n234. Sachen's vision and the texts associated with it are the subject of a skeptical treatment in Davidson 2005, 315–21.

200. DR's note: These are the *Teaching on the Secret Path*, the *Profound Path*, *Virūpa's Protectors*, and *Virūpa's System of Vajravidaraṇa.*

201. The references here are to the seventy-two tantras and four Dharmas that do not pass beyond the boundary wall, transmitted to Sachen in a vision of Virūpa, mentioned above.

202. DR's note: Those students who were closer to Sachen were known as his sons, while those who were further from him were known as his nephews.

203. Here the author follows the Tsarpa interpretation of the identity of Sachen's eleven commentaries, following Mangto Ludrub and Khyentse Wangchug. An older interpretation, following Musepa Dorje Gyaltsen, does not include the *Zangripugma* and *Mangchungma*, having in their place the *Bandema* and *Denbuma*. This latter list actually matches the eleven texts of Sachen's commentaries that have survived to the present day (although as the author notes here, not all have a surviving textual transmission). Each of the eleven commentaries, and the different traditions of listing the eleven, are

discussed in Stearns 2001, 16–25. Davidson (2005, 303–11) analyzes the commentaries and the chronology of their composition.

204. The long version of the *Asengma* is no longer extant. See Stearns 2001, 18.

205. These lines appear in Sapaṇ's *Biography of the Great Lama Jetsun*, 584–85. A version of the lines also appears in Sakya Paṇḍita's *Clarification of the Meaning through Symbols*, 205. See also the discussion in Davidson 2005, 351.

206. These lines are also from Sakya Paṇḍita's *Clarification of the Meaning through Symbols*, 206.

207. These are discussed in Davidson 2005, 306–7.

208. On a different enumeration by Jetsun Dragpa Gyaltsen, see Sobisch 2002.

209. The book in question is the *Yellow Book* compiled by Jetsun Dragpa Gyaltsen. All twenty-four texts listed below are found together in parts 2 and 3 of the *Yellow Book* (SLL, 11:11–191). Ten of these texts are by Dragpa Gyaltsen; the others are by Sachen Kunga Nyingpo. The names of the texts in the list given in the present work are in condensed form; the full titles given in translation here are from the printed edition. The compilation of the *Yellow Book* is discussed in Stearns 2001, 32–35, and Davidson 2005, 356–59.

210. Dragpa Gyaltsen's list has the following three texts at this point: (1) *Condensed Fire Ritual for Removing Obstacles*, (2) *Removing Obstacles by Washing*, and (3) *Removing Obstacles with Tsatsa*. However, in the printed edition of the *Yellow Book*, number 3 is presented not as a separate text but as a subsection of 2. This would explain the reference to two texts in the present list. It would also clear up a discrepancy in the table of contents for the *Yellow Book*, which states that there are twenty-four texts but lists twenty-five (see SLL 11:4).

211. This is Sachen's *Asengma*.

212. These verses describe the contents of the *Yellow Book* contained in sections 4 to 9.

213. The above three lines refer to six texts by Dragpa Gyaltsen, some of which are found in SLL, 11:191–260.

214. The four texts on clearing away hindrances are found in SLL, 11:260–67. The three sādhanas are in SLL, 11:267–92.

215. These three texts are not in the current edition of the *Yellow Book*. The commentary on the fourteen root downfalls called *Dispelling Errors* is found in SKB, 7:255–378.

216. All of the texts before this point are considered part of the extensive path. They are followed by two texts detailing the medium and concise path (SLL, 11:292–300), and then by a group of nine texts that include the four great central pillars (SLL, 11:300–323) and the five Dharmas that produce realization (SLL, 11:323–44).

217. The scriptural connections (*lung sbyor*) are four texts connecting the practices of the Lamdre with citations from the scriptures. The two histories (*chos 'byung*) are two short histories of the Lamdre by Dragpa Gyaltsen—the first histories of the Lamdre ever written.

218. "Aspects of the path" (*lam gyi cha rkyen*) refers to a genre of writing on issues that may arise during practice.

219. In the Sakya tradition, *guardian* (*mgon po*) usually refers specifically to the protector Mahākāla.

220. Varuci's *Mahākālasādhana*, translated by Amoghavajra and Bari, is in the Tengyur (Q4207).
221. See Q4912.
222. See Q2635 and Q2647.
223. See Q67–69.
224. There have been several lamas bearing the epithet Ngogpa (Rngogs pa). The ones in question here may be the translator Ngog Lotsāwa Loden Sherab (1059–1109) and his uncle Ngog Legpai Sherab (n.d), the founder of Sangpu Monastery.
225. The brother of Putra is called Batra. The Monpa brother and sisters are the Guardian of the Tent along with Śrīdevī (Palden Lhamo) and Ekajaṭi. See Nebesky-Wojkowitz 1956, 50–51.
226. The Skin Mask Guardian (Sebag Gonpo, or Sebag Yeshe Gonpo) is a form of Mahākāla. The physical representation of this protector that was brought to Tibet is a dance mask (*'chams sku*), and the guardian is also referred to here as the "dance mask." The protector is also known as the Flying Black Skin Mask (Sebag Nagpo Purshe).
227. The Skin Mask statue became one of the "four wondrous objects of worship" (*ngo mtshar ba'i rten bzhi*) at Sakya. Its whereabouts are no longer known (Schoening 1990, 43).
228. On these three forms, see Nebesky-Wojkowitz 1956, 60–61.
229. On these forms of the Four-Faced Mahākāla, see Nebesky-Wojkowitz 1956, 61–62.
230. The Khasarpaṇa image of Avalokiteśvara, which also features in the biographies of Virūpa and Drogmi Lotsāwa (above), is discussed in Stearns 2001, 209–10.
231. The Vairocana mentioned here is probably Vairocanarakṣita, an Indian paṇḍita who visited and taught in Tibet in the twelfth century. See *Blue Annals* (Roerich 1996, 844–47).
232. Uru ("the central horn") is a region name dating from the imperial administration of Tibet; Uruto is at the western end of the Kyichu River valley.
233. According to Davidson 2005, 297, Bari Lotsāwa's sojourn in central Tibet lasted fifteen years.
234. There is a short boundary protection ritual (*srung 'khor*) for Bhayanāsa by Sachen Kunga Nyingpo (SKB 2:284–86).
235. The stūpa discussed here is probably the Namgyal Chorten, one of Sakya's "four wondrous objects of worship." Bari is also said to have built a temple around the stūpa, and in the eighteenth century a larger stūpa was built over the Namgyal Chorten. For this reason the Namgyal Chorten was relatively undamaged by the destruction of Sakya in the 1960s. See Schoening 1990, 14.
236. These five topics comprise chapters 5 to 9 of the present translation.
237. This title does not appear in the Kangyur, but the passage quoted here seems to be a substantially edited version of a prophecy that appears in the fifth chapter of the *Kuśalamūlaparidhara Sūtra* (Q769, 99a–100b). The majority of the sūtra prophecy is not cited, including portions before and after the cited lines, as well as several verses after lines 2, 11, 25, and 40 of this citation. Also, lines 31–37 of this citation appear in a different position in the sūtra prophecy, after the final lines of this citation.
238. I have translated this line based on the version in the sūtra: *de tshe sems can blta bar spro ba med.*

239. I have translated this line based on the version in the sūtra: *de dag thams cad shes pas tshogs par 'gyur.*
240. These verses are from chapter 9 of the *Saddharmapuṇḍarīka Sūtra.* In the sūtra this prophecy is given by the Buddha to Ānanda regarding his future life as a buddha.
241. Zhitogpa Kunga Rinchen (1339–99) was a Sakya throne holder. See Heimbel 2011 for an overview of biographical sources for Ngorchen Kunga Zangpo's life.
242. The *Three Perceptions* (*snang gsum*) are the texts comprising the preliminary practices for the Lamdre. The term refers to three levels of perception: the impure (*ma dag pa*) perception of an ordinary being, the visionary or "experiential" (*snyams*) perception of a yogin, and the pure (*dag pa*) perception of a buddha.
243. The six yogas (*sbyor drug*) refers to the six-branch vajra yoga (*rdo rje rnal 'byor yan lag drug pa*) of Kālacakra tantra. In the later tradition, they are included in the eight chariots of the practice lineage; see the beginning of chapter 9.
244. DR's note: There is a Collected Works in one volume.
245. For a discussion of this and other versions of the list of abbots at Ewam Choden, see Jackson 1989b. Many of the names here include official titles, particularly that of Khenchen "great abbot." Later titles often include the names of one of the four houses of Ngor, Penkhang (also known as Pende), Tartse, Khangsar, and Luding, with candidates for the abbacy taken from one of these houses in turn.
246. DR's note: Jamyang was watched over by Sapaṇ. There are many works by him.
247. DR's note: There is a Collected Works in one volume.
248. DR's note: There is a Collected Works in fifteen volumes.
249. The "nephew line" (*dbon rgyud*) refers to the line of patrilinial descent via the nephew. At points in this list and elsewhere, "nephew" (*dbon*) is sometimes used as shorthand for "in the nephew line."
250. DR's note: On this occasion the teachings of Ngorchen Dorje Chang were sent to Karjam. He greatly furthered the teachings, having been told in a prophecy that he would do so.
251. There is a Collected Works in one volume, including a Lamdre instruction manual.
252. DR's note: There is a Collected Works in four volumes.
253. DR's note: There are a few works by him.
254. DR's note: There are three volumes of excellent teachings, including *The Vajra Garland.*
255. DR's note: Born into the lineage of Ozer Senge, the commander-in-chief of Sakya. There is a single book of his works, containing many excellent teachings.
256. DR's note: This was the beginning of the Gerpeb succession of abbots.
257. DR's note: He was appointed stand-in throne holder of Tartse.
258. DR's note: He also went to Derge in order to honor Khenchen Jampaiyang Sangye Puntsog.
259. DR's note: He established the hermitage of Yilhung Lhagyal in the thirteenth fire-pig year (1767).
260. DR's note: He was made throne holder for seven years.
261. These are the five topics mentioned elsewhere: Prajñāpāramitā, Madhyamaka, Pramāṇa, Vinaya, and Abhidharma.
262. That is to say, Yagton (Yag) is paired either with Rendawa (Zhon) or Rongton (Rong).

263. Bu and Dol are Buton and Dolpopa. Nya and Tson are Nyawon Kunga Pal and Tsondru Pal. Yag and Zhon are Yagton Sangye Pal and Rendawa Zhonu Lodro. The two lineages are Buton—>Tsondru Pal—>Yagton and Dolpopa—>Nyawon—>Rendawa. Other sources for this tradition are discussed in Cabezon and Dargyay 2007, 295.
264. Gar Tongtsen was the most important minister of Songtsen Gampo's reign. He and his sons continued to hold great power after the death of Songtsen Gampo.
265. See Roloff 2009 and Harter 2011 on Rendawa's philosophical views.
266. The text has *dka' chen bzhi*, but this should probably be corrected to *bka' chen bzhi*, which indicates the four textual traditions emphasized in the Kadam curriculum: Prajñāpāramitā, Pramāṇa, Vinaya, and Abhidharma. See Dreyfus 2003, 144.
267. Kazhipa (*bka' bzhi pa*) is an honorific title indicating mastery of the four textual transmissions.
268. That is, exposition, composition, and debate.
269. Text has *sa ma bya* "earth-bird year," which would be 1369 or 1429.
270. The *Blue Annals* dates the founding of Nalendra to the wood-hare year (1435). See Roerich 1996, 1081.
271. The *five eyes* (*spyan lnga*) are: (1) the physical eye (*sha'i spyan*), (2) the divine eye (*lha'i spyan*), (3) the eye of knowledge (*shes rab kyi spyan*), (4) the eye of Dharma (*chos kyi spyan*), and (5) the eye of wisdom (*ye shes kyi spyan*).
272. On the title Kachupa (*bka' bcu pa*), "master of the ten textual traditions," see Dreyfus 2003, 144.
273. See Dreyfus 2003, 144.
274. The text has iron-horse year (*lcags rta*), which would be 1450 or 1510.
275. DR's note: The stream of the teaching center at the great temple of Sakya itself also began in this place.
276. According to van der Kuijp 1983, 121, Tanag Tubten Nampar Gyalwai Ling was founded in 1472, Nyenyo Jago Shong in 1489, and Je Tubten Yangpachen in 1490.
277. *Skye tshal dgon ma lag drug.* According to van der Kuijp 1983, 120, the complex is also known as "The six children of Mother Kyetsal" (*skyed tshal ma bu drug*). All six monasteries specialized in the study of Pramāṇa.
278. The commentary indicated here is probably Gorampa's *Yum don rab gsal.* There is a different interpretation of this in Cabezon and Dargyay 2007, 36.
279. Sachen's commentary is *Explanation of the Vajrabhairavakalpa Tantra.*
280. This commentary by Gorampa does not seem to be extant.
281. See Cassor 2011 for an overview of Gorampa's works on Madhyamaka.
282. GSB, 7:1–453.
283. GSB, 8:1–125.
284. Not identified.
285. GSB, 2:1–383.
286. GSB, 3:1–667.
287. GSB, 4:1–160.
288. GSB, 4:161–357.
289. GSB, 4:359–475.
290. GSB, 4:477–720.

291. GSB, 5:511–751.
292. These are the two famous treatises on the Madhyamaka: *Illuminating Certainty* (*Nges don rab gsal*, GSB, 5:1–415) and *Distinguishing the View* (*Lta ba'i shan byed*, GSB, 5:417–510).
293. Not identified.
294. GSB, 9:1–323.
295. GSB, 9:489–619.
296. GSB, 9:325–488.
297. GSB, 1:95–107.
298. Not identified.
299. GSB, 12:31–177.
300. GSB, 13:279–631.
301. Several works related to Guhyasamāja are found in GSB volumes 10 and 11.
302. Not identified.
303. Gorampa traveled to Sakya and taught there in the final year of his life.
304. According to Kunga Drolchog's *Detailed Biography of the Great Paṇḍita Śākya Chogden* (18.7), Bagton was a contemporary of Rongton and a disciple of Yagton. Śākya Chogden is considered to be the rebirth of both the master Yagton and the disciple Bagton. The title Mapam indicates that this master was considered an emanation of Maitreya. The *Detailed Biography* (6.1–7.6) suggests that Yagton, Rongton, and Śākya Chogden were all emanations of Maitreya (personal communication from Volker Caumanns, 2009).
305. While the text suggests the "lower terrace" (*bang rim*), this seems to be the name of a hamlet near Sangpu. See Kunga Drolchog's *Detailed Biography,* 8.6. Personal communication from Volker Caumanns, 2009.
306. Text has water-sheep year (1463). There is some confusion concerning the correct date of Rongton's death in the Tibetan sources. According to Kunga Drolchog's *Detailed Biography* (53.6), Rongton died in the twelfth month of the iron-horse year, which is early 1451. But the *Detailed Biography* is not correct on this point. Rongton died in the twelfth month of the earth-snake year, which is early 1450. This is testified by sources such as the biography of Rongton written by Śākya Chogden (361.7) and also his *Gsol 'debs dang mgur 'bum gyi skor* (472.5). Personal communication from Volker Caumanns, 2009; see also Jackson 1989a, 8.
307. "The new Mañjuśrī" is Tsongkhapa. Around this time there were serious sectarian tensions in central Tibet. As a consequence of an order given by the Neudzong ruler, who was a patron of the Gelugpas, in 1442 Śākya Chogden and other Sakyapas were forced to abandon their own Sakya tradition and to join religious classes under the tutelage of Gelug teachers. See Kunga Drolchog's *Detailed Biography*, 26.7 and 27.5. The text here implies that Tsongkhapa's texts were taught in order to convert Śākya Chogden to Tsongkhapa's philosophical position. During that time Śākya Chogden also studied at Sera. The *Detailed Biography* makes a comparison with Dharmakīrti's studies with non-Buddhists, which he later used to refute their doctrines (see Chattopadhyaya and Chimpa 1970, 230–33). Similarly, Śākya Chogden first studied the works of Tsongkhapa and later refuted Tsongkhapa's arguments in his *Overview of the Madhyamaka*. Personal communication from Volker Caumanns, 2009.

308. For more on this text by Darpaṇa Ācārya, see Stearns 2001, 172n15.
309. For a discussion of the four transmission lineages of Hevajra, see Davidson 1992, 109ff.
310. See chapter 8, where the three cycles of benefit to others are included among the Sakya yoga tantra practices.
311. This trio, the *nang brtag rgyud gsum*, often appear together as three key topics of study in the Kagyu tradition. The *Profound Inner Meaning* (*Zab mo nang gi don*) is a work by the Third Karmapa Rangjung Dorje.
312. Text also has "in the wood-hare year" which would be 1435 or 1495, but Śākya Chogden would have been twenty-eight in 1457 (a fire-ox year).
313. The eighteen texts of great renown are discussed at the beginning of chapter 8 of the present text.
314. Not identified.
315. These are presumably the famous works by Sonam Tsemo.
316. The bodhisattva trilogy is Puṇḍarīka's commentary on the *Kālacakra Tantra*, Vajragarbha's commentary on the *Hevajra Tantra*, and Vajrapāṇi's commentary on the *Cakrasaṃvara Tantra*.
317. These gifts included a statue of the Buddha and the Dharma robes of Chogyal Pagpa; see Kunga Drolchog's *Detailed Biography*, 78.5ff.
318. The three foundations (*gzhi gsum*) are (1) *poṣadha*, the purification ritual (*gso sbyong*), (2) *varṣavasana*, the summer retreat (*dbyar gnas*), and (3) *pravāraṇa*, the closing of the summer retreat (*dgag dbye*).
319. SSB, 12:1–319.
320. Probably SSB, 3:1–161 and 3:163–561.
321. See SSB, 6:1–229, 342–72, and 372–415; SSB, 5:1–280.
322. Kunga Drolchog, *Detailed Biography*, 141–12.
323. These episodes are related in more detail in Kunga Drolchog's *Detailed Biography* (19.4–20.2; 159.5ff and 111.5–112.6). On the second episode, see Komarovski 2007, 126. On the third episode, see also Vitali 2004. Personal communication from Volker Caumanns, 2009.
324. DR's note: According to some Dharma histories, it was the month of Sel. Translator's note: The Tibetan text gives the date as the eighth cycle, whereas it must be the ninth.
325. Zhuchen Tsultrim Rinchen's collected works can have been published several times. The most recent and most extensive collection, in eleven volumes, is *Zhu chen tshul khrims rin chen gyi gsung 'bum* (Kathmandu: Sachen International [Guru Lama]), 2005.
326. The ten religious activities are (1) transcribing the teachings, (2) worshiping, (3) making donations, (4) listening to the teachings, (5) reading the teachings, (6) comprehending the teachings, (7) instructing others, (8) reciting holy works, (9) contemplation, and (10) meditation.
327. The three ways a student delights a teacher are with respect, offerings of food, and meditation.
328. The "three vajra thrones" are the places in the maṇḍala in which are situated the (1) buddhas and bodhisattvas, (2) male and female peaceful deities, and (3) male and female wrathful deities. The phrase may refer simply to all of these types of deities, as seems to be the case here.

329. Gendun Gyatso (1492–1542), the second Dalai Lama, was the abbot of Tashi Lhunpo. As stated here, Tsarchen Losel Gyatso began his career in the Gelug tradition before turning to Sakya teachers.
330. Only four volumes of his writings are extant. His journal of his journey across Tsang is translated in Stearns 2012.
331. DR's note: There are four volumes of these, primarily on the hearing lineage.
332. DR's note: His marvelous words on both sūtra and mantra are contained in eleven volumes of his collected works.
333. The father and son are Tsarchen Losel Gyatso and Jamyang Khyentse Wangchug.
334. That is to say, the teachings of this lineage spread to the Gelug school as well.
335. This name, meaning "the lord of Dharma, the eighteenth," is here linked to the day of Choje Rinpoche's passing. An alternative oral tradition links the name to the tenth abbot, Chetsun Jamyang Donyo Gyaltsen, who is said to have received eighteen precious items from the Chinese emperor. The present text mentions several items bestowed upon Chetsun Jamyang Donyo Gyaltsen but not eighteen. The honorific name of the recent Nalendra abbots has been Chogye Trichen.
336. During and after the establishment of Gelug rule over central Tibet in the seventeenth century, the abbacy of Nalendra was removed from the Sakya and held only by Gelug monks. The two abbots mentioned are from the Gelug school and of relatively low rank, as is emphasized here.
337. "Master of science" translates the Tibetan *rig gnas slob dpon*.
338. This temple, called Trashi Rabten, was inaugrated in 1975.
339. Chetsun Trichen Ngawang Khyenrab Tubten Legshe Gyatso Chog, generally known as Chogye Trichen, passed away in January 2007 at his monastery in Lumbini.
340. DR's note: Four volumes of his works are extant.
341. Tendzin Nyendrag also served as the twenty-second abbot of Nalendra.
342. On these texts see Jinpa 2006.
343. The Vajramālā collection derives from the twelfth-century Indian master Abhayākaragupta and contains forty-eight empowerments. It is included in the Compendium of All Tantras. The Ocean of Sādhanas is a collection of sādhanas, also attributed to Abhayākaragupta, collected in the Tengyur (Q4221–4466). The Hundred Sādhanas of Bari, from Bari Lotsāwa, contains seventy-seven permissions, while the Nartang Hundred contains thirty-six permissions; both are included in the Compendium of Sādhanas.
344. The three deities in this empowerment are Mañjuśrī, Avalokiteśvara, and Vajrapāṇi.
345. On Gelongma Palmo and her transmission of Avalokiteśvara practices, see Vargas-O'Brien 2001.
346. The "ultimate secret yoga" (*rnal 'byor gsang mtha'*) is a category of tantra described in the *Cakrasaṃvara Tantra*, and is often used as a synonym for the tantra itself.
347. The White Vajravārāhī "Illuminating Insight" (*phyag dkar gsal byed*) is connected with the Prajñāpāramitā.
348. The Tibetan text has *thugs rje chen po tshe bum lugs*, corrected here to *thugs rje chen po tshe bum tshem bu pa lugs*.
349. The esoteric instruction tradition (*man ngag lugs*) is Virūpa's tradition—that is, the

Lamdre. The commentarial tradition (*'grel pa lugs*) is that of Ḍombī, who did not receive the Lamdre.

350. DR's note: Whether there is a specific transmission for this needs to be investigated.
351. The following list contains mainly thematic groups of texts, most are which are found in the Sakya Lamdre Literature Series (SLL in bibliography).
352. On the causal empowerment, see Davidson 1992, 127.
353. See Stearns 2001, 257n253.
354. *Lam bsdus te bsgrub pa'i lung sbyin pa*. See Stearns 2001, 237n136.
355. The *Book of Blazing Fire* (*Me 'bar ma*) is attributed to Dagchen Lodro Gyaltsen (1444–95). However, I have not been able to locate it nor the supplementary volumes mentioned here (Tib. *Dud sol pod* and *Gyi ljang pod*).
356. "Invocation" here translates *gnas dbabs*.
357. DR's note: In certain places, such as Gongkar Dorje Den and Trashi Choje, there are a great many sādhana practices that mix the Sakya and Buton traditions.
358. For an English translation of the biography of Jamyang Khyentse Wangpo by Jamgon Kongtrul Lodro Taye, see Akester 2012.
359. The eight chariots are discussed in Stearns 2001, 4–7. All of these systems except numbers 6 and 8 are treated in chapter 10 of the present work. The six yogas of Kālacakra derive from the *Kālacakra Tantra*, were translated into Tibetan in the eleventh century, and were the speciality of the Jonang school. The deity yoga of three vajras, also related to the six yogas of Kālacakra, was brought to Tibet from Oḍḍiyāna by Orgyenpa Rinchenpal in the thirteenth century. Both lineages were rare by the nineteenth century.
360. Yutog Yonten Gonpo (1126–1202) is credited with laying the foundation of the Tibetan medical tradition through his transmission of the *Four Tantras*.
361. This paragraph has been moved from folio 149a in the original Tibetan text, where it appears out of sequence after the line: "At the age of twenty, Khyentse Rinpoche traveled to Central Tibet."
362. These Indian textbooks on Sanskrit grammar, translated into Tibetan, form the basis for the study of Sanskrit in the Sakya school, and the first two in particular are still used for learning Sanskrit. The *Kalāpa* is better known in Sanskrit as the *Kātantra*. On the translation and transmission of this grammatical literature in Tibet, see Verhagen 1994.
363. This name is allusive of Sanskrit poetics. The "six faces" (*gdong drug*, Skt. *sadmukha*) is said to refer either to the Ganges River (which has six main sources) or the god Kārtika, son of Śiva.
364. On the eighteen books of great renown (*pu sti grags chen bco brgyad*), see the beginning of chapter 8 of the present work. The five books of virtuous scripture (*dge phyogs bka' pod lnga*) are Pramāṇa, Madhyamaka, Prajñāpāramitā, Abhidharma, and Vinaya.
365. The ten great transmissions (*bka' chen bcu*) usually refer to the five main scriptural texts (see previous note) and their respective commentaries.
366. Sūtra, illusion, and mind (*mdo rgyud sems*) refer to the *Sūtra Encompassing All Intentions*, the *Māyājāla Tantras*, and the Mind Series of the Great Perfection. Space (*klong*) is not usually part of this set but here must refer to the Space Series (*klong sde*) of the Great Perfection.

367. The trio of lama, perfection, and compassion (*bla rdzogs thugs gsum*) refers to guru yoga, the great perfection (*rdzogs chen*), and the Great Compassionate One (Mahākaruṇika).

368. The *Hundred Instructions* (*khrid brgya*) of Jonang Jetsun Kunga Drolchog (1507–66), containing meditative instructions from various traditions—primarily the Lamdre of the Sakyapas, the esoteric instructions of the Shangpa Kagyu, and the six-branch yoga of the Jonangpas—is found in volume 8 of the *Treasury of Oral Precepts*. On Kunga Drolchog, see Stearns 1999, 64–67.

369. Gyalse Zhenpen Taye (1800–1855/69) was based in Dzogchen Monastery in Kham but traveled throughout Tibet to compile and publish a major collection of the Nyingma transmitted (*bka' ma*) texts. This passage indicates that he presented copies of these to Jamyang Khyentse Wangpo, who ensured that they were propagated in the Nyingma monasteries of Kham, such as Palyul, where some of these texts, apparently, were no longer in circulation.

370. This paragraph concerns the Compendium of All Tantras, the compilation of which is discussed in detail in the section on Loter Wangpo. Current printings of the Compendium of All Tantras contain well over a hundred empowerments.

371. The *Treasury of Oral Instructions*.

372. The three blazes (*'bar ba gsum*) are (1) warmth in the body, (2) power in the speech, and (3) realization in the mind. The three gatherings are (1) in the day, disciples, (2) in the night, ḍākinīs, and (3) at all times, food and resources.

373. Jamyang Khyentse Wangpo is considered to have manifested five emanations after his death: of body, speech, mind, qualities, and activities. Wutaishan (in Shanxi Province, China) is considered the home of the bodhisattva Mañjuśrī.

374. Many of the names of the texts in this list are short forms or nicknames. The four small tantric texts (*rgyud chung bzhi*) are: (1) the *Hevajra Tantra*, (2) *Ornament to Beautify the Jewel Tree* (an explanation of Dragpa Gyaltsen's *Jewel Tree*), and (3) *Ornament to Beautify the Three Means* (an explanation of Sonam Tsemo's *Classes of Tantra*), both by Ngorchen Konchog Lhundrub, and (4) *Distinguishing the Three Vows* by Sakya Paṇḍita. The seven texts necessary for all (*kun tu dgos pa'i gzhung bdun*) are: (1) the *Three Perceptions* and (2) the *Three Continua* (the preliminary and main practices of the Lamdre), (3) the *Jewel Tree* by Dragpa Gyaltsen, (4) *Classes of Tantra* by Sonam Tsemo, (5) *Tantra Fragments* by Sachen Kunga Nyingpo, (6) the *Overview* by Dragpa Gyaltsen (a summary of topics in the *Classes of Tantra* and the *Jewel Tree*), and (7) the *Commentary on the Hymn to Nairātmyā* by Sakya Paṇḍita. The list of seven texts enumerated here differs slightly from that in Stearns (2006, 660n455), which does not contain the *Three Perceptions* and *Three Continua* and instead includes two hymns by Dragpa Gyaltsen. Stearns says the list of seven are enumerated by their short titles in a verse by Dragpa Gyaltsen quoted by Tsangjampa Dorje Gyaltsen (1424–98) in *River of Explication*, 3a.

375. The eight realizations (*abhisamaya*) derive from the *Abhisamayālaṃkāra*; they are: knowing all aspects (*sarvākārajñatā*), knowing the path (*mārgajñatā*), knowing all things (*sarvājñatā*), realization of all aspects (*sarvākārābhisaṃbhoda*), peak realization (*mūrdhābhisaṃbhoda*), graduated realization (*anupūrvābhisaṃbhoda*), momentary realization (*ekakṣaṇābhisaṃbhoda*), and dharmakāya. See the discussion of these in Taniguchi 2004.

376. "Group sādhana practice" translates *sgrub mchod chen mo*.
377. Tartse Khenchen Jampa Kunga Tenpai Gyaltsen (1829–70) died in his forty-first year. As mentioned above, he was a student of Jamyang Khyentse Wangpo.
378. Lhundrub Teng Monastery was founded by Derge Botar Trashi Senge (*sde dge bo thar bkra shis seng ge*) in the fifteenth century.
379. The three white masters are Sachen Kunga Nyingpo, Sonam Tsemo, and Dragpa Gyaltsen. "White" refers to their lay status, as against Sakya Paṇḍita and Chogyal Pagpa, known as "the two red ones."
380. The two masters are referred to here only as "the two Mañjuvajras" (*rje 'jam pa'i rdo rje rnam gnyis*).
381. As mentioned earlier, Jamyang Khyentse Wangpo was recognized as the rebirth of Ngor Tartse Khenchen Jampa Namkha Chime, but it does not seem to be him referred to here. It may be Tartse Khenchen Namkha Palzang (1532–1602), who had the title of Paṇchen; however, he did not live to the age of seventy-five. There is an earlier Sakya lama called Paṇchen Namkha Palzang (1464–1529) who did live to the age of seventy-five but did not hold the post of Tartse Khenchen.
382. The four modes are the literal (*tshig*), general (*spyi*), hidden (*sbas*), and ultimate (*mthar thug*).
383. The three deities of immortality are Amitāyus, White Tārā, and Uṣṇīṣavijayā.
384. The five auspicious circumstances are teacher, retinue, place, teaching, and time.
385. A *kaṭora* (Skt.) is a small ritual vessel.
386. This is Dezhung Rinpoche Kunga Gyaltsen (1885–1952).
387. The esoteric instruction tradition of Hevajra (*kye rdo rje man ngag lugs*) is the Hevajra instruction of Virūpa, another name for the Lamdre.
388. The lineages of the profound view (*zab mo lta ba*) and vast activity (*rgya chen spyod pa*) are the lineages of the bodhisattva vow in the Madhyamaka (Mañjuśrī, Nāgārjuna) and Cittamātra (Maitreya, Asaṅga) traditions.
389. The *Shejama* (*shes bya ma*) verse is in praise of Sakya Paṇḍita.
390. Khenpo Zhenga's full religious name was Zhenpen Chokyi Nangwa. He was educated in the Nyingma tradition but later was associated with the Sakya tradition as well. He composed interlinear commentaries (*mchan 'grel*) on thirteen classics of Indian Buddhism, which were the main study texts in the college at Dzongsar and the other study centers he established. See Jackson 2003, 26–30, and Bayer 1999.
391. David Jackson's account (2003, 172–77), based on Dhongthog Rinpoche's full biography of Khenchen Dampa, adds that Khenpo Shenga questioned the use of studying Pramāṇa.
392. Kusho (*sku zhabs*) is a respectful form of address, akin to "sir."
393. Dezhung Anjam Rinpoche should not be confused with Dezhung Rinpoche Jampa Kunga Tenpai Nyima (1906–1987), the subject of the biography by David Jackson (2003). Dezhung Anjam Rinpoche was instrumental in having the latter recognized as an incarnate lama; see Jackson 2003, 34–35.
394. Several refuge prayers begin with the phrase "Encompassing all refuges" (*skyabs gnas kun 'dus*), including prayers to Mañjuśrī.
395. Gsung 'bum, 1:1–42.

396. Not identified.

397. Gsung 'bum, 1:311–42.

398. Gsung 'bum, 1:267–76.

399. Kaḥtog Orgyen Chokyi Gyatso was the third person to hold the title of Kaḥtog Situ (a Nyingma role not related to the Kagyu Tai Situ). He was the nephew and student of Jamyang Khyentse Wangpo and a student of Loter Wangpo as well.

400. The second Zurmang tulku here is the Tenth Trungpa Chokyi Nyinje, the predecessor of Chogyam Trungpa.

401. The three roots are the lama, the yidam, and the ḍākinī.

402. Jamyang Khyentse Chokyi Lodro moved from Kaḥtog to Dzongsar at the age of fifteen, where he was installed as the monastery's throne holder.

403. That is, the Heart Essence (*snying thig*) collections of Longchenpa and Jigme Lingpa.

404. These are the terma of Terdag Lingpa.

405. Dongyu Chokyi Nyima was the eighth Khamtrul Rinpoche (1931–80).

406. This three-volume set of collected ritual practices, lacking publication information, is available at TBRC, reference number W1PD5284.

407. These were students of Sakya Paṇḍita.

408. The six great books (*pod chen drug*) seem to be the same as the six great topics, i.e., Prajñāpāramitā, Pramāṇa, Vinaya, Abhidharma, Madhyamaka, and the three vows.

409. This work is often simply called *Ngor Chojung* (*Ngor chos 'byung*).

410. Contained in SLL volumes 1–8.

411. DR's note: There is a printed version of this work up to the biography of Zhalu Khenchen kept in Drepung.

412. Contained in SLL volumes 1–8.

413. See Ame Zhab's Bka' 'bum (Kathmandu: Sa skya rgyal yongs gsung rab slob gnyer khang, 2000) for his histories of Cakrasaṃvara (16:283–612; 19:1–532), Guhyasamāja (11:475–792; 12:491–590; 13:1–192), Yamāntaka (13:521–640; 15:105–246), and Mahākāla (25:1–492). There is a brief historical introduction to the tradition of Vajrakīlāya in 8:1–6.

414. Tsarchen Losel Gyatso's Dharma Cycle of Mahākāla (*Nag po chen po'i chos skor*) is available on TBRC as a scanned manuscript, reference number W1CZ1045. See also the collection with the name, without author information, at W1KG13693.

415. These texts are not in the Gsung 'bum of Ngawang Chodrag (1572–1641).

416. For an overview and discussion of the sources on the decline of the Dharma, see Nattier 1991.

417. This discussion is based on the hermeneutical triad of *dgongs gzhi* ("basis in intention"), *dgos pa* ("motive"), and *dngos la gnod byed* ("literal inconsistency"). See chapter 7 of Ruegg 2010 for a detailed analysis.

418. On this quotation, see Sørensen 1994, 154n433.

419. The discussion here is of traditional Tibetan chronologies. See Bechert 1991 for an overview of modern scholarly calculations of the dates of the Buddha.

420. The alternative names for the years given here are from a system in which each year of the sixty-year cycle has its own name. The year of arising (*rab tu skyes*, or *rab byung*) is the first year in the cycle. The year of abundance (*'byor ba*, also known as *rnam byung*)

is the second. The virtuous year (*dge byed*) is the thirty-sixth. The all-subduing year (*thams cad 'dul*) is the twenty-first, and the all-holding year (*kun 'dzin*) is the twenty-second. See Schuh 1973 and the table in Cornu 1997, 80–81.

421. The ruler of Guge mentioned here is Tri Namkha Wangpo (Khri Nam mkha'i dbang po, b. 1409). See Heimbel 2011, 74.

422. The year of insects (*srin bu*) refers to the forty-ninth year of the sixty-year cycle.

423. This text has been translated into English; see Trichen 1983.

Bibliography

Abbreviations

GSB: Go rams pa gsung 'bum. *The Collected Works of Kun-mkhyen Go-rams-pa Bsod-nams-seng-ge*. 13 vols. Dehradun: Sakya College, 1979. W11249.

Q: Bka' 'gyur and Bstan 'gyur (Qianlong / Peking edition).

SKB: Sa skya bka' 'bum. *The Collected Works of the Founding Masters of the Sa-skya*. 15 vols. Dehradun: Sakya Centre, 1992–93. W22271.

SLL: Sa skya Lam 'bras Literature Series. 27 vols. Dehradun: Sakya Centre, 1983–85. Comprising *Lam 'bras slob bshad* (vols. 1–21), W23649; and *Lam 'bras tshogs bshad* (vols. 22–27), W23648.

SSB: Śākya mchog ldan gsung 'bum. *The Complete Works (Gsuṇ 'bum) of Gser-mdog Paṇchen Śakya-mchog-ldan*. 24 vols. New Delhi: Ngawang Tobgyel, 1995. W23200.

W: Reference number of the Tibetan Buddhist Resource Centre (tbrc.org).

Tibetan and Sanskrit

Scripture

Aṣṭamahāsthānacaityastotra. Gnas chen po brgyad kyi mchod rten la bstod pa. Q2024, 2025.

Avataṃsaka Sūtra. Sangs rgyas phal po che'i mdo. Q761.

Bhadrakalpikā Sūtra. Bskal pa bzang po pa zhes bya ba theg pa chen po'i mdo. Q762.

Buddhakapāla Tantra. Sangs rgyas thod pa zhes bya ba rnal 'byor ma'i rgyud kyi rgyal po. Q63.

Buddhasamāyoga Tantra. Sangs rgyas thams cad dang mnyam par sbyor ba'i rgyud. Q8.

Cakrasaṃvara Tantra. 'Khor lo sdom pa'i rgyud. Q30.

Candra Vyākaraṇa Sūtra. Tsandra pa'i mdo. Q5767.

Candragarbha Sūtra. Zla ba'i snying po'i mdo. Q743.

Candraguhyatilaka Tantra. Zla gsang thig le zhes bya ba rgyud. Q111.

Catuḥpīṭha Tantra. Rnal 'byor ma'i rgyud kyi rgyal po chen po dpal gdan bzhi pa. Q67.

Ḍākārṇavamahāyoginī Tantra. Mkha' 'gro rgya mtsho chen po rnal 'byor ma'i rgyud. Q19.

Dupai Do. Dgongs pa 'dus pa'i mdo. In Rnying ma rgyud 'bum, 16: 2–617. Thimphu, Bhutan: National Library, 1982.

Ghanavyūha Sūtra. Stug po bkod pa'i mdo. Q778.

Graded Presentation of the Sūtras. Mdo sde rnam gzhag rim pa. Not identified.

Guhyasamāja Tantra. Gsang ba 'dus pa rtsa ba'i rgyud. Q81.

Hevajra Tantra. Kye rdo rje'i rgyud / Brtag gnyis. Q10.

Kālacakra Tantra. Dus kyi 'khor lo'i rgyud. Q4.

Kātantra Vyākaraṇa Sūtra. Ka lā pa'i mdo. Q5775.
Karaṇḍavyūha Sūtra. Za ma tog bkod pa'i mdo. Q784.
Karmaśataka. Karma sha taṃ / Las brgya tham pa. Q1007.
Karmavibhaṅga. Las rnam par 'byed pa. Q1005.
Karuṇāpuṇḍarīka Sūtra. Snying rje chen po'i pad ma dkar po'i mdo. Q779.
Kuśalamūlaparigrāha-bodhisattvapiṭaka Sūtra. Dge ba'i rtsa ba yongs su 'dzin pa'i byang chub sems dpa'i sde snod kyi mdo. Not identified; see Q769.
Kṛṣṇayamāri Tantra. Gshin rje gshed dgra nag po'i rgyud. Q103.
Laṅkāvatāra Sūtra. Lang kar gshegs pa'i mdo. Q775.
Mahākāla Tantra. Mgon po mngon par 'byung ba'i rgyud. Q62.
Mahāmāya Tantra. Ma hā mā ya'i rgyud / Sgyu 'phrul chen po'i rgyud. Q64.
Mañjuśrīmūla Tantra. 'Jam dpal gyi rtsa ba'i rgyud. Q162.
Mañjūśrīnāmasaṃgīti. Jam dpal mtshan yang dag par brjod pa. Q2.
Māyājāla Tantras. Sgyu 'phrul 'dra ba'i rgyud. Q102.
Nighaṇṭu. Sgra sbyor bam po gnyis pa. Q5833.
Pangkong Sūtra of a Hundred Homages. Spang bkong phyag brgya pa'i mdo. Q993.
Parinirvāṇa Sūtra. So sor thar pa'i mdo. Q1031.
Pitāputrasamāgama Sūtra. Yab sras mjal ba'i mdo. Q760, 16.
Prajñāpāramitā in a Hundred Thousand Verses. See *Śatasāhasrikā.*
Prātimokṣa Sūtras. So thar gyi mdo gnyis. (1) *So sor thar pa'i mdo.* Skt. *Prātimokṣa Sūtra.* Q1031. (2) *Dge long ma'i so sor thar pa'i mdo.* Skt. *Bhikṣuṇīprātimokṣa Sūtra.* Q1033.
Raktayamāri Tantra. Gshin rje gshed dmar po'i rgyud. Q109.
Ratnaguṇasañcayagāthā. Yon tan rin po che sdud pa tsigs su bcad pa. Q5190.
Ratnakūṭa Sūtra. Dkon mchog brtsegs pa'i mdo. Q760.
Ratnamegha Sūtra. Dkon mchog sprin pa'i mdo. Q897.
Samādhirāja Sūtra. Ting nge 'dzin gyi rgyal po'i mdo. Q795.
Saṃpuṭa Tantra. Kha sbyor gyi rgyud / Yang dar par sbyor ba'i rgyud. Q26.
Saṃvara Tantra. Bde mchog gi rgyud. Q16.
Saṃvara Vajraḍāka Tantra. Bde mchog rdo rje mkha' 'gro'i rgyud. Q18.
Sandhivyākaraṇa Tantra. Dgongs pa lung bstan pa'i rgyud. Q83.
Ṣaṇmukhīdhāraṇī. Sgo drug pa'i gzungs. Q3518.
Sarasvatī Vyākaraṇa Sūtra. Dbyangs can sgra mdo. Q5886.
Śatasāhasrikā. 'Bum / Shes rab kyi pha rol tu phyin pa stong phrag brgya pa. Q730.
Savapnanirdeśa Sūtra. Rgyal po kri kri'i rmi lam lung bstan pa'i mdo. Q760, 4.
Sitātapatrādhāraṇī. Gdugs dkar de bzhin gshegs pa'i gtsug tor nas byung ba'i gdugs dkar mo can gzhan gyis mi thub ma zhes bya ba'i gzungs. Q204 and 205.
Śmaśānālaṅkāra Tantra. Dur khrod nag po rgyud. Q47.
Supratiṣṭha Tantra. Rab tu gnas pa'i rgyud. Q118.
Sūtra on Repaying Kindness. Drin lan bsab pa'i mdo. Q1022.
Tārāmūlakalpa Tantra. Rgyud ral pa gyen brdzes. Q469.
Tattvasaṃgraha Tantra. De bzhin gshegs pa thams cad kyi de kho na nyid bsdus pa zhes bya ba theg pa chen po'i mdo. Q112.
Vajrabhairava Tantra. 'Jigs byed kyi rgyud. Q53.
Vajrabhairavakalpa Tantra. Rdo rje 'jigs byed kyi rtog pa'i rgyud / Rtog pa bdun pa. Q106.

Vajramālā Tantra. Rdo rje 'phreng ba'i rgyud. Q82.
Vajrapāṇyabhiṣeka Tantra. Lag na rdo rje dbang bskur ba'i rgyud. Q130.
Vajrapañjara Tantra. Rdo rje gur zhes bya ba'i rgyud. Q11.
Vidyottama Tantra. Rig pa mchog gi rgyud. Q402.
Vinayakṣudrāgama. Lung phran tshegs / Dul ba phran tshegs kyi gzhi. Q1035.
Yamāri Tantras. Gshin rje gshed kyi rgyud. Probably refers to the *Kṛṣnayamāri Tantras*, Q103, 104, 107. May also refer to the *Raktayamāri Tantra*, Q109.

Authored Works

Abhayākaragupta. *Munimatālaṃkāra. Thub pa'i dgongs rgyan.* Q5299.
Amarasiṃha. *Amarakośa. Mngon brjod a ma ra ko sha / 'chi med mdzod.* Q5819.
Ame Zhab Ngawang Kunga Sonam. *Dharma History of Demchog and the Protector. Bde mchog dang mgon po'i chos 'byung.* Dehradun: Sakya Center, 1985. W22433.
———. *Lamdre History: An Ocean of Excellent Explanation. Yongs rdzogs bstan pa rin po che'i nyams len gyi man ngag gsung ngag rin po che'i byon tshul khog phub dang bcas pa rgyas par bshad pa legs bshad 'dus pa'i rgya mtsho.* New Delhi: Ngawang Tobgay. W10308.
———. *Miraculous Shower of Blessings: The Life Story of Muchen Sangye Gyaltsen. Mus chen sangs rgyas rgyal mtshan gyi rnam thar byin rlabs kyi char 'bebs ngo mtshar sarga gsum pa.* Dehra Dun: Sakya Centre, 1974. W10329.
———. *Sakya Lineage History. Sa skya gdung rabs.* In Bka' 'bum, 3:7–656. Kathmandu: Sa skya rgyal yongs gsung rab slob gnyer khang. W29307.
———. *Treasury of Miracles: A Family History of the Sakya. Sa skya'i gdung rabs ngo mtshar bang mdzod.* New Delhi: Tashi Dorje, Delhi, 1975. TBRC W30132.
Āryadeva. *Caryāmelāpakapradīpa. Spyod pa bsdus pa'i sgron ma.* Q2668.
———. *Jñānasārasamuccaya. Ye shes snying po kun las btus pa.* Q5251.
———. *Madhyamakacatuḥśataka. Dbu ma bzhi brgya.* Q5246.
Asaṅga. *Abhidharmasamuccaya. Chos mngon pa kun las btus pa.* Q5550.
Aśvaghoṣa. *Jātakamālā. Skyes pa'i rabs kyi rgyud.* Q5650.
———. *Vajrayānamūlāpattisaṃgraha. Rdo rje theg pa rtsa ba'i ltung ba bsdus pa.* Q3303.
Atiśa. *Bodhipathapradīpa. Byang chub lam gyi sgron ma.* Q5343.
Bari Lotsāwa. Hundred Sādhanas of Bari. *Ba ri brgya rtsa.* In Compendium of Sādhanas, edited by Khyentse Wangpo and Loter Wangpo, 12:1–133. Kangra: Sherap Gyaltsen. W23681.
Bhāvaviveka. *Tarkajvālā. Rtog ge 'bar ba.* Q5256.
Bhavideva. *Gurupañcāśikā. Bla ma lnga bcu pa.* Q4544.
Bhavyakīrti. *Cakrasaṃvarasyapañjikāśūramanojñā. Dpal 'khor lo sdom pa'i dka' 'grel dpa' bo'i yid du 'ong ba.* Q2121.
Buton Rinchen Drub. *Bright Lamp Illuminating the Six Divisions. Sgron ma mtha' drug rab gsal.* In Gsung 'bum, 9:147–688. Lhasa: Zhol par khang, 2000. W1934.
Candrakīrti. *Madhyamakāvatāra. Dbu ma la 'jug pa.* Q5262.
———. *Pradīpodyotana. 'Grel chen sgron ma gsal ba.* Q2650.
Candranandana. *Candrikāprabhāsa. Yan lag brgyad pa'i snying po'i rnam par 'grel pa tshig gi don gyi zla zer.* Q5800.

Cho Namgyal, Tubtenpa. *Necklace of Fresh Flowers. Me tog gsar pa'i do shal.* In *Bod kyi rgyal rabs phyogs bsdebs*, 225–405. Dharamsala: Library of Tibetan Works and Archives, 1985. W24011.

Chogyal Pagpa. *Endowed with Purity. Brtag gnyis kyi 'grel pa dag ldan chung ba.* SKB, 13:279–334.

———. *Verses on the Defeat of the Daoist Teachers. Zin shing gi ston pa btul ba'i tshigs bcad.* SKB, 15:637–39.

Chogye Trichen Legshe Gyatso. *Condensed Dharma History of Sakya. Sa skya'i chos 'byung bsdus pa.* Dharamsala: Shes rig par khang, 1969. W00KG09736.

———. *Clarifying Explanation of the Oral Lineage of the Nalendra Abbatial Succession. Nalendra'i gdan rabs snyan brgyud bstan pa'i gsal byed.* Not identified.

Daṇḍin. *Kāvyādarśa. Snyan ngag me long.* Q5789.

Dezhung Anjam Rinpoche Jampa Kunga Tenpai Gyaltsen. *Drops of Nectar. Bdud rtsi thigs pa.* In Gsung 'bum, 1:215–65. Kathmandu: Sa skya rgyal yongs gsung rab slob gnyer khang. W1KG11946.

———. *Lamp for the Precious Daily Practice of the Vinaya. 'Dul ba lag len rin chen sgron me.* In Gsung 'bum, 1:407–56. Kathmandu: Sa skya rgyal yongs gsung rab slob gnyer khang. W1KG11946.

———. *Recognizing the Ground of All. Kun gzhi ngos 'dzin.* In Gsung 'bum thor bu, 133–81. New Delhi: Dhongthog Rinpoche, 1977. W23816.

———. *Rosary of Wonderful Jewels. Ngo mtshar nor bu'i phreng ba.* New Delhi: Gonpo Dorje, 1981. W2CZ6645

Dharmakīrti. *Nyāyabindu. Rigs pa'i thigs pa.* Q5711.

———. *Pramāṇavārttika. Tshad ma rnam 'grel.* Q5709.

Dharmottara. *Pramāṇaviniścaya. Tshad ma rnam par nges pa.* Q5710.

Dignāga. *Pramāṇasamuccaya. Tshad ma kun btus.* Q5700.

Ḍombī Heruka. *Innate Accomplishment. Lhan cig skyes grub.* SLL, 11:387–400.

———. *Nairātmyāyoginīsādhana. Bdag med rnal 'byor ma'i sgrub thabs.* Q2435.

Dragpa Gyaltsen. *Causal Continuum of the Ālaya. Kun gzhi rgyu rgyud.* SLL, 11:128–31.

———. *Dentsog. Gdan stsogs kyi yi ge.* SLL, 11:131–35.

———. *Extensive, Medium, and Condensed Empowerments for the Phase of the Path. Lam dus kyi dbang rgyas 'bring bsdus gsum.* SLL, 11:154–58.

———. *Hymn to the Father Hevajra in Daṇḍaka Meter. Yab kyi bstod pa daṇḍaka'i mchan.* In *Sngags skor*, 500–506. Beijing: Mi rigs dpe skrun khang, 2004. W29976.

———. *Four Authenticities. Tshad ma bzhi'i yi ge.* SLL, 11:158–61.

———. *Guidance for the Seven Practices of the Vital Winds in the Context of the Path of a Worldly Person. 'Jig rten pa'i lam gyi skabs su rlung gi sbyor ba bdun gyis lam khrid.* SLL, 11:173–83.

———. *Immaculate Ornament: Hymn to the Mother Nairātmyā. Yum gyi bstod pa dri ma med pa'i rgyan.* In *Sngags skor*, 507–13. Beijing: Mi rigs dpe skrun khang, 2004. W29976.

———. *Jewel Tree. Ljon shing.* SKB, 6:1–277.

———. *Maintaining the Drops. Thig le'i srung ba.* SLL, 11:170–71.

———. *Ornament for the Vajrapañjara. Rdo rje gur gyi rgyan zhes bya ba'i rnam 'grel.* SKB, 7:1–145.

———. *Overview. Rgyud sde spyi'i rnam gzhag dang rgyud kyi mngon par rtogs pa'i stong thun sa bcad.* SKB, 6:279–323.

———. *Commentary on Bodhicitta. Byang chub sems 'grel.* SLL, 11:400–406.

———. *Removing Obstacles by Washing. Grib mkhrus gyi sel ba.* SLL, 11:167–69.

———. *Removing Obstacles with Tsatsa. Sā tstshas sel ba.* SLL, 11:169–70.

———. *Short Tantra of Maitrīpa's Khecarī. Mai tri'i mkha' spyod kyi rgyud chung.* SKB 8:111–13.

———. *Signs of Death in the Context of the Vase Empowerment for the Practice of Dying; Including the Yogic Postures and the Cheating of Death. Bum dbang gi 'da' ka ma'i skabs su 'chi ltas/ 'khrul 'khor / 'chi bslu dang bcas pa.* SLL, 11:138–44.

———. *Six Oral Precepts. Gdams ngag drug gi yi ge.* SLL, 11:161–63.

———. *Tantra Fragments. Rgyud sde'i dum bu.* SKB, 6:661–90.

———. *Triple Cycle of Breathing. Byin rlabs tshar gsum khug pa.* SKB, 6:377–82.

———. *Yellow Book. Pod ser.* SLL, 11:9–345.

Dragyab Dongkam Trichen Ngawang. *Key to a Thousand Doors of Profound Meaning: A Catalog of the Pround Ocean of Dharma, the Compendium of All Tantras. Dam chos rgya mtsho'i rgyud sde kun btus kyi dkar chag zab don sgo brgya 'byed pa'i lde'u mig.* In Compendium of All Tantras, edited by Loter Wangpo, 249–646. Delhi: N. Lungtok and N. Gyaltsan, 1971–72. W21295.

Drubpa Zhuchen. *Lamp. Mar me.* Not identified.

Durjayacandra. *Suparigraha. Bzang po yongs gzung.* Q2369.

Gorampa Sonam Senge. *Benefit of Others Permeating Everything. Gzhan phan kun mkhyab.* GSB, 10:253–392.

———. *Essential Nectar of Great Bliss. Bde chen bcud kyi snying po.* GSB, 13:215–70.

———. *Conquering the Obstacles to the Benefit of Others. Gzhan phan gnod spong.* GSB, 10:407–62.

———. *Illuminating Saṃsāra and Nirvāṇa. Khor 'das rab gsal.* GSB, 8:395–459.

———. *Illuminating the Meaning of the Mother. Yum don rab gsal.* GSB, 6:1–639.

———. *Illuminating the Supreme Sages. Skyes bu mchog gi gsal byed.* GSB, 8:127–267.

———. *Illuminating the Topics. Gnad kyi gsal byed.* GSB, 12:557–693.

———. *Illuminating Those Who Entered Absorption. Snyoms 'jug rab gsal.* GSB, 8:269–401.

———. *Samantabhadra's Sun. Kun tu bzang po'i nyi ma.* GSB, 2:1–383.

———. *Threefold Miracle. Ngo mtshar gsum ldan.* GSB, 4:161–357.

Guṇaprabha. *Vinaya Sūtra. 'Dul ba mdo / Mdo rtsa.* Q5619.

Harśadeva. *Nāgānanda. Klu kun tu dga' ba'i zlos gar.* Q5654.

Indrabhūti. *Complete Path of the Consort. Phyag rgya'i lam skor.* SLL, 11:461–79.

Jampa Kunga Tenpai Gyaltsen. *The Hundred Empowerments: A Beautiful Garland of Jewels. Dbang brgya nor bu'i phreng mdzes.* Not identified.

Jñānagarbha. *Satyadvāyavibhaṅgha. Bden pa gnyis rnam par 'byed pa.* Q5283.

Jñānaśrī. *Instructions Guarding Against Disturbances in the Bodily Elements. 'Byung ba lus 'khrugs kyi bar chad srung ba'i man ngag.* SLL, 13:399–400.

Kamalaśīla. *Bhāvanākrama. Bsgom pa'i rim pa.* Q5310–12.

———. *Madhyamakāloka. Dbu ma snang ba.* Q5287.

Kāṇha (Kṛṣṇācarya). *Olapati (Drops of Spring). O la pa ti ste dpyid kyi thig le.* Q2168.

———. *Straightening the Crooked. Yon po bsrang ba.* SLL, 11:457–61.

Khyentse Wangpo, Jamyang. *Garden of Miraculous Flowers. Ngo mtshar u dumba ra'i dga' tshal.* In *The Collected Works (Gsuṅ 'bum) of the Great 'Jam-dbyaṅs Mkhyen-brtse'i-dbaṅ-po.* Gangtok: Gonpo Tseten, 1977–80. SLL, 8:1–235.

Khyentse Wangpo and Loter Wangpo, eds. Compendium of Sādhanas. Sgrub thabs kun btus. 14 vols. Dehradun: G. T. K. Lodoy, N. Gyaltsen, N. Lungtok, 1970. W23681.

Konchog Lhundrub, Ngorchen. *Great Ship for Entering the Ocean of Teachings: A History of the Dharma. Chos byung bstan pa'i rgya mtshor 'jug pa'i gru chen brtsams 'phro / Ngor chos 'byung.* New Delhi: Ngawang Topgay, 1973. W30267.

———. *Family History of the Sakya. Sa skya pa'i gdung rabs.* In *E wam bka' 'bum,* 17:273–468. Beijing: Krung go'i bod rig pa dpe skrun khang, 2009–10. W1KG8320.

Kongton Wangchug Drupa. *Biography of Sonam Senge. Bsod nams seng ge'i rnam thar.* New Delhi: T. G. Dhongthog, 1973.

Kuddālapāda. *Inconceivable. Bsam mi khyab.* SLL, 11:347–62.

Kunga Drolchog. *Detailed Biography of the Great Paṇḍita Śākya Chogden. Shā kya mchog ldan gyi rnam thar zhib mo rnam par 'byed pa.* SSB, 16:1–233.

Kunga Lodro, Jamgon. *Supplement to the Treasury of Miracles, a Family History of Sakya. Sa skya'i gdung rabs ngo mtshar bang mdzod kyi kha skong.* Beijing: Mi rigs dpe skun khang, 1991.

Kunga Wangchug, Ngorchen, ed. *Little Red Book. Pu sti dmar chung.* SLL, 13:1–469.

Kunga Zangpo, Ngorchen, *Sunlight That Spreads the Teachings. Bstan pa rgyas pa'i nyin byed.* In *Kye rdor rnam bshad,* 7–140. New Delhi: Trayang and Jamyang Samten, 1976. W18115.

Lama Dampa Sonam Gyaltsen. *Black Book. Pod nag.* SLL, 16:1–598.

———. *Miraculous Manifestation. Bla ma rgyud pa'i rnam thar ngo mtshar snang ba.*

Longchenpa. *Fourfold Heart Essence. Snying thig yab bzhi.* New Delhi: Trulku Tsewang, Jamyang and L. Tashi, 1971. W1KG9720.

Loter Wangpo, ed. Compendium of All Tantras. Rgyud sde kun btus. Delhi: N. Lungtok and N. Gyaltsan, 1971–72. W21295.

Maitreya. *Bodhisattvabhūmi. Rnal 'byor spyod pa'i sa las/ byang chub sems dpa'i sa.* Q5538.

———. *Sūtrālaṃkāra. Mdo sde rgyan.* Q5521.

———. *Uttaratantraśāstra. Rgyud bla ma.* Q5525.

Mangto Ludrub Gyatso. *Chronology. Bstan rtsis chos 'byung gsal ba'i nyin byed lhag bsam rab dkar.* Lhasa: Bod ljongs mi dmangs dpe skrun khang, 1987. W10247.

Marton. *Incisive Vajra. Zhib mo rdo rje.* Full edition and translation in Stearns 2001.

Nāgabodhi. *Guhyasamāja-maṇḍalopāyikā-viṃśatividhi. 'Dus pa'i dkyil 'khor chog nyi shu pa.* Q2693.

Nāgārjuna. *Commentary on Bodhicitta. See under* Dragpa Gyaltsen.

———. *Jantupoṣaṇabindu. Skye bo gso thig.* Q5822.

———. *Mūlamadhyamakakārikā. Dbu ma rtsa ba'i tshig le'ur byas pa.* Q5224.

———. *Pañcakrama. Rim pa lnga pa.* Q2667.

———. *Suhṛllekha. Bshes pa'i phrin yig.* Q5682.

———. *Sūtrasamuccaya. Mdo kun las btus pa.* Q5330.

———. *Tantrasamuccaya. Rgyud kun las btus pa.* Not identified.

———. *Yogaśataka. Sbyor ba brgya pa.* Q5795.

Nārotapa/Nāropa. *Purifying the Threefold Suffering. Sdug bsngal gsum sel.* SLL, 13:406–10.

Ngawang Chodrag. *Blossoming Lotus Grove: A Setting for the Lamdre. Lam 'bras khog phub gsung ngag bstan pa'i pad tshal bzhad pa.* SLL, 26:151–96.

———. *A Setting of Beautiful Jewels: Lectures on the Six Great Books. Pod chen drug gi 'bel gtam rin chen mdzes pa'i phra tshom pa.* Thimphu: Kunsang Topgyel and Mani Dorje, 1979. W10298.

Ngawang Kunga Sonam. *See* Ame Zhab.

Ngawang Lozang Gyatso (Fifth Dalai Lama). *Song of the Spring Queen. Dpyid kyi rgyal mo'i glu dbyangs.* Varanasi: Kalsang Lhundrup, 1967. W1KG20999.

Ngor Ponlob Ngawang Legdrub. *Three Vows: The Ornament of the Guru's Intention. Sdom gsum 'jam dbyangs bla ma'i dgongs rgyan.* In *Sdom gsum*, 1:312–436. Beijing: Mi rigs dpe skrun khang, 2004. W29981.

Ngorchen. *See* Konchog Lhundrub; Kunga Wangchug; Kunga Zangpo.

Norzang Gyatso and Pugpa Lhundrub. *Oral Transmission of the Karuṇāpuṇḍarīka. Pad dkar zhal lung.* Rewalsar: Zigar Drukpa Kargyud Institute, 1985. W30118.

Prajñākaragupta. *Esoteric Instructions Guarding Against the Hindrances of External Demons. Phyi rol gdon gyi bar chad srung ba'i man ngag.* SLL, 13:398–99.

Prajñāvarman. *Devātiśayastotraṭīkā. Lha las phul du byung bar bstod pa'i 'grel pa.* Q2005.

Prajñendraruci/Vīravajra. *Ratnajvāla. Rin chen 'bar ba.* Q2380.

Ratnākaraśānti. *Chandoratnākara. Sdeb sbyor rin chen 'byung gnas.* Q5790, 5791, 5903.

Ratnavajra. *Stotraviṃśaka. Bstod pa nyi shu pa.* Q4922.

———. *Esoteric Instructions Guarding Against Hindrances to Mental Concentration. Ting nge 'dzin sems kyi bar chad srung ba'i man ngag.* SLL, 13:400–401.

Rongton Sheja Kunrig. *Illuminating the Meaning. Rnam bshad tshig don rab tu gsal ba.* New Delhi: Ngawang Topgay, 1972. W30455.

Sachen Kunga Nyingpo. *Asengma. A seng ma.* SLL, 11:188–91.

———. *Auma. A 'u ma.* SLL, 29:161–295.

———. *Characteristics of the Mudrā in the Insight Wisdom Initiation. Shes rab ye shes kyi phyag rgya'i mtshan nyid.* SLL, 11:147–48.

———. *Condensed Fire Ritual for Removing Obstacles. Grib sel gyi sbyin sregs bsdus pa.* SLL, 11:166–67.

———. *Dagyalma. Zla rgyal ma.* SLL, 27:397–529.

———. *Eight Topics of the Lord in the Context of the Fourth Empowerment. Dbang bzhi pa'i skabs su dbang phyug don brgyad.* SLL, 11:186–87.

———. *Explanation of the Vajrabhairavakalpa Tantra. 'Jigs byed rtog pa bdun pa'i ṭī kā.* SKB, 2:173–199.

———. *Five Dependent Arisings. Rten 'brel lnga.* SLL, 11:163–66.

———. *Fourteen Syllables of the Bhaga. Bha ga'i yi ge bcu bzhi.* SLL, 11:183–85.

———. *Garland of Pearls. Mu tig phreng ba.* SKB, 2:305–673.

———. *Gatengma. Sga theng ma.* SLL, 28:149–491.

———. *Hymn to Glorious Virūpa. Dpal ldan bi rū pa la bstod pa.* SKB, 1:1–6.

———. *Hymn to Zhangton Possessing the Supreme Qualities. Zhang ston la bstod pa yon tan mchog mnga' ma.* SKB, 1:6–7.

———. *Mangchungma. Mang chung ma.* Not extant.
———. *Method for Reciting the Hundred Syllables. Yig brgya'i 'don thabs.* SLL, 11:171–73.
———. *Nyagma. Gnyags ma.* SLL, 11:21–128.
———. *Oral Precepts on the Fourth Bardo. Bar do bzhi pa'i gdams ngag.* SLL, 11:151–54.
———. *Physical Maṇḍala in the Twenty Dharmas of the Path. Lam la sogs pa'i chos nyi shu la lus kyi dkyil 'khor.* SLL, 11:135–38.
———. *Practice of Dying According to the Fourth Initiation. Bzhi pa'i 'da' ka ma.* SLL, 11:148–51.
———. *Practice of Dying of the Vase Empowerment. Bum dbang 'da' ka ma.* SLL, 11:144–46.
———. *Realization That Opens Up the Thirteenth Bhūmi. Sa bcu gsum pa phyed kyi mgon rtogs.* SLL, 11:187–88.
———. *Seal of the Four Cakras. 'Khor bzhi'i rgya.* SLL, 11:185–86.
———. *Sedonma. Sras don ma.* SLL, 12:1–446.
———. *Yoga of the Drops. Thig le'i rnal 'byor.* SLL, 11:146–47.
———. *Yumdonma. Yun don ma.* SLL, 29:1–159.
———. *Zangripugma. Zangs ri phug ma.* Not extant.
———. *Zhujema. Zhu byas ma.* SLL, 27:1–189.
Śākya Chogden. *Chariot of the Sun: A Commentary on the Difficult Points of the Vinaya Sūtra. Mdo sde'i dka' 'grel nyi ma'i shing rta.* SSB, 22:1–265.
———. *Commentary on the Difficult Points of the Abhidharmasamuccaya. Kun btus dka' 'grel.* SSB, 14:1–339.
———. *Commentary on the Saṃvara Tantra. Bde mchog gi rnam bshad.* SSB, 8:1–193.
———. *Cosmic Ocean Discoursing on Dharmakīrti's Seven Treatises: Commentary (Ṭīkā) on the Treasury of Logic. Rigs gter ṭī kā sde bdun ngag rol.* SSB, 19:447–749.
———. *Cosmic Ocean of Nectar: Rituals for the Three Foundations. Gzhi gsum cho ga bdud rtsi'i rol mtsho.* SSB, 22:267–310.
———. *Explanation of the Karmaśataka. Las brgya'i ṭi ka ba.* SSB, 22:311–525.
———. *Garland of Ocean Waves: A Traditional Commentary on the Prajñāpāramitā. Shes rab kyi pha rol tu phyin pa'i dka' 'grel bzhed tshul rgya mtsho'i rlabs kyi phreng ba.* SSB, 11:157–587.
———. *Golden Spoon of Excellent Explanations: Questions and Answers. Legs bshad gser gyi thur ma.* SSB, 6:439–647.
———. *Great Verification of Pramāṇa. Tshad ma'i mtha' gcod chen mo.* SSB, 19:1–137.
———. *Harbor for the Fortunate: An Explanation of the Mūlamadhyamakakārikā. Rtsa shes ṭi kā skal bzang 'jug ngogs.* SSB, 5:1–280.
———. *Hundred Gates to Liberation: A Commentary on the Guhyasamāja Tantra. Gsang 'dus rnam bshad rnam par thar pa'i sgo brgya pa.* SSB, 7:405–606.
———. *Illumination of Logic: A Commentary on the Difficult Points of the Pramāṇavārttikakārikā. Rnam 'grel gyi dka' 'grel rigs pa'i snga ng ba.* SSB, 19:169–445.
———. *Key to the Essential Points of the Definitive Meaning: An Explanation of the Madhyamakāvatāra. 'Jug ṭī kā nges don gnad kyi lde'u mig.* SSB, 5:281–457.
———. *Ocean of Explanation: A Detailed Outline of the Abhidharmakośa. Mdzod kyi mtha' bcad bye brag bshad mtsho.* SSB, 20:11–619 and 21:11–355.
———. *Overview of the Madhyamaka. Dbu ma'i stong mthun che chung gnyis.* SSB, 4:433–605.

———. *Samantabhadra's Cosmic Ocean: An Explanation of Pramāṇa. Tshad ma'i ṭī kā kun bzang rol mtsho / Shāk ṭīk.* SSB, 18:189–693.
Sakya Paṇḍita. *Advice of Mañjuśrī.* 'Jam dpal zhal lung. Delhi: Dpal ldan sa skya'i gsung rab, 1995. W23697.
———. *Biography of the Great Lama Jetsun. Bla ma rje btsun chen po'i rnam thar.* SKB, 10:576–98.
———. *Bouquet of Flowers: A Treatise on Composition. Sdeb sbyor sna tshogs me tog gi chun po.* SKB, 10:530–69.
———. *Clarification of the Meaning through Symbols. Brda don gsal ba.* SLL, 13:205–12.
———. *Clarifying the Sage's Intention. Thub pa'i dgongs pa gsal ba.* SKB, 10:1–197.
———. *Commentary on the Hymn to Nairātmyā. Bdag med ma'i bstod 'grel.* In *Sngags skor*, 188–238. Beijing: Mi rigs dpe skrun khang, 2004. W29976.
———. *Distinguishing the Three Vows. Sdom gsum gyi rab tu dbye ba.* SKB, 18:1–96.
———. *Entrance Gate for the Learned. Mkhas pa rnams 'jug pa'i sgo.* SKB, 10:325–447.
———. *Joyful Entrance: A Treatise on Drama. Zlos gar gyi bstan bcos rab dga'i 'jug pa.* Not extant (see Jackson 1987, 83).
———. *Letter to the Buddhas of the Ten Directions. Phyogs bcu'i sangs rgyas kyi 'phrin yig.* SKB, 12:109–37.
———. *Precious Treasury of Excellent Sayings. Legs par bshad pa'i rin po che'i gter.* SKB, 10:199–243.
———, ed. *Profound Path. Lam zab. Lam zab mo bla ma'i rnal 'byor.* SLL, 13:375–98.
———. *Scholar's Mouthwash: A Treatise on Poetry. Snyan ngag mkhas pa'i kha rgyan.* SKB, 12:542–48.
———. *Summary of Grammar. Sgra nye bar bsdus pa.* SKB, 10:502–3.
———, ed. *Teachings on the Secret Path. Lam sbas bshad.* SLL, 18:27–32.
———. *Treasury of Logic. Tshad ma rigs pa'i gter.* SKB, 11:1–49.
———. *Treasury of Words. Tshig gi gter.* SKB, 10:505–30.
Śākyaprabha. *Prabhāvati. 'Dul ba 'od ldan.* Q5627.
Sangye Puntsog. *Garland of Gems: The Succession to the Throne of Ewam. E wam chos gdan gyi gdan rabs nor bu 'phreng ba.* SLL, 25:1–52.
Śāntarakṣita. *Madhyamakālaṃkāra. Dbu ma rgyan.* Q5284.
Śāntideva. *Bodhicaryāvatāra. Byang chub sems dpa'i spyod pa la 'jug pa.* Q5272.
———. *Śikṣāsamuccaya. Kun btus gnyis.* Q5336.
———. *Sūtrasamuccaya. Mdo kun las btus pa.* Not extant.
Śāntipa. *Unified Meaning of Sūtra and Tantra. Mdo rgyud kyi don bsre.* SLL, 13:395–98.
Saroruhavajra (also Padmavajra). *Guhyasiddhi. Gsang ba grub pa.* Q3061.
———. *Hevajrasādhana of Saroruha. Sgrub thabs mtsho skyes.* Q2347.
———. *Nine Methods of the Profound Development Stage. Bskyed rim zab pa'i tshul dgu.* SLL, 11:419–45.
Smṛtijñānakīrti. *Vacanamukhāyudhopama. Smra ba'i sgo mtshon cha.* Q5784.
Sonam Tsemo. *Bodhicaryāvatāra Commentary. Byang chub sems dpa'i spyod pa la 'jug pa 'grel pa.* SKB, 5:439–669.
———. *Classes of Tantra. Rgyud sde spyi'i rnam gzhag.* SKB, 3:1–147.
———. *Easy Introduction for Children. Byis pa bde blag tu 'jug pa.* SKB, 4:635–51.

———. *Introduction to the Dharma. Chos la 'jug pa'i sgo.* SKB, 4:525–633.

———. *Summary of the Saṃputa Tantra. Sam pu ta'i rgyud kyi bsdus don.* SKB 3:709–53.

Tagtsang Lotsawa. *Knowing All the Philosophical Systems. Grub mtha' kun shes.* Thimphu: Kunzang Topgyel and Mani Dorje, 1976. W1CZ2515.

———. *Knowing All the Sūtra Sets. Mdo sde kun shes.* Not identified.

———. *Knowing All the Tantra Sets. Rgyud sde kun shes.* Not identified.

Tongrawa Kunga Legdrub. *Blue Book. Pod sngon.* SLL, 31:1–673.

Tsangjampa Dorje Gyaltsen. *River of Explication. Rnam bshad chu rgyun.* In *Sngon byon pa'i sa skya pa'i mkhas pa rnams kyi sngags skor*, 2:371–636. Kathmandu: Sa skya rgyal yongs gsung rab slob gnyer khang, 2003. W1KG4312.

Tsarchen Losel Gyatso. *Sunlight of Explanation. Rnam bshad nyi zer.* SLL, 10:327–581.

Tumi Sambhota / Tonmi Sambhota. *Basic Grammar in Thirty Verses. Sum cu pa.* In *Sgra dang sdeb sbyor*, edited by Mkhan po dam chos zla bas bsgrigs, 3–6. Lanzhou: Kan su'u mi rigs dpe skrun khang, 2004. W29032.

———. *Guide to Signs. Rtags kyi 'jug pa.* In *Sgra dang sdeb sbyor*, edited by Mkhan po dam chos zla bas bsgrigs, 7–10. Lanzhou: Kan su'u mi rigs dpe skrun khang, 2004. W29032.

Vāgbhaṭa. *Vaidyāṣṭāṅga. Sman dpyad yan lag brgyad pa.* Q5799.

Vāgīśvarakīrti. *Illuminating the Recollection of the Innate. Gnyug ma dran gsal.* SLL, 13:401–2.

———. *Letterless Mahāmudrā. Phyag rgya chen po yi ge med pa.* SLL, 11:406–19.

Vasubandhu. *Abhidharmakośa. Chos mngon pa'i mdzod tshig le'ur byas pa.* Q5590.

———. *Abhidharmakośabhāṣya. Chos mngon pa'i mdzod bshad pa / Mdzod 'grel.* Q5591.

———. *Saṃbhāraparikathā. Tshogs kyi gtam.* Q5666.

Vasumitra. *Vibhāṣākośa. Bye brag tu bshad pa / Bye brag bshad mdzod chen mo.* Extant only in Chinese (Taisho 1545).

Vibhūticandra. *Piṇḍīkṛtasādhana. Sgrub thabs mdor byas.* Q2701.

Vimuktisena. *Pañcaviṃśatisāhasrikāloka. Nyi khri snang ba / Shes rab kyi pha rol tu phyin pa stong phrag nyi shu lnga pa'i man ngag gi bstan bcos mngon par rtogs pa'i rgyan gyi 'grel pa.* Q5185.

———. *Great Commentary on the Pañcaviṃśatisāhasrikā. Nyi khri 'grel chen / Shes rab kyi pha rol tu phyin pa stong phrag nyi shu lnga pa'i man ngag gi bstan bcos mngon par rtogs pa'i rgyan gyi tshig le'ur byas pa'i rnam par 'grel pa.* Q5186.

Vinitadeva. *Triśatakārikā. Tshig le'ur byas pa sum brgya pa'i rnam par bshad pa.* Q5628.

Virūpa. *Divisions of the Empowerment. Dbang gi rab dbye.* SLL, 11:41–43.

———. *Vajra Lines. Rdo rje tshig rkang.* SLL, 11:10–19.

Zhuchen Tsultrim Rinchen. *Cosmic Ocean of Confident Endeavor. Gnyer gdengs can rol pa'i chu gter.* Dehradun: D. Gyaltsen, 1970. W23863.

———. *New Moon That Increases the Miraculous Ocean. Ngo mtshar chu gter 'phel ba'i zla ba gsar pa.* In *Sde dge bstan 'gyur*, 11:3–1007. Delhi: Karmapae Choedhey. 1982–5. W23703.

Anonymous and Rediscovered (Terma) Works

Kachem Kakholma. Bka' chems bka' khol ma. Lanzhou: Kan su'u mi rigs dpe skrun khang, 1991. W20856.

Maṇi Kabum. Ma ṇi bka' 'bum. New Delhi: Trayang and Jamyang Samten, 1975. W19225.

Testimony of Ba. Sba bzhed. Beijing: Mi rigs dpe skrun khang, 1980. W20000. See Wangdu and Diemberger 2000.

Other References

Akester, Matthew. 2012. *The Life of Jamyang Khyentse Wangpo.* New Delhi: Shechen Publications.

Amipa, Sherab Gyaltsen. 1976. *A Waterdrop from the Glorious Sea: A Concise Account of the Advent of Buddhism in General and the Teachings of the Sakyapa Tradition in Particular.* Rikon, Switzerland: Tibetan Institute.

Bayer, Achim. 1999. *The Life and Works of mKhan-po gZhan-dga' (1871–1927).* Master's thesis, University of Hamburg.

Bechert, Heinz, ed. 1991. *The Dating of the Historical Buddha: Die Datierung des historischen Buddha.* Göttingen: van den Hoeck & Ruprecht.

Cabezón, José Ignacio, and Geshe Lobsang Dargyay. 2007. *Freedom from Extremes: Gorampa's "Distinguishing the Views" and the Polemics of Emptiness.* Boston: Wisdom Publications.

Cassor, Constance. 2011. "Gorampa Sonam Sengé on the Refutation of the Four Extremes." *Revue d'Etudes Tibétaines* 22: 121–37.

Chattopadhyaya, Alak, and Lama Chimpa. 1970. *Taranātha's History of Buddhism in India.* Lhasa: Indian Institute of Advanced Study.

Cornu, Phillipe. 1997. *Tibetan Astrology.* Boston: Shambhala.

Davenport, John T. 2000. *Ordinary Wisdom: Sakya Pandita's Treasury of Good Advice.* Boston: Wisdom Publications.

Davidson, Ronald M. 1992. "Preliminary Studies on Hevajra's Abhisamaya and Lam 'bras Tshogs-bshad." In *Tibetan Buddhism: Reason and Revelation*, edited by Steven Goodman and Ronald Davidson, 107–32. Albany: State University of New York Press.

———. 2002. *Indian Esoteric Buddhism: A Social History of the Tantric Movement.* New York: Columbia University Press.

———. 2005. *Tibetan Renaissance: Tantric Buddhism in the Rebirth of Tibetan Culture.* New York: Columbia University Press.

Dreyfus, Georges. 2003. *The Sound of Two Hands Clapping: The Education of a Tibetan Buddhist Monk.* Berkeley: University of California Press.

Dudjom, Jigdral Yeshé Dorje. 1991. *The Nyingma School of Tibetan Buddhism: Its Fundamentals and History*, translated by Gyurme Dorje and Matthew Kapstein. Boston: Wisdom Publications.

Everding, Karl-Heinz. 2002. "The Mongol States and Their Struggle for Dominance over Tibet in the 13th Century." In *Tibet, Past and Present*, edited by Henk Blezer, 109–29. Leiden: Brill.

Harter, Pierre-Julien. 2011. "Doxography and Philosophy: The Usage and Significance of School Denominations in Red mda' ba gzhon nu blo gros' *Ornament of the Proofs of Consciousness.*" *Revue d'Etudes Tibétaines* 22: 93–119.

Heimbel, Jörg. 2011. "Biographical Sources for Researching the Life of Ngor chen Kun dga' bzang po (1382–1456)." *Revue d'Études Tibétaines* 22: 47–91.

Hoog, Constance. 1983. *Prince Jiṅ-Gim's Textbook of Tibetan Buddhism: The Śes-bya rab-gsal (Jñeya-prakaśa) by Phags-pa Blo-gros rgyal-mtshan dPal-bzaṅ-po of the Sa-skya-pa.* Leiden: Brill.

Jackson, David P. 1987. *Entrance Gate for the Wise: Sa-skya Paṇḍita on Indian and Tibetan Traditions of Pramāṇa and Philosophical Debate.* 2 vols. Vienna: Arbeitskreis für Tibetische und Buddhistische Studien, Universität Wien.

———. 1989a. *The Early Abbots of 'Phan-po Na-lendra.* Vienna: Arbeitskreis für Tibetische und Buddhistische Studien, Universität Wien.

———. 1989b. "Sources on the Chronology and Succession of the Abbots of Ngor E-wam-chos-ldan." *Berliner Indologische Studien* 4.5: 49–94.

———. 2003. *A Saint in Seattle: The Life of the Tibetan Mystic Dezhung Rinpoche.* Boston: Wisdom Publications.

Jinpa, Thupten. 2006. *Mind Training: The Great Collection.* Boston: Wisdom Publications.

Komarovski, Yaroslav. 2007. "Echoes of Empty Luminosity: Reevaluation and Unique Interpretation of Yogācāra and Niḥsvabhāvavāda Madhyamaka by the Fifteenth Century Tibetan Thinker Śākya mchog ldan." PhD diss., University of Virginia.

Martin, Dan. 2013. "The Highland Vinaya Lineage: A Study of a Twelfth-Century Monastic Historical Source, the 'Transmission Document' by Zhing-mo-che ba." In *Tibet After Empire: Culture, Society and Religion between 850–1000*, edited by Christoph Cüppers, Robert Mayer, and Michael Walter, 239–65. Lumbini, Nepal: Lumbini International Research Institute.

Nattier, Jan. 1991. *Once Upon a Future Time: Studies in a Buddhist Prophecy of Decline.* Berkeley: Asian Humanities Press.

Nebesky-Wojkowitz, René de. 1956. *Oracles and Demons of Tibet: The Cult and Iconography of the Tibetan Protective Deities.* London: Oxford University Press.

Obermiller, E. 1986 [1931–32]. *The History of Buddhism (Chos ḥbyung) by Bu-ston. I The Jewellery of Scripture, II The History of Buddhism in India and Tibet.* New Delhi: Sri Satguru Publications.

Petech, Luciano. 1990. *Central Tibet and the Mongols: The Yuan Sa-skya Period of Tibetan History.* Serie orientale Roma. Rome: Instituto italiano per il Medio ed Estremo Oriente.

Rhoton, Jared, 2002. *A Clear Differentiation of the Three Codes: Essential Distinctions among the Individual Liberation, Great Vehicle, and Tantric Systems: The Sdom Gsum Rab Dbye and Six Letters.* Albany: State University of New York Press.

Roerich, Nicholas, trans. 1996 [1949]. *The Blue Annals.* Delhi: Motilal Banarsidass.

Roloff, Carola. 2009. *Red mda' ba: Buddhist Yogi-Scholar of the Fourteenth Century.* Wiesbaden: Dr Ludwig Reichert Verlag.

Ruegg, David Seyfort 1981. *The Literature of the Madhyamaka School of Philosophy in India.* Wiesbaden: Otto Harrossowitz.

———. 2004. "Aspects of the Investigation of the (Earlier) Indian Mahāyāna." *Journal of the International Association of Buddhist Studies* 27.1: 3–62.

———. 2010. *The Buddhist Philosophy of the Middle: Essays on Indian and Tibetan Madhyamaka.* Boston: Wisdom Publications.

van Schaik, Sam van. 2011. "A New Look at the Invention of the Tibetan Script." In *New*

Studies of the Old Tibetan Documents: Philology, History and Religion, edited by Yoshiro Imaeda et al., 45–96. Tokyo: ILCAA, 2011.

van Schaik, Sam, and Imre Galambos. 2012. *Manuscripts and Travellers: The Sino-Tibetan Documents of a Tenth-Century Buddhist Pilgrim.* Berlin: de Gruyter.

Schoening, Jeffrey D. 1990. "The Religious Structures at Sakya." In *Reflections on Culture: Essays in Memory of Turrell V. Wylie,* edited by Lawrence Epstein and Richard Sherburne, 11–47. Lewiston/Queenston/Lampeter: The Edwin Mellon Press.

Schuh, Dieter. 1973. *Untersuchungen zur Geschichte der Tibetischen Kalenderrechnung.* Wiesbaden: Steiner Verlag.

Shoju Inaba. 1963. "The Lineage of the Sa skya pa: A Chapter of the Red Annals." *Memoirs of the Research Department of the Toyo Bunko* 22: 107–23.

Smith, E. Gene. 2001. *Among Tibetan Texts.* Boston: Wisdom Publications.

Snellgrove, David. 1959. *The Hevajra Tantra: A Critical Study.* London: Oxford University Press.

Sobisch, Jan-Ulrich. 2002. "The 'Records of Teachings Received' in the Collected Works of A mes zhabs: An Untapped Source for the Study of Sa skya pa Biographies." In *Tibet Past and Present,* edited by Henk Blezer, 161–79. Leiden: Brill.

———. 2007. *Life, Transmissions, and Works of A-mes-zhabs Ngag-dbang-kun-dga'-bsod-nams, the Great 17th Century Sa-skya-pa Bibliophile.* Verzeichnis der orientalischen Handschriften in Deutschland 38. Stuttgart: Franz Steiner Verlag.

Sørensen, Per K. 1994. *Tibetan Buddhist Historiography: The Mirror Illuminating the Royal Genealogies, An Annotated Translation of the XIVth Century Tibetan Chronicle: rGyal-rabs gsal-ba'i me-long.* Wiesbaden: Harrossowitz Verlag.

Stearns, Cyrus. 1999. *The Buddha from Dolpo: A Study of the Life and Thought of the Tibetan Master Dolpopa Sherab Gyaltsen.* New York: State University of New York Press.

———. 2001. *Luminous Lives: The Story of the Early Masters of the Lam 'bras Tradition in Tibet.* Boston: Wisdom Publications.

———. 2006. *Taking the Path as the Result: Core Teachings of the Sakya Lamdré Tradition.* Boston: Wisdom Publications.

———. 2012. *Song of the Road: The Poetic Travel Journal of Tsarchen Losal Gyatso.* Boston: Wisdom Publications.

Suzuki, Teitaro. 1904. "The First Buddhist Council." *The Monist* 14: 253–82.

Taniguchi, Fujio. 2004. "Mārgajñatā in the Abhisamayālaṅkāra." In *Three Mountains and Seven Rivers: Prof. Musashi Tachikawa's Felicitation Volume,* edited by Musashi Tachikawa et al., 97–105. New Delhi: Motilal Banarsidass.

Tatz, Mark. 1987. "The Life of the Siddha-Philosopher Maitrīgupta." *Journal of the American Oriental Society* 107 (4): 695–711.

Trichen, Chogay. 1983. *The History of the Sakya Tradition: A Feast for the Minds of the Fortunate.* Translated by Jennifer Stott. Bristol: Ganesha Press.

Tucci, Guiseppe. 1949. *Tibetan Painted Scrolls,* 3 vols. Rome: Libreria della Stato.

Uebach, Helga. 1987. *Nel-pa Paṇḍita's Chronik Me-tog Phreṅ-wa: Handschrift der Liberary of Tibetan Works and Archives, Tibetischer Text in Faksimile, Transkription und Übersetzung.* Munich: Kommission für Zentralasiatische Studien, Bayerische Akademie der Wissenschaften.

van der Kuijp, Leonard. 1983. *Contributions to the Development of Tibetan Buddhist Epistemology: From Eleventh to the Thirteenth Century*. Wiesbaden: F. Steinder.

Vargas-O'Brien, Ivette M. 2001. "The Life of dGe slong ma dPal mo: The Experience of a Leper, Founder of a Fasting Ritual, a Transmitter of Buddhist Teachings on Suffering and Renunciation in Tibetan Religious History." *Journal of the International Association for Tibetan Studies* 24: 157–86.

Verhagen, Pieter. 1994. *A History of Sanskrit Grammatical Literature in Tibet*, vol. 1. Leiden: Brill.

Vitali, Roberto. 2004. "Gur lha khang ma, 'The Tent Which Is a Temple,' Donated to Shakya mchog ldan by the Mustang Ruler bKra shis mgon." *Tibet Journal* 29.3: 65–74.

Wangdu, Pasang, and Hildegard Diemberger. 2000. *dBa bzhed: The Royal Narrative Concerning the Bringing of the Buddha's Doctrine to Tibet.* Vienna: Verlag der Österreichischen Akademie der Wissenschaften.

Index

A

Abhirati (*Mngon dga'*), 65

Acala (*Mi gyo ba*), 56, 59, 122, 147, 153, 173, 193, 237n50

Ajātaśatru (*Ma skyes dgra*), 28–29

Ajitamitra (*Mi pham bshes gnyen*), 89, 244n167

Akaniṣṭha (*'Og min*), 17, 19, 22, 27, 130, 190

Akaramati (7th c., *A ka ra ma ti*), 40

Amdo Dragom Zhabdrung Konchog Tenpa Rabgye (1801–66, *A mdo brag sgom zhabs drung dkon mchog bstan pa rab dgyes*), 185–86

Ame Zhab (*A myes zhabs*). *See* Jamgon Ame Zhab Kunga Sonam Wangpo

Amitāyus (*Tshe dpag med*), 173, 176, 179, 182, 193, 256n383

Amitāyus Nirmāṇakāya (*Tshe dpag med sprul sku*), 179

Amoghapāśa (*Don yod zhags pa*), 173

Amoghavajra (11th c., *Don yod rdo rje*), 92, 110, 121, 246n187, 248n220

Ānanda (~5th c. BCE, *Kun dga' bo*), 23, 29–30, 125–27, 235n16, 249n240

Ānandabhadra (*Kun dga' bzang po*). *See* Ngorchen Kunga Zangpo

Aṅgulimālā (~5th c. BCE, *Ser mo'i 'phreng ba*), 23

Arāḍakālāma (*Rloms pa ring 'phur*), 21

Arapacana Mañjuśrī (*'Jam dbyangs a ra pa tsa na*), 174

Ārya Kṛṣṇa (~4th c. BCE, *'Phags pa nag po*), 30

Āryadeva (3rd c., *Arya de wa*), 33–34, 37, 143, 150, 172

Asaṅga (4th/5th c., *Thogs med*), 11, 35–37, 57, 59, 143–44, 148–49, 154, 172, 256n388

Aścaryavajra (*Mgo mtshar rdo rje*), 82

Aseng, Khampa (12th c., *Khams pa a seng*), 59, 94, 100–101, 225–26

Aśoka, King (304–232 BCE, *Rgyal po mya ngan med, Dharma A shwa ka*), 30, 80

Aśvaghoṣa (2nd c., *Rta dbyangs*), 33–34, 243n152

Āṭavī (*'Brog*), 24

Atiśa (982–1054, *A ti sha*), 37–38, 45, 47, 55–56, 69, 132, 174, 176, 216, 229

Avadhūti (*A wa dhu ti pa*), 81–82, 91, 244n172

B

Ba Rinchen Sungwa (8th c., *Dbas rin chen srung ba*), 41

Ba Selnang (8th c., *Sba gsal snang*), 39

Bagton Śākya Ozer (14–15th c., *Bag ston shā kya 'od zer*), 147, 251n304

Bairotsana (8th c., *Bai ro tsa na*), 41, 47, 71

Balmo Ravine (*Bal mo grog*), 56, 98, 238n68

Balpo (*Bal po*), 54

Bari Lotsāwa Rinchen Drag (1040–1111, *Ba ri lo tsā ba rin chen grags*), 55–57, 107–11, 120–23, 180, 248n220, 253n343

Barompa Darma Wangchug (1127–94, *'Ba' rom pa dar ma dbang phyug*), 49
Barpug (*Bar phug*), 83
Barpug Rong (*Bar phug rong*), 122
Bartang (*Bar thang*), 86
Begtse (*Beg tse*), 12, 119, 181
Bhadra (*Bzang po*), 30
Bhadra, Captain (*Ded dpon bzang po*), 135
Bhairava (*'Jigs byed*), 48, 88, 142, 153, 156–57, 175, 182, 193, 202
Bhaiṣajyaguru (*Sman bla*), 173
Bhaiṣajyavana (*Sman gyi nags*), 24
Bhallika (~5th c. BCE, *Bzang skyong*), 22
Bhavyakīrti (*Skal ldan grags pa*), 26
Bhayanāsa (*Bha ya na sa*), 129, 248n234
Bhīmeśvara (*Bh mi sa ra*), 79
Bhotarāhula, the Indian yogin (*Bho ta ra hu la*), 58
Bhṛkuṭī (*Khro gnyer can*), 40
Bhurukuṃkūṭa (*Sme brtsegs*), 174
Bhurukuṃkūṭī (*Sme brtsegs ma*), 174
Bhūtaḍāmara (*Byung po 'dul byed*), 122, 192
Bidhaka (*Bi dha ka*), 33
Biji (12th c., *Bi ji*), 62, 65, 240n95
Bimbisāra (*Gzugs can snying po*), 38
Black Brahman, "the butcher" (*Bram nag bshan pa*), 181
Black-Cloaked One Wielding a Copper Knife (*Ber nag zangs ri can*), 112, 180
Black Jambhala (*Dzam nag*), 174
Black Goddess (*Lha mo nag po*), 112
Black Mañjuśrī (*'Jam dpal nag po*), 109, 156, 179
Black Siṃhamukha (*Seng ge nag po*), 181
Black Yama (protector, *Gshin nag*), 112
Black Yamāntaka (*Gshin rje nag po*), 175, 182
Blue Siṃhamukha (*Seng ldong sngon mo*), 109, 179
Bodhgaya (*Rdo rje gdan*), 16, 59, 87, 109, 112, 114
Bodhisattva Dawa Gyaltsen (12th c., *Byang sems zla ba rgyal mtshan*), 60, 101
Bodhisattva Jinpa (11th c., *Byang sems sbyin pa*), 64
Bodong Khenchen Ngamding Mawa Labsum Gyaltsen (1526–77, *Bo dong mkhan chen rngam sding ma ba bslab gsum rgyal mtshan*), 163
Bodong Chogle Namgyal (1375–1451, *Bo dong phyogs las rnam rgyal*), 226–27
Bokharwa Maitri Dondrub Gyaltsen the Fourth (16th c., *Bod mkhar ba mai tri don grub rgyal mtshan bzhi*), 162
Bom Lungda (*'Bom lung mda'*), 141
Brahmā (*Tshangs pa*), 14, 18–20, 22
Brahman, the (*Bram ze*), 115
Brawolung (*Bra bo lung*), 55
Buchog Nyi (17th c., *Bu chog gnyis*), 154
Buddhagupta (8th c., *Sangs rgyas gsang ba*), 41
Buddhajñānapāda (9th c., *Sangs rgyas ye shes zhabs*), 238n73
Buddhanandi (*Buddha nandi*), 33
Buddhaśrī (*Buddha shrī*), 128–29
Bum Rabjampa Cho Dondrub (15th c., *Bum rab 'byams pa chos don grub*), 141, 220
Bumtragsum, Paṇḍita (15th c., *Paṇḍita 'bum phrag gsum*), 141
Buton (14th c., *Bu ston*), 130, 136, 144, 160–62, 226–27, 237n47, 244n160, 250n263, 254n357

C

Caityagiri (*Mchod rten ri*), 24
Cakrasaṃvara (*'Khor lo bde mchog*), 26, 48, 50, 55, 59, 72, 78, 88, 90–91, 101, 107–8, 115, 119–20, 123, 131, 142–44, 148–49, 152, 156, 175, 182, 193, 222, 235n10, 243n147, 244n160, 252n316, 253n346, 257n413
Caṇḍika (~10th c., *Tsaṇḍi ka*), 78
Candragomin (7th c., *Tsandra go mi*), 37

Candrakīrti (7th c., *Zla grags pa*), 34–35, 143, 145, 148, 172, 192
Central Asia (*Rgya nag mthil*), 64
Central Tibet (*Dbus gtsang*), 44, 55, 65, 120, 136, 138, 142, 167, 185, 202, 217, 223, 244n163, 248n233, 251n307, 253n336, 254n361
Chag Drachom (11th c., *Chag dgra bcom*), 46
Chag Lotsāwa (1197–1264, *Chag lo tsā ba*), 65
Chagen Wangchug Gyaltsen (14th c., *Cha rgan dbang phyug rgyal mtshan*), 87, 95–96
Chagna, Drogon (1239–67, *'Gro mgon phyag na*), 68–69
Chagtsal Ridge (*Phyag rtsal sgang*), 55
Chalung Dorje Dragzong (*Cha lung rdo rje'i brag rdzong*), 161
Cham Lhakhang (*Lcam lha khang*), 58
Chamdo (*Chab mdo*), 198
Chandaka (~5th c. BCE, *'Dun pa*), 20
Changkya Rolpai Dorje (1717–86, *Lcang skya rol pa'i rdo rje*), 221
Chapa Chokyi Senge (1109–69, *Phya pa chen po chos kyi seng ge*), 60, 70
Che Khyidrug, Lotsāwa (~9th c., *Lo tsā ba lce khyi 'brug*), 165
Chekhawa (1102–76, *'Chad kha ba*), 48
Chemo Namkha of Penyul (11th c., *'Phan yul gyi mched mo nam mkha'*), 92
Chenga Tsultrim Darma (15th c., *Spyan lnga tshul khrims dar ma*), 139
Chengawa (1038–1103, *Spyan nga ba*), 48
Chenpo Paljor Gyatso (15th c., *Chen po dpal 'byor rgya mtsho*), 140
Chetsun Chogye Trichen Rinpoche (*Lce btsun bco rgyad khri chen rin po che*). *See* Chetsun Trichen Ngawang Khyenrab Tubten Legshe Gyatso Chog
Chetsun Dorje Chang Ngawang Lodro Nyingpo (*Lce btsun rdo rje 'chang ngag dbang blo gros snying po*). *See* Khangsar Khenchen Dorje Chang Ngawang Lodro Nyingpo
Chetsun Gachen Khyabdag Nyingpo (18th c., *Lce btsun dga' chen khyab bdag snying po*), 175
Chetsun Gendun Trashi Paljor (19th c., *Lce btsun dge 'dun bkra shis dpal 'byor*), 164, 168
Chetsun Jamyang Donyo Gyaltsen (15th c., *Lce btsun 'jam dbyangs don yod rgyal mtshan*), 166, 253n335
Chetsun Khyenrab Choje Rinpoche (1436–97, *Lce btsun mkhyen chos rje rin po che*), 130, 165–66, 168, 253n335
Chetsun Khyenrab Jampa Ngawang Lhundrub (1633–1703, *Lce btsun mkhyen rab byams pa ngag dbang lhun grub*), 72, 163, 165, 167, 169, 175
Chetsun Khyentse Rabten (*Lce btsun mkhyen brtse rab brtan*). *See* Chogyepa Khyentse Rabten
Chetsun Ngawang Kunkhyen (18th c., *Lce btsun ngag dbang kun mkhyen*), 167
Chetsun Ngawang Sonam Gyaltsen (*Lce btsun ngag dbang bsod nams rgyal mtshan*). *See* Khangsar Khenchen Ngawang Sonam Gyaltsen
Chetsun Rinchen Khyentse Wangpo (20th c., *Lce btsun rin chen mkhyen brtse dbang po*), 168
Chetsun Tendzin Nyendrag (19th c., *Lce btsun bstan 'dzin snyan grags*), 168–69, 253n341
Chetsun Tenpai Wangchug Chogdrub (19th c., *Lce btsun bstan pa'i dbang phyug mchog grub*), 167–68
Chetsun Trichen Ngawang Khyenrab Tubten Legshe Gyatso Chog (1920–2007, *Lce btsun khri chen ngag dbang mkhyen rab thub bstan legs bshad rgya mtsho mchog*), 2, 9, 164, 168–69, 232–33, 253n339

Chidrumpa Seche family (*Phyi 'brum pa se lce tsho*), 93
Chim Namkha Drag (1210–85, *Mchims nam mkha' grags*), 225, 227
Chime Dorje (18th c., *Chi med rdo rje*), 201
Chiring (*Spyi ring*), 53
Chiwo Lhepa Jangchub O (13th c., *Spyi bo lhas pa byang chub 'od*), 63
Chiwo Lhepa Jose (13th c., *Spyi bo lhas pa jo sras*), 67
Cho Pal Zangpo (15th c., *Chos dpal bzang po*), 130
Chogro Lui Gyaltsen (9th c., *Cog ro klu'i rgyal mtshan*), 41, 45, 47, 128, 237n42
Chogro Zhongpa Driche Śāka Tson (11th c., *Lcog ro gzhong pa 'bri lce shā ka btson*), 93
Chogyal Pagpa (*Chos rgyal 'phags pa*). *See* Pagpa Lodro Gyaltsen
Chogye Trichen Legshe Gyatso (*Bco rgyad khri chen legs bshad rgya mtsho*). *See* Chetsun Trichen Ngawang Khyenrab Tubten Legshe Gyatso Chog
Chogye Trichen Ngawang Kunga Khyenrab (*Bco rgyad khri chen ngag dbang kun dga' mkhyen rab*). *See* Chetsun Ngawang Kunkhyen
Chogyepa Khyentse Rabten (17th c., *Chos rgyas pa mkhyen brtse rab brtan*), 72, 164, 167
Choje Gonpo Wangchugpa (15th c., *Chos rje mgon po dbang phyug pa*), 147
Choje Kunga Paljor (15th c., *Chos rje kun dga' dpal byor*), 147
Choje Rinpoche (*Chos rje rin po che*). *See* Khyenrab Choje Rinpoche
Choje Śākya Lodropa (15th c., *Chos rje shā kya blo gros pa*), 147
Choje Sangrinpa (15th c., *Chos rje sangs rin pa*), 147
Choje Tugje Palsang (15th c., *Chos rje thugs rje dpal bzang*), 147
Chokor Lhunpo (*Chos 'khor lhun po*), 141
Chokyi Gyaltsen (15th c., *Chos kyi rgyal mtshan*), 71
Cholung Kachupa Choje Palzang (15th c., *Chos lung bka' bcu pa chos rje dpal bzang*), 139
Chomden Rigpai Raldri (1227–1305, *Bcom ldan rig pa'i ral gri*), 138, 225
Chomden Rigral (*Bcom ldan rig ral*). *See* Chomden Rigpai Raldri
Chudu (*Chu 'dus*), 130
Chudu Khetsunpa (*Chu 'dus mkhas btsun pa*), 130
Chumig (*Chu mig*), 60, 63, 131, 239n89
Chushul (*Chu shul*), 46

D

Dagchen Dorje Chang (*Bdag chen rdo rje 'chang*). *See* Dagchen Lodro Gyaltsen
Dagchen Jamyang Rinchen (1258–1306, *Bdag chen 'jam dbyangs rin chen*), 154, 241n120
Dagchen Kunga Legjung (1308–41, *Bdag chen kun dga' legs 'byung*), 71
Dagchen Kunga Samdrub (d. 1572, *Bdag chen kun dga' bsam grub*), 71
Dagchen Lodro Gyaltsen (1444–95, *Bdag chen blo gros rgyal mtshan*), 71–72, 159, 220, 262n335
Dagchen Lodro Wangchug (b. 1402, *Bdag chen blo gros dbang phyug*), 70, 149, 241n123
Dagchen Trashi Rinchen (1824–65, *Bdag chen bkra shis rin chen*), 74–75, 242n134
Dagchen Zhitogpa Kunga Rinchen (1339–99, *Bdag chen zhi thog pa kun dga' rin chen*), 128
Dagpo Dao Zhonu (*Dwags po zla 'od gzhon nu*). *See* Gampopa
Dagpo Gyaltsewa Jangpa Ngawang Sonam Gyaltsen (17th c., *Bdag po rgyal rtse ba byang pa ngag dbang bsod nams rgyal mtshan*), 132, 163

Dagpo Trashi Namgyal (15th c., *Dwags po bkra shis rnam rgyal*), 130, 140

Dagpo Onpo Paṇchen Trashi Namgyal (*Dwags po dbon po paṇ chen bkra shis rnam rgyal*). *See* Dagpo Trashi Namgyal

Ḍākinīpata (*Dā ka na pa ta*), 79

Ḍamarupa (~10th c., *Ḍa ma ru pa*), 81

Dānaśīla (9th c., *Dā na shī la*), 42, 45

Dānaśīla (12th c., *Dā na shī la*), 63

Dantig (*Dan tig*), 44

Dar Drangmoche (*'Dar grang mo che*), 161

Dar Ladrang (*'Dar bla brang*), 161

Dartsedo (*Dar rtse mdo*), 167, 204, 208

Datse Sarpa Ngawang Tendzin Norbu (20th c., *Zla tshes gsar pa ngag dbang bstan 'dzin nor bu*), 169

Dawa Gyaltsen, Bodhisattva (12th c., *Byang sems zla ba rgyal mtshan*), 60, 101, 174

De Tsugon (10th c., *Lde gtsug mgon*), 43

Denma (*Ldan ma*), 154

Denma Drung Kunga Rinchen (15th c., *Ldan ma drung kun dga' rin chen*), 130, 224

Densa Kar Samdrub Ling (*Ldan sa dkar bsam grub gling*), 154

Denyul Langtang (*Ldan yul glang thang*), 43

Derge (*Sde dge*), 157, 172, 183, 187–89, 194, 198, 203–5, 210–11, 216, 224–25, 249n258

Derge Lhundrub Teng (*Sde dge lhun grub steng*), 164, 189, 194, 210, 216, 224–25, 256n378

Devikoṭa (*De bi ko ṭi*), 80

Dezhin Shegpa (1384–1415, *De bzhin gshegs pa*), 49

Dezhung Chogtrul Anjam Rinpoche (1885–1952, *Sde gzhung mchog sprul a 'jam rin po che*), 200, 205, 208–15, 256n386

Dezhung Chogtrul Rinpoche Kunga Gyaltsen (*Sde gzhung mchog sprul rin po che kun dga' rgyal mtshan*). *See* Dezhung Chogtrul Anjam Rinpoche

Dezhung Monastery (*Sde gzhung dgon pa*), 167, 204

Dezhung Tulku Nyendrag Lungrig Nyima (d. 1898, *Sde gzhung sprul sku snyan grags lung rigs nyi ma*), 203, 232

Dezhung Rinpoche Kunga Tenpai Nyima (*Sde gzhung rin po che*). *See* Tharlam Dezhung Lungrig Tulku Jampa Tenpai Nyima

Dhānyakaṭaka (*'Bras spungs*), 26

Dharmapāla (11th c., *Dharma pā la*), 45, 237n45

Dharmapālarakṣita (1268–87, *Dharma pā la rakṣita*), 68–70, 241n120

Dharmatāśīla (9th c., *Dharma tā shī la*), 42

Dhītika (~4th c. BCE, *Dhi dhi ka*), 38, 236n24

Dhṛṭaka (~5th c. BCE, *Dhi dhi ka*), 33, 236n24

Dhūmāṅgārīdevī (*Dud sol lha mo*), 112, 180

Dignāga (ca. 480–540, *Phyogs kyi glang po*), 36–37, 63, 148, 171, 240n98

Ding (*Ding*), 58, 96

Dingri (*Ding ri*), 49–50, 138

Dingri Kunpang Chenpo (n.d., *Ding ri kun spangs chen po*), 50

Dīpaṃkara (*Mar me mdzad*), 18, 28, 132

Dipaṃkarabhadra (~10th c., *Mar me mdzad bzang po*), 117

Dogyal Namtrul Chetsun Khyenrab Tendzin Lhundrub (17th c., *Gdong rgyal rnam 'phrul lce btsun mkhyen rab bstan 'dzin lhun grub*), 167

Dokham (*Mdo khams*), 120, 141, 154, 183, 201

Dokhampa Palden Tose (15th c., *Mdo kham pa dpal ldan thod se*), 139

Ḍombī Heruka (~10th c., *Ḍombi he ru*

ka), 41, 57, 80–82, 92, 108, 242n142, 243n146, 244n168, 246n184
Ḍombīpa (*Ḍombi pa*). *See* Ḍombī Heruka
Dome Lingkhawa Aseng (*Mdo smad gling kha ba a seng*). *See* Aseng, Khampa
Dongag Rabjam Mawa Jamyang Sangye Senge (1504–69, *Mdo sngags rab byams smra ba 'jam dbyangs sangs rgyas seng ge*), 131
Dongton (13th c., *Ldong ston*), 67
donkey-faced Cakrasaṃvara (*Bde mchog bong zhal can*), 175
Dokongwa (~12th c., *Do kong ba*), 225
Doring Kunpang Chenpo (1449–1524, *Rdo ring kun spangs chen po*), 153
Doringpa Kunzang Chokyi Nyima (*Rdo ring pa kun bzang chos kyi nyi ma*), 104, 160–61
Dorje Chang Dragshul Trinle Rinchen (1871–1935, *Rdo rje 'chang drag shul 'phrin las rin chen*), 75
Dorje Chang Jampa Ngawang Kunga Tendzin Trinle (1884–1963, *Rdo rje 'chang byams pa ngag dbang kun dga' bstan 'dzin phrin las*), 169
Dorje Chang Kunga Zangpo (*Rdo rje 'chang kun dga' bzang po*). *See* Ngorchen Kunga Zangpo
Dorje Chang Wangchug Rabten (1558–1636, *Rdo rje 'chang dbang phyug rab brtan*), 72, 87, 163–64
Dorje Den (*Rdo rje gdan*). *See* Gongkar Dorje Den
Dorje Drag (*Rdo rje brag*), 164
Dorje Gyaltsen (17th c., *Rdo rje rgyal mtshan*), 166
Dorje Rinchen (8th c., *Rdo rje rin chen*), 54, 120
Dorje Rinchen (1819–67, *Rdo rje rin chen*), 74, 185, 242n132
Dorje Tsugtor (~10th c., *Rdo rje gtsug tor*), 54
Dorje Ying (*Rdo rje dbyings*), 42
Dorpe (*Rdo spe*), 140
Dragkar Sempa Chenpo (15th c., *Brag dkar sems dpa' chen po*), 130
Dragpa Gyaltsen, Jetsun (1147–1216, *Rje btsun grags pa rgyal mtshan*), 59–65, 69, 95, 97, 99–103, 108, 110, 141, 177, 191, 204, 210, 219, 226, 239n79, 240n93, n99, n103, 245n174, nn176–77, nn179–80, n183, 246n193, 247nn208–10, n213, n217, 255n374, 256n379
Dragpa Gyaltsen (1336–1376, *Grags pa rgyal mtshan*), 71
Dragpa Rinchen Dondrub (15th c., *Grags pa rin chen don grub*), 130
Dragra Dorje Chang (*Brag ra rdo rje 'chang*). *See* Dragra Jamyang Chokyi Nyima
Dragra Jamyang Chokyi Nyima (19th c., *Brag ra 'jam dbyangs chos kyi nyi ma*), 207, 209
Dragra Trashi Gyatso (19th c., *Brag ra bkra shis rgya mtsho*), 215, 218
Dragtengpa Yonten Tsultrim (11th c., *Brag steng pa yon tan tshul khrims*), 113
Dragtog Sonam Zangpo (15th c., *Brag thog bsod nams bzang po*), 135
Dragtse Senagpa (11th c., *Shang gi brag rtse se nag pa*), 92
Dragtsewa Losal Tendzin (19th c., *Brag rtse ba blo gsal bstan 'dzin*), 73
Dragyab (*Brag g.yab*), 198
Dragyab Dongkam Trichen Ngawang Damcho Gyatso (19th c., *Brag g.yab gdong kaṃ khri chen ngag dbang dam chos rgya mtsho*), 232
Dragzongma (*Brag rdzong ma*), 157, 192–93, 202
Drangti Darma Nyingpo (12th c., *'Brang ti dar ma snying po*), 57, 227, 238n72
Drangti Khenchen Drubpai Wangchug Jampa Namkha Samdrub (1696–1754, *Brang ti mkhan chen grub pa'i dbang*

phyug byams pa nam mkha' bsam grub), 73, 132
Drangti Khenchen Drubpai Wangchug Namkha Sangye (16th c., *Brang ti mkhan chen grub pa'i dbang phyug nam mkha' sangs rgyas*), 132
Drangti Khenchen Jampa Kunga Tenpai Gyaltsen (1829–70, *Brang ti'i mkhan chen thams cad mkhyen pa byams pa kun dga' bstan pa'i rgyal mtshan*), 133, 188, 191–93, 199, 256n377
Drangti Khenchen Jangchub Sempa Rigyai Khyabdag Naljor Jampal Zangpo (1789–1864, *Brang ti mkhan chen byang chub sems dpa' rigs brgya'i khyab bdag rnal 'byor 'jams dpal bzang po*), 133, 184–85
Drangti Khenchen Namkha Rinchen (1624–69, *Drang ti mkhan chen nam mkha' rin chen*), 132
Drangti Khenchen Tamche Khyenpa Jampa Kunga Tenpai Gyaltsen (*Brang ti mkhan chen thams cad mkhyen pa byams pa kun dga' bstan pa'i rgyal mtshan*). *See* Drangti Khenchen Jampa Kunga Tenpai Gyaltsen
Drangti Khenchen Tamche Khyenpa Jampa Namkha Chime (1763–1820, *Brang ti mkhan chen thams cad mkhyen pa byams pa nam mkha' 'chi med*), 133, 184, 224, 256n381
Drangti Namka Chime (*Brang ti nam mkha' 'chi med*). *See* Drangti Khenchen Tamche Khyenpa Jampa Namkha Chime
Drangyul (*Sbrang yul*), 94
Dratonpa Yonten Gyatso (15th c., *Grwa ston pa yon tan rgya mtsho*), 140
Drenchog Chogleg Dorje (16th c., *'Dren mchog mchog legs rdo rje*), 166
Drenchog Namkha Palzang (1611–72, *'Dren mchog nam mkha' dpal bzang*), 132
Dreyul Kyetsal (*Bras yul skyed tshal*), 140–42
Drida Zalmogang (*Bri zla zal mo gang*), 201
Drigung Kyobpa (12th c., *'Bri gung skyob pa*), 49
Dro Sherab Drag (12th c., *'Bro shes rab grags*), 46
Drogmi Lotsāwa (*'Brog mi lo tsā ba*). *See* Drogmi Śākya Yeshe
Drogmi Śākya Yeshe (993–1072?, *'Brog mi shākya ye shes*), 46, 54–56, 78, 82–98, 108, 110, 243n143, nn149–50, n154, n156, 244nn156–60, 245n183, 248n230
Drogon Chogyal Pagpa (*'Gro mgon chos rgyal 'phags pa*). *See* Pagpa Lodro Gyaltsen
Drogsa (*Brog sa*), 255
Drolma Palace (*Sgrol ma pho brang*), 210, 242n131
Drom Depa Tonchung (11th c., *'Brom des pa ston chung*), 92, 95
Drompa Gyang (*Grom pa rgyang*), 87
Dromton Gyalwai Jungne (1004–1064, *'Brom ston rgyal ba'i 'byung gnas*), 45, 48
Dropugpa Śākya Senge (19th c., *'Bro phug pa Shākya seng ge*), 74
Drozang Nyingpo (~12th c., *'Gro bzang snying po*), 174
Dru Sibui Ngagchang Gonsarwa Sonam Chopel (1527–1603/10, *Bru si bu'i sngags 'chang dgon gsar ba bsod nams chos 'phel*), 163, 220
Drubchen Dragpugpa Sonam Pal (1277–1350, *Grub chen brag phug pa bsod nams dpal*), 103
Drubtob Yonten Palzang (13th c., *Grub thob yon tan dpal bzang*), 67, 103
Drubtob Yontenpal (*Grub thob yon tan dpal*). *See* Drubthob Yonten Palzang
Drubwang Ratnabhadra (19th c., *Grub dbang ratna bha dra*), 75

Drum Yeshe Gyaltsen (10th c., *Grum ye shes rgyal mtshan*), 45
Drungche Rinchen Wangyal (19th c., *Drung che rin chen dbang rgyal*), 183
Drungchen Tsultrim Gyaltsen (19th c., *Drung chen tshul khrims rgyal mtshan*), 201
Drub (13th c., *Grub*), 65
Drubpa Yonten (14th c., *Grub pa yon tan*), 128
Drubpa Zhuchen (n.d., *Sgrub pa zhu chen*), 111
Drubchen Chokyi Lama (*Grub chen chos kyi bla ma*). *See* Karma Pakshi
Drubchen Sangye Gyatso (*Grub chen sangs rgyas rgya mtsho*). *See* Khedrub Sangye Gyatso
Drubchog Konchog Lodro (15th c., *Grub mchog dkon mchog blo gros*), 130
Drubkhangpa Palden Dondrub (1563–1636, *Sgrub khang dpal ldan don grub*), 132, 182, 220
Drubtson Kunga Cholha (19th c., *Sgrub brtson kun dga' chos lha*), 203
Ducho (*Dus mchod*), 165
Dugyal Pawo Totrengchen (*Sdud rgyal dpa' bo thod 'phreng can*), 238n63
Dulwa Dzinpa Chenpo Jamyang Gyaltsen (19th c., *Dul ba 'dzin pa chen po 'jam dbyangs rgyal mtshan*). *See* Gapa Lama Jamyang Gyaltsen
Durjayacandra (10th c., *Mi thub pa zla ba*), 60, 89, 244n168
Dusong Mangpoje (7th c., *'Dus srong mang po rje*), 41
Dusum Khyenpa (1110–93, *Dus gsum mkhyen pa*), 49, 226, 237n57
Dutsi Chemchog (*Bdud rtsi che mchog*), 237n49
Dzamling Chergu Wangdu (19th c., *'Dzam gling che rgu dbang sdud*), 74
Dzing Namgyal Gonpo Yeshepa (*'Dzing rnam rgyal mgon po ye shes pa*), 196
Dzingpo Dzong (*'Dzing spo 'dzong*), 195
Dzogchen Khenpo Zhenga Rinpoche (1871–1927, *Rdzogs chen mkhan po gzhan dga' rin po che*), 206–8, 210, 256n390
Dzonglungpa (15th c., *Rdzong lung pa*), 227
Dzongpa Kunga Gyaltsen (1382–1436, *Rdzong pa kun dga' rgyal mtshan*), 137, 219–20
Dzongsar Khyentse Jamyang Chokyi Lodro (1893–1959, *Rdzong gsar mkhyen brtse 'jam dbyangs chos kyi blo gros*), 1, 200, 205, 208–9, 211, 214–18, 233, 236n1, 257n402
Dzongsar Trashi Lhatse (*Rdzong gsar bkra shis lha rtse*), 189, 194, 198, 215, 225
Dzongshar Bodrugpa Choje Losel Puntsog (18th c., *Rdzong shar bod 'brug pa chos rje*), 164

E

Eastern Tibet (*Smad*), 1, 43–45, 87
Ekādaśamukha (*Bcu gcig zhal*), 173
Ewam Choden (*E waṃ chos ldan*), 130–34, 142, 144, 156, 164, 193, 206, 209, 223, 249n245
Ewam Khangsar Khenchen Dampa Rinpoche (*E waṃ khang gsar mkhan chen dam pa rin po che*). *See* Khangsar Ngawang Khyentse Tubten Nyingpo
Ewam Luding Khenchen Gyalse Jamyang Chokyi Nyima (*E waṃ klu sdings mkhan chen rgyal sras 'jam dbyangs chos kyi nyi ma*). *See* Luding Gyalse Jamyang Chokyi Nyima
Ewampa Chenpo (*E waṃ pa chen po*). *See* Ngorchen Kunga Zangpo

F

Fierce and Brilliant Lord (*Drag po gzi ldan dbang phyug*). *See* Kṣetrapāla
Fifth Dalai Lama (*Gong sa lnga pa*). *See* Ngawang Losang Gyatso

Flower Courtyard (*Me tog ra ba*), 70, 241n118, 242n126
Four-Faced Black Strongman (*Stobs 'phrog nag po gdong bzhi*). *See* Kṣetrapāla
Four-Faced Guardian (*Mgon po zhal bzhi*). *See* Kṣetrapāla

G
Ga Kyegu Dondrub Ling (*Sga skye rgu don grup gling*), 172, 194, 200, 203, 205, 213, 224
Ga Rabjampa Chokyi Gyalpo Kunga Yeshe (12th c., *Sga rab byams pa chos kyi rgyal po kun dga' ye shes*), 201
Game Dzinda (*Sga smad 'dzin mda'*), 201
Gampopa (1079–1153, *Sgam po pa*), 48
Gaṇapati (*Tshogs bdag*), 108, 111, 178
Ganden Kunso (12th c., *Dga' ldan kun bsod*), 68
Ganden Nampar Gyalwai Ling (*Dga' ldan rnam par rgyal ba'i gling*). *See* Riwo Ganden
Ganden Trashi Pal (~12th c., *Dga' ldan bkra shis dpal*), 68
Gandhāra (*Ga dha ra*), 31, 59
Gapa Lama Jamyang Gyaltsen (1870–1940, *Sga pa bla ma 'jam dbyangs rgyal mtshan*), 146, 200, 205, 208, 213
Gar Tongtsen (7th c., *Mgar stong btsan*), 137, 250n264
Garbharipa (*Garbha ri pa*), 82
Gartar (*Mgar thar*), 133
Garton Jamyang Sherab Gyatso (1396–1474, *'Gar ston 'jam dbyangs shes rab rgya mtsho*), 130–31
Garwang Chokyi Wangchug (*Gar dbang chos kyi dbang phyug*), 49
Gato (*Sga stod*), 198, 224
Gaton Naljor Wangchug Kunga Nyima (20th c., *Sga ston rnal 'byor dbang phyug kun dga' nyi ma*), 211
Gaton Ngawang Legpa (*Sga ston ngag dbang legs pa*), 2, 201–6, 211–13, 215, 221
Gavāṃpati (~5th c. BCE, *Ba lang bdag*), 29
Gawai Shenyen (n.d, *Dga' ba'i bshes gnyen*), 227
Gayadhara (*Ga ya dha ra*), 82–87, 91–92, 98, 110, 179–80, 243n149, n151, 243nn158–59
Gazi Lodro Senge (15th c., *Ga zi blo gros seng ge*), 138
Gekyab (~10th c., *Dge skyabs*), 54
Gelong Kunlo (13th c., *Dge slong kun blo*), 68
Gelongma Palmo (~11th c., *Dge slong ma dpal mo*), 173, 253n345
Gendun Drubpa (1391–1474, *Dge' 'dun grub pa*), 58
Gendun Gyatso (1492–1542, *Dge 'dun rgya mtsho*), 160, 253n329
Geshe Dondrub (15th c., *Dge shes don grub*), 130
Geshe Melhang Tserwa (12th c., *Dge bshes mes lhang tsher ba*), 57
Getong (~10th c., *Dge mthong*), 54
Gewa Gyaltsen (5th c., *Dge ba rgyal mtshan*), 139, 149, 165
Gewa Rabsal (10th c., *Dge ba rab gsal*), 44, 87, 144n163
Ghanavyūha (*Nyams dga'*), 17
Glittering Lake in Yardrog (*Yar 'brog g.yu mtsho*), 138
Go Khugpa Lhetse (*'Gos khug pa lhas btsas*). *See* Go Lotsāwa
Go Lotsāwa (11th c., *'Gos lo tsā ba*), 46, 85–86, 90, 119, 226, 243n156
Godan Khan (1206–51, *Go dan*), 64
golden realms of the north (*Byang phyogs kyi 'jigs rten gyi khams gser mdog can*), 59
Gomde Trahrel (15th c., *Sgom sde khra hral*), 139
Gongkar Dorje Den (*Gong dkar rdo rje gdan*), 136, 224, 254n357

Gongpa Rabsal (*Dgongs pa rab gsal*). *See* Gewa Rabsal
Gonjo Jinzang (15th c., *Gon jo sbyin bzang*), 140–41
Gonjo Yeshe Pal (14th c., *Gon jo ye shes dpal*), 136
Gonpo Ngodrub Palbar (1801–56, *Mgon po dngos grub dpal 'bar*), 74
Gonsarwa Sonam Chopel (*Dgon gsar ba bsod nams chos 'phel*). *See* Dru Sibui Ngagchang Gonsarwa Sonam Chopel
Gorampa (*Go rams pa*). *See* Gowo Rabjampa Sonam Senge
Gorum (*Sgo rum*). *See* White Gorum Zimchil
Govindacaṇḍa (~10th c., *Go binda tsandra*), 79
Gowo Rabjampa Sonam Senge (1429–89, *Go bo rab 'byams pa bsod nams seng ge*), 130–31, 141–47, 153, 219–20, 227, 232, 250n278, 251n303
Gowo Rabjampa Sherab Pal (15th c., *Go bo rab 'byams pa shes rab dpal*), 140–41
Grahamāṭṛkā (*Gza' yum*), 173
Gṛdhrakūṭa Mountain (*Bya rgod 'phung po'i ri*), 23–24
Great Fifth (*Lnga pa chen po*). *See* Ngawang Losang Gyatso
Great Red Gaṇapati (*Tshogs bdag dmar chen*), 108, 178
Great Yellow Vaiśravaṇa (*Rnam sras ser chen po*), 174
Guardian, the (*Mgon po*). *See* Mahākāla
Guardian of the Tent (*Gur gyi mgon po*), 129, 179–80, 202, 204, 212–13, 248n225
Guge (*Gu ge*), 138, 230, 258n421
Guge Paṇchen (*Gu ge paṇ chen*). *See* Guge Paṇḍita Dragpa Gyaltsen
Guge Paṇḍita Dragpa Gyaltsen (1415–86, *Gu ge paṇḍita grags pa rgyal mtshan*), 130
Guhyasamāja (*Gsang ba 'dus pa*), 26, 34, 48, 72, 88, 115–16, 137, 142, 146, 149, 156, 175, 182, 193, 222, 251n301
Guhyasamāja Akṣobhya (*Gsang 'dus mi bskyod pa*), 182
Guṇaprabha (9th c., *Yon tan 'od*), 37, 145, 154, 171, 194, 202
Gung (*Gung*), 65, 220
Gungri Gungtsen (7th c., *Gung ri gung btsan*), 41
Gungru Gyaltsen Zangpo (15th c., *Gung ru rgyal mtshan bzang po*), 139
Gungru Sherab Zangpo (15th c., *Gung ru shes rab bzang po*), 130, 142, 165
Gungtang (*Gung thang*), 57–58, 98
Guru Chokyi Wangchug (1212–70, *Gu ru chos kyi dbang phyug*), 47, 225
Guru Chowang (*Gu ru chos dbang*). *See* Guru Chokyi Wangchug
Guru Mahāyogin (11th c., *Bla ma ma ha yo gi*), 121
Guru Ratnasambhava (*Bla ma rin 'byung*), 177
Guru Rinpoche (*Gu ru rin po che*). *See* Padmasambhava
Guru Sendhepa Ratnakīrti (11th c., *Bla ma sendhe pa rin chen grags pa*), 115–17
Gya Śākya Zhonu (11th c., *Gya shā kya gzhon nu*), 87
Gyagarpa Sherab Gyaltsen (1436–95, *Rgya gar pa shes rab rgyal mtshan*), 71, 224
Gyalse Khyentse Ozer (1904–53, *Rgyal sras mkhyen brtse 'od zer*), 205
Gyalse Togme (1285–1369, *Rgyal sras thogs med*), 142, 182
Gyaltsa Kunden Repa (12th c., *Rgyal tsha kun ldan ras pa*), 49
Gyaltsab (*Rgyal tshab*). *See* Gyaltsab Darma Rinchen
Gyaltsab Dampa Kunga Wangchug (1424–78, *Rgyal tshab dam pa kun dga' dbang phyug*), 130–31, 149

Gyaltsab Darma Rinchen (1364–1432, *Rgyal tshab dar ma rin chen*), 50, 226
Gyaltsewa Ngawang Sonam Gyaltsen (1598–1674, *Rgyal rtse ba ngag dbang bsod nams rgyal mtshan*), 132, 153
Gyalwa Lhachog Senge (1468–1535, *Rgyal ba lha mchog seng ge*), 131
Gyalwa Men (15th c., *Rgyal ba sman*), 141
Gyalwa Sherab (15th c., *Rgyal ba shes rab*), 135
Gyalwa Yang Gonpa (13th c., *Rgyal ba yang dgon pa*), 65
Gyalwai Sherab (11th c., *Rgyal ba'i shes rab*), 45
Gyalwang Sonam Gyatso (1543–88, *Rgyal dbang bsod nams rgya mtsho*), 163
Gyama (*Rgya ma*), 151
Gyengong temple (*Rgyan gong dgon pa*), 46, 63, 87, 244n163
Gyichuwa Dralhabar (11th c., *Sgyi chu ba dgra lha 'bar*), 57, 98
Gyijang Ukarwa (11th c., *Gyi ljang dbu dkar ba*), 92
Gyijo Dawai Ozer (11th c., *Gyi jo zla ba'i 'od zer*), 85, 243n158
Gyipen (10th c., *Gyi phan*), 44
Gyolwa Khampa Gateng (12th c., *Gyol ba khams pa sga theg*), 101

H
Haklenayaśas (*Ha ka li ka na ya nā sha*), 33
Haribhadra (8th c., *Seng ge bzang po*), 37, 239n77
Harinanda (13th c., *'Phrog byed dga' bo*), 64
Hayagrīva (*Rta mgrin*), 174
Heruka (*Her ru ka*), 36, 54, 86, 175–76, 237n49
Heshang Mahāyāna (8th c., *Ha shang ma ha yan*), 41
House of Dungcho (*Dus mchod bla brang*), 70–71, 242n128
House of Lhakhang (*Lha khang bla drang*), 70–71, 216, 242n127
House of Rinchen Gang (*Bla drang rin chen sgang*), 70–71
House of Zhitog (*Gzhi thog bla brang*), 70
Hukarche (13th c., *Hu dkar che*), 70

I
Indra (*Brgya byin*), 21–22
Indrabhūti, King (~10th c., *Rgyal po indra bhū ti*), 108, 178, 245n181
Indrabhūti, the Great (*Indra bhū ti chen po*), 26–27, 32, 91, 245n181
Indraketu (*Dbang po'i tog*), 17
Īśvarasena (7th c., *Dbang phyug sde*), 36

J
Jago Pungpo (*Bya rgod phung po*), 151
Jambudvīpa (*'Dzam bu'i gling*), 11, 17–18, 24, 26–27, 30, 33, 37, 125, 137, 227, 234
Jamchen Rabjampa Sangye Pal (1412–86, *Byams chen rab 'byams pa sangs rgyas dpal*), 140–43, 220, 224
Jamchenpa (1383–1445, *Byams chen pa*), 50
Jamgon Ame Zhab Kunga Sonam Wangpo (1597–1659, *'Jam mgon a mes zhabs kun dga' bsod nams dbang po*), 2, 72–75, 86–87, 163, 221–22, 232, 238n70, 242n129, 243n149, nn151–56, 244n159, nn161–62, 257n413
Jamgon Dorje Rinchen (*'Jam mgon rdo rje rin chen*). *See* Dorje Rinchen (1819–67)
Jamgon Kongtrul Lodro Taye (1813–99, *'Jam mgon kongs sprul blo gros mtha' yas*), 51, 185–88, 192, 196, 199, 203, 205, 214–15, 254n358
Jamgon Kunga Gyaltsen (1819–67, *'Jam mgon kun dga' rgyal mtshan*), 74
Jamgon Kunga Lodro (1729–1783, *'Jam mgon kun dga' blo gros*), 72–74, 163–64, 182, 220

Jamgon Lhundrub Palden (1624–97, *'Jam mgon lhun grub dpal ldan*), 132
Jamgon Ngagi Wangpo Kunga Lodro (*'Jam mgon ngag gi dbang po kun dga' blo gros*). *See* Jamgon Kunga Lodro
Jamgon Sangye Palzang (*'Jam mgon sangs rgyas dpal bzang*). *See* Tsungme Kheshing Drubpa Jamgon Sangye Palzang
Jamgon Sangye Puntsog (*'Jam mgon sangs rgyas phun tshogs*). *See* Khenchen Jampaiyang Sangye Puntsog
Jamgon Sonam Rinchen (1705–41, *'Jam mgon bsod nams rin chen*), 72
Jamgon Trashi Lhundrub (*'Jam mgon bkra shis lhun grub*). *See* Tsang Dokharwa Khenchen Trashi Lhundrub
Jamgon Wangdu Nyingpo (1763–1809, *'Jam mgon dbang sdud snying po*), 74
Jampa Cho Trashi (19th c., *Byams pa chos bkra shis*), 202
Jampa Kunga Tendzin (*Byams pa kun dga' bstan 'dzin*). *See* Tartse Khenchen Jampa Kunga Tendzin
Jampa Kunga Trashi (1558–1603, *Byams pa kun dga' bkra shis*), 132, 224, 232
Jampa Lingpa, Je (15th c., *Rje byams pa gling pa*), 136
Jampa Ngawang Lhundrub (*Byams pa sngags dbang lhun grub*). *See* Chetsun Khyenrab Jampa Ngawang Lhundrub
Jampa Ngawang Namgyal (17th c., *Byams pa sngags dbang rnam rgyal*), 72
Jampa Ngawang Sangye Tendzin (18th c., *Byams pa ngag dbang sangs rgyas bstan 'dzin*), 169
Jampa Ngawang Tendzin Nyendrag (*Byams pa ngag dbang bstan 'dzin snyan grags*). *See* Chetsun Tendzin Nyendrag
Jampa Ngawang Tendzin Trinle (18th c., *Byams pa ngag dbang bstan 'dzin phrin las*), 169
Jampa Palden Chodze (19th c., *Byams pa dpal ldan chos mdzad*), 133–34, 200
Jampa Palden Zangpo (1789–1864, *Byams pa dpal ldan bzang po*), 133
Jampa Tsultrim Lhundrub (1676–1729, *Byam pa tshul khrims lhun grub*), 132, 156
Jampa Tsultrim Palzang (1675–1710, *Byams pa tshul khrims dpal bzang*), 132
Jampal Dragpa (16th c., *'Jam dpal grags pa*), 71
Jampal Tendzin Trinle (19th c., *'Jam dpal bstan 'dzin 'phrin las*), 202
Jamyang Choje (15th c., *'Jam dbyangs chos rje*), 160
Jamyang Choje, Tashi Palden (1379-1449, *'Jam dbyangs chos rje*), 50
Jamyang Chokyi Je Konchog Dragpa (b. 1716, *'Jam dbyangs chos kyi rje dkon mchog grags pa*), 133, 221
Jamyang Chokyi Lama Sangye Yeshe (18th c., *'Jam dbyangs chos kyi bla ma sangs rgyas ye shes*), 73, 133, 224
Jamyang Damcho Gyaltsen (16th c., *'Jam dbyangs dam chos rgyal mtshan*), 166
Jamyang Dewai Dorje (18th c., *'Jam dbyangs bde ba'i rdo rje*), 221
Jamyang Donyo Gyaltsen (1310–44, *'Jam dbyangs don yod rgyal mtshan*), 70–71, 166
Jamyang Dragpai Pal (*'Jam dbyangs grags pa'i dpal*). *See* Dzongpa Kunga Gyaltsen
Jamyang Gyaltsen (*'Jam dbyangs rgyal mtshan*). *See* Gapa Lama Jamyang Gyaltsen
Jamyang Khyenrab Taye (20th c., *'Jam dbyangs mkhyen rab mtha' yas*), 200
Jamyang Khyentse Chokyi Lodro (*'Jam dbyangs mkhyen brtse chos kyi blo gros*). *See* Dzongsar Khyentse Chokyi Lodro
Jamyang Khyentse Wangchug (1524–68,

'Jam dbyangs mkhyen brtse dbang phyug), 161–63, 165, 177, 220, 236n2, 244n161, n169, 246n194, n203, 253n333
Jamyang Khyentse Wangpo Kunga Tenpai Gyaltsen (1820–92, *'Jam dbyangs mkhyen brtse dbang po kun dga' brtan pa'i rgyal mtshan*), 182, 184–90, 192, 194–201, 203, 205, 214, 217, 221, 225, 254n358, 255n369, n373, 256n377, n381, 257n399
Jamyang Konchog Lhundrub (*'Jam dbyangs dkon mchog lhun grub*). *See* Konchog Lhundrub
Jamyang Kunga Chozang (1433–1503, *'Jam dbyangs kun dga' chos bzang*), 130, 141, 153, 220
Jamyang Kunga Sonam Lhundrub (1571–1642, *'Jam dbyangs kun dga' bsod nams lhun grub*), 132, 166
Jamyang Legpai Lodro (19th c., *'Jam dbyangs legs pa'i blo gros*), 199, 203
Jamyang Namkha Gyaltsen (16th c., *'Jam dbyangs nam mkha' rgyal mtshan*), 71, 166
Jamyang Ngagi Wangpo (1517–84, *'Jam dbyangs ngag gi dbang po*), 166
Jampaiyang Ngawang Legdrub (*'Jam pa'i dbyangs ngag dbang legs grub*). *See* Ponlob Ngawang Legrub
Jamyang Rinchen Dorje (1837–1901, *'Jam dbyangs rin chen rdo rje*), 133–34, 198, 203, 224
Jamyang Sangye Palzang (*'Jam dbyangs sangs rgyas dpal bzang*). *See* Tsungme Kheshing Drubpa Jamgon Sangye Palzang
Jamyang Sangye Yeshe (*'Jam dbyangs sangs rgyas ye shes*). *See* Jamyang Chokyi Lama Sangye Yeshe
Jamyang Sherab (20th c., *'Jam dbyangs shes rab*), 233
Jamyang Sherab Dragpa Pal (15th c., *'Jam dbyangs shes rab grags pa dpal*), 149
Jamyang Sherab Gyatso (1396–1474, *'Jam dbyangs shes rab rgya mtsho*). *See* Garton Jamyang Sherab Gyatso
Jamyang Sherab Gyatso (d. 1873, *'Jam dbyangs shes rab rgya mtsho*), 133
Jamyang Sherab Gyatso from Ngari (15th c., *Mnga' ris pa 'jam dbyangs shes rab rgya mtsho*), 140
Jamyang Sonam Wangchug (17th c., *'Jam dbyangs bsod nams dbang phyugs*), 72
Jamyang Sonam Wangpo (*'Jam dbyangs bsod nams dbang po*). *See* Sakyapa Jamyang Sonam Wangpo
Jang Dagchen Palden Chokyong (15th c., *Byang bdag chen dpal ldan chos skyong*), 135
Jangchub O (11th c., *Byang chub 'od*), 45, 63, 112
Jangchub Sempa Chenpo Sangye Tendzin (d. 1705, *Byang chub sems dpa' chen po sangs rgyas bstan 'dzin*), 132
Jangchub Sempa Kunga Bum (15th c., *Byang chub sems dpa' kun dga' 'bum*), 141
Jangchub Sempa Zhonu Gyalchog (*Byang chub sems dpa' gzhon nu rgyal mchog*). *See* Sempa Chenpo Zhonu Gyalchog
Jarbuwa of Uyug (12th c., *U yug gi dbyar sbu ba*), 102
Jaṭilakāśyapa (*Lteng rgyas 'od srung ral pa can*), 23
Jāyasena (12th c., *Dza ya se na*), 61
Jāyaśrī (~10th c., *Dza ya shrī*), 82
Jayulwa (1075–1138, *Bya yul ba*), 225
Je Tubten Yangpachen (*Jad thub bstan yangs pa can*), 141, 250n276
Je Donyo Pal (*Rje don yod dpal*). *See* Khedrub Donyo Palwa
Jepa (12th c., *Rje pa*), 60
Jetāri (~10th c., *Sgra las rnam rgyal / Dze tā ri*), 72
Jetsun Doringpa Kunpang Kunzang Chokyi Nyima Loden Sherab Gyaltsen Palzangpo (*Rje btsun rdo*

ring pa kun spangs kun bzang chos kyi nyi ma blo ldan shes rab rgyal btsan dpal bzang po). *See* Doringpa Kunzang Chokyi Nyima
Jetsun Gorumpa Kunga Legpa (*Rje btsun sgo rum pa kun dga' legs pa*). *See* Khyabdag Gorumpa Kunga Legpai Jungne
Jetsun Khacho Wangmo (18th c., *Rje btsun mkha' spyod dbang mo*), 73
Jetsun Tamdrin Wangmo (19th c., *Rje btsun rta mgrin dbang mo*), 75
Jetsunma Pema Trinle Wangmo (19th c., *Rje btsun ma padma phrin las dbang mo*), 200
Jigdral Ngawang Kunga Sonam (b. 1929, *'Jigs bral ngag dbang kun dga' bsod nams*), 74–75
Jigme Gyalwai Nyugu (1765–1843, *'Jigs med rgyal ba'i myu gu*), 185
Jigme Wangyal (*'Jigs med dbang rgyal*). *See* Kunga Nyingpo
Jigten Choto (*'Jig rten mchod bstod*), 237n39
Jinakīrti (~10th c., *Rgyal ba grags*), 78
Jinamitra (8th c., *Rgyal ba'i bshes gnyen*), 41, 45
Jinkim, Prince (*Jin kim*), 68, 241n113
Jñānagarbha (8th c., *Ye shes snying po*), 238n75
Jñānapāda (9th c., *Ye shes zhabs*), 97, 115, 238n73
Jñānaśrīmitra (975–1025, *Dznyā na shrī mi tra*), 37
Jñānavajra (12th c., *Dzanyā na badzra*), 58, 108
Joden Sonam (13th c., *Jo gdan bsod nams rgyal mtshan*), 75
Jodenpa Kunga Namgyal (*Jo gdan pa kun dga' rnam rgyal*). *See* Tuton Kunga Namgyal
Jomo Auma (12th c., *Jo mo 'a 'u ma*), 101
Jomo Magchungma (12th c., *Jo mo mang chung ma*), 101
Jonang Jetsun Kunga Drolchog (1507–66, *Jo nang rje bstun kun dga' grol mchog*), 255n368
Jonang Kunkhyen Chenpo Pal Mikyo Dorje (1243–1313, *Jo nang kun mkhyen chen po dpal mi bskyod rdo rje*), 95
Jose Gyalpo (12th c., *Jo sras rgyal po*), 97–98
Jvālamukhī (*Kha 'bar ma*), 121
Jvālinī Cave (*'Bar ba'i phug*), 24

K

Kachupa Jinzang (*Bka' bcu pa sbyin bzang*). *See* Gonjo Jinzang
Kachupa Sherab Senge (15th c., *Bka' bcu pa shes rab seng ge*), 147
Kāmarāja (*Kag chol*), 178
Kaḥtog Mahāpaṇḍita Situ Chokyi Gyatso (*Kaḥ thog ma hā paṇḍita situ chos kyi rgya mtsho*). *See* Kaḥtog Situ Panchen Orgyen Chokyi Gyatso
Kaḥtog Situ Panchen Orgyen Chokyi Gyatso (1880–1925, *Kaḥ thog situ paṇ chen o rgyan chos kyi rgya mtsho*), 200, 214
Kālacakrapāda (~10th c., *Dus 'khor zhabs pa*), 37
Kāmadhenu (~10th c., *Ka ma dhya nu*), 27
Kamalaśīla (8th c., *Ka ma la shī la*), 42, 136, 138, 203, 238n75
Kāmarūpasiddhi (~10th c., *Ka ma ru pa sa dhi dha*), 79
Kamgom (12th c., *Kaṃ sgom*), 49
Kangyurwa Gonpo Sonam Chogden (*Bka' 'gyur ba mgon po bsod nams mchog ldan*). *See* Khyabdag Kangyurwa Chenpo Nesarwa Won Rinpoche Gonpo Sonam Chogden
Kāṇha (~10th c., *Nag po pa*), 80–81, 91–92, 98, 108, 245n179
Kaniṣka (2nd c., *Ka niṣka*), 31
Kapila(vastu, *Ser skya*), 19–20, 24

Kar Śākya Drag (15th c., *Dkar shā kya grags*), 140, 201
Karchung (*Skar chung*), 50
Karjam (*Dkar 'byams*), 249n250
Karma Chagme (1613–78, *Karma chags med*), 49
Karma Chokyi Senge (20th c., *Karma chos kyi seng ge*), 205
Karma Konchog Zhonu (14th c., *Karma dkon mchog gzhon nu*), 137
Karma Pakshi (1206–83, *Karma pa kshi*), 49
Karmapa Tegchog Dorje (1798–1868, *Karma pa theg mchog rdo rje*), 186
Karmayama (*Las gshin*), 175
Karmo Nyida (*Dkar mo nyi zla*), 54, 73, 120, 238n63
Karṇikāvana (*Na rgyan*), 31
Karse Jamgon Chogtrul (1904–1954, *Kar se 'jam mgon mchog sprul*), 215
Kashmir (*Kha che*), 31, 36, 112, 117
Kāśyapa Buddha (*'Od srungs*), 28, 31, 39
Kathmandu (*Yam bu*), 121, 244n165
Kauśāmbī (*Kau sham+bhi*), 24
Kawa Paltseg (8th c., *Ska ba dpal brtsegs*), 41, 47, 237n42
Kazhipa, abbot of Kyormolung (14th c., *Skyor mo lung gi mkhan chen bka' bzhi pa*), 137
Kewang (10th c., *Ke wang*), 44
Khachar Jangchub Sempa (15th c., *Kha char byang chub sems dpa'*), 149
Khadiravaṇī Tārā (*Seng ldeng nags sgrol*), 174
Kham (*Khams*), 1, 43–44, 48–49, 59, 92, 129–30, 139–42, 164, 167–68, 185–86, 188, 192, 194, 205–6, 224, 234, 241n119, 255n369
Khamje college Shedrub Dargyeling (*Khams bye bshad grwa bshad grub dar rgyas gling*), 208
Khampa Lungpa (1023–1115, *Kham pa lung pa*), 48
Khampa Use (*Khams pa dbu se*). *See* Dusum Khyenpa
Khangsar Khenchen Dorje Chang Ngawang Lodro Nyingpo (d. 1905, *Khang gsar mkhan chen rdo rje 'chang ngag dbang blo gros snying po*), 133, 202
Khangsar Khenchen Dorje Chang Ngawang Lodro Zhenpen Nyingpo (*Khang gsar mkhan chen rdo rje 'chang ngag dbang blo gros gzhan phan snying po*). *See* Khenchen Dampa
Khangsar Khenchen Jampa Sonam Zangpo (*Khang gsar mkhan chen byams pa bsod nams bzang po*). *See* Khangsarwa Drubpai Wangchug Jamgon Jampa Sonam Zangpo
Khangsar Khenchen Ngawang Sonam Gyaltsen (19th c., *Khang gsar mkhan chen ngag dbang bsod nams rgyal mtshan*), 133–34, 232
Khangsar Khenchen Tsungme Ngawang Lodro Tendzin (19th c., *Khang gsar mkhan chen mtshungs med ngag dbang blo gros bstan 'dzin*), 133
Khangsar Ngawang Khyentse Tubten Nyingpo (1913–88, *Khang gsar ngag dbang mkhyen brtse thub bstan snying po*), 134
Khangsar Ngawang Yonten Gyatso (20th c., *Khang gsar ngag dbang yon tan rgya mtsho*), 134, 205
Khangsarwa Drubpai Wangchug Jamgon Jampa Sonam Zangpo (1689–1749, *Khang gsar ba grub pa'i dbang phyug 'jam mgon byams pa bsod nams bzang po*), 72, 132, 156
Khangsarwa Khenchen Jampa Sonam Lhundrub (1714–45, *Khang gsar ba mkhan chen byams pa bsod nams lhun grub*), 133
Khangsarwa Ngawang Chokyong Zangpo (b. 1723, *Khang gsar ba ngag dbang chos skyong bzang po*), 133
Khangsarwa Ngawang Lodro Zangpo

(19th c., *Khang gsar ba ngag dbang blo gros rgyal mtshan*), 133
Kharag (*Kha rag*), 85
Khartse Chang Rawa Lodro Zangpo (15th c., *Mkhar rtse lcang ra ba blo gros bzang po*), 153
Ḳhasarpaṇa (*Kha sar pā ṇi*), 80, 89, 115, 243n143, 248n230
Khau Dragzong Nagpo (*Kha'u brag rdzong nag po*), 160
Khecara (*Mkha' spyod*), 84–85
Khecarī (*Mkha' spyod ma*), 91, 107–8, 178, 187, 193, 202–3, 211, 217, 221, 245n173
Khedrub (*Mkhas grub*). *See* Khedrub Geleg Palzang
Khedrub Chenpo Jampa Kunga Sonam (d. 1787, *Mkhas grub chen po byams pa kun dga' bsod nams*), 133
Khedrub Chenpo Sangye Rinchen (*Mkhas grub chen po sangs rgyas rin chen*). *See* Muchen Sangye Rinchen
Khedrub Dawa Zangpo (15th c., *Mkhas grub zla ba bzang po*), 130
Khedrub Donyo Palwa (15th c., *Mkhas grub don yod dpal ba*), 140
Khedrub Geleg Palzang (1385–1438, *Mkhas grub dge legs dpal bzang*), 50, 135, 226–27
Khedrub Gyatso (19th c., *Mkhas grub rgya mtsho*), 199
Khedrub Palden Dorje (1411–82, *Mkhas grub dpal ldan rdo rje*), 130–31
Khedrub Sangye Dragpa (18th c., *Mkhas grub sangs rgyas grags pa*), 133
Khedrub Sangye Gyatso (18th c., *Mkhas grub sangs rgyas rgya mtsho*), 225
Khedrub Sempa Chenpo Chetsun Tendzin Zangpo (16th c., *Mkhas grub sems dpa' chen po lce btsun bstan 'dzin bzang po*), 220, 225
Khenchen Dampa (1876–1952, *Mkhan chen dam pa*), 1, 75, 134, 200, 205–10, 221, 232, 236n1, 256n391
Khenchen Dorje Chang Palden Chokyong (1702–69, *Mkhan chen rdo rje 'chang dpal ldan chos skyong*), 132–33, 221, 224–25
Khenchen Dorje Pal (*Mkhan chen rdo rje dpal*). *See* Tsangma Dorje Pal
Khenchen Jampaiyang Sangye Puntsog (1649–1705, *Mkhan chen 'jam pa'i dbyangs sangs rgyas phun tshogs*), 132, 182, 220–21, 224, 232, 249n258
Khenchen Jamyang Palchog Gyaltsen (1599–1673, *Mkhan chen 'jam dbyangs dpal mchog rgyal mtshan*), 132
Khenchen Khachar (15th c., *Mkhan chen kha phyar*), 142
Khenchen Kunga Tenpai Lodro (1822–44, *Mkhan chen kun dga' bstan pa'i blo gros*), 133, 224
Khenchen Labsum Gyaltsen (*Mkhan chen bslab gsum rgyal mtshan*). *See* Bodong Khenchen Ngamding Mawa Labsum Gyaltsen
Khenchen Ngawang Chodrag (1572–1641, *Mkhan chen ngag dbang chos grags*), 72, 86, 141, 163, 177, 220–22, 227, 232, 257n415
Khenchen Ngawang Khyenrab Jampal Nyingpo (1868–1949, *Mkhan chen ngag dbang mkhyen rab 'jam dpal snying po*), 133
Khenchen Rigdzin Zangpo (19th c., *Mkhan chen rig 'dzin bzang po*), 185
Khenchen Sangye Puntsog (*Mkhan chen sangs rgyas phun tshogs*). *See* Khenchen Jampaiyang Sangye Puntsog
Khenchen Trashi Lhundrub (*Mkhan chen bkra shis lhun grub*). *See* Tsang Dokharwa Khenchen Trashi Lhundrub
Khenchen Tsultrim Lhundrub (*Mkhan chen tshul khrims lhun grub*). *See* Jampa Tsultrim Lhundrub
Khenchen Wangchug Palzang (15th c.,

Mkhan chen dbang phyug dpal bzang), 141
Khenchen Yagpa (*Mkhan chen g.yag pa*). *See* Yagton Sangye Pal
Khenchen Zhenpen Chokyi Nangwa (*Mkhan chen gzhan phan chos kyi nang ba*). *See* Dzogchen Khenpo Zhenga Rinpoche
Khenpo Deno Changwa Yonten Zangpo (20th c., *Mkhan po sde snod 'chang ba yon tan bzang po*), 9
Khenpo Dragpa Senge (13th c., *Mkhan po grags pa seng ge*), 65
Khenpo Jamyang Kunga Namgyal (19th c., *Mkhan po 'jam dbyangs kun dga' rnam rgyal*), 205
Khenpo Jangsempa (15th c., *Mkhan po byang sems pa*), 147
Khenpo Lodro Gyaltsen (20th c., *Mkhan po blo gros rgyal brtsan*), 205
Khenpo Lozang Namgyal (15th c., *Mkhan po blo bzang rnam rgyal*), 165
Khenpo Ngaga (1879–1940, *Mkhan po ngag dga'*), 205
Khenpo Samten Lodro (1868–1931, *Mkhan po bsam gtan blo gros*), 200, 205, 215, 218, 224
Khenpo Yonten Zangpo (1927–2010, *Mkhan po yon tan bzang po*), 75
Khenpo Zhenga (*Mkhan po gzhan dga'*). *See* Dzogchen Khenpo Zhenga Rinpoche
Kherge Jangchub Pal (13th c., *Kher gad byang chub dpal*), 46
Khetsun Chodrag Gyatso (*Mkhas btsun chos grags rgya mtsho*), 203
Khetsun Namkha Legpa (1305–43, *Mkhas btsun nam mkha' legs pa*), 70, 241n123
Khewang Ratnaśrībhadra (15th c., *Mkhas dbang ratna shrī bha dra*), 139
Khon Barkye (*'Khon bar skyes*), 53–54
Khon Gyichuwa Dralhabar (12th c., *'Khon sgyi chu ba dgra lha 'bar*), 57, 98
Khon Konchog Gyalpo (1034–1102, *'Khon dkon mchog rgyal po*), 54–56, 92, 98, 122, 219
Khon Nāgendrarakṣita (8th c., *'Khon nā gendra rakṣhi ta*), 120
Khon Palpoche (*'Khon dpal po che*). *See* Khonpa Jegung Tag
Khon Rog Sherab Tsultrim (11th c., *'Khon rog shes rab tshul khrims*), 54
Khondung Śākya Gyaltsen (15th c., *'Khon gdung shā kya rgyal mtshan*), 153
Khonpa Jegung Tag (8th c., *'Khon pa rje gung stag*), 54
Khore (*Kho re*). *See* Yeshe O
Khuna Sherab Gyatso (*Khu na shes rab rgya mtsho*). *See* Khuna Chogtrul Jamyang Sherab Gyatso
Khuna Chogtrul Jamyang Sherab Gyatso (1877–1942, *Khu na mchog sprul 'jam dbyangs shes rab rgya mtsho*), 191, 202
Khuwo Jigdral Choying Dorje (1875–1932, *Khu bo 'jigs bral chos dbyings rdo rje*), 185
Khyabdag Gorumpa Kunga Legpai Jungne (1477–1544, *Khyab bdag sgo rum pa kun dga' legs pa'i 'byung gnas*), 162, 201
Khyabdag Kangyurwa Chenpo Nesarwa Won Rinpoche Gonpo Sonam Chogden (1603–59, *Khyab bdag bka' 'gyur ba chen po gnas gsar dbon rin po che mgon po bsod nams mchog ldan*), 162–64
Khyenrab Jampa Ngawang Lhundrub (*Khyen rab byams pa ngag dbang lhun grub*). *See* Chetsun Khyenrab Jampa Ngawang Lhundrub
Khyenrab Chokyi Ozer (1889–1960s, *Mkhyen rab chos kyi 'od zer*), 205
Khyenrab Ngedon Zangpo (19th c., *Mkhyen rab nges don bzang po*), 168
Khyenrab Trinle Zangpo (15th c., *Mkhyen rab 'phrin las bzang po*), 165
Khyentse Rabten (*Mkhyen brtse rab*

brtan). *See* Chogyepa Khyentse Rabten
Khyentse Wangchug (*Mkhyen brtse dbang phyugs*). *See* Choje Gonpo Wangchugpa (15th c.)
Khyentse Wangpo (*Mkhyen brtse dbang po*). *See* Jamyang Khyentse Wangpo Kunga Tenpai Gyaltsen
Khyin Lotsāwa (11th c., *Khyin lo tsā ba*), 54, 98
Khyung Rinchen Drag (12th c., *Khyung rin chen grags*), 57
Khyungpo Naljor (1079–1127, *Khyung po rnal 'byor*), 48, 237n54
Kodragpa Sonam Gyaltsen (1182–1261, *Ko brag pa bsod nams rgyal mtshan*), 95
Konchog Gyaltsen (19th c., *Dkon mchog rgyal mtshan*), 199
Konchog Lhundrub (1497–1557, *Dkon mchog lhun grub*), 71, 76, 131, 182, 220–21, 227, 232, 255n374
Kongpo Lodro Wangchug (14th c., *Kong po blo gros dbang phyug*), 137
Kongton Wangchug Drub (15th c., *Kong ston dbang phyug grub*), 146–47
Kosala (*Ko sa la*), 38
Koṭalipa (*Ko ṭa li pa*), 106
Kṛṣṇācārya (*Nag po spyod pa*). *See* Kāṇha
Kṛṣṇamunirāja (6th c., *Thub rgyal*), 36
Kṣetrapāla (*Zhing skyong*), 12, 115–19, 153, 181, 208, 248n229
Kubilai Khan. *See* Sechen
Kukkuripa (n.d., *Ku ku ri pa*), 33, 206
Kumārata (n.d., *Ku mā ra ta*), 33
Kunga Bar (12th c., *Kun dga' 'bar*), 59
Kunga Gyaltsen (1310–58, *Kun dga' rgyal mtshan*), 71, 242n126
Kunga Gyaltsen, the great abbot of Dro (15th c., *Gros mkhan chen kun dga' rgyal mtshan*), 138
Kunga Gyaltsen Palzangpo. *See* Sakya Paṇḍita Kunga Gyaltsen Palzangpo
Kunga Gyatso (18th c., *Kun dga' rgya mtsho*), 155
Kunga Jamyang (19th c., *Kun dga 'jam dbyangs*), 203
Kunga Khedrub Wangpo, the Rikhug tulku (18th c., *Kun dga' mkhas grub dbang po ri khug sprul sku*), 73–74
Kunga Legpa (15th c., *Kun dga' legs pa*), 71, 242n126
Kunga Legpa Zangpo Pal (14th c., *Kun dga' legs pa bzang po dpal*), 71, 242n127
Kunga Lodro, the imperial preceptor (1299–1327, *Kun dga' blo gros, ti shrī*), 70, 241n120, 242n124, nn126–27
Kunga Lodro (1729–83, *Kun dga' blo gros*). *See* Jamgon Kunga Lodro
Kunga Lodro (19th c., *Kun dga' blo gros*), 208
Kunga Nyima (1309–82, *Kun dga' nyi ma*), 70
Kunga Nyingpo (1850–99, *Kun dga' snying po*), 74–75, 202
Kunga Nyingpo (1092–1158, *Sa kya pa chen po*). *See* Sachen Kunga Nyingpo
Kunga Pende Gyatso (19th c., *Kun dga' phan bde rgya mtsho*), 74
Kunga Sonam (19th c., *Kun dga' bsod nams (khri chen)*, 74
Kunga Tenpai Gyaltsen (20th c., *Kun dga' bstan pa'i rgyal mtshan*), 75
Kunga Tenpai Lodro (*Kun dga' bstan pa'i blo gros*). *See* Khenchen Kunga Tenpai Lodro
Kunga Trashi, the Nenga Rigpai Paṇḍita (19th c., *Kun dga' bkra shis gnas nga rigs pa'i paṇḍi ta*), 74
Kunkhyen Dorje Denpa Kunga Namgyal (*Kun mkhyen rdo rje gdan pa kun dga' rnam rgyal*). *See* Tuton Kunga Namgyal
Kunkhyen Namkha Sonam (~14th c., *Kun mkhyen nam mkha' bsod nams*), 220

Kunkhyen Sangye Pal (*Kun mkhyen sangs rgyas 'phel*). *See* Jamchen Rabjampa Sangye Pal
Kunkhyen Shero (14th c., *Kun mkhyen shes [rab] 'od [zer]*), 137–38
Kunkhyen Trashi Namgyal (*Kun mkhyen bkra shis rnam rgyal*). *See* Dagpo Trashi Namgyal
Kunkhyen Yagpa (*Kun mkhyen g.yag pa*). *See* Yagton Sangye Pal
Kurukulle (*Ku ru ku lle*), 108, 176, 178–79
Kurukulle Garbhasuvarṇasūtra Śrī (*Ku ru ku lle dpal mo gser gyi snying thag can*), 108
Kusālipa (11th c., *Ku sā li pa*), 115
Kusara (7th c., *Ku sa ra*), 41
Kuśinagara (*Grong khyer rtswa can*), 23
Kuvana (*Ku pa na*), 31
Kyangdul (*Rkyang 'dul*), 63
Kyareng the Bloodless (*Skya reng khrag med*), 54
Kyawo Kadang (*Skyo bo kha gdangs*), 59
Kyegu Monastery (*Skyes dgu dgon*). *See* Ga Kyegu Dondrub Ling
Kyegu Dondrub Ling (*Skyes dgu don grub gling*). *See* Ga Kyegu Dondrub Ling
Kyergangpa Chokyi Rinchen (1154–1217, *Skyer sgang pa chos kyi rin chen*), 48, 173, 237n54
Kyichu River (*Skyid chu*), 42, 248n232
Kyide (10th c., *Skyid lde*), 43
Kyirong (*Skyid rong*), 83–85, 89, 120
Kyo Ojung (n.d., *Skyo 'od 'byung*), 175
Kyoda Drula Ngawang Chodzin (19th c., *Skyo mda' gru bla ngag dbang chos 'dzin*), 199
Kyoda Sonam Wangchug (n.d., *Skyo mda' bsod nams dbang phyug*), 180
Kyog Duldzin (11th c., *Skyogs 'dul 'dzin*), 45
Kyormolung (*Skor mo lung*), 66
Kyoton Sonam Lama (12th c., *Sko ston bsod nams bla ma*), 50
Kyura Akyab (11th c., *Skyu ra a skyabs*), 55

L

Lab Lama Dogyu Gyatso (1832–88, *Lab bla ma mdo rgyud rgya mtsho*), 155
Lachen Kunga Gyaltsen (14th c., *Bla chen kun dga' rgyal mtshan*), 71
Lalitavajra (n.d., *Lā li ta badzra*), 33
Lama Dampa Sonam Gyaltsen (1312–75, *Bla ma dam pa bsod nams rgyal mtshan*), 50, 70, 86, 135, 159, 177, 219, 226, 242n124
Lama Gyichuwa (11th c., *Bla ma sgyi chu ba*), 57, 96, 98
Lama Mal (*Bla ma mal*). *See* Mal Lotsāwa
Lama Nam (*Bla ma nam*). *See* Namkha-upa Chokyi Gyaltsen
Lama Ozer Śākya (13th c., *Bla ma 'od zer shā kya*), 65
Lama Palden Gyalpo (15th c., *Bla ma dpal ldan rgyal po*), 130
Lama Sachen (*Bla ma sa chen*). *See* Sachen Kunga Nyingpo
Langdarma (9th c., *Glang dar ma*), 42–44
Langtang (*Glang thang*), 43, 151
Langtangpa (1054–1123, *Glang thang pa*), 48
Lato Jangyab (*La stod byang rgyab*), 123
Lato Wangyal (12th c., *Stod dbang rgyal*), 108, 179
Laton Konchog Bar (12th c., *La ston dkon mchog 'bar*), 48
Legpa Gyaltsen (15th c., *Legs pa rgyal mtshan*), 147
Legshe Kunga Pel (18th c., *Legs bshad kun dga' 'phel*), 154–55
Lha Lama Yeshe O (*Lha bla ma ye shes 'od*). *See* Yeshe O
Lha Totori Nyentsen (n.d., *Lha tho tho ri gnyan btsan*), 39
Lhade (11th c., *Lha lde*), 45
Lhakhang Khenchen Jampal Zangpo

(20th c., *Lha khang mkhan chen 'jam dpal bzang po*), 75
Lhari Rolpa (*Lha ri rol pa*), 38
Lhatse (*Lha rtse*), 83, 87, 89–90
Lhatsun Jangchub O (*Lha btsun byang chub 'od*). *See* Jangchub O
Lhatsun Kali (11th c., *Lha btsun ka pa li*), 92
Lhatsun Sonam Lhundrub (15th c., *Lha btsun bsod nams lhun grub*), 166
Lho (*Lho*). *See* Lhopa Kunkhyen Rinpoche Palzang
Lhopa Kunkhyen Rinpoche Palzang (13th c., *Lho pa kun mkhyen rin chen dpal bzang*), 65, 103
Liangzhou (*Ling chu rtse*), 64
Lingje Repa (1128–88, *Gling rje ras pa*), 49
Ling Gotse (*Gling 'go rtse*), 207
Lingtopa Rinchen Namgyal (14th c., *Gling stod pa rin chen rnam rgyal*), 137
Litang (*Li thang*), 198, 204, 210
Litang Betsang Choje Khyenrab Gyatso (19th c., *Li thang be tshong chos rje mkhyen rab rgya mtsho*), 200
Litang Geshe Jampa Puntsog (19th c., *Li thang dge bshes byams pa phun tshogs*), 185
Litang Yonru (*Li thang g.yon ru*), 201
Lo Lotsāwa (13th c., *Glo lo tsā ba*), 65
Geshe Lozang Chokyi Gawa (20th c., *Dge bshes blo bzang chos kyi dga' ba*), 205
Lochen Dharmaśrī (1654–1717, *Lo chen dharma shrī*), 44–45
Lochen Kyabchog Pal (15th c., *Blo chen skyabs mchog dpal*), 128, 138
Lodri Khenpo (n.d., *Lo dri mkhan po*), 30
Lodro Chokyongwa (15th c., *Blo gros chos skyong ba*), 149
Lodro Gyatso Drima Mepai O (*Blo gros rgya mtsho dri ma med pa'i 'od*). *See* Jamyang Khyentse Wangpo Kunga Tenpai Gyaltsen
Logkya Jose Chodragpa (13th c., *Klog skya jo sras chos grags pa*), 101
Lokaśrī (n.d., *Lo ka shrī*), 111–12
Lokya Sherab Tseg (11th c., *Klog skya shes rab brtsegs*), 123
Lopa Chenga Konchog Dragpa (16th c., *Lo pa spyan lnga dkon mchog grags pa*), 166
Lopa Choje Chenga Kunga Dorje (15th c., *Lo pa chos rje spyan snga kun dga' rdo rje*), 165
Lobpon Chen Chenpo (11th c., *Slob dpon spyan chen po*), 123
Lobpon Dragpa Ozer (15th c., *Slobs dpon grags pa 'od zer*), 149
Lobpon Jamyang Dragpa (n.d., *Slobs dpon 'jam dbyangs grags pa*), 156
Lobpon Rinchen Gyaltsen (1238–79, *Slob dpon rin chen rgyal mtshan*), 68, 70, 103, 241n111, n118, n120, n122
Lobpon Yeshe Jungne (1238–74, *Slob dpon ye shes 'byung gnas*), 68, 70, 241n119
Lord Khumbu (11th c., *Rje khum bu*), 95, 246n189
Lord of the Charnel Grounds and his consort (*Dur khrod kyi bdag po yab yum*), 119
Lord of yogins (*Rnal 'byor dbang phyug*). *See* Vīrupa
Losemtso (n.d., *Blo sems 'tsho paṇḍi ta*), 39
Loten Zhipa (15th c., *Blo brtan bzhi pa*), 148–49
Loton (*Lo ston*), 87, 244n163
Lotsāwa Zhang Yeshe Dorje (14th c., *Lo tsā ba zhang ye shes rdo rje*), 136
Lower Drompa (*Grom pa smad*), 66
Lower Nyang (*Nyang smad*), 46, 63, 87
Lowo (*Glo bo*), 151–53
Lowo Khenchen (16th c., *Glo bo mkhan chen*), 227
Lowo Lotsāwa (13th c., *Glo bo lo tsā ba*), 67

Lub Lotsāwa (11th c., *Klubs lo tsā ba*), 45
Luding Gyalse Jamyang Chokyi Nyima (1872–1926, *Klu lding rgyal sras 'jam dbyangs chos kyi nyi ma*), 75, 134
Luding Jamyang Tenpai Nyima (20th c., *Klu lding 'jam dbyangs bstan pa'i nyi ma*), 134
Luding Jamyang Tubten Lungtog Gyaltsen (20th c., *Klu lding 'jam dbyangs thub bstan lung rtogs rgyal mtshan*), 134, 210
Ludrub Gyatso (*Klu grub rgya mtsho*). *See* Mangto Ludrub Gyatso
Luipa (~9th c., *Llu'i pa*), 148, 175, 182, 193
Lumbini (*Lum+bi ni*), 19, 168, 253n339
Lume Tsultrim Wangchug (10th c., *Klu mes tshul khrims dbang phyug*), 44–45
Lungtengpa Geshe Konchog Kyab (11th c., *Lung steng pa dge bshes dkon mchog skyab*), 122
Lupa (14th c., *Klu pa*), 159, 179
Lutsa Tagpo Ochen (*Kla tsha stag po 'od can*), 53

M

Ma Chokyi Sherab (b. 1055, *Rma chos kyi shes rab*), 49
Machig Dorje Den (13th c., *Ma cig rdo rje gdan*), 70
Machig Drubpai Gyalmo (12th c., *Ma cig grub pa'i rgyal mo*), 95, 174, 176, 193, 246n189
Machig Gyalmo (*Ma cig rgyal mo*). *See* Machig Drubpai Gyalmo
Machig Jodro (13th c., *Ma cig jo 'gro*), 70
Machig Khabmema (13th c., *Ma cig khab smad ma*), 70
Machig Labdron (*Mag gcig lab sgron*). *See* Machig Labkyi Dronma
Machig Labkyi Dronma (1055–1153, *Mag gcig lab kyi sgron ma*), 50, 168
Machig Odron (12th c., *Ma cig 'od sgron*), 59
Machig Zhangmola (11th c., *Ma cig zhang mo la*), 56
Magadha (*Yul dbus*), 14, 19, 31, 81–82
Magzorma (*Dmag zor ma*), 181
Mahādeva (~2nd c. BCE, *Lha chen po*), 30
Mahākāla (*Nag po chen po*), 55, 58 66, 68–69, 84, 109–14, 153, 177, 179–80, 182, 238n69, 247n219, 248nn226–27, n229, 257n413. *See also* Guardian of the Tent, Kṣetrapāla, Skin Mask Wisdom Guardian
Mahākāla and his consort (*Mgon po lcam dral*), 66
Mahākāla Guardian of the Tent (*Nag po chen po gur gyi mgon po*). *See* Guardian of the Tent
Mahākāla, Four-Faced (*Nag po gdong bzhi*). *See* Kṣetrapāla
Mahākaruṇika (*Thugs rje chen po*), 173, 176, 193, 255n367
Mahākāśyapa (~5th c. BCE, *'Od srungs chen po*), 29–31
Mahāmāya, Queen (~5th c. BCE, *Dam pa sgyu 'phrul chen mo*), 19
Mahāmāya (*Ma hā mā ya*), 48, 88
Mahāmayūrī "Overcoming the Poisons" (*Dug dbang rma bya*), 175
Mahāpaṇḍita Tartse Namkha Palzang (1532–1602, *Ma hā paṇḍita thar rtse nam mkha' dpal bzang*), 131, 256n381
Maitreya (*Byams pa*), 17–18, 32, 35, 63, 137, 143, 145, 149, 151, 154, 168, 172, 191, 193, 217, 251n304, 256n388
Maitrīpa (12th c., *Me tri pa*), 48, 91, 108, 178, 244n172, 245n173
Maja Jangtson (d. 1185, *Rma bya byang brtson*), 63
Makkolam (*Sa dkar can*), 24
Mal Lotsāwa (11th c., *Mal lo tsā ba*), 46, 55, 57–58, 95, 108–11, 113, 120–21, 123
Malgyo Lodro Dragpa (*Mal gyo blo gros grags pa*). *See* Mal Lotsāwa
Malgyowa (*Mal gyo ba*). *See* Mal Lotsāwa

Mamo Botong (*Ma mo rbod gtong*), 237n49
Mangkhar (*Mang mkhar*), 54, 70, 82, 84, 101, 160
Mangkhar Topowa Tomo Dorjetso (11th c., *Mang mkhar ba stod po ba bstod mo rdo rje mtsho*), 92
Manglam Zhigpa (~11th c., *Mang lam zhig pa*), 95
Mangsong Mangtsen (7th c., *Mang srong mang btsan*), 41
Mangto Ludrub Gyatso (1523–96, *Mang thos klu grub rgya mtsho*), 163, 220, 227, 235
Mangyul (*Mang yul*), 43, 84, 89
Mañjughoṣa (*'Jam dbyangs*), 66, 69
Mañjuśrī (*'Jam dpal*), 11, 31, 36, 41, 55–57, 59–60, 62–63, 69, 73, 109, 122, 132, 148, 150, 156, 161, 168, 174, 179, 182, 184, 191, 198, 203, 212, 214, 216–17, 233, 253n344, 255n373, 256n388
Mañjuśrī cave (*'Jam dpal brag*), 98, 246n196
Mañjuśrīvarman (8th c., *'Jam dpal go cha*), 35
Mañjuvajra (*'Jam pa'i rdo rje*), 35, 116, 175, 182, 256n380
Mankhar Tubten Gepel (*Mang khar thub bstan dge 'phel*), 161
Manota (*Ma no ta*), 33
Mapam Namtrul Khenchen Yagton Zhab (*Ma pham rnam 'phrul mkhan chen g.yag ston zhabs*). *See* Yagton Sangye Pal
Mar (*Dmar*). *See* Mar Śākyamuni
Mar Chogyal (13th c., *Dmar chos rgyal*), 103
Mar Śākyamuni (9th c., *Smar shā kya mu ni*), 44–45, 65, 103
Māra (*Mdud*), 15–16, 18, 21, 27, 30
Markhampa Dragpa Zangpo (15th c., *Dmar khams pa grags pa bzang po*), 130, 139, 420
Marpa Chokyi Lodro (1012–97, *Mar pa chos kyi blo gros*), 46, 48, 90, 195, 237n55, 244n165
Marpa Drubtob Sherab Yeshe (1135–1203, *Smar pa grub thob shes rab ye shes*), 49
Marton Gyaltsen Ozer (15th c., *Dmar ston rgyal tshan 'od zer*), 130
Masang Chije (*Ma sangs spyi rje*), 53
Mase Lodro Rinchen (1386–1423, *Rma se blo gros rin chen*), 49
Mesho (*Smad shod*), 225
Meton Tsonpo (11th c., *Mes ston tshon po*), 48
Meu Tonpa (11th c., *Me'u ston pa*), 48
Milarepa (1052–1135, *Mi la ras pa*), 48
Mindroling (*Smin grol gling*), 45, 185, 216
Minling Trichen Sangye Kunga (19th c., *Smin gling khri chen sangs rgyas kun dga'*), 185
Minyag Khepa Norbu Tendzin (19th c., *Mi nyag mkhas pa nor bu bstan 'dzin*), 203
Minyag Prajñājvāla (~11th c., *Mi nyag pra dznyā dzwā la*), 102
Mitra Śāntivarman (n.d., *Bshes gnyen zhi ba'i go cha*), 115
Mogchogpa Rinchen Tsondru (12th c., *Rmog lcogs pa rin chen rtson 'grus*), 48
Mogton (12th c., *Rmog ston*), 60
Mongo Ravine (*Mon 'gro grog*), 56, 98 238n68
Mongolia (*Hor*), 4, 65–70, 132, 167, 240nn104–5
Monpa brothers and sisters (*Mon pa ming sring*), 112, 248n225
Mopa Drangag (*Mod pa drag sngags*), 237n49
Morchen Ngawang Kunga Lhundrub (1654–1726, *Rmor chen ngag dbang kun dga' lhun grub*), 156, 163–64, 182, 221, 225
Mount Kukkuṭapāda (*Ri bo bya rkang can*), 35
Mount Meru (*Ri rab kyi zom*), 14
Mawai Wangchug Khenchen Sonam

Paljor (19th c., *Smra ba'i dbang phyug mkhan chen bsod nams dpal 'byor*), 133
Mṛgajā (~5th c. BCE, *Ri dwags skyes*), 20
Mu Namkhai Naljor (15th c., *Mus nam mkha'i rnal 'byor*), 138
Mu Tugje Palzang (15th c., *Mus thugs rje dpal bzang*), 141
Muchen (*Mus chen*). *See* Muchen Sempa Chenpo Konchog Gyaltsen
Muchen Konchog Gyaltsen (*Mus chen dkon mchog rgyal mtshan*). *See* Muchen Sempa Chenpo Konchog Gyaltsen
Muchen Sangye Gyaltsen (1542–1618, *Mus chen sangs rgyas rgyal mtshan*), 72, 232
Muchen Sangye Rinchen (1450–1524, *Mus chen sangs rgyas rin chen*), 131, 166
Muchen Sempa Chenpo Konchog Gyaltsen (1388–1469, *Mus chen sems dpa' chen po dkon mchog rgyal mtshan*), 103, 130–31, 137, 139, 142–43, 146, 149, 159, 182, 193, 220
Mugulung (*Mu gu lung*), 82, 90, 93, 160
Mune Tsepo (d.798, *Mu ne btsad po*), 42
Mupa Tugje Palwa (15th c., *Mus pa thugs rje dpal ba*), 153
Murampa Konchog Dragpa (15th c., *Mus ram pa dkon mchog grags pa*), 153
Murug Tsepo (d. 804, *Mu rug btsad po*), 42
Mutagmo (*Mus stag mo*), 209
Mutig Tsepo (8th c., *Mu tig btsad po*), 42

N

Nāga, the Elder (~2nd c. BCE, *Gnas brten klu*), 30
Nāgabodhi (n.d., *Klu'i byang chub*), 34
Nāgārjuna (~2nd c., *Klu grub*), 11, 15, 33–35, 37, 143, 145, 148, 154, 256n388
Nāgārjuna (~9th c., *Klu grub*), 91, 172–73, 193, 238n73, 245n177
Nāgendrarāja (*Klu dbang rgyal po*), 173
Nagtso Lotsāwa (1011–64, *Nag tsho lo tsā ba*), 45–46
Nairañjanā (*Nai rany+dza na*), 21
Nairātmyā (*Bdag med lha mo*), 77–79, 92, 148, 176–77, 246n184
Naked One Wielding a Copper Knife (*Gcer bu zangs ri can*), 112, 180
Nālandā, India (*Nā lendra*), 35, 78–79
Nālendra, Tibet (*Nā lendra*), 138, 142, 147, 151, 159, 163–69, 210, 223, 232, 250n270, 253nn335–36, n341
Naljor Jampal Zangpo, Khenchen (*Rnal 'byor 'jam dpal bzang po, mkhan chen*). *See* Drangti Khenchen Jangchub Sempa Rigyai Khyabdag Naljor Jampal Zangpo
Naljorpa Unyon Kunga Zangpo (15th c., *Rnal 'byor pa dbus smyon kun dga' bzang po*), 153
Namde Osung (9th c., *Gnam lde 'od srungs*), 43
Namgyal (15th c., *Rnam rgyal*), 140
Namkabum (12th c., *Nam mkha' 'bum*), 225
Namkha Legpa (n.d., *Nam mkha' legs pa*), 71. *See also* Khetsun Namkha Legpa
Namkha Tenpa, Paṇḍita (15th c., *Paṇḍita nam mkha' bstan pa*), 140
Namkha Trashi (*Nam mkha' bkra shis*). *See* Namkha Trashi Gyaltsen
Namkha Trashi Gyaltsen (b. 1458, *Nam mkha' bkra shis rgyal mtshan*), 71, 154
Namkhai Nyingpo (8th c., *Nam mkha'i snying po*), 41
Namkhau Kyelhe (*Nam kha'u skyed lhas*), 118
Namkhaupa Chokyi Gyaltsen (11th c., *Gnam kha'u pa chos kyi rgyal mtshan*), 55, 57, 96, 109, 118–19
Namkhaur Darma Gyaltsen (*Gnam kha'ur dar ma rgyal mtshan*). *See* Namkhaupa Chokyi Gyaltsen
Namri Songtsen (6th c., *Gnam ri srong btsan*), 40

Namse Gyaltsen (14th c., *Rnam sras rgyal mtshan*), 71
Namtang Karpo in Dringtsam (*'Bring mtshams gnam thang dkar po*), 84
Nanam Dorje Dudjom (8th c., *Sna nam rdo rje bdud rjoms*), 135
Nanda (~5th c. BCE, *Cung dga' bo*), 23
Nangchen Tsangda Purpa Lama Rinpoche (19th c., *Nang chen gtsang mda' phur pa bla ma rin po che*), 198
Naro Bande (12th c., *Sna ro ban de*), 102
Nāropa (*Nā ro pa*). *See* Nārotapa
Nārotapa (11th c., *Nā ro ta pa*), 37, 58, 88, 108, 112, 178, 187, 193, 203, 221, 236n34
Nartang Lotsāwa Saṅghaśrī (15th c., *Snar thang lo tsā ba sanga shrī*), 139
Nartang Paljor Lingpa Khangsar Khenchen Sonam Gyatso (1617–67, *Snar thang dpal 'byor gling pa khang gsar mkhan chen bsod nams rgya mtsho*), 132
Nedong Tsetsog Khenchen Yolwa Zhonu Lodro (1527–99, *Sne gdong rtse tshogs mkhan chen yol ba gzhon nu blo gros*), 162–63
Nelpa Paṇḍita (*Nel pa paṇḍi ta*), 162
Nepal (*Lho bal*), 39–41, 43, 83, 88, 117, 120–22, 217
Nesar Chogtrul Namkha Legpa (18th c., *Gnas gsar mchog sprul nam mkha' legs pa*), 73, 241n123
Nesarwa Dorje Chang Wangchug Rabten (*Gnas gsar ba rdo rje 'chang dbang phyug rab brtan*). *See* Dorje Chang Wangchug Rabten
Nesarwa Jamyang Khyentse Wangchug (*Gnas gsar ba 'jam dbyangs mkhyen brtse dbang phyug*). *See* Jamyang Khyentse Wangchug
Nesarwa Ngawang Kunga Legpai Jungne (1704–60, *Gnas gsar ba ngag dbang kun dga' legs pa'i 'byung gnas*), 73, 156, 163–64, 220–21
Ngadag Palkhortsen (9th c., *Mnga' bdag dpal 'khor btsan*), 43
Ngagchang Dragpa Lodro (1563–1617, *Sngags 'chang grags pa blo gro*), 72
Ngagchang Kunga Rinchen (*Sngags 'chang kun dga' rin chen*). *See* Sakyapa Ngagchang Chenpo Kunga Rinchen
Ngagi Wangchug (17th c., *Sngags gi dbang phyug*), 71
Ngagi Wangpo Kunga Lodro (*Ngag gi dbang po kun dga' blo gros*). *See* Jamgon Kunga Lodro
Ngamring Khenpo (15th c., *Ngam rings mkhan po*), 135
Ngamringpa Sangye Samdrub (15th c., *Ngam ring pa sangs rgyas bsam grub*), 140
Ngari (*Mnga' ris*), 43, 45, 53, 73, 92, 98, 110, 112–13, 117, 129, 131–32, 151, 167, 203, 205, 208
Ngarig Khyenpa Odzong Geshe Lozang Jinpa (20th c., *Lnga rigs mkhyen pa 'o rdzong dge bshes blo bzang sbyin pa*), 205
Ngaripa Selwai Nyingpo (11th c., *Mnga' ris pa gsal ba'i snying po*), 92
Ngawang Chenpo Kunga Rinchen (1517–84, *Ngag dbang chen po kun dga' rin chen*), 71–72
Ngawang Chodrag (*Ngag dbang chos grags*). *See* Khenpo Ngawang Chodrag
Ngawang Chokyong Zangpo (*Sngags dbang chos skyong bzang po*). *See* Khangsarwa Ngawang Chokyong Zangpo
Ngawang Khedrub Gyatso (*Ngag dbang mkhas grub rgya mtsho*). *See* Penkhang Ngawang Khedrub Gyatso
Ngawang Kunga Legpai Jungne (1308–41, *Ngag dbang kun dga' legs pa'i 'byung gnas*), 71, 242n126
Ngawang Kunga Rinchen (19th c., *Ngag dbang kun dga' rin chen*), 74

Ngawang Kunga Rinchen (1902–50, *Ngag dbang kun dga' rin chen*), 75
Ngawang Kunga Tegchen Palbar Trinle Wangi Gyalpo (b. 1945, *Ngag dbang kun dga' theg chen dpal 'bar 'phrin las dbang gi rgyal po*), 75–76, 210
Ngawang Kunga Trashi (1654–1711, *Ngag dbang kun dga' bkra shis*), 72
Ngawang Lodro Nyingpo (19th c., *Ngag dbang blo gros snying po*). *See* Khangsar Khenchen Dorje Chang Ngawang Lodro Nyingpo
Ngawang Lodro Zhenpen Nyingpo (*Ngag dbang blo gros gzhan phan snying po*). *See* Khenchen Dampa
Ngawang Losang Gyatso (1617–82, *Ngag dbang blo gsang rgya mtsho*), 40, 163–64, 166–67, 220, 237n39, 241n112
Ngawang Norbu Gyenpa (20th c., *Ngag dbang nor bu rgyan pa*), 71
Ngawang Samten Lodro (*Ngag dbang bsam brtan blo gros*). *See* Khenpo Samten Lodro
Ngawang Shedrub Gyatso (19th c., *Ngag dbang bshad grub rgya mtsho*), 201
Ngawang Sonam Gyaltsen (*Ngag dbang bsod nams rgyal mtshan*). *See* Khangsar Khenchen Ngawang Sonam Gyaltsen
Ngawang Tendor (*Ngag dbang brtan rdor*). *See* Ngawang Tenpa Dorje
Ngawang Tenpai Dorje (16th c., *Ngag dbang bstan pa'i rdo rje*), 177, 27
Ngawang Tutob Wangchug (20th c., *Ngag dbang mthu thob dbang phyug*), 74
Ngawang Yonten Gyatso (*Ngag dbang yon tan rgya mtsho*). *See* Khangsar Ngawang Yonten Gyatso
Ngog Legpai Sherab (11th c., *Rngog legs pa'i shes rab*), 46, 248n224
Ngog Lotsāwa Loden Sherab (1059–1109, *Rngog lo tsā ba blo ldan shes rab*), 57, 225, 248n224
Ngogton Chodor (12th c., *Rngog ston chos rdor*), 48
Ngonga Chodei Khenpo Palden Sangye (15th c., *Mngon dga' chos sde'i mkhan po dpal ldan sangs rgyas*), 130
Ngor Ewampa Pankhang Khenchen Jampa Palden Chodze (*Ngor e waṃ pa phan khang mkhan chen byams pa dpal ldan chos mdzad*). *See* Jampa Palden Chodze
Ngor Tartse Khenchen Jampa Namkha Chime (*Ngor thar rtse mkhan chen byams pa nam mkha' 'chi med*). *See* Drangti Khenchen Tamche Khyenpa Jampa Namkha Chime
Ngorchen Konchog Lhundrub (*Ngor chen dkon mchog lhun grub*). *See* Konchog Lhundrub
Ngorchen Kunga Zangpo (1382–1456, *Ngor chen kun dga' bzang po*), 12, 103, 114 125–35, 140, 142, 144, 146, 148–49, 151, 154, 156, 159, 165, 171, 177, 182, 193, 202, 204, 219–20, 224–25, 227, 230–32, 235n2, 249n241, n250
Ngorchen Sangye Yeshe (*Ngor chen sangs rgyas ye shes*). *See* Jamyang Chokyi Lama Sangye Yeshe
Ngorchen Sonam Zangpo (*Ngor chen bsod nams bzang po*). *See* Khangsarwa Drubpai Wangchug Jamgon Jampa Sonam Zangpo
Ngulton Rinwang (12th c., *Rngul ston rin dbang*), 48
Nordzingyi Tigle (*Nor 'dzin gyi thig le*), 160
Norzang Gyatso (1423–1513, *Nor bzang rgya mtsho*), 229
Nub (13th c., *Nub*), 65, 219. *See also* Nub Lachen Jangnying
Nub Lachen Jangnying (n.d., *Gnubs bla chen byang snying*), 47, 225
Nyag Zhirawa Wangchug Gyaltsen (12th c., *Gnyags gzhi ra ba dbang phyug rgyal mtshan*), 102

Nyagre Palgyi Gyaltsen (15th c., *Nyag re dpal gyi rgyal tshan*), 130
Nyagrodha cave (*Nyā gro dha'i phug*), 29
Nyame Gyergom Chenpo (1090–1171, *Mnyam med gyer sgom chen po*), 49
Nyan Nganpa Jamyang Khache (15th c., *Snyan ngan pa 'jam dbyangs kha che*), 138
Nyangdran Chokyi Seng (11th c., *Nyang bran chos kyi seng*), 225
Nyangdren Pabongkha (*Nyang bran pha bong kha*), 41
Nyangomla Monkharwa (11th c., *Myang bsgom la smon mkhar ba*), 95
Nyangto Tsechenpa Dorje Gyaltsen (15th c., *Nyang stod rtse chen pa rdo rje rgyal mtshan*), 153
Nyangtopa Sherab Legpa (15th c., *Nyang stod pa shes rab legs pa*), 140
Nyangtsa Dring (13th c., *Nyang tsha 'bring*), 65
Nyatri Tsenpo (*Gnya' khri btsan po*), 38–39, 43
Nyawon Kunga Pal (1285–1379, *Nya dbon kun dga' dpal*), 220, 226, 250n263
Nyen Lotsāwa (11th c., *Gnyan lo tsā ba*), 108, 115–19, 179, 243n143
Nyen Osung (13th c., *Gnyan 'od gsung*), 67
Nyen Tsugtor Gyalpo (*Gnyan gtsug tor rgyal po*). *See* Nyenpul Jungwa Tsugtor Gyalpo
Nyenchen Sonam (13th c., *Gnyan chen bsod nams*), 103
Nyenpul Jungwa Tsugtor Gyalpo (12th c., *Gnyan phul byung ba gtsug tor rgyal po*), 61, 101
Nyenton (*Gnyan ston*). *See* Nyenton Bepai Naljor
Nyenton Bepai Naljor (11th c., *Gnyan ston sbas pa'i rnal 'byor*), 48, 226, 237n54
Nyenyo Jago Shong (*Gnyan yod bya rgod gshongs*), 141, 162, 250n276
Nyetang Chodzong (*Snye thang chos rdzong*), 148
Nyetang Lotsāwa (*Snye thang lo tsā ba*). *See* Paṇchen Loten Zhipa
Nyetangpa Dragpa Senge (13th c., *Snye thang pa grags pa seng ge*), 67
Nyitricham (*Nyi khri lcam*). *See* Tra Puma Nyitricham

O

ocean of ḍākinīs (*Mkha' 'gro rgya mtsho*), 182
Oḍḍiyāna (*O rgyan / U ḍyana*), 25–27, 32–33, 55, 59, 80, 160, 246n192, 254n359
Ode (11th c., *'Od lde*), 43, 45
Odzong Geshe Lozang Jinpa (1834–95, *'O rdzong dge bshes blo bzang sbyin pa*), 203, 205
Old Utse (*Dbu rtse rnying ma*), 60, 66, 240n103
Onchang Peme Trashi Gepel temple (*'On cang rdo dpe med bkra shis dge 'phel gyi gtsug lag khang*), 42
Ongom (1116–69, *Dbon sgom*), 49
Onpo Norpel (14th c., *Dbon po nor 'phel*), 135
Onpo Shertsul (12th c., *Dbon po sher tshul*), 96
Orgyen Mindroling (*O rgyan smin grol gling*). *See* Mindroling
Orgyen Rinchenpal (1230–1309, *O rgyan rin chen dpal*), 184, 254n359
Orgyenpa (*O rgyan pa rin chen dpal*). *See* Orgyen Rinchenpal
Ozer Senge (n.d., *'Od zer seng ge*), 249n255

P

Padampa Sangye (12th c., *Pha dam pa sangs rgyas*), 49
Padmanarteśvara (*Padma gar dbang*), 175
Padmasambhava (8th c., *Padma sambha

wa), 41, 47, 54, 120, 216, 237n48, 246n192
Padmaśrī (12th c., *Padma shrī*), 58
Pagmodrupa Dorje Gyalpo (*Phag mo gru pa rdo rje rgyal po*), 49, 102, 226, 237n57
Pagpa Lodro Gyaltsen (1235–80, *'Phags pa blo gros rgyal mtshan*), 28, 66–69, 103, 131, 144, 220, 225, 240nn104–9, 241nn111–14, n118, 252n317, 256n379
Paki (*Pha ki*), 116
Palbumtrag Sumpa Jampa Cho Dondrub (15th c., *Dpal 'bum phrag gsum pa byams pa chos don grub*), 130
Palchen Onpo (1150–1203, *Dpal chen 'od po*), 62, 69, 140n94
Palcho (*Dpal chos*). *See* Khenchen Dorje Chang Palden Chokyong
Palchog Dangpo, Lotsāwa (12th c., *Lo tsā ba dpal mchog dang po*), 61
Palde (10th c., *Dpal lde*), 43
Palde Rigpagon (10th c., *Dpal lde rig pa mgon*), 43
Palden Chogyi Langpo (19th c., *Dpal ldan phyogs kyi glang po*), 74
Palden Dorje Dema (15th c., *Dpal ldan rdo rje bde ma*), 136
Palden Lhamo (*Dpal ldan lha mo*), 248n225
Palden Lodro Gyaltsen (*Dpal ldan blo gros rgyal mtshan*). *See* Penkhang Khenchen Palden Lodro Gyaltsen
Paldren (14th c., *Dpal 'dren*), 128
Palmo Paltang (*Dpal mo dpal thang*), 90
Palpung Situ Rinpoche Pema Wangchog Gyalpo (1886–1952, *Dpal spungs si tu rin po che padma dbang mchog rgyal po*), 205
Pamtingpa brothers (11th c., *Pham mthing pa sku mched*), 123, 244n165
Paṇchen Lhawang Lodro (15th c., *Paṇ chen lha dbang blo gros*), 141
Paṇchen Ngawang Chodrag (*Paṇ chen ngag dbang chos grags*). *See* Khenchen Ngawang Chodrag
Pārśva, Bhikṣu (*Dge slong rtsibs*), 33
Patsab Nyima Drag (b. 1055, *Pa tshab nyi ma grags*), 46
Pedrugpa Chagtsang Tongol (11th c., *Phad drug pa phyug gtsang mthong rgol bya ba*), 93
Pema Dudul Wangchug (1792–1853, *Padma bdud 'dul dbang phyug*), 74
Pema Karpo (1527–92, *Padma dkar po*), 227
Pende Khenchen Palden Lodro Gyaltsen (*Phan bde mkhan chen dpal ldan blo gros rgyal mtshan*). *See* Penkhang Khenchen Palden Lodro Gyaltsen
Penkhang Jamyang Kunzang Tubten Chokyi Gyaltsen (19th c., *Phan khang 'jam dbyangs kun bzang thub bstan chos kyi rgyal mtshan*), 134
Penkhang Khenchen Palden Lodro Gyaltsen (1840–1900, *Phan khang mkhan chen dpal ldan blo gros rgyal mtshan*), 133
Penkhang Ngawang Khedrub Gyatso (d. 1969, *Phan khang ngag dbang mkhas grub rgya mtsho*), 134, 210
Penkhang Ngawang Kunga Tenpai Gyaltsen (1863–99, *Phan khang ngag dbang kun dga' bstan pa'i rgyal mtshan*), 133
Penkhang Ngawang Lodro Tegchog Tenpai Gyaltsen (20th c., *Phan khang ngag dbang blo gros theg mchog bstan pa'i rgyal mtshan*), 134
Penpo (*Phan po*), 138
Penyul (*Phan yul*), 92, 165
Penyulpa Upa Dropoche (11th c., *'Phan yul pa dbus pa grod po che*), 92
Playful Vidyādharī (*Rig pa 'dzin pa rtsen ma*), 108
Pobdarwa Lochen Zhonu Pal (15th c., *Spob dar ba lo chen gzhon nu dpal*), 140

Podrang Zhiwa O (11th c., *Pho brang zhi ba 'od*), 46
Ponlob Ngawang Legdrub (b. 1811, *Dpon slob ngag dbang legs grub*), 186, 224
Ponpo Hill (*Dpon po ri*), 55
Potala (*Po ta la*), 59, 89, 115
Potowa (1027–1105, *Po to ba*), 48
Prajñācakra (*Shes rab 'khor lo*), 173
Prajñāgupta (11th c., *Shes rab gsang ba*), 55, 92, 238n65, 246n187
Prajñākara (*Shes rab byung gnas*), 37
Prajñāpāla (11th c., *Pra dz+nyā pā la*), 45
Prajñāvarman (8th c., *Shes rab go cha*), 38
Prasenajit (~5th c. BCE, *Gsal rgyal*), 38
Protectress of Mantra (*Sngags srung ma*), 184
Puchungwa (1031–1106, *Phu chung ba*), 48
Pugpa Lhundrub (15th c., *Phug pa lhun grub*), 229
Puhrang (*Pu hrangs*), 43, 117
Puhrang Lochung (*Pu hrangs lo chung*), 57
Puhrang Lotsāwa Zhonu Sherab (11th c., *Pu hrangs lo tsā ba gzhon nu shes rab*), 55, 83
Puntsog Gyaltsen (19th c., *Phun tshogs rgyal mtshan*), 199
Puntsog Palace (*Phun tshogs pho brang*), 1, 242n131
Pūrṇamati (*Gang blo ma*), 173
Pūrṇika (~2nd c., *Rtsibs legs*), 31
Putra and his brother and sister (*Pu tra lcam dral*), 73, 112, 248n225

R

Ra Chorab (11th c., *Rwa chos rab*), 46
Ra Dorje Drag (b. 1016, *Rwa rdo rje grags*), 46, 175
Ra Lotsāwa (*Rwa lo tsā ba*). *See* Ra Dorje Drag
Rabjam Gon (13th c., *Rab byams mgon*), 65
Rabjam Sheja Kunzig Khedrub Ngawang Damcho (d.1804, *Rab byams shes bya kun gzigs mkhas grub ngag dbang dam chos*), 133
Rabjam Sherab Chopel (19th c., *Rab byams shes rab chos 'phel*), 202
Rabjampa Lhawang Lodro (15th c., *Rab byams pa lha dbang blo gros*), 147
Rāgavajra (*Chags pa rdo rje*), 178. *See also* Gaṇapati
Rāhula (*Rā hu la*), 33
Rājagṛha (*Rgyal po'i khab*), 21, 24, 28–29, 31
Raktayamāri (*Gshed dmar*), 142, 222
Ramoche (*Ra mo che*), 40
Ratnarakṣita (9th c., *Ratna rakṣita*), 42
Ratnavajra (11th c., *Rin chen rdo rje*), 37, 89, 244n171
Rāvaṇa (*Sgra sgrogs pa*), 24
Red Jambhala (*Dzam dmar*), 109, 179
Red Tārā (*Sgrol dmar*), 174
Red Vasudhārā (*Nor rgyan ma dmar po*), 108, 179
Renda (*Red mda'*), 137
Rendawa Zhonu Lodro (1349–1412, *Red mda' ba gzhon nu blo gros*), 50, 137, 220, 226, 249n262, 250n263, n265
Reton Konchog Gyalpo (11th c., *on dkon mchog rgyal po*), 92
Rigdzin Pema Trinle (1641–1717, *Rig 'dzin padma 'phrin las*), 164
Rigpai Wangchug Gewa Gyaltsen (*Rin pa'i dbang phyug dge ba rgyal mtshan*). *See* Gewa Gyaltsen
Rinchen Gyaltsen (*Rin chen rgyal mtshan*). *See* Lobpon Rinchen Gyaltsen
Rinchen Lodro (15th c., *Rin chen blo gros*), 140
Rinchen Mingyur Gyaltsen (*Rin chen mi 'gyur rgyal mtshan*). *See* Sharchen Rinchen Mingyur Gyaltsen
Rinchen Palzang (16th c., *Rin chen dpal bzang*), 160

Rinchen Zangpo (958–1055, *Rin chen bzang po*), 45–46, 107, 110, 112–13
Riwo Ganden (*Ri wo dga' ldan*), 50, 129, 163, 226
Rong Lotsāwa (13th c., *Rong lo tsā ba*), 65
Rong Me Karmo Tagtsang (*Rong rme dkar mo stag tshang*), 216
Rong Mentang (*Rong sman thang*), 206
Rongchung Sherab Pal (15th c., *Rong chung shes rab dpal*), 139
Rongton Donyo Pal (*Rong ston don yod dpal*). *See* Khedrub Donyo Palwa
Rongton Mawai Senge (*Rong ston smra ba'i seng ge*). *See* Rongton Sheja Kunrig
Rongton Sheja Kunrig (1367–1437, *Rong ston shes bya kun rig*), 131, 136–40, 142, 147, 149, 151, 165, 168–69, 219–20, 249n262, 251nn304–6
Rongurmig (*Rong ngur smrig*), 57
Ṛṣipatana (*Drang srong lhung ba*), 22
Rulag (*Ru lag*), 87
Rūpati (*Ru pa ti*), 38
Rutsa Zhangkyab (15th c., *Ru tsha zang skyabs*), 141

S

Sa Lotsāwa Jamyang Kunga Sonam (1485–1533, *Sa lo tsā ba 'jam dbyangs kun dga' bsod nams*), 71, 220
Śabala Garuḍa (*Rdo rje khyung khra*), 176
Sachen Kunga Nyingpo (1092–1158, *Sa chen kun dga' snying po*), 49, 56–62, 69, 93, 95–102, 104, 108–14, 119–20, 122–23, 144, 148, 206, 225–26, 245n174, n177, n180, 247n209, 248n234, 255n374, 256n379
Sahajalilata (~10th c., *Lha cig skyes pa'i rol pa*), 108
Sāketu (*Sgra bcas*), 24
Sakhul Terlung Dilgo (*Sa khul gter lung de'u mgo*), 184
Sakya Chenpo Jamyang Namkha Gyaltsen (*Sa skya chen po 'jam dbyangs nam mkha' rgyal mtshan*). *See* Jamyang Namkha Gyaltsen
Śākya Chogden Drime Legpai Lodro (1428–1507, *Shā kya mchog ldan dri med legs pa'i blo gros*), 2, 130, 147–53, 162–64, 220, 227, 232, 251nn304–7, 252n312
Śākya Daṇḍapāṇi (~5th c. BCE, *Shā kya lag na be con*), 20
Śākya Dondrub (15th c., *Shā kya don grub*), 166
Śākya Lodro (11th c., *Shā kya blo gros*), 54
Sakya Paṇḍita Kunga Gyaltsen Palzangpo (1182–1251, *Sa skya paṇḍita kun dga' rgyal mtshan dpal bzang po*), 10, 13–14, 62–66, 88, 102–3, 111, 141, 145, 148, 150, 154, 162, 191, 201, 204, 222, 226, 229–30, 234, 235n1, 239n79, 247nn205–6, 255n347, 256n379, 256nn389–90, 257n407
Sakya Trizin (*Sa skya khri 'dzin*). *See* Ngawang Kunga Tegchen Palbar Trinle Wangi Gyalpo
Śākya Zangmo (15th c., *Shā kya bzang mo*), 147
Śākya Zangpo (d. 1270, *Shā kya bzang po*), 129
Sakyai Zurchepa Rinchen Gyaltsen (18th c., *Sa skya'i zur 'chad pa rin chen rgyal mtshan*), 73
Sakyapa Jamyang Sonam Wangpo (1559–1621, *Sa skya pa 'jam dbyangs bsod nams dbang po*), 72, 163, 166
Sakyapa Ngagchang Chenpo Kunga Rinchen (1517–84, *Sa skya pa sngags 'chang chen po kun dga' rin chen*), 166, 200
Śākyasena (11th c., *Shākya se na*), 45
Śākyaśrī, the Kashmiri paṇḍita (1127–1225, *Kha che paṇ chen shākya shrī*), 46, 61, 63, 129, 180, 229
Sakyong Lama Kunga Trinle (18th c., *Sa skyong bla ma kun dga' 'phrin las*), 157, 225

Śākyaprabha (8th c., *Śā kya 'od*), 37
Salo Jampal Dorje (16th c., *Sa lo 'jam dpal rdo rje*), 166
Salo Kunga Sonam (*Sa lo kun dga' bsod nams*). *See* Sa Lotsāwa Jamyang Kunga Sonam
Salo Ngagchang Kunga Rinchen (*Sa lo sngags 'chang kun dga' rin chen*). *See* Sakyapa Ngagchang Chenpo Kunga Rinchen
Saltong Shogom (12th c., *Gsal stong shwo sgom*), 237n57
Samantabhadra (*Kun tu bzang po*), 31, 39
Samantara (*Sa mantara*), 34
Śaṃkara (8th c., *Bde 'byed*), 35
Śaṃkara, the brahman (~7th c., *Bram ze shaṃ ka ra*), 41
Saṃvara (*Bde mchog*). *See* Cakrasaṃvara
Śāṇavāsa (~5th c. BCE, *Sha na gos can*), 30
Sangan Sa Dupa (*Sa ngan sa'i mdud pa*), 214
Sangdag Palchen Onpo (19th c., *Gsang bdag dpal chen 'od po*), 74
Saṅghabhadra (*'Dus bzang*), 36
Saṅghanandi (*Saṃ ghā nandi*), 33
Saṅghaśrī (13th c., *Saṃ ga shrī*), 63
Sangpu Neutog (*Gsang phu ne'u thog*), 60, 137, 140, 147–48, 240n95, 248n224, 251n305
Sangye Chopel (18th c., *Sangs rgyas chos 'phel*), 155
Sangye Palzang (*Sangs rgyas dpal bzang*). *See* Tsungme Kheshing Drubpa Jamgon Sangye Palzang
Sangye Puntsog (*Sangs rgyas phun tshogs*). *See* Khenchen Jampaiyang Sangye Puntsog
Sangye Tonpa (1207–78, *Sangs rgyas ston pa*), 48, 237n54
Sangye Tseten (16th c., *Sangs rgyas tshe brtan*), 71
Śāntarakṣita (725–88, *Zhi ba 'tsho*), 39, 41, 155, 192, 237n48, 238n75
Śāntideva (8th c., *Zhi ba lha*), 35, 37, 143–44, 191, 203
Śāntigarbha (8th c., *Shānti garbha*), 41
Śāntipa (~10th c., *Shānti pa*), 37
Saptākṣara (*Yi ge bdun pa*), 123
Saraha (~9th c., *Sa ra ha*), 33, 37
Saroruha (*Mtsho skyes*). *See* Saroruhavajra
Saroruhavajra (~9th c., *Mtsho skyes rdo rje*), 63, 65–66, 91, 176
Sarvavid Vairocana (*Kun rig*), 146, 149, 156–57, 175, 185, 192
Sazang Ganden (*Sa bzang dga' ldan*). See *Tarlam Sazang Namgyaling*
Sazang Mati Paṇchen (1294–1376, *Sa bzang Ma ti paṇ chen*), 50, 225
Sazang Pagpa Zhonu Lodro (1372–1475, *Sa zang 'phags pa gzhon nu blo gros*), 128
Se Karchungwa (*Se mkhar chung ba*). *See* Seton Kunrig
Se Yeshe Tsondru (11th c., *Se ye shes brtson 'grus*), 87
Sechen (1215–1294, *Se chen*), 67, 69, 132, 240n105, 241n113, n119
Secret Mantra Roar (*Gsang sngags sgra*), 178
Segom Dragkyab (11th c., *Bse sgom brag skyabs*), 95
Segom Jangye (11th c., *Bse sgom byang ye*), 93
Sekhar Chodrag (20th c., *Bse mkhar chos grags*), 205
Sempa Chenpo Pema Zangpo (15th c., *Sems dpa' chen po padma bzang po*), 139
Sempa Chenpo Zhonu Gyalchog (15th c., *Sems dpa' chen po gzhon nu rgyal mchog*), 130, 136–37, 139
Senge Gyaltsen (14th c., *Seng ge rgyal mtshan*), 138
Sepa Kunlo (15th c., *Se pa kun blo*), 130
Sera (*Se ra*), 129, 251n307
Sera Rabjampa Trashi Gyaltsen (18th

c., *Se ra rab byams pa bkra shis rgyal mtshan*), 155
Seton Kunrig (1029–1116, *Se ston kun rig*), 56, 92–93, 96, 98, 244n159
Shab (*Shab*), 66, 115, 128
Shab Gonga (*Shab sgo lnga*), 58
Shabto Dzilungpa Khenchen Jampa Sheja Zangpo (17th c., *Shab stod rdzi lung pa mkhan chen byams pa shes bya bzang po*), 132
Shang (*Shang*), 92
Shang Chokor (*Shang chos 'khor*), 128
Shar (*Shar*). *See* Sharpa Yejung
Shar Minyag Seu Gyalpo (n.d., *Shar mi nyag se'u rgyal po*), 133
Sharchen Kunga Trashi (*Shar chen kun dga' bkra shis*). *See* Jampa Kunga Trashi
Sharpa Yejung (d. 1261, *Shar pa ye 'byung*), 65
Sharchen Mingyur Gyaltsen (*Shar chen mi 'gyur rgyal mtshan*). *See* Sharchen Rinchen Mingyur Gyaltsen
Sharchen Rinchen Mingyur Gyaltsen (b. 1717, *Shar chen rin chen mi 'gyur rgyal mtshan*), 133, 156, 200 224
Sharchen Sherab Jungne (1596–1653, *Shar chen shes rab 'byung gnas*), 132
Sharchen Yeshe Gyaltsen (d. 1406, *Shar chen ye shes rgyal mtshan*), 128–29, 136
Sharpa Dukhorwa Yeshe Rinchen (13th c., *Shar pa dus 'khor ba ye shes rin chen*), 68
Sharpa Jamyang Rinchen Gyaltsen (*Shar pa 'jam dbyangs rin chen rgyal mtshan*). *See* Dagchen Jamyang Rinchen
Sharwapa (1070–1141, *Shar ba pa*), 48
Shedrub Dargyeling (*Shes grub dar rgyas gling*), 208
Sheldrong (*Shel grong*), 151
Sheltsa Gyalpo (*Shel tsha rgyal po*), 53
Shen Dorseng (12th c., *Gshen rdor seng*), 226
Sherab Dorje (15th c., *Shes rab rdo rje*), 140
Sherab Pal (13th c., *Shes rab dpal*), 66
Sherab Yonten (10th c., *Shes rab yon tan*), 54
Sheu Lotsāwa Kunga Chodrag (16th c., *She'u lo tsā ba kun dga' chos grags*), 166
Shojo Champurmo (12th c., *Shos jo lcam phur mo*), 59
Siddhārtha (~5th c. BCE, *Rgyal bu don grub*), 13–28, 62
Śīlamañju (8th c., *Shī la mandzu*), 41
Śīlendrabodhi (9th c., *Shī lendra bo dhi*), 42
Siṃha Vikrīḍita (~10th c., *Seng ge rnam par brtsen pa*), 82
Siṃhala (*Singa la*), 34
Siṃhanāda (*Senge sgra*), 173, 179
Siṃhanāda the Protector and Liberator (*Senge sgra'i ngag srung 'grol*), 179
Śiśumāra Hill (*Byis pa gsod*), 24
Situ Pema Nyinje Wangpo (1774–1853, *Si tu padma nyin byed dbang po*), 186
Six-Armed Guardian (*Mgon po phyag drug pa*), 184
Skin Mask Wisdom Guardian (*Bse 'bag ye shes mgon po*), 110–14, 238n69, 248n226–27
Sky-Soaring Vajragaruḍa (*Rdo rje khyung khra*), 109, 179
Smṛtijñānakīrti (11th c., *Smrī ti*), 43, 150, 201
So Yeshe Wangchug (10th c., *So ye shes dbang phyug*), 47
Sochungwa (12th c., *So chung ba*), 49
Sogpo Lhatsun Yeshe Dondrub (19th c., *Sog po lha btsun ye shes don grub*), 186
Somanātha (*So ba na thar*), 80
Somapūri (*So ma pū ri*), 78
Sonam Dorje (*Bsod nams rdo rje*). *See* Nyenpul Jungwa Tsugtor Gyalpo
Sonam Gyaltsen Palzangpo (15th c., *Bsod nams rgyal mtshan dpal bzang po*), 147

Sonam Tendzin Wangpo (17th c., *Bsod nams bstan 'dzin dbang po*), 166
Sonam Tsemo, Lobpon Rinpoche (1142–82, *Slob dpon rin po che bsod nams rtse mo*), 59–62, 65, 69, 99–101, 131, 150, 210, 239n86, 252n315, 255n374, 256n379
Sonam Tso (19th c., *Bsod nams mtsho*), 184
Songtsen Gampo (605–49, *Srong btsan sgam po*), 40–41, 47, 250n265
Śraddhākaravarman (11th c., *Shra ddhā ka ra warma*), 110, 112–13
Śramaṇa Devī (*Lha mo shra ma ṇa*), 174
Śrāvastī (*Mnyam yod*), 24
Śrī Dharmapāla (*Dpal ldan chos skyong*). *See* Virūpa
Śrī Siṃha (~8th c., *Shrī sing ha*), 136
Śrīparvata (*Dpal gyi ri*), 91
Sthāvarā the earth goddess (*Sa'i lha mo brtan ma*), 21
Sthiramati (~ 2nd c. BCE, *Yid brtan*), 30
Subhadra (~5th c. BCE, *Rab bzang*), 23
Subhutiśrīśānti (11th c., *Su bhu ti shrī shanti*), 45
Sudarśana (~4th c. BCE, *Legs mthong*), 30
Śuddhodana, King (~5th c. BCE, *Zas gtsang*), 19
Sugataśrī (13th c., *Su ga ta shrī*), 63
Sukhāvati (*Bde ba can*), 59, 146, 230
Sūkṣmadīrgha (11th c., *Phra la, paṇḍita*), 43
Sumpa Lotsāwa (12th c., *Sum pa lo tsā ba*), 108
Sunanda (~5th c. BCE, *Rab dga'*), 23
Sunaśata (*Su na sha ta*), 33
Sungkye Tendzin Gyalse Khedrub Tensal (15th c., *Gsung skyes bstan 'dzin rgyal sras mkhas grub bstan gsal*), 141
Surendrabodhi (9th c., *Su rendra bo dhi*), 42
Sūryavajra (n.d., *Nyi sbas*), 176
Svastika (~5th c. BCE, *Bkra shis*), 21
Śvetaketu (*Dam pa tog dkar po*), 16, 18

T

Taglung Tangpa Trashipal (1359–1424, *Stag lung thang pa bkra shis dpal*), 49
Tagpuwa Chokyi Wangchug (18th c., *Stag phu ba chos kyi dbang phyug*), 221
Tagpuwa Losang Tenzin (18th c., *Stag phu ba blo bzang bstan rgyan*), 221
Tagtsang Lotsāwa (*Stag tshang lo tsā ba*). *See* Tsang Tagtsang Lotsāwa Drapa Sherab Rinchen
Tamdrin (*Rta mgrin*). *See* Hayagrīva
Tanag (*Rta nag*), 43, 66, 147
Tanag Serling (*Rta nag gser gling*), 143
Tanag Tubten Nampar Gyalwai Ling (*Rta nag thub bstan rnam par rgyal ba'i gling*), 141, 144, 147, 172, 209, 224, 250n276
Tanagpa Shengom Rogpo (11th c., *Rta nag pa gsher sgom rog po*), 92
Tangtong Gyalpo (1385–1464, *Thang stong rgyal po*), 130, 206, 224
Tārā (*Sgrol ma*), 36, 38, 40, 43, 56, 59, 62, 70, 108, 116, 120, 122, 174, 182, 193, 203–4, 210, 237n50, 256n383
Tārā who clears away all obstacles (*Sgrol ma bar chad kun sel*), 174
Tarlam Dezhung Lungrig Tulku Jampa Tenpai Nyima (1906–87, *Thar lam sde gzhung lung rigs sprul sku byams pa kun dga' bstan pa'i nyi ma*), 1–2, 210, 234
Tarlam Sazang Namgyaling (*Thar lam sa bzang rnam rgyal gling*), 129, 204
Tartse Dorje Chang Jampa Kunga Tendzin (*Thar rtse rdo rje 'chang byams pa kun dga' bstan 'dzin*). *See* Tartse Khenchen Jampa Kunga Tendzin
Tartse Dorje Chang Namkha Chime (*Thar rtse rdo rje 'chang nam mkha' 'chi med*). *See* Tartse Khenchen Namkha Chime

Tartse Jampa Namkha Kunzang Tenpai Gyaltsen (1907–40, *Thar rtse byams pa nam mkha' kun bzang bstan pa'i rgyal mtshan*), 134
Tartse Jamyang Kunga Tenpai Gyaltsen (1933–87, *Thar rtse 'jam dbyangs kun dga' bstan pa'i rgyal mtshan*), 134
Tartse Jamyang Kunzang Tenpai Gyaltsen (20th c., *Thar rtse 'jam dbyangs kun bzang bstan pa'i rgyal mtshan*), 134
Tartse Jamyang Kunzang Tubten Chokyi Gyaltsen (20th c., *Thar rtse 'jam dbyangs kun bzang thub bstan*), 134
Tartse Khenchen Dorje Chang Jampa Kunga Tendzin (*Thar rtse mkhan chen rdo rje 'chang byams pa kun dga' bstan 'dzin*). *See* Tartse Khenchen Jampa Kunga Tendzin
Tartse Khenchen Jampa Kunga Tendzin (1776–1852, *Thar rtse mkhan chen byams pa kun dga' bstan 'dzin*), 74, 133, 184, 186, 190
Tartse Khenchen Namkha Chime (1765–1820, *Thar rtse mkhan chen nam mkha' 'chi med*), 73, 164
Tartse Namkha Samdrub (*Thar rtse nam mkha' bsam grub*). *See* Drangti Khenchen Drubpai Wangchug Jampa Namkha Samdrub
Tegchen Choje Kunga Trashi (1349–1425, *Theg chen rdo rje kun dga' bkra shis*), 136, 220
Terdag Lingpa (1646–1714, *Gter bdag gling pa*), 135, 138, 149, 220
Tese, the Khotanese lotsāwa (*Thi li se lo tsā ba*), 39
Three Lhamo Yugu Sisters (*Lha mo dbyug gu spun gsum*), 179
Thunderous Drumbeat, The (*Rnga sgra*), 182
tiger-riding guardian (*Stag zhon*), 181
Tingkham (*Sting khams*), 130
Tinuma, Lhamo (*Lha mo ti nu ma*), 109, 179
Togom Jangchub Sherab (12th c., *Stod sgom byang chub shes rab*), 102
Togtsa Pawo Tag (n.d., *Thog tsha dpa' bo stag*), 53
Tonchung (*Ston chung*). *See* Drom Depa Tonchung
Tongmon House (*Mthong smon bla brang*), 135
Tongmon Monastery (*Mthong smon dgon*), 165, 168–69
Tongra Kunga Legdrub (16th c., *Stong ra kun dga' legs grub*), 166, 177
Tongrawa (*Stong ra ba*). *See* Tongra Kunga Legdrub
Tonmi Sambhoṭa (*Thon mi sambho ṭa*). *See* Tumi Saṃbhota
Toyon Lhatsun Dondrub Gyaltsen (1792–1855, *Tho yon lha btsun don grub rgyal mtshan*), 199
Tra Puma Nyitricham (12th c., *Khra phu ma nyi khri lcam*), 62, 65
Trapuṣa (~5th c. BCE, *Ga gon*), 22
Trapuwa Sangye Zangpo (15th c., *Phra phu ba sangs rgyas bzang po*), 153
Trashi (16th c., *Bkra shis*), 160
Trashi Lhunpo (*Bkra shis lhun po*), 160, 253n329
Trashi Rinchen (14th c., *Bkra shis rin chen*), 128. *See also* Dagchen Trashi Rinchen
Trashigon (10th c., *Bkra shis mgon*), 43
Trehor (*Tre hor*), 1, 198, 204, 211
Trehor Nyadrag Monastery (*Tre hor nya brag dgon*), 204
Tri Maṇḍala (*Kri maṇḍal*), 70, 241n117
Tri Ralpachen (*Khri ral pa can*). *See* Tritsug Detsen
Tri Trashi Tsegpapal (9th c., *Khri bkra shis brtsegs pa dpal*), 43
Trichen Sangye Tenpa (17th c., *Khri chen sangs rgyas bstan pa*), 225
Tride Tsugtsen, "the bearded ancestor" (d. 754, *Khri sde gtsug btsan mes ag tshom can*), 41

Tride Yumten (9th c., *Khri lde yum brtan*), 43
Tridu Kalzang (*Khri 'du skal bzang*), 203
Trikyi Nyimagon (9th c., *Khri kyi nyi ma mgon*), 43
Trinle Chopel (20th c., *Phrin las chos 'phel*), 205
Trinle Nampar Rolpa Jamyang Chokyi Lodro (*Phrin las rnam par rol pa 'jam dbyangs chos kyi blo gros*). *See* Dzongsar Khyentse Jamyang Chokyi Lodro
Trisong Detsen (742–800, *Khri srong lde'u btsan*), 41–42, 54, 128, 237n48
Tritsug Detsen (d. 841, *Khri gtsug lde btsan*), 42
Trogma retreat (*Prog ma dgon*), 46
Trolungpa Sonam Chopal (17th c., *Spro lung pa bsod nams chos dpal*), 72
Trom Dokog (*Khrom rdo khog*), 225
Trom Gyalwa Jangchub (n.d., *Khrom rgyal ba byang chub*), 225
Tropu Jampai Pal (1173–1225, *Khro phu byams pa'i dpal*), 46
Trotsang Onpo Druglha (11th c., *Khro tshang dbon po 'brug lha*), 49
Trulnang (*'Phrul snang*), 40
Trungpa Chokyi Nyinje (1879–1939, *Drung pa chos kyi nyin byed*), 257n400
Tsalpa Rinchen Gyaltsen (15th c., *Tshal pa rin chen rgyal mtshan*), 153
Tsamo Rongpa Shapamo Jocham Gyaltsen (11th c., *Tsha mo rong pa shab pa mo jo lcam rgyal msthan*), 93
Tsang (*Gtsang*), 43, 63, 131, 138, 140, 164, 186, 188, 190, 205, 230, 244n163, 253n330. *See also* Tsang Rabsal
Tsang Chumig (*Gtsang chu mig*). *See* Chumig
Tsang Nagpa (13th c., *Gtsang nag pa*), 62
Tsang Rabsal (9th c., *Gtsang rab gsal*), 44–45
Tsang Tagtsang Lotsāwa Drapa Sherab Rinchen (b. 1405, *Gtsang stag tshang lo tsā ba sgra pa shes rab rin chen*), 153–54
Tsang Tobgyal Chokor Gang (*Gtsang thob rgyal chos 'khor sgang*), 154
Tsangchug Zhungpel Kyawa Tsungme Sonam Palden (1669–1713, *Gtsang phyug gzhung spel skya ba mtshungs med bsod nams dpal ldan*), 132
Tsang Dokharwa Khenchen Trashi Lhundrub (1672–1739, *Gtsang mdo mkhar ba mkhan chen bkra shis lhun grub*), 132–33, 156–57, 220, 225
Tsangjampa Dorje Gyaltsen (1424–98, *Gtsang byams pa rdo rje rgyal mtshan*), 255n374
Tsangkha meditation centre (*Gtsang kha dgon pa*), 61, 102
Tsangma Dorje Pal (13th c., *Gtsang ma rdo rje dpal*), 46, 172
Tsangmepa Gyergom Sewo (11th c., *Gtsang smad pa gyer bsgom se bo*), 92
Tsangnag Pugpa Sherab Ozer (13th c., *Gtsang nag phug pa shes rab 'od zer*), 65
Tsangpa Sempa Chenpo Konchog Gyaltsen (*Gtsang pa sems dpa' chen po dkon mchog rgyal mtshan*). *See* Muchen Sempa Chenpo Konchog Gyaltsen
Tsangrong Jamchen (*Gtsang rong byams chen*), 140
Tsangse Gyepai Loden Dongdrug Gawai Langtso (*Tshang sras dgyes pa'i blo ldan gdong drug dga' ba'i lang tsho*). *See* Jamyang Khyentse Wangpo Kunga Tenpai Gyaltsen
Tsarchen Losel Gyatso (*Tshar chen blo gsal rgya 'tsho*), 104, 160–65, 253n329, n333, 257n414
Tse Bhrūṃ Choje Karma Tutobpa (18th c., *Tshe bhrūṃ chos rje karma mthu stobs pa*), 155
Tsechen Kunga Nyingpo (n.d., *Brtse chen kun dga' snying po*), 73

Tsede (11th c., *Rtse lde*), 117
Tsedong (*Rtse gdong*), 71, 132
Tsedong Rinchen Gang (*Rtse gdong rin chen sgang*), 154
Tsedong Sisum Namgyal (*Rtse gdong srid gsum rnam rgyal*), 209, 224
Tsedong Trichen Gendun Trashi Paljor (*Rtse gdong khri chen dge 'dun bkra shis dpal 'byor*). *See* Gendun Trashi Paljor
Tsedong Trichen Khyenrab Tendzin Lhundrub (18th c., *Rtse gdong khri chen mkhyen rab bstan 'dzin lhun grub*), 164
Tsedong Trichen Kunga Sonam Lhundrub (*Rtse gdong khri chen kun dga' bsod nams lhun grub*). *See* Jamyang Kunga Sonam Lhundrub
Tsegpa Wangchug Senge (13th c., *Rtsegs pa dbang phyug seng ge*), 63
Tsegye (*Tshes brgyad*), 165
Tsembupa (n.d., *Tshem bu pa*), 176
Tsetang (*Rtsed thang*), 136, 140
Tsetang Sanglhun (15th c., *Rtse thang sangs lhun*), 141
Tsewa Chenpo (19th c., *Rtse ba chen po*), 74
Tsewang Paljor (19th c., *Tshe dbang dpal 'byor*), 184
Tsezhi (*Tshes bzhi*), 165
Tsog (*Tshogs*). *See* Tsogom Kunga Palzang
Tsungme Konchog Palden (1526–90, *Mtshungs med dkon mchog dpal ldan*), 131
Tsogom Kunga Palzang (1210–1307, *Tshogs sgom kun dga' dpal bzang*), 65, 67, 103, 219
Tsogom Kungapal (*Tshogs sgom kun dga' dpal*). *See* Tsogom Kunga Palzang
Tsoje Karma Ngawang (18th c., *Tsho 'byed karma ngag dbang*), 155
Tsoje Lhagon (18th c., *Tsho byed lha mgon*), 154
Tsongkhapa Lozang Dragpa (1357–1419, *Tsong kha pa blo bzang grags pa*), 50, 137, 148, 226, 236n32, 251n307
Tsongtsun Sherab Senge (10th c., *Tshong btsun shes rab seng ge*), 87, 244n163
Tsultrim Gyalpo (10th c., *Tshul khrims rgyal po*), 54
Tsungme Kheshing Drubpa Jamgon Sangye Palzang (1700–45, *Mtshungs med mkhas shing grub pa 'jam mgon dangs rgyas dpal bzang*), 133, 156, 201, 224
Tsungme Puntsog Dondrub (18th c., *Mtshungs med phun tshogs don grub*), 133
Tsurton Wange (11th c., *Mtshur ston dbang nge*), 48
Tsurton Zhonseng (13th c., *Tshur ston gzhon seng*), 63
Tubten Dongag Cho (*Thub bstan mdo sngags chos*), 204
Tubten Khedrub Gyatso (20th c., *Mthu brtan mkhas grub rgya mtsho*), 74
Tubten Legshe Zangpo (19th c., *Thub bstan legs bshad bzang po*), 199
Tubten Nampar Gyalwa (*Thub bstan rnam par rgyal ba*). *See* Tanag Tubten Nampar Gyalwai Ling
Tubten Rawame (*Thub bstan ra ba smad*), 164
Tukwan Losang Chokyi Nyima (1737–1802, *Thu'u bkwan blo bzang chos kyi nyi ma*), 221
Tulku Lungrig Nyima (*Sprul sku lung rigs nyi ma*). *See* Tarlam Dezhung Lungrig Tulku Jampa Tenpai Nyima
Tulku Anjam Rinpoche (*Sprul sku a 'jam rin po che*). *See* Dezhung Chogtrul Anjam Rinpoche
Tumi Sambhoṭa (7th c., *Thu mi sambho ṭa*), 40, 135, 150, 199, 237n41
Tuṣita (*Dga' ldan*), 17–18, 35, 137, 139
Tuton Kunga Namgyal (1432–96, *Thu ston kun dga' rnam rgyal*), 103, 135–36

U

U (*Dbus*), 43, 45, 92, 129, 136, 140, 164, 186, 188, 205
Udayana (*Tshar byed*), 38
Udraka (~5th c. BCE, *Lhag spyod*), 21
Udyāna (*Skyed mos tshal*), 20
Ug (*Dbugs*), 96
Upa Marton Gyatso Rinchen (15th c., *Dbus pa dmar ston rgya mtsho rin chen*), 139
Upagupta (*Nyes sbas*), 30
Upāli (~5th c. BCE, *Nye ba 'khor*), 29
Upper Drompa (*Grom pa stod*), 66, 230
Upper Nyang (*Nyang stod*), 65
Upper Shab (*Shab stod*), 115
Use (*Dbu se*), 53
Uṣṇīṣa (*Uṣhṇī ṣha*), 116
Uṣṇīṣasitātapatrā (*Gtsug gtor gdugs dkar po*), 173
Uṣṇīṣavijayā (*Gtsug gtor rnam par rgyal ma*), 122, 129–30, 182
Uyug (*U yug*), 102

V

Vādisiṃha (*Seng ge smra ba*), 173
Vāgīśvarakīrti (~10th c., *Ngag gi dbang phyug grags*), 37, 88, 92, 245n183
Vairocana Abhisaṃbodhi (*Rnam snang mngon byang*), 193
Vairocanarakṣita (12th c., *Bai ro tsa na*), 119, 248n231
Vaiśālī (*Yangs pa can*), 20–21, 24, 30
Vajra seat (*Rdo rje gdan*), 14, 109, 214
Vajrabhairava (*Rdo rje 'jigs byed*). *See* Bhairava
Vajramahākāla (*Rdo rje nag po chen po*). *See* Mahākāla
Vajrapāṇi (*Phyag na rdor rje*), 26, 31–32, 42, 55, 69, 114, 174–76, 182, 201, 252n316, 253n344
Vajrapāṇi "Overcoming Death" (*Phyag na rdo rje 'chi 'joms*), 175, 182
Vajrapāṇi "Overcoming the Demons" (*Phyag na rdo rje 'byung po 'dul byed*), 201
Vajrasāna, the elder (11th c., *Rdo rje gdan pa chen po*), 48, 108, 115, 117, 121, 237n52
Vajrasāna, the younger (*Rdo rje gdan pa chung ba*). *See* Amoghavajra
Vajravārāhī (*Rdo rje 'phag mo*), 32, 108, 121, 175, 253n347
Vajravega (*Rdo rje shugs*), 176
Vajravidaraṇa (*Rdo rje rnam 'joms*), 122, 173, 177, 182
Vanaprastha (10th c., *Nags khrod pa*), 82, 98
Vanaratna, Paṇḍita (1384–1468, *Paṇḍita nags kyi rin chen*), 149
Vārāṇasī (*Wa ra ṇa si*), 21–22, 24, 79
Vararuci (n.d., *Mchog sred*), 110–11, 113
Vasubandhu (~5th c., *Dbyigs gnyen*), 33, 36–37, 43, 63, 143, 145, 148–49, 154, 227, 236n24
Vasumatī (*Dbyig ldan*), 23
Vasumitra (*Ba su mi tra*), 31
Vasunanda (*Ba su nanda*), 236n24
Vatsa (*Pad sa la*), 38
Veṇapura (*'Od ma'i grong*), 24
Vetālī (*Ro langs*), 175
Vigatāśoka (3rd c. BCE, *Mya ngan bral*), 30
Vijayasenā (~10th c., *Rnam par rgyal ba'i sde*), 78
Vikramaśīla (*Bi kā ma shī la*), 37, 88, 236n34, 244n166
Vimala (*Dri ma med pa*), 65, 190
Vimalamitra (8th c., *Bi ma la mi tra*), 41
Vimalasvabhāva (*Dri med 'byung gnas*), 31
Vimaloṣṇīṣa (*Gtsug gtor dri med*), 173
Vimuktisena (~6th c., *Grol sde*), 37, 57, 236n32
Vinītadeva (8th c., *Dul ba'i lha*), 30, 78, 236n19
Vīrasena, King (~3nd c. BCE, *Dpa' bo'i sde*), 30
Vīravajra, Bhikṣu (10th c., *Dge slong*

dpa' bo rdo rje), 82–83, 89–90, 92, 244nn168–170
Virūpa (~10th c., *Bi rwa pa*), 11, 33, 58, 60, 73, 77–85, 87, 89–91, 95, 98–100, 102, 104, 110, 131–32, 160, 177, 204, 206, 221, 223, 239n80, n81, 242n130, 243nn144–46, 248n230, 253n349, 256n387
Viśuddha Heruka (*Yang dag he ru ka*), 54
Viśuddhaprabhā (*'Od zer dri med*), 173, 193
Visukalpa (*Bi su kalpa*), 33
Viśvamātṛ (*Sna tshogs yum*), 176
Viśvāmitra (~5th c. BCE, *Kun gyi bshes gnyen*), 20
Vṛjiputra (~5th c. BCE, *Bri dzi bu*), 29

W

Wangchug Kyi (14th c., *Dbang phyug skyid*), 137
Wangchug Rabten (*Dbang phyug rab brtan*). *See* Dorje Chang Wangchug Rabten
Wangla Kunga Tenzin (18th c., *Dbang bla kun dga' bstan 'dzin*), 156
western Tibet (*Stod*), 43–46. *See also* Ngari
White Acala (*Mi g.yo dkar po*), 147, 173
White Gaṇapati (*Tshogs bdag dkar po*), 178
White Gorum Zimchil (*Sgo rum gzim spyil dkar po*), 56, 69, 114, 128, 238n69, 240n103, 241n115
White Guardian (*Mgon dkar*), 115, 181
White Jambhala (*Dzam dkar*), 174
White Jambhala "Dragon Youth" (*Dzam dkar 'brug gzhon*), 174
White Prajñāpāramitā (*Sher phyin dkar mo*), 176
White Pratisarā (*Sor 'brang dkar mo*), 176
White Tārā (*Sgrol dkar*), 182, 203–4
White Vajravārāhī "Illuminating Insight" (*Phag dkar shes rab gsal byed*), 175, 253n347
White Zimchil (*Gzim spyil dkar po*). *See* White Gorum Zimchil
Wutaishan (the five-peaked mountain, *Ri bo rtse lnga*), 67, 190, 255n373

Y

Yadrug Silima (*G.ya' 'brug si li ma*), 53
Yagton Sangye Pal (1348–1414, *G.yag ston sangs rgyas dpal*), 128, 135–38, 147, 219, 226, 249n262, 250n263, 251n304
Yagyal Khepai Wangchug Tsondru Pal (14th c., *Ya gyal mkhas pa'i dbang phyug brtson 'grus dpal*), 136
Yagyal Khepai Wangpo Jamchen Rabjampa Sangye Pal (*Ya gyal mkhas pa'i byams chen rab 'byams pa sangs rgyas dpal*). *See* Jamchen Rabjampa Sangye Pal
Yagyu (14th c., *G.yag g.yu*), 136
Yalung (*G.ya lung*), 54, 101
Yama (*Gshin rje*). *See* Yamāntaka
Yamāntaka (*Gshin rje gshed*), 50, 72, 111, 112, 149, 161, 182, 222, 237n49, 257n413
Yangchen Drinpar Chagpa Pal Mangdu Topa Ludrub Gyatso (*Dbyangs chen mgrin par chags pa dpal mang du thos pa klu sgrub rgya mtsho*). *See* Mangto Ludrub Gyatso
Yangkharwa Dremo Kone (11th c., *G.ya mkhar ba dbrad mo dkon ne*), 93
Yapang Kye (*G.ya' spang skyes*), 53
Yar (*Yar*), 44
Yargyab Onpo Paṇchen Sonam Namgyal (15th c., *Yar rgyab dbon po paṇ chen bsod nams rnam rgyal*), 139
Yarlung Chogtrul Rinpoche Namkha Legpa Lhundrub (16th c., *Yar lung mchog sprul rin po che nam mkha' legs pa lhun grub*), 163
Yarlung Trashi Chode (17th c., *Yar lung bkra shis chos sde*), 162
Yarlungpa Mara Serpo (12th c., *Yar klung pa sma ra ser po*), 50

Yarpo Gyamoche (12th c., *G.yar po rgya mo che*), 48
Yaśas (3rd c. BCE, *Grags pa*), 30
Yaśodharā-Gopā (~5th c. BCE, *Go pa grags 'dzin ma*), 20
Yellow Jambhala (*Dzam ser*), 174
Yellow Parṇaśabarī (*Ri khro ma ser mo*), 174
Yelpa Drubtob Yeshe Tsegpa (1134–94, *Yel pa grub thob ye shes brtsegs pa*), 49
Yerangpa (11th c., *Ye rangs pa*), 120
Yermo Tangpa (*Dbyer mo thang pa*), 120
Yerpa (*Yer pa*), 43
Yeru (*G.yas ru*), 59
Yeru Khato (*G.yas ru kha stod*), 123
Yeshe Jungne (1238–74, *Ye shes 'byung gnas*), 68, 70, 241n129
Yeshe O (947–1024, *Ye shes 'od*), 43, 44–45, 112
Yilhung Lhagyal (*Yid lhung lha rgyal*), 249n259
Yo (*G.yo*). *See* Yo Gejung
Yo Gejung (9th c., *G.yo dge 'byung*), 44
Yoga Choding (15th c., *Yo ga chos sdings*), 135
Yolwa Dorje Chang Zhonu Lodro (*Yol ba rdo rje 'chang gzhon nu blo gros*). *See* Nedrong Tsetsog Khenchen Yolwa Zhonu Lodro
Yongdzin Konchog Pel (1445–1514, *Yongs 'dzin dkon mchog 'phel*), 131, 144, 147
Yongdzin Lodro Gyatso (19th c., *Yongs 'dzin blo gros rgya mtsho*), 74
Yongdzin Paṇḍita Palden Chokyi Gyaltsen (19th c., *Yongs 'dzin paṇḍita dpal ldan chos kyi rgyal mtshan*), 133, 190
Yonru Betsang Choje Khedrub Gyatso (20th c., *G.yon ru be tshang chos rje mkhas grub rgya mtsho*), 211
Yonten Jungne (n.d., *Yon tan 'byung gnas*), 62
Yonten Lhundrub (19th c., *Yon tan lhun grub*), 203
Yonten Ozer (15th c., *Yon tan 'od zer*), 130
Yukharmo (*G.yu mkhar mo*), 122
Yumbu Lagang (*Yum bu bla sgang*), 39
Yunnan, China (*Ljang*), 70
Yuring (*G.yu ring*), 53
Yutog Yonten Gonpo (1126–1202, *G.yu thog yon tan mgon po*), 184

Z

Zangchen Chogle Namgyal (15th c., *Bzang chen phyogs las rnam rgyal*), 130
Zangden Kachupa (15th c., *Bzang ldan bka' bcu pa*), 139
Zangdong (*Zangs sdong*), 58
Zangpo Gyaltsen (17th c., *Bzang po rgyal mtshan*), 72
Zangpo Pal, Dagnyi Chenpo (1262–1324, *Bdag nyid chen po bzang po dpal*), 70, 241n120
Zangri Pugpa (12th c., *Zangs ri phug pa*), 101
Zangskar Pagpa Sherab (11th c., *Zangs dkar 'phags pa shes rab*), 46
Zangtsa Sonam Gyaltsen (1184–1239, *Zangs tsha bsod nams rgyal mtshan*), 65, 69–70, 241n111
Zarwa Kalden Yeshe (d. 1207, *Zar ba skal ldan ye shes*), 49
Zechen Rabjampa Pema Sangag Tendzin (1731–1805, *Ze chen rab 'byams padma gsang sngags bstan 'dzin*), 156
Zemogang (*Ze mo sgang*), 154
Zepa Lodro Gyatso (15th c., *Bzad pa blo gros rgya mtsho*), 139
Zhabchung Zekyog (12th c., *Zhabs cung zad kyog*), 101
Zhabdrung Ngawang Norbu (17th c., *Zhabs drung ngag dbang nor bu*), 169
Zhabdrung Rinpoche Trashi Gyatso (*Zhabs drung rin po che bkra shis rgya mtsho*). *See* Dragra Trashi Gyatso
Zhalu Khen Rinpoche Sonam Chogden (16th c., *Zhwa lu mkhan rin po che bsod nams mchog ldan*), 163

Zhalu Khenchen (*Zhwa lu mkhan chen*). *See* Dorje Chang Wangchug Rabten
Zhalu Kuzhang Khyenrab Choje (*Zhwa lu sku zhang mkhyen rab chos rje*). *See* Khyenrab Choje Rinpoche
Zhalu Losal Tenkyong (*Zhwa lu blo gsal bstan skyong*). *See* Zhalupa Rinchen Losal Tenkyong
Zhalupa Rinchen Losal Tenkyong (b. 1804, *Zhwa lu pa rin chen blo gsal bstan skyong*), 185–86
Zhama Caṇḍi (11th c., *Zha ma tsaṇḍi*), 95
Zhama Machig Gyalmo (*Zha ma ma cig rgyal mo*). *See* Machig Drubpai Gyalmo
Zhang Konchog Pal (d. 1307, *Zhang dkon mchog dpal*), 68, 103
Zhang Olkawa from Drangyul (12th c., *Sbrang yul gyi zhang 'ol ka ba*), 94
Zhang Tsultrim Drag (12th c., *Zhang tshul khrims grags*), 61
Zhang Yeshe De (8th c., *Zhang ye shes sde*), 41, 47, 237n42
Zhang Yudragpa Tsondru Dragpa (1123–93, *Zhang g.yu brag pa brtson 'grus grags pa*), 49
Zhang Lotsāwa (13th c., *Zhang lo tsā ba*), 65
Zhangom Choseng (12th c., *Zhang sgom chos seng*), 48
Zhangton Chobar (1053–1135, *Zhang ston chos 'bar*), 58, 93–98, 100, 246n190, n197
Zhangton Zijibar (11th c., *Zhang ston gzi brjid 'bar*), 93, 246n190
Zhangse Marwa (~11th c., *Zhang gse dmar ba*), 102
Zhangzhung (*Zhang zhung*), 43, 45
Zhangzhung Lingkhawa (12th c., *Zhang zhung gling kha ba*), 49
Zhechen Mahāpaṇḍita Gyurme Tutop Namgyal (b. 1787, *Zhe chen ma hā paṇḍita 'gyur med mthu stobs rnam rgyal*), 184–85
Zhegon (*Zhe dgon*), 128
Zheri Kyetsal Ogma (*Bzhad ri skyed tshal*), 141
Zhonu Senge (15th c., *Gzhon nu seng ge*), 139
Zhuchen Lhagsam Tenpai Gyaltsen (19th c., *Zhu chen lhag bsam bstan pa'i rgyal btsan*), 199
Zhuchen Paṇḍita (*Zhu chen paṇḍita*). *See* Zhuchen Tsultrim Rinchen
Zhuchen Tsultrim Rinchen (1697–1774, *Zhu chen tshul khrims rin chen*), 154–58, 220, 224, 232, 252n325
Zhudon Dorje Kyab (13th c., *Zhu don rdo rje skyabs*), 63
Zhudon Sonam Rinchen (15th c., *Zhu don bsod nams rin chen*), 140
Zhudrag Marwa (11th c., *Zhu brag dmar ba*), 102
Zhuje Ngodrub (n.d., *Zhus rje dngos grub*), 100–101
Zhungya Ngodrub Palbar (16th c., *Gzhung brgya dngos grub dpal 'bar*), 141, 220
Zimwog Jampa Tendzin Nyendrag (*Gzim 'og byams pa bstan 'dzin snyan grags*). *See* Chetsun Tendzin Nyendrag
Zimwog Tongmon (*Gzim 'og mthong smon*). *See* Tongmon Monastery
Zimwog Tulku Tendzin Trinle (*Gzim 'og sprul sku bstan 'dzin phrin las*). *See* Jampa Ngawang Tendzin Trinle
Zimwogpa Ngawang Tendzin Trinle (*Gzim 'og pa ngag dbang bstan 'dzin 'phrin las*). *See* Jampa Ngawang Tendzin Trinle
Zu Dorje Gyaltsen (11th c., *Gzus rdo rje rgyal mtshan*), 45
Zur Sherab Jungne (11th c., *Zur shes rab 'byung gnas*), 47
Zurpoche Śākya Junge (1002–62, *Zur po che shā kya 'byung gnas*), 92, 243n154

About the Author

Dhongthog Rinpoche was one of the most important scholars of the Sakya school in the twentieth century. Born in 1933 in the Trehor region of eastern Tibet, he was identified as the fifth in the tulku lineage of Dhongthog Monastery. He studied under a number of renowned teachers, including Jamyang Khyentse Chokyi Lodro (1893–1959). In 1957 he left Tibet for India and worked for many years at Tibet House in New Delhi, where he wrote several works, including this history of the Sakya school. In 1979 he moved to Seattle, where he founded the Sapan Institute, continued to write, and worked closely with Dezhung Rinpoche (1906–87). He passed away in Seattle in January 2015.

About the Translator

Sam van Schaik received his PhD from the University of Manchester in 2000 for his work on the Dzogchen texts of Jigme Lingpa, published as *Approaching the Great Perfection*. He is currently a senior researcher in the International Dunhuang Project at the British Library, where he works on early Tibetan Buddhist manuscripts. He has also studied and translated some of the key works by masters of the Sakya school. Recent publications include *Tibet: A History*.

Also Available from Wisdom Publications

The Nyingma School of Tibetan Buddhism
Its Fundamentals and History
Dudjom Rinpoche
Translated and Edited by Gyurme Dorje and Matthew Kapstein

"A landmark in the history of English-language studies of Tibetan Buddhism."—*History of Religions*

Freeing the Heart and Mind
Introduction to the Buddhist Path
His Holiness Sakya Trizin

In his first book, His Holiness Sakya Trizin shares foundational wisdom for starting on the Buddhist path alongside essential teachings from great masters like Virupa, Sakya Pandita, and Jamyang Khyentse Wangpo.

Taking the Result as the Path
Core Teachings of the Sakya Lamdré Tradition
The Library of Tibetan Classics
Translated by Cyrus Stearns

"Students of the Lamdré will rejoice to see these often enigmatic Tibetan yoga manuals transformed into such lucid English."—David P. Jackson, curator, the Rubin Museum of Art

A Saint in Seattle
The Life of the Tibetan Mystic Dezhung Rinpoche
David P. Jackson

The inspiring biography of one of the greatest scholar-yogis of our time—the Sakya luminary Dezhung Rinpoche, who in 1960 became one of the first lamas to transmit Tibetan Buddhism in the West.

The Three Levels of Spiritual Perception
A Commentary on the Three Visions
Deshung Rinpoche
Translated by Jared Rhoton

A classic guide to the Lamdré meditation tradition by one of the Sakya school's most celebrated teachers in the West.

Luminous Lives
The Story of the Early Masters of the Lam 'bras Tradition in Tibet
Cyrus Stearns

"A seminal manuscript history of its earliest practitioners and masters, and a detailed description of the Lam 'bras teachings."—*Tricycle*

Freedom from Extremes
Gorampa's "Distinguishing the Views" and the Polemics of Emptiness
José I. Cabezón and Geshe Lobsang Dargyay

"A magnificent translation of a pivotal Tibetan examination of the nature of reality. Essential for comprehending the variety of views on the middle ground."—Jeffrey Hopkins, University of Virginia

Hermit of Go Cliffs
Timeless Instructions from a Tibetan Mystic
Cyrus Stearns

An inspiring collection of beautiful and accessible tantric songs from the meditation master Gyalwa Godrakpa (1170–1249).

To Dispel the Misery of the World
Whispered Teachings of the Bodhisattvas
Ga Rabjampa
Translated by Rigpa Translations
Foreword by Khenpo Appey

"For anyone yearning to lead a saner and more altruistic life in these troubling times, the practice of lojong, or 'training the mind' in compassion, is a simply priceless tool."—Sogyal Rinpoche

About Wisdom Publications

Wisdom Publications is the leading publisher of classic and contemporary Buddhist books and practical works on mindfulness. To learn more about us or to explore our other books, please visit our website at wisdompubs.org or contact us at the address below.

Wisdom Publications
199 Elm Street
Somerville, MA 02144 USA

We are a 501(c)(3) organization, and donations in support of our mission are tax deductible.

Wisdom Publications is affiliated with the Foundation for the Preservation of the Mahayana Tradition (FPMT).